T0330632

AMERICA AND THE THIRD WORLD

AMERICA AND THE THIRD WORLD
Revolution and Intervention

JOHN L. S. GIRLING

Volume 80

Routledge
Taylor & Francis Group

LONDON AND NEW YORK

First published in 1980

This edition first published in 2011
by Routledge
2 Park Square, Milton Park, Abingdon, Oxon, OX14 4RN

Simultaneously published in the USA and Canada
by Routledge
711 Third Avenue, New York, NY 10017

Routledge is an imprint of the Taylor & Francis Group, an informa business

First issued in paperback 2013

© 1980 John L. S. Girling

British Library Cataloguing in Publication Data
A catalogue record for this book is available from the British Library

ISBN 13: 978-0-415-60130-6 (hbk)
ISBN 13: 978-0-415-84603-5 (pbk)
eISBN 13: 978-0-203-83577-7 (Volume 80)

Publisher's Note
The publisher has gone to great lengths to ensure the quality of this reprint but
points out that some imperfections in the original copies may be apparent.

Disclaimer
The publisher has made every effort to trace copyright holders and welcomes
correspondence from those they have been unable to contact.

America and the Third World

Revolution and Intervention

John L. S. Girling
Research School of Pacific Studies
Australian National University

Routledge & Kegan Paul
London, Boston and Henley

First published in 1980
by Routledge & Kegan Paul Ltd
39 Store Street, London WC1E 7DD,
Broadway House, Newtown Road,
Henley-on-Thames, Oxon RG9 1EN and
9 Park Street, Boston, Mass. 02108, USA

Set in Baskerville by
Oxprint, Oxford

British Library Cataloguing in Publication Data

Girling, John Lawrence Scott

America and the Third World.
1. United States – Foreign relations – 1977 –
2. Underdeveloped areas – Foreign relations
I. Title
327.73'0172'4   E872   79-41056

ISBN 0 7100 0318 8

Contents

Preface		vii
Acknowledgments		xii
1	Perspectives on the Third World	1
	Perspectives applied: practice	3
	Perspectives compared	8

Part one ★ REVOLUTION

	Introduction	15
2	Revolutionary motivation	19
	Peasant participants	21
	Motivation and mobility	25
	Opposition and order	28
	Concept and conditions	31
	Case studies: Philippines, Thailand, Vietnam	33
3	Structural context	46
	Catalytic insurrection: Cuba	47
	Why failure?	52
	An alternative: national resistance	64
	Another alternative: urban insurgency	68
	The Chinese way	74
	Prospects	76
4	General theory of revolution?	78
	Universal theory, specific conditions	79
	Political, psychological, systemic theories	89

Part two ★ INTERVENTION

	Introduction	103

5 US foreign policy: two perspectives   107
    Security and pluralism   110
    Dominance and dependence   111
    Perspectives compared   113
    Conclusion   118

6 America and the Third World:
    from involvement to intervention   122
    Global involvement   124
    Strategic-economic nexus   132
    Stages of intervention   139
    America in a 'bind'   147

7 Limited war   152
    Education in the Cold War   153
    Military solutions preferred   155

8 Counter-insurgency: analysts and operators   162
    Contract research   165
    Neutrality of technicians   167
    'Suppression'   171
    SMASH   177

9 Implications of involvement   185
    Nixon Doctrine: two views   187
    Push and pull: global alarms   190
    Manipulation from below   192
    Politics and morals: the linkage   197
    Deep involvement   199
    Prospects   205

10 Conclusion: the global condition   208
    Strategic disengagement   209
    Total engagement   212
    Intermediate strategy   213
    Solution?   219

    Notes   222
    Index   273

Preface

American foreign policy is characterised by global involvement. This involvement is the result of the drastic changes in the international configuration of force brought about by the Second World War and its aftermath: the elimination or diminution of all former great powers, except one; America's monopoly, then superiority, and now parity (with its chief rival) in the possession of nuclear weapons; the vast expansion of the American economy (the power-house of the allied war effort); and finally the challenge to America's interest in a stable world order posed both by domestic instability in non-communist countries and by the alternative model of world order which rival powers seek to achieve: these last two factors, indigenous instability and communist capacities and intentions, are causally linked in American global perceptions.

From the American standpoint, global involvement thus reflects the transformation of the USA from an economic power to a military, political and economic super-power – from regional power, in the Western hemisphere, to international power. From the standpoint of the way in which society is organised, politically and economically ('domestic structure') in most Third World countries, America's global involvement represents the latest manifestation of a system of patronage which is of mutual (though unequal) benefit to both patron and client: the patron provides protection, a share in the wealth generated, and a semblance of participation in the common endeavour; in return the clients – the military, political and economic élites in Third World countries – provide loyalty, economic facilities and the wherewithal, in terms of joint or individual action, to maintain security. Thus American 'involvement' is far more than a formal relationship between 'sovereign states', whether allies, 'friends' or neutrals: it is the sum of the military, political and economic connections between the major components of the American domestic structure and their functional 'counterparts' (which vary from those that are fused in one institution to more or less separate military, political and economic entities) comprising the domestic structures of Third World countries. It is this overall network of relationships which is the object of my investigation.

My approach is to put forward three propositions which I seek to test in the body of the work. My first proposition is that American policy-makers' overriding interest is in the stability of the global system of interlocking relationships. To test this proposition requires an examination both of the professed aims and the actual performance of American policy with regard to the Third World.

My second proposition is that the interest of American policy-makers, which is largely supported by the American public, coincides with the interests of the decision-makers in the great majority of the countries of the Third World. To test this proposition requires an examination of the military, political and economic components of these domestic structures and their international relations.

My third proposition is that this global system 'normally' operates peacefully, but that it is subject to internal and external challenges, as noted above. If these challenges are believed to be serious ones, Third World rulers attempt to suppress them by force; and their employment of force escalates as the 'threat' increases. But if indigenous coercion fails to remove the threat, then the patron's intervention (again, in various forms and escalating to meet an increased threat) is necessary to maintain the system: i.e. to preserve each part of the system, on the assumption that the strength of the chain is that of its weakest link.[1] Crises, military, political or economic, are the *test* of the system.

To substantiate or disprove this (complex) proposition requires an examination: first of internal instability in countries of the Third World which, potentially at least, culminates in the overthrow of the established order; and second of external (adversary) instigation or manipulation of dissidence aimed to derive unilateral advantage from changes in the overall balance of forces.

The investigation carried out in this study proceeds in reverse order: in the first part I examine both the subjective (motivational) factors conducive to instability and revolt in the Third World and the objective (structural) conditions facilitating or 'depressing' the emergency of revolutionary movements; finally in the second part I examine American globalism as it varies in its response to changes in the above environment (and to its perceptions of those changes) from 'involvement' to 'inter-vention'. Chapter 5 clears the ground for the investigation of US foreign policy by first testing an alternative proposition: that, in *addition* to strategic or economic interests, the liberal-democratic values of a pluralist society also significantly affect the formulation and conduct of America's global policy.

Chapter 1 provides the conceptual framework used in this study. Its limits are set, at one end of the spectrum, by pluralist conceptions; at the other end, by Marxist conceptions. The former are favourable to the assumptions underlying American foreign policy, perceive the mutual benefits arising from America's relations with the Third World, and advocate system-maintenance. The latter are critical of the assumptions, 'benefits' and system, respectively. The pluralist approach underlines the autonomy of political parties and interest groups and on these grounds infers the indeterminacy of foreign policy – or rather the diversity of foreign policies in a given society, each corresponding to the separate interests of the various groups involved. The Marxist approach, to the contrary, emphasises the class nature of society and insists that foreign and domestic policies are indivisible: they do not vary according to the separate interests of formally independent institutions, but are determined by the dominant class interests of that society.

Besides the range of perspective offered by this framework, there are two further advantages. First of all, pluralism and Marxism are complementary with regard to the particular insights that may be derived from each of them (as integrated theories they are, of course, mutually exclusive). Pluralism reflects the primacy given to politics: state sovereignty, constitutional freedoms, party autonomy. Marxism reflects the primacy given to economics: critically, in terms of exploitation, class society, and the uneven development of production; prescriptively, in terms of revolution, an end to exploitation, and the release of productive energy. The Marxist analysis, I shall argue, explains more adequately than does pluralism *the realities* of most Third World countries, while pluralist perspectives are more significant in discerning the *possibilities* of autonomous development in those countries.[2] My aim is to make use of this complementarity of political and economic insights in a 'structural' approach, which identifies dominant patterns of behaviour through historical research, in ways suggested by Gunnar Myrdal and Osvaldo Sunkel.

The second advantage is that pluralism and Marxism provide (or provided) unifying conceptions of the variety of countries under consideration, which range from India with its vast population to African mini-states, from systems of military, bureaucratic or party domination to those of personal leadership, and from near-subsistence agricultural economies to highly-differentiated, technologically-oriented economies. 'Developmental' pluralists, comparing political systems in the Third World, have classified the enormous variety of political structures according to their stage of development, defined in terms of the 'Anglo-American model'. Similarly, developmental economists perceive these countries at different stages of economic progress, leading to the 'take-off' phase of self-sustaining growth modelled on modern corporate capitalism. Marxists, in turn, reduce the variety of economic mechanisms and forms of government to order under the unifying concept of the global imperialism-dependence system. The economic growth of Third World countries, where it takes place, is not the result of autonomous development, but reflects the requirements of the capitalist world. As Marx himself put it, in a form acceptable to developmental pluralists, 'the country that is more developed industrially only shows, to the less developed, the image of its own future'.[3] However insufficient, on the one hand, or dogmatic, on the other, these unifying conceptions may be, they do provide a set of 'manageable' perspectives for the investigation of countries whose sheer number and range of differences would defeat a more empirically-based approach.

I also include an assessment of longer-term prospects. What I have stated above does not imply that the situation of super-power hegemony (each dominant in its own sphere, in spite of important defections, and at times accepting, at other times contesting, that of the other) will remain unchanged. For there are certain trends in regard both to the internal situation of Third World countries and the international environment, which qualify (although they also reinforce) my argument. These trends lead away from the bipolarity of the immediate post-war years to a more fragmented world. What this means for imperial patron–client relations – should these tendencies be fulfilled – is discussed in terms of domestic conditions (at the end of chapter 3) and of international and regional patronage (at the end of chapter 9). Such long-term prospects, over the next decade or more, are set out as a counterpoint to my analysis of the current situation.

One final comment. The analysis that follows focuses on 'revolutionary situations' – typically those of rural-based insurgencies, although other forms of struggle are not excluded – which have clear-cut implications for US global policy. For the objectives of the revolutionaries are the overthrow of the established regime, usually an ally or friend of the

USA, and the radical restructuring of society; and the practical result, internationally, is alignment with a major communist power. The Iranian type of revolution, by contrast, is more problematic: it has destroyed an ally of the USA, but aims at a theocratic transformation, of which the outcome is uncertain;[4] and it is non-aligned.

The potential for both the radical and the 'fundamentalist' type of revolution is evident in the Third World. But the latter type, foreshadowing growing uncertainty and instability, has no less disturbing implications for US foreign policy. This is because renewed instability in areas of the Third World coincides with the build-up of Soviet power and its expansion of influence: a build-up which stems from determination never again to suffer the humiliation experienced during the Cuban missile crisis;[5] and an expansion which profits from the unaccustomed hesitancy of the USA induced by Watergate and Vietnam. Both factors produce a deteriorating strategic environment for the USA, which prompts it to build up its own strength, in turn. . . .

This closing-in and overlapping of spheres of influence, resulting from Soviet expansion, reduces the arena of 'exclusive' US involvement. If there is less opportunity for 'automatic' US intervention, in the style of the 1950s and 1960s, there is all the more possibility of entanglement with the rival power.

Acknowledgments

'The path of revolution is always tortuous, never straight', said Chairman Mao, contemplating the extraordinary vicissitudes of the revolutionary movement in China. The analogy fits only too well the subject of this book and my experience in writing and rewriting it. All the more reason, then, for me to thank most warmly those who have encouraged me to persevere with, and to improve, this work.

I am deeply indebted, as can readily be seen within, to such outstanding scholars as Barrington Moore, Eric Wolf, Gunnar Myrdal, Jacques Lambert, Osvaldo Sunkel, and James Scott for their studies of revolutions and social structure in the Third World; and I have been inspired, whether in agreement or dissent, by the rewarding foreign policy studies of such diverse authors as Stanley Hoffmann, Susanne Bodenheimer, Franz Schurmann, Melvin Gurtov, Hedley Bull, and Henry Kissinger himself. But the views expressed in this book are my own.

Finally, I owe special thanks to George Kahin, and to David Chandler, W. A. Woode, Jamie Mackie, and Milton Osborne; to two anonymous readers for Cornell University Press; to friends at the Australian National University, including Anthony Reid, Stephen FitzGerald, Arthur Stockwin, John Vincent and the late Sisir Gupta; and above all to Nina, who shared the experiences, pleasurable and otherwise, which went into making this book.

1 ★ *Perspectives on the Third World*

In my investigation I use the 'adversary' procedure; comparing pluralist conceptions with those of rival, and opposite, Marxist conceptions. Given their basic assumptions, both cannot be correct; if one is right, the other will be wrong. However, both may be wrong. Each theory is more than a logically consistent and interrelated set of parts: each purports to explain the basic social features of the world we live in.[1] Thus it should be possible to test the validity of each theory by applying them to concrete situations.

Such a test is essential, because those with different perspectives on domestic society (autonomous parties, corporations, unions, etc., versus institutional structures dependent on international capitalism) arrive at different *international* conclusions. My own approach, as we shall see, while not accepting the validity either of the thesis (a society of sovereign states) or the antithesis (imperialist *economic* motivation) absorbs elements of the two in the concept of imperial 'patronage' of client regimes. It is the nature of these regimes that this chapter is about. But this synthesis, too, will be tested to see if it provides an adequate explanation of global involvement.

Consider, for example, three countries in Southeast Asia which have many aspects in common and yet in important fields appear to be moving in very different directions: these are the Philippines, Thailand and (South) Vietnam. Even a brief examination of their historical development and the current situation raises interesting questions. How can we account for the fact that countries with similar basic characteristics (mainly rural populations, largely rice-growing agriculture, relatively under-developed economies with low levels of industrialisation) should experience such different forms of rule, both today and in the past? Are these diverse forms an implicit manifestation of pluralism? Or are they the relatively unimportant, if differentiated, aspects of 'super-structures' which rest on the underlying, shared reality of élite ownership of the means of production, domination of the polity, and exploitation of the masses? Such inquiries form the subject-matter of part 1 of this work.

Although my basic purpose is a study of foreign policy, yet the importance of proceeding from an analysis of the *internal* conditions of the countries concerned cannot be emphasised too strongly:[2]

> it is the elements within a nation which determine the effect of inter-national situations upon the national reality. It would be too easy to replace internal dynamics by external dynamics. Were it possible, we would be spared the study of the dialectic of each movement of a global process and could instead substitute for the analysis of different con-crete situations a generalised and abstract formula.

Responses to domestic questions determine the range of possible answers to *international* questions. To take the latter first – at one end of the scale, can American involvement in the affairs of the three countries be explained by the 'attraction' of one pluralist society to the pluralist elements in the others? To enlarge the questions, i.e., in terms of global power, is involvement in Southeast Asia an integral part of a grand design to safeguard pluralism against its totalitarian enemies throughout the world? Alternatively, is there little or no correlation between the domestic values of a super-power and its foreign policy, especially in times of stress: whether that policy is basically one of strategic containment (with overtones of democratic rhetoric); or of balance of power accompanied by détente; or a combination of both relying on methods of *realpolitik*? Moving from pluralist and strategic to economic motivation, is American power exercised globally to achieve and maintain optimum conditions for the secure and profitable expansion of 'liberal capitalist' enterprise,[3] more or less regardless of regimes in the countries in which it operates? Or, at the other end of the scale, is 'American imperialism' – that is, the concentrated economic power of corporate capitalism working in unison with the coercive power of the state machine – striving to 'integrate the capitalist world' under its hegemony?[4] American 'involvement' in the Third World thus provides the opportunity to test the validity both of the pluralist conception (a voluntary alliance of free nations to maintain a stable world order) and of the neo-Marxist (imperialism-dependence) conception, as discussed in part 2.

An analysis starting with internal conditions, as I have argued, provides both the evidence for testing theories (which are ultimately of global scope) and an illustration of methodologies – the way in which pluralists and Marxists perceive the subject. But in examining Third World countries it is useful to consider a further, intermediate, category – the concept of patron–client relations. The latter supplements, but is not a substitute for, either Marxism or pluralism.

Whereas the latter theories are both analytic (ways of investigating society) *and* prescriptive (incorporating values that can and should be realised), the concept of patron–client relations is purely analytic: it explains a mode of behaviour that exists: the concept, as such, does not imply a judgment in terms of goals to be achieved. Patron–client relations can be subsumed under either Marxist or pluralist perspectives: for such relations can be perceived as a traditional, largely unstructured, form of behaviour which will be superseded in the course of modernisation (whether of the pluralist or Marxist variety) by more 'rational', impersonal and institutionalised patterns of activity. The patron–client concept does, however, present a useful corrective to pluralist and Marxist perspectives, where the prescriptive element – and this is both strength and weakness – tends to invade the analytic.

Perspectives applied: practice

In the following section, I shall apply these three perspectives to one country, the Philippines. In constitutional terms this country has been, although it no longer is, one of the most plausible candidates for the award of pluralism in the developing world; yet the social and political relations between Filipinos indicate the importance of patron and client; and the land tenure system appears to justify the Marxist critique. In all three respects the Philippines is an appropriate case study, but it is, of course, merely one example out of many, all of which require empirical investigation.

First of all, to describe the pluralist perspective based on the Anglo-American model. Exponents of this point of view consider that a 'modern political system' is characterised by a relatively high degree of differentiation, explicitness and functional distinctiveness of political and governmental structures. The political process is governed by the 'input-output' model of systems analysis, derived from economic theory, whereby 'raw' inputs, i.e. the demands on and the supports for the system, are converted into finished outputs, that is decisions. The conversion process is activated by political socialisation and recruitment, and by mechanisms of interest articulation and aggregation. The key role of interest groups (organisations of industrialists, trade unions, civic groups and the like) is to 'process raw claims', i.e., formulate specific demands, 'in an orderly way and in aggregable form', meaning that they are combined to form alternative courses of action – through the party system, the legislature and the bureaucracy.[5]

Now, according to 'developmental' pluralists, the Philippines 'stands out as the most advanced and integrated' among the 'mixed systems of Africa–Asia' – i.e. those that combine modern concepts with traditional practices. The Philippine system represents a 'fusional adaptation' of the two sectors with the emergence of a 'fairly homogeneous political culture'. Indeed 'the discontinuities between the modern élite subsociety and the mass are much less marked than in other transitional systems.' There is a comparatively high degree of functional distinctiveness of the political and governmental structures; and competing parties are instruments through which political 'brokers' endeavour to aggregate the largest possible number of interests:[6]

> In the performance of the governmental functions the Philippine legislature is fully participant, the bureaucracy is far less dominant in the performance of political functions than in most other African–Asian systems, the judiciary is independent, and the army is apolitical.

Another well-known developmental theorist sums up: 'Popular demands for change are reflected in a competitive political process and thus much of the dynamics for change is to be found in the operation of the political functions.'[7]

There could hardly be a greater contrast between this rather touching belief in the democratic process in the Philippines and the severely critical analysis of the Marxists. Thus: 'U.S. imperialism, domestic feudalism and bureaucrat capitalism prevent the Filipino people from making use of their natural resources to their own advantage.'[8] The 'semi-feudal' character of Philippine society chiefly results from the impact of US monopoly capitalism on the old feudal mode of production. As for the 'bureaucrat capitalists' running the state machine at all levels, their role is to serve imperialism and feudalism. They cannot be expected to change their basic semi-colonial and semi-feudal policies. It is only to deceive the people that they may make themselves out to be 'populists', 'nationalists', 'democrats' or even 'socialists'. But they will never hesitate to turn 'outright fascists' and employ military force to quell the revolutionary masses.[9] Marxists, of course, derive their political analysis from their assessment of the socio-economic 'foundation'. In a country like the Philippines, where two-thirds of the population is rural, land ownership is crucial. Marxists quote official figures to show that the rate of tenancy increased from 18 per cent in 1903 to 50 per cent in 1961, while as much as 41 per cent of the total farm area was owned (in 1953) by a mere 0.36 per cent of the population. This 'landlord class will never surrender its ownership of vast lands voluntarily', according to the Marxist thesis. It will always make use of its political power to serve its interests. The army, police, courts and prisons are at its service. Landowners have their own private armies to put down rivals, defend their particular interests, and to attack the revolutionary mass movement. Because 'the landlords themselves are officials of the reactionary government', their power extends into every agency. As big financiers of electoral campaigns, 'they are found in decisive positions in all the reactionary political parties'.[10]

The apparent autonomy of the party system is a sham. The two major parties, the Nacionalista Party and the Liberal Party, have never expressed any basic policy difference with regard to the fundamental problems of 'U.S. imperialism, feudalism and bureaucrat capitalism'. The stalwarts of both parties at every level can shift from one party to the other. 'These puppet political parties have always been alike as the [American] Democratic Party and the Republican Party or Coca-Cola and Pepsi-Cola are.' Their differences are at the most factional and cliquish. They are preoccupied with quarrelling over the spoils of colonial office. 'Indeed, the big bureaucrats are characteristically big compradors and big landlords themselves. . . . They are capitalists by converting the entire government into a private enterprise from which they draw enormous private profits.'[11]

Finally, the patron–client perspective focuses, neither on class policy dictated by economic ownership, nor on constitutional forms reflecting a variety of interests, but on the pattern of personal relations. From this point of view, the Philippine polity, unlike most Western democracies, is structured less by organised interest groups or by individuals perceiving themselves in class or occupational categories 'than by a network of mutual aid relationships between pairs of individuals', typically the prosperous patron and the poor client.[12] The four major aspects of patron–client relationships in the Philippines are these: patronage and reciprocity; gentry power and factions; identical political parties; and satisfied clients.

The Philippine political process is dominated by an élite drawn largely from among those who can afford to be patrons, i.e., landowners, employers and professional men. 'Members of this élite, ranging themselves under the banners of two national parties, compete with each other for elective offices.' Each is supported by his kinsmen, rich or poor, by his non-kinsmen clients, and by whoever else among the 'little people' of his community can be induced, by offers of material or other rewards, to vote for him.

> The two rival parties in each province are structured by vertical chains of dyadic patron–client relationships extending from great wealthy political leaders in each province down to lesser gentry politicians in the towns, down further to petty leaders in each village, and down finally to the clients of the latter – the ordinary peasantry.

Thus both parties contain among their leaders and supporters members of all social strata, of all occupational groups, and of all regions.[13]

The Philippines, however, is divided between the wealth of the 'big people', rooted in the unequal distribution of land, and the 'chronic state of insecurity and need' of the 'little people'. Yet the former are traditionally expected to come to the aid of the latter in times of crisis either by providing the necessities of life or by relaxing the burden of obligations (debts or share of the crop) on an individual basis. This social pattern, long antedating the introduction of national elections, has been taken over almost intact into the political system.[14] The political leader, from the national down to the provincial and village level, provides satisfaction to his clients (access to public funds, jobs, local projects) while clients at each level demonstrate their loyalty by delivering the vote.

In conclusion, it is clear that each perspective of the same country produces a different political assessment. Indeed the contrast between pluralist and Marxist interpretations – in the constitutional era – is so striking that it brings to mind President Kennedy's wry query, on the return of a military and a civilian official from Vietnam with contradictory reports: 'You two did visit the same country, didn't you?'[15] However, even from the pluralist perspective, as modified by the patron–client assessment, it is evident that Philippine pluralism is characteristic of the élite – 1 or 2 per cent of the population at most;[16] and that this type of pluralism, reflecting diversity of territory and personality (including rivalry between 'family dynasties' and within them), is far removed from the *functionalist* pluralism of democratic theory.

Thus if we set aside democratic pluralism, which is the appearance rather than the reality, the crucial issue is between the Marxist and patron–client approaches. Both basically *agree* on the fused political and economic power of the landlords, rooted in the unequal division of land, and expressed in the form of a landowner-dominated party system and electoral contest for office. The two parties, with the same social basis and the same 'interest' in politics, like the 'Ins' and 'Outs' of eighteenth-century England,[17] are as 'identical' as Coca-Cola and Pepsi-Cola.[18]

There are three major *differences* between the Marxist and patron–client approaches: on the dominant role ascribed to US 'monopoly capitalism' by the Marxists (rather than focusing on Japanese or indigenous capital); on whether or not the mass of poor people benefit from patron–client relations or, a related issue, are merely 'deceived' into taking part in the electoral process; and finally on the potential for reform in the countryside and cities or the 'necessity' of armed peasant struggle. One element significantly missing from all three analyses is the emerging 'middle classes': it is only briefly referred to as the hope of pluralism, as the ambivalent middle strata for the Marxists ('unity and struggle') and as a small, but growing, component of the network of patron–client relations.

Here I shall only touch on the crucial question of reformism or revolution. The Marxist argument that the electoral system is one of 'deception' is too dogmatic; but given the economic conditions in the Philippines, I believe the patron–client assumption of widespread satisfaction is no less wide of the mark. However, there are three things to consider. First, 'semi-feudal' attitudes and activities – help and protection by the patron in return for 'service' and loyalty by the client – are not insignificant, especially when reinforced (as they often are) by kinship ties. Second, to a certain extent Filipino voters are 'willing victims' of the electoral ritual; belief in the democratic myth offers psychological compensation for material deprivation. Finally, and the most telling point of all – the constitutional system did not last. After only two decades of independence it was already breaking down. President Marcos's authoritarian 'new society', relying on his wealthy relatives and intimates, on the armed forces (greatly increased in size) and on the civilian bureaucracy, denotes both the failure of pluralism and the insufficiency of patronage;[19] but it has yet to validate, not so much the Marxist analysis, as its Maoist prescription – the efficacy of armed revolt.

Perspectives compared

To sum up the implications of the previous section with regard to the two major perspectives: Marxism asks the right questions, but does not always provide the right answers; pluralism gives the right answers to certain questions (such as what functions are needed for the model of a modern society?) but for many countries these may not be the right questions. Essentially, Marxism insists on a conflict model of society: this is verified or disproved in a given country by the existence or otherwise of feudal or capitalist exploitation; its international form is imperialism. Pluralism (and 'patronage'), on the other hand, insist on a consensus model of society; this is verified or disproved by the existence or absence of a harmony of interests (under capitalism) or of reciprocity of obligations and advantages (under feudal or 'semi-feudal' patronage systems); its international form is interdependence.

The 'consensus' values of pluralism are liberal (individual liberty, freedom of choice) and democratic (government by consent of the governed). These noble ideals take on three practical forms. First, separation of powers to prevent arbitrary or authoritarian infringement of liberty: in the pluralist idiom this is 'competitive autonomy'. The second form is that of representative government, implying power-sharing and harmony of interests: the pluralist concept is 'bargaining culture'. And finally, popular sovereignty is analogous to consumer sovereignty: free choice is exercised through the electoral system (the free market system). Indeed, as one writer puts it: 'Voters choose their representatives on the basis of stated preferences. Government . . . is similar to the productive unit and manufactures decisions, which the public evaluates through the electoral mechanism.'[20]

The 'consumer' thesis is not only the political expression of laissez-faire economics but also reflects the positive correlation observed by the 'developmental' theorists between economic development and political competitiveness. To elaborate: economic development is associated with the growth of a middle class and the diffusion of middle-class values and institutions: such values are seen as an 'instrumental' orientation towards government as opposed to an 'affective' orientation: 'it is instrumental when it takes the form of a bargain with consequences realistically spelled out'.[21] Institutions, too, are characterised by specialised functional differentiation resulting from an ever more complex division of labour. Instrumental orientation and functional differentiation are prerequisites of pluralism, which may be understood as competition within a framework of consensus. This is how the bargaining culture reconciles the problem of order (representative *government*) with that of freedom (majority *choice*).

Yet in spite of its economic derivation, pluralist theory minimises or denies the impact of economic forces on political processes. Just as the 'output' components – legislature, executive and judiciary – are independent, i.e., operate under a system of checks and balances, so too are the 'inputs' from 'society' regulated and processed by *separate* mechanisms of interest articulation (ideally, 'associational interest groups' explicitly representing interests)[22] and of interest aggregation. The latter is performed by combining interests in alternative courses of action for the voter–consumer to choose between them. Separation of powers (functions) and the 'boundary' between society and polity are fundamental tenets of pluralism.

But what of the relevance of pluralism? However much the pluralist model of pragmatic interest-oriented coalitions transcending class divisions[23] approximates to the political process in the Western democracies,[24] it bears little resemblance to the situation in most of the 'developing countries'. Everywhere the states of the 'free world', or rather the rulers of those states, are turning towards authoritarianism. To update Rousseau: nations are born free (on independence day), but we see them everywhere in chains. The erosion of pluralist institutions in the Philippines (poor boundary maintenance because of the direct impingement of 'society' – that is, gentry-business power – on the polity) is no isolated instance. While the electoral overthrow in 1977 of authoritarianism in India remains a shining exception (though it does little to improve socio-economic conditions), it is the Philippine example that has been followed by the collapse of the elaborate competitive autonomous bargaining culture in the Lebanon, the bloody ending of the democratic experiment in Thailand, the rejection of a middle-class, welfare-oriented parliamentary democracy in Uruguay, and the brutal suppression of political liberty, free communication and economic association, for workers and peasants, in Chile. To go back a little in history: even the Sukarno regime, rightly criticised for its adventurist foreign policy and its economic failures, was far more pluralist in form and reality – the thriving mass organisations of peasants and workers, the religious and regional groups, the functional associations, the proliferation of parties – than the 'new order' of Suharto and the generals that took its place.

Even from the pluralist perspective, it is evident that the political characteristics of the Third World are either the breakdown of pluralism or its 'illegitimate' functioning. The first occurs as a result of the flood of raw unprocessed claims from 'society' which either overload the mechanism of interest articulation and aggregation, etc., or, worse, by-pass it altogether. The second is the case – by far the most common occurrence – wherever 'institutional interest groups', such as the military or the civilian bureaucracy, contrary to their explicit functions of defence and administration, usurp the role of interest articulation and aggregation in their own interests. Developmental pluralism provides no theoretical explanation why this 'overloading' or these distortions take place (and so frequently). It merely classifies what has happened case by case.[25]

Marxist theories, to the contrary, provide a powerful explanatory tool.[26] What the pluralists perceive as 'breakdown' the Marxist sees as revolutionary change: 'At a certain stage of development, the material forces of production in society come in conflict with the existing relations of production', that is, property relations; in an epoch of social revolution the change in the economic foundation transforms the 'entire immense superstructure' – the legal, political, religious, philosophical forms in which 'men become conscious of this conflict and fight it out'.[27] As for the typical abuse of power – strictly, abuse of functions – by the military or bureaucrats which, to the pluralists, represents an immature stage of development, because of the predominance of 'traditional' over 'modern' attitudes, to the Marxist this is the *normal* state of affairs. The government of a capitalist state is the executive committee of the bourgeoisie.[28] Such a government is designed to further capitalist expansion, through the exploitation of its victims, by drawing up appropriate rules of the game; identical parties, elections without choice, partial legislation, coercion of opposition, and an independent judiciary to safeguard the existing 'rights of property'.

Even though both pluralists and Marxists have theories to explain 'breakdown' and 'illegitimacy' in Third World countries, the difference between them is fundamental. The one perceives the situation as it approximates to the Western model: its analysis, and more significantly its prescription, are determined by that goal. Similarly Marxists perceive the situation in terms of the class character and the 'uneven development' of formally independent countries; their analysis and prescription are determined by the goal of revolution. In sum, pluralists look for (and sometimes find) *autonomous* entities in society; Marxists look for (and frequently find) structures of *dominance and dependence*, whose internal antagonisms give rise to forces opposed to that dependence.

Each theory excludes the other. To the one, the declared autonomy of churches, trade unions, political parties, judges, parliaments and cabinets is either illusory or intended to deceive. To the other, the emphasis on structural dependence is equally incorrect or misleading: to pluralists, the situation is one, or is potentially one, of bargaining, resulting in mutual – if not always equal – advantage, for the good of the whole. From the Marxist viewpoint, states are moving towards revolution; instances of autonomy are merely cross-currents in the tide of fundamental change. From the pluralist viewpoint, autonomy is the counterpart of the more specialised division of labour which both creates and is created by growth economies; externally, too, through the diversification of exports (and export markets) developing countries attain greater autonomy in the world market system as they approach the take-off stage.

Is it possible to have it both ways?[29] In my view it is, on the assumption that while both observe the same society, the pluralists look forward to the *possibilities* in society; the Marxists analyse the current *realities*. If there were no possibilities of pluralism in landowner-dominated societies, how could pluralist democracy ever have come into being in England, the USA and Western Europe?[30] Conversely the patron–client analysis – to round off the argument – in effect looks *backward* to the origins of those 'feudal' obligations, personal ties and reciprocal arrangements which still exist and indeed permeate behaviour in many Third World countries. As a general rule the client is subject to exploitation because he has so little bargaining power. But he does get some benefit in return for his arduous services: in physical terms, protection and subsistence; and, above all, he gets (or used to get) what Marxists usually ignore or deny – that is, psychological satisfaction from the sense of belonging to a community, to an ordered, if hard, way of life in an uncertain and frequently hostile world. How else could the patron–client system have endured so long?

To conclude: it is my contention that one can 'use' Marxism against pluralism – to examine the nature and extent of economic power, in any one country, regionally or globally, and the political processes by which economic interests are promoted and achieved. But one can also use pluralism against Marxism: to understand the possibilities of autonomous development, in particular of the state machine, the authoritarian leader, the military and elements of the bourgeoisie (including organised labour in many Third world countries), any or all of which may stand above classes, act with a sense of social responsibility and even represent the 'national interest'.

The strength of the Marxist perspective, as I have argued, is that it treats society as a whole; it seeks to establish the relationship between economic conditions and political processes. The utility of Marxism, however, is limited by its determinism, which does not sufficiently allow for various non-economic possibilities, or for different kinds of economic change. The strength of pluralism is exactly the opposite: that is, its openness to autonomous development. Its weakness, too, is the obverse of Marxism's strength, for it abstracts political issues from the socio-economic context; it treats them separately and therefore neglects or minimises the relationship between them.

Thus a given situation may vary greatly according to perspective. The same country, as I have shown in the case of the Philippines, may be quite unrecognisable from the other's perspective: it becomes a different country. This, as the current example of Vietnam makes clear, has enormous implications for policy-making and for the outcomes of those policies. Yet I believe that both are valid (if inadequate) perspectives. How can one overcome this dilemma?

My suggestion, therefore, is a further synthesis. It is to add a third dimension to the contemporary 'cross-section' analysis of Marxism and pluralism, by utilising the historical approach. It is historical research, above all, that enables one to discern the outstanding developments and thus identify the dominant patterns of behaviour in a particular society, or in international society. Given a long enough period of history, the underlying structural conditions may readily be distinguished from those features, often seen as significant or urgent at the time, which turn out to be superficial or ephemeral.

What is the relevance of this approach to my study? It is this. From an historical perspective, American involvement in the Third World is revealed, not just as a matter of shared perceptions (with Third World élites) of a common threat, or as the policy platform of a particular administration, or as an affinity between democratic societies – though all these at times and places may attain importance. Instead, American involvement results from the structure of American military, political and economic power and the way it intermeshes with the structures of power in Third World societies. These societies, in turn, face structural changes (largely as a result of this, or previous forms of 'intermeshing') which may lead to economic growth, but also to instability and unrest. The latter is the challenge which reinforces, but may also break, the 'intermeshing structure' described in its domestic and international aspects in this study.

Part one
★REVOLUTION★

Introduction

The *fact* of revolution and the *fear* of revolution have dominated American policy towards the Third World for more than a quarter of a century. Both fact and fear converge in the belief that 'indigenous' insurgencies and urban mass struggles as well as explicitly communist-led revolutions can be manipulated – at first by 'international communism', then either by Moscow or Peking – in a chain reaction of revolt against 'transitional' structures of authority in one Third World country after another. This is seen as a 'universal' threat, encompassing America's own security; thus it requires an equivalent response. The latter takes the form not only of indirect, i.e. 'preventive', measures but also of direct intervention, as in the Vietnam war. The range of options has been widened to include intervention by proxy by both sides (similar to Stalin's technique in Korea) as in Angola.

Thus two types of threat to an American-based 'world order' are intertwined: the one derived from indigenous circumstances – ideologically subversive or revolutionary movements threatening the internal stability of America's allies and friends; the other the result of great power rivalry (stemming from incompatible 'national interests') pursued by the expansion of military power or political and economic influence, or all three. This traditional form of rivalry is capable of exploiting ideological alignments on the one hand, and nationalistic causes – ranging from Third World countries' demands for greater political or economic independence to internal upheavals and ethnic separatism – on the other. At any one time, the ideological (as in the Cold War) or the national issue (in the era of détente) may predominate; or, as in the past, they may be inextricably combined – as in the European wars of religion and territorial aggrandisement.

15

Now consider the contemporary threats to world order posed by unrest, dissidence, revolt and revolution in the present environment: the heady fusion of African nationalism and anti-colonial fervour against racist regimes in southern Africa; turbulence and uncertainty in the Middle East and Southeast Asia; religious, ethnic, linguistic and economic tensions in south Asia; the ominous overtones of the Arab–Israel conflict; and the 'norm' of resistance and repression in Latin America. Given the potential for international crises in all these regions, can one assume that détente between the West and the communist powers on the one hand, and the post-Vietnam doctrine of self-reliance for America's friends and allies on the other, have put an end to the 'necessity' of global intervention?

This question needs to be broken down into two specific questions. First, in the environment outlined above, what are the possibilities of unrest being transformed into insurgencies or mass struggles and culminating in successful revolutions? I try to answer this question in the first part of this study. Second, given the ambiguous experiences of the past and the changes in the American domestic structure, what will be the likely reaction of US policymakers to current problems and probable trends in the external environment? This is the subject-matter of the second part.

First, an overview of internal struggle. Its characteristics in the past and of necessity (if it is to be effective) in the future, are summed up in four words: revolution, authority, mobilisation and welfare. The aim and motivation of revolutionaries is to overthrow the existing order. Protracted rural-based insurgency in alliance with urban elements is the typical form it takes, and is likely to take even in increasingly urbanised countries, if it is to achieve this aim. (Urban guerrilla warfare is a variant, depending mainly on disruption and attrition to erode the will and strength of the opposing regime: attacking the very nerve centre of power, the insurgents gamble on spectacular success despite the odds on a crushing defeat.) It is a contest for authority; the insurgents seek to substitute over ever-widening spheres their own authority for that of the incumbents. The way to do this is by mobilising popular energies. And the issue at stake is the people's welfare. But the latter entails a cruel paradox. In both communist and 'nationalist' revolutions the immediate issue of welfare rallies popular, especially rural, support. But once the struggle is won, popular welfare either becomes subordinate to the usually exploiting rule of a new élite (as Frantz Fanon bitterly observed), or else it is crudely fitted into a more or less dogmatic Marxist framework. Yet there is an important qualification: the Chinese model of authoritative allocation and control of manpower and resources is a dire necessity for countries, large or small, where population presses heavily on limited resources – whether limited physically or by structural constraints. In such countries the theoretical alternative of free ownership and reliance on market incentives – for the majority of people – can only be an illusion.

Second, the likelihood of revolution. Under the circumstances of many countries in the Third World, subjected as they are to the stresses of economic change, population pressures, ethnic rivalries and social polarisation, popular discontent may be transformed into rebellion. But whatever the global fears of American strategists, experience suggests that of dozens of uprisings, on a local or national scale, few will possess those special qualities of revolutionary mobilisation and of governmental ineptitude and critical weakness that made possible both a Cuba and a Vietnam. As I argue in this study, structural conditions in most of Latin America and much of Africa and Asia have so far served to depress the opportunities both for rural-based insurgency in the Chinese or Vietnamese style and for the type of 'catalytic' insurrection that erupted in Cuba. These conditions are the product of underdevelopment: peasant dependence, radical 'rootlessness', military caste loyalties, and middle-class absorption in the ruling system.

Third, the possibility of change. The four categories mentioned above are *pivotal* strata of society. Peasant deference, apathy or traditionalism may be transformed into opposition and struggle when segments of the peasantry (varying from landless labourers to tenant farmers and small and 'middle' owner-cultivators) become aware of their depressed situation and of the possibility of change. The amateurism of radical intellectuals may develop into 'professionalism' and the 'economism' of organised and unorganised workers may develop into radicalism by dint of experience in coping with repression, in working with other strata of society, and in organising an appropriate response. Soldiers under stress may disobey, mutiny or desert. The 'national bourgeoisie' may be alienated by the refusal of an intransigent élite leadership to provide 'middle-class' members with a genuine opportunity for political participation, by insecurity, economic crisis, and so on. Indeed a severe and abrupt worsening of the economic situation of a Third World country, confronting the expectations aroused by a period of slow but steady growth, may be the catalyst of revolutionary change.

Fourth, the symbiotic factor. A revolutionary situation results from the symbiosis of structural conditions and individual, group or class motivation. Revolutionary motivation (awareness of the *need* to change the 'old ways' and of the *possibility* of doing so) reflects the structural context (conditions of ownership, work, wealth, authority, security and 'justice' that are no longer bearable) and in turn transforms that context, successfully or otherwise, by its impact on those conditions. Thus structures give rise to motivation (whether in the form of deference or resistance) and motivation transforms (reinforces or undermines) structures.

The chapters, below, stem from this analysis. Chapter 2, which I confess does not always make for easy reading, emphasises motivation – but in specific contexts. Chapter 3 emphasises social structures, but also examines the problem the other way round: why, it asks, did revolution not break out, or if it did break out, not succeed, in countries where social and economic conditions were apparently conducive to revolt? The final chapter in part 1 considers the relationship between unique factors and common elements in revolutionary situations: the dialectic of autonomous development and 'global processes'.

2 * Revolutionary motivation

In any revolutionary situation there are four analytically distinct factors: social forces, i.e. impoverished sectors of the population and groups striving for upward mobility, as opposed to those with an interest in maintaining the existing order; consciousness on the part of the former that change is necessary, and possible; new forms of leadership and organisation; and substantial extrinsic pressures, ranging from economic dislocation on the one hand to political penetration and military intervention on the other.

These four factors operate dynamically: changes in social, economic and political structures, whether internally or externally derived, are changes in the relationships between individuals and groups in society; these changing relationships stimulate an awareness of 'unjustifiable' differences in societal roles and institutions; new roles and institutions are formed in response to this awareness; and these newly-formed structures express new relationships between individuals and groups in society, in an endless chain of causation.

Concretely, the main 'motive forces' of revolution in the Third World are particular categories of peasants; their motivation and awareness are the result of changes in the way in which they live and work; their desire to realise their new aims is blocked by the existing institutional framework; they are joined by dissatisfied urban elements – from among students, workers, teachers, professionals, clerks, artisans, migrants, 'marginals' and the unemployed – whose aims of improvement are similarly obstructed by the 'old order'; the latter are divided in their response to the challenge: and their authority is undermined, because their legitimising role of 'patronage' with regard to their following has been eroded by economic changes – and perhaps totally displaced through foreign intervention.

Such is the *concept* of a revolutionary process in the Third World, which has to be *realised*, if it is realised, under the specific conditions of a given society. Wherever conditions in areas of the Third World conform to the concept, then such conditions reflect Lenin's 'fundamental law' of revolution – with two important changes. The first is the substitution of peasants for 'proletariat' (or their incorporation, through loss of land ownership, in the proletariat). The second is the substitution of protracted struggle for rapid insurrection. The revolutionary law asserts the irreconcilable antagonism between the possessor and the dispossessed, which will be brought to its inevitable climax by the very processes generated by society itself (and by the international society).

Lenin's apocalyptic, Manichean vision of society is expressed in the famous formula: On the side of the 'oppressed masses', awareness of misery, accompanied by the desire and the determination to change that situation; on the side of the 'ruling classes', internal 'contradictions' aggravated by an often externally-derived crisis. 'Only when the *"lower classes" do not want* the old way, and when the *"upper classes" cannot carry on in the old way* – only then can revolution triumph.'[1] Lenin continues:[2]

> This truth may be expressed in other words; revolution is impossible without a nationwide crisis (affecting both the exploited and the exploiters). It follows that for revolution it is essential, first, that a majority of the workers (or at least a majority of the class-conscious, thinking, politically active workers) should fully understand that revolution is necessary and be ready to sacrifice their lives for it, secondly, that the ruling classes should be passing through a governmental crisis, which draws even the most backward masses into politics . . . weakens the government and makes it possible for the revolutionaries to overthrow it rapidly.

From this duality springs the third element of a revolutionary situation, which is the more or less rapid polarisation of society and the 'mobilising' effect this has on the 'hitherto apathetic' masses, drawing them into the struggle. The crisis of confidence affecting leaders of the regime thus has its counterpart in the conscious withdrawal of confidence in the regime by those who were formerly trusting, acquiescent or obedient.

The fourth element in a revolutionary situation is the ability of revolutionary leaders to analyse, understand and investigate a particular society and their tactical skill in 'seizing the moment' to launch the offensive – a mastery demonstrated by all the great revolutionaries from Lenin to Ho Chi Minh.

My aim in this chapter is to examine the *realisation* of the revolutionary concepts outlined above. I shall briefly discuss: first, the categories of peasants motivated to revolt and the contexts in which they do so; second, the problem of social consciousness – awareness of the need for change and the possibility of change – and the spread of this awareness; third, the actual or potential 'forces of opposition', including urban elements, versus the 'forces of order' in society; and finally, after considering universal and unique factors, examples of a revolution that failed (the Philippines), a partial revolution (Thailand) and a revolution that was 'carried through to the end' (Vietnam).

Peasant participants

Eric Wolf's major study of peasant wars in this century provides an excellent framework for discussion. After examining revolutions in Mexico, Russia, China, Vietnam, Algeria and Cuba, he concludes:[3]

> [The] peasant rebellions of the twentieth century . . . are but the parochial reactions to major social dislocations, set in motion by overwhelming societal change. The spread of the market has torn men up by their roots, and shaken them loose from the social relationships into which they were born. Industrialisation and expanded communication have given rise to new social clusters. . . . Traditional political authority has eroded or collapsed; new contenders for power are seeking new constituencies for entry into the vacant political arena. Thus when the peasant protagonist lights the torch of rebellion, the edifice of society is already smouldering and ready to take fire.

It is the spread of capitalist relations that has upset the traditional equilibrium of rural societies, creating three interlocking crises: the demographic crisis – the enormous pressure of increasing population on resources; the ecological crisis – the change from subsistence to commercial agriculture threatening customary peasant ways of combining resources to reduce risks and improve stability; and finally the crisis of authority:[4]

> The development of the market produced a rapid circulation of the élite. The manipulators of the new 'free-floating resources' – labour bosses, merchants, industrial entrepreneurs – challenged the

inherited power of the controllers of fixed social resources – the
tribal chief, the mandarin, the landed nobleman. . . . [Commerciali-
sation] deranged the numerous middle-range ties between centre
and hinterland, urban and rural sectors . . . at the very same time it
also lessened the ability of power-holders to perceive and predict
changes in the rural area.

Widespread social dislocation is a necessary condition for peasant
rebellion: but it is not a sufficient condition. Nor is extensive privation a
sufficient condition; 'if it were', as Trotsky said, 'the masses would be
always in revolt'.[5] Which among the various strata of the rural
population has both the motivation and the *ability* to rebel?

Although poor peasants and landless labourers are the most deprived,
they depend on landlords for the largest part of their livelihood, and have
no 'tactical power' of their own to launch a sustained revolt; they are
without sufficient resources, Wolf argues, to serve in the struggle for
power.[6] However, revolution cannot be carried on, Hamza Alavi asserts,
without the participation of the poor peasants;[7] and his assertion is
borne out by the Russian, Chinese and Vietnamese revolutions. Mao's
own experience is that 'leadership by the poor peasants is absolutely
necessary. Without the poor peasants there would be no revolution.'
Mao distinguished between the 'utterly destitute' 20 per cent of the
Chinese peasantry (without land or money) and the 'less destitute' 50
per cent (tenants, semi-owners, and handicraft workers), both of which
comprised the poor peasants, which 'have always been the main force in
the bitter fight in the countryside'.[8] (Middle peasants, in Mao's view,
were 'vacillating'; to them revolution would not bring much good: 'they
have rice in their pots and no creditors knocking on their doors.' But it
was 'essential' they join the poor-peasant-dominated associations.) Yet
Mao also spoke in an undifferentiated way of the 'several hundred
million peasants' rising like a mighty storm – a force so swift and violent
that no power will be able to hold it back.[9]

Rich peasants, on the other hand, can be excluded as initiators of
revolt: as employers of the labour of others, as money-lenders, and as
notables co-opted by the state machine, they exercise local power in
alliance with external power-holders.[10] Consider, for example, the rural
élite in India, who own more land than the average, are ritually pre-
eminent and, as village leaders, serve as a transmission belt between
central authority and the rural masses; in return for these services, there
is virtually no tax on land, official ceilings on holdings (where they exist)

are around 30 acres, and landless labourers who take to violence against the system are regularly shot down by the authorities.[11] Rich peasants are unlikely to embark on rebellion. But under certain circumstances they may take part in it: e.g. they may be motivated to unite with other peasants in an 'anti-feudal' struggle (as in China against the warlords and Kuomintang); and they are likely to join other rural and urban elements in a 'nationalist' revolution – as in China against the Japanese, and as in Vietnam against the French.

The third category is that of landowning middle peasants. They have secure access to their land, which is cultivated by family labour and, unlike poor peasants, have sufficient resources for 'tactical mobility'. It is the middle peasant, the main bearer of peasant tradition, who is the most vulnerable to economic changes: 'He is in a balancing act . . . [which] is continually threatened by population growth, the encroachment of rival landlords, the loss of rights to grazing, forest and water', and by falling prices and unfavourable market conditions. The middle peasant has the motive and the ability to resist.[12]

In the fourth place there are 'peripheral' – poor but 'free' – peasants outside the domain of landlord control. Peasants living in frontier zones, in mountainous areas, or who are ethnically or linguistically distinct from the surrounding population, are also tactically mobile.[13] It was in such 'peripheral' regions, from Mao's experience of the late 1920s and early 1930s, that 'one or more small areas under Red political power' could survive even when 'completely encircled by the White regime'. Such areas must be neither 'too close to the enemy's big political centres', where they would be dangerously exposed, nor yet too far away to exert any influence on the population.[14] Free peasants are also a force for revolt.

Finally, there are the tenant farmers renting family-size holdings: they are likely to play a key role wherever the intense competition for land as a result of heavy population pressure has driven up the price of land – and hence of rents – for they are the most visibly exploited group. This is because under conditions of highly productive land, a large supply of cheap labour and little mechanisation, it is in the landlord's interest to 'maximise his surplus' and not his agricultural production: the landlord gets high rents, where there is great land hunger, without making an effort. Such 'rent capitalism', as opposed to 'entrepreneurial capitalism', is not only conducive to rural instability – and to the mobilisation of the peasantry – but is particularly widespread in Asia.[15]

But to the question whether 'mobilisation' leads to revolution, the evidence is contradictory. On the one hand, the high incidence of tenancy and subsistence holdings in southeast China and in the Red River and Mekong Deltas of Vietnam is clearly associated with the spread of peasant rebellion. On the other hand similar rural conditions in India and Java did not result in large-scale, organised, sustained revolutionary movements. In Kerala, for example, overpopulation and inequality of ownership accompanied by a high degree of literacy transformed rural resentment into political action: but Communist Party control of the state of Kerala (for a time) was emasculated by the superior power of Congress operating at the centre. Similarly, the Indonesian Communist Party (PKI) developed wide support among the landless labourers, tenants and smallholders in densely populated east and central Java; but it functioned within the Javanese context of vertical (not class) structures – *aliran* – integrating in each 'stream' different socio-economic groups possessing common religious or cultural values.[16] The very success of the PKI's 'accommodation' to the environment made it incapable of directing the tide of protest to destroy the obstacles in its path. By pursuing a 'gradualist, moderate and flexible' strategy, relying on traditional patron–client and authority relationships, the PKI was able to organise on a mass basis, but failed to attain the goal of national power.[17]

Yet all the evidence indicates that some form of peasant alliance with radical urban elements is essential for the transformation of peasant discontent – or rebellion – into organised revolution. As Barrington Moore succinctly puts it:[18]

Whether or not this [rural revolutionary] potential becomes politically effective depends on the possibility of a fusion between peasant grievances and those of other strata. By themselves the peasants have never been able to accomplish a revolution. . . . The peasants have to have leaders from other classes.

This fusion is not effected easily. The peasant, in particular, is handicapped by the nature of his work and competition with his fellows for scarce resources; both the dispersion and the individualism of the peasant makes it difficult to pass from passive recognition of wrongs to political participation as a means to put them right.[19] The main barrier to peasant mobilisation is precisely *isolation*: physical isolation – separate holdings, lack of communication, desire for self-sufficiency; social isolation – rural stratification, extent of illiteracy, remoteness from towns; and psychological isolation – the apparent impregnability of the rural power structure undercutting the motivation for change.[20] Despite these obstacles, the process of rural rebellion necessarily involves a new awareness of the situation and the will to change it. Such a change in peasant motivation is essential to the revolutionary alliance between peasants and urban movements.

Motivation and mobility

How do peasants, traditionally-oriented, dispersed, and often divided in their interests, become aware of the need for change and of the possibilities of collective action to bring it about? Two basic factors are involved: the objective transformation of social and economic conditions outlined above: population pressures, competition for land, crop prices, systems of tenure and so on; and the subjective relationship among peasants and between peasants and landlords. As for the latter, where links between overlord and peasant are strong, as Barrington Moore points out, the tendency towards peasant rebellion or revolution is feeble.[21] But these links are also a compound of subjective and objective factors.

For a sense of community is dissipated precisely by economic and demographic changes which result in severe competition between landlord and peasant for land or other resources and thus in the failure of the 'exchange relationship' between the two.[22] The landowner is *expected* to perform various services to the community – providing security, settling disputes, behaving generously, giving help in times of sickness or drought, and so on – in return for the surplus he extracts from the peasantry. As in the feudal system, 'the contributions of those who fight, rule and pray must be obvious to the peasant, and the peasants' return payments must not be grossly out of proportion to the services received'. These folk conceptions of justice have a rational and realistic basis; landlord practices departing from this basis are likely to need deception and force the more they do depart from it.[23]

The rural norm of social relations is *reciprocity*: either between equals, reflected in customary 'mutual aid' practices, such as helping with the harvest and building a house for other villagers, with the expectation of similar help in return; or between unequals, as above, where informal social controls help to redistribute wealth or impose specific obligations on the patron with regard to his 'following'.[24] The peasant in effect bestows legitimacy even on a relationship between unequals so long as the expected performance and reciprocity of rights and obligations are recognised and carried out. This is because the peasant's sense of 'rights' – a 'just' price, a fair rent – is derived, not so much from considerations of what does or does not constitute 'exploitation', but from the fundamental need for survival: for the peasant this means the assurance of a stable income and subsistence security. The penalties for those at the margin of survival are so severe, indeed fatal, that he has no other choice.[25]

Now the spread of commercialism, growth of population and shortage of land (referred to above) not only directly threaten peasant stability and survival – they erode the customary (subjective) relations between landlord and peasants. Throughout the colonial period in Southeast Asia, Scott points out:[26]

the major changes in agrarian life produced a growing tenant class that was increasingly at the mercy of landowners for its livelihood and security. The growth of markets and the cash economy meant new instabilities in tenant income due to price fluctuations. . . . As demographic pressure on arable land mounted, and as a growing class of landless competed for tenancies, the landowner could use his tactical advantage to impose more onerous conditions. . . . Through its legal system and coercive [capacity] the colonial state enforced contracts, put down unrest, and made it politically possible for the landowner to extract the maximum advantage from his economic power.

The stiffening of tenancy terms was accompanied by tension and unrest. As tenant defiance grew, so landlords relied more heavily on the courts and the colonial police to maintain order, and they hired toughs and watchmen to enforce the terms of tenancy. The world economic crisis of the 1930s marked a watershed in agrarian relations: landlords, hard-pressed, tried to pass on the costs; they called in existing debts, tightened tenancy provisions, and dismissed defaulting tenants. These new hardships often constituted a direct threat to peasant subsistence, for they came on top of a collapse in crop prices and subsidiary employment opportunities. The peasant response was often violent, with major rebellions in Burma, Vietnam and the Philippines.[27]

The diffusion of a monetary economy and, with it, of contractual rather than customary social obligations, thus has three major effects. First, it tends to widen the material gap between landowners and rich, or enterprising, peasants on the one hand, and growing numbers of disadvantaged tenant farmers (including sharecroppers), smallholders and landless labourers on the other. Second, the transformation of superior-subordinate relations from patronage to managerialism and' from personal (if arbitrary) behaviour to impersonal legal enforcement upsets existing concepts of right and wrong, and compels an awareness among peasants of the new and disturbing world they live in. Third, peasant consciousness of change is not merely a by-product of modernisation; it is directly and continually stimulated by the very processes involved: new means of communication, diffusion of education, opportunities for social or geographical mobility, alternative forms of employment, and exposure to novel possibilities – with expectations to match. The dislocating effect of modernisation is, of course, offset by the advantages it can bring: access to consumer goods, mass communications, transport, opportunities for education, material improvement, social advancement, and so on. Whether or not the disadvantages outweigh the benefits in any individual country is a matter for empirical investigation.

The *nationalist* revolutions in Indonesia and Algeria demonstrate the social consequences of modernisation – as regards urban as well as rural strata – in much the same way as do the communist-led revolutions in China and Vietnam. Wertheim shows how the social mobility of the traditionally higher strata in Indonesian society had been furthered by Dutch educational and administrative practices. However, the colonial 'caste' system precluded them from achieving positions within the government commensurate with their educational qualifications. It is from within this frustrated élite that nationalist leaders arose. What contributed to the popular basis of the nationalist movement, however, was the emergence of small traders, especially in Java. This was due especially to the introduction of a money economy and to increasing shortage of land, which drove many peasants into trade. The economic crisis of the early 1930s seriously affected their opportunities in two ways. It curtailed the distribution of commodities and the collection of agricultural products for export. It led to increasing competition from the large number of landless peasants who turned towards commerce, swamping the urban markets with petty traders, and thus contributing to the pattern of 'shared poverty'. Even though the broad mass of Javanese peasants had practically no prospect of vertical mobility, there was significant horizontal mobility: movement to the towns, employment as plantation workers and under the Japanese occupation shipment overseas as forced labourers or work on fortifications and in the mines within Indonesia. Now the Javanese peasants actively participated in the post-war revolutionary struggle against the Dutch. This suggests to Wertheim the importance, and perhaps necessity, of increased horizontal mobility – bringing people together from different areas, thus facilitating the creation of nation-wide organisations and communications – in promoting a pre-revolutionary situation.[28]

In Algeria, too, while reformist Islam was one source of nationalism (emphasising the connection between Islam and the Arabic language), the other source lay in the development of an Algerian semi-proletariat. This came about in two ways. The first was through the decay of the traditional pattern of Algerian sharecropping. The introduction of French legal codes allowed sharecroppers to abandon their landlords and seek work elsewhere. The result was a wholesale exodus from the wheatfields into better paid, but seasonal and therefore precarious, work in the vineyards. The second arose from the movement of mountain Kabyles, facing extreme population pressures, into towns to become traders, storekeepers, transport workers, police, bank clerks, porters and miners. At the same time there was massive recruitment of Algerians, and especially Kabyles, to the labour force in France – amounting to well over half a million people by 1950. This had two major effects: the inculcation of French socialist ideas and organising methods among the migrants; and the rapid creation and diffusion of Algerian nationalism once the migrants returned home to find that they could do little to realise their aspirations in a *colon*–dominated society. These two developments – reformist Islam providing the cultural form for a new network of social relations between clusters of middle peasants and sons of the urban élite; and the city-ward migration of peasants, especially Kabyles, bringing them into contact with urban, industrial and professional ways of life – contributed decisively to the outbreak of the Algerian national revolt.[29]

Opposition and order

'Intolerable social and economic conditions had created the conditions for revolution', declared one of the foremost communist commanders in China in the 1930s; 'it was only necessary to give leadership, form and objectives to this rural mass movement.'[30] This statement sums up concisely the three major components of a revolutionary situation:

substantial strata of the peasantry as the 'motive force' of revolution; organisation and leadership by non-peasant or ex-peasant elements, especially intellectuals – surrogate for the 'proletariat' of Marxist mythology; and finally the 'blindness' of the existing order, whose incapacity or unwillingness to remedy 'intolerable' conditions deprives it of all legitimacy. Let us examine or re-examine these components.

First comes emphasis on the peasant struggle. In the conditions of the Third World, contrary to Lenin's Eurocentric formula, it is elements of the peasantry rather than the proletariat which have the motive and the ability to rebel. Indeed the organised 'proletariat' in most Third World countries is small or negligible; and in many countries it has become part of the 'institutionalised' status quo rather than an alienated and disruptive force. It follows that insurgency rather than revolution in Lenin's sense is characteristic of social upheavals in countries where the rural population is either substantial or overwhelming. In this situation revolutionaries cannot expect the urban general strike or nationwide insurrection of Lenin's prescription to be effective: this was the lesson of the disastrous attempts to 'seize cities' in southern China in the late 1920s and early 1930s. Instead they are compelled, by force of circumstance, to revert to protracted, rural struggle aimed at gradually changing the balance of forces in their favour. It is Mao's doctrine of 'encirclement of the cities by the countryside'. The form it takes is shown in a classic passage by General Vo Nguyen Giap describing the war against the French:[31]

> Guerrilla warfare is the form of fighting . . . of the people of a weak and badly equipped country who stand up to an aggressive army which possesses better equipment and technique . . . avoiding the enemy when he is stronger and attacking him when he is weaker, now scattering, now regrouping our forces, now wearing out, now exterminating the enemy, determined to fight him everywhere, so that wherever the enemy goes he would be submerged in a sea of armed people.

Second comes the urban alliance. The leadership and organisation of the peasant masses must be seen in its social context – that of the actual or potential 'forces of opposition' deployed against the prevailing 'forces of order' in a given society. The former consists basically of four elements: the depressed, but not necessarily radicalised, peasant strata; a small working class, whose organised members have become an institutionalised if subordinate element of the political and economic order; intellectuals, a significant number of whom (whether as students, teachers, members of the free professions and occasional radicals in the ranks of the bureaucracy and the military) are potentially or actually revolutionary, but who are also 'vacillating' and unstable; and finally the rootless slum dwellers, migrants from overpopulated rural areas, the unorganised, casual labourers or hangers-on in the inflated service sectors, Marx's *lumpenproletariat*, 'the street' of Middle Eastern riots and demonstrations, the 'city mob', Marcuse's 'substratum of the outcasts and outsiders, the exploited and persecuted of other races and other colours': that elementary force whose 'opposition is revolutionary even if their consciousness is not'.[32]

What formula for revolution emerges from these disparate segments of the forces of opposition confronting the 'forces of order'? The latter comprise the traditional 'establishment' of military conservatives, landed interests and religious orthodoxy; the 'new élite' from the bureaucracy, the professions and the financial, industrial and commercial middle classes; and finally those who aspire to upward social mobility from among the self-employed and the white-collar workers. One thing is evident: it is only when substantial elements of the 'middle classes' desert 'order' for opposition – or, to put it more concretely, when increasing disorder makes even opposition seem preferable to support of the status quo – only then can a nation-wide revolution take place.

Thus the third factor is governmental crisis. This is when the state of equilibrium between the potential forces of opposition and the forces of order – the 'normal' situation – is upset by the impact or even the threat of catastrophic change: internally, as a result of economic or political crisis; externally, chiefly as the result of war. It is then that the 'moment of truth' confronts the peasants when landlord exactions, heavy taxation, military depredations and official abuses, combined with crop failures, threaten their very existence: in turn, the middle classes, bankrupted by inflation, are driven to poverty and the verge of starvation. (In industrial countries, however, this may lead to fascism, not communism.) Both the rural and urban population then know that it is impossible to go on as before. The stark evidence of the need for change and the possibility of change breaks the psychological bonds of habitual obedience, compels a withdrawal of confidence in the regime, inspires the awakening from apathy to action:[33]

> In revolutions, as well as counter-revolutions and civil wars, there comes a crucial point when people suddenly realise that they have

irrevocably broken with the world they have known and accepted all their lives. For different classes and individuals this momentary flash of a new and frightening truth will come at successive points in the collapse of the prevailing system.

Concept and conditions

However plausible the concept of a 'revolutionary situation' – arising out of peasant mobilisation, urban dissidence and governmental crisis – conditions in the Third World, seemingly conducive to just such an outcome, in practice have produced different and even contradictory results. This is the case even though most Third World countries have broadly similar (inegalitarian) social structures, are subjected to the same global (capitalist) processes and their dislocating effects, and experience marked political instability. These factors are basic to the revolutionary process. And yet, taking the Third World as a whole, effective and sustained revolution (in contrast to sporadic outbursts of violence) is the exception rather than the rule.

There are two ways to explain this major problem. One considers the apparent (temporary) diversity to be merely the reflection of an underlying *universal* reality;[34] this reality can be expressed in the form of models, which may, however, be modified from time to time. The other, agnostic, approach takes refuge in empiricism: it pursues investigation on a case-by-case basis; this may provide a more satisfying explanation of the particular role of indigenous factors than does the universalist approach, but it ignores the wider, and especially the long-term, implications.

For the universalists, appearance and reality coincide in the great revolutions: in Russia, China, Vietnam. Admittedly, these hardly accord with the original Marxist model of revolutions breaking out in the most developed capitalist countries, where the contradictions are most acute.[35] But they do conform to the modified Leninist law of 'uneven economic and political development': this states that 'the front of capitalism will be pierced where the chain of imperialism is weakest', not necessarily in the advanced industrialised countries.[36] The second innovation follows from the first. Lenin in effect abandoned Marx's theory of distinct epochs – the epoch of bourgeois rule running its predestined course before it makes way for its successor, the proletarian revolution. Instead Lenin envisaged a continuous revolutionary process transforming the bourgeois-democratic into the socialist revolution – i.e. not permitting the bourgeoisie to 'call a halt' to revolution once it had gained power and thus, as happened repeatedly in nineteenth-century France, to suppress its working-class allies. For Lenin, therefore, revolutionaries must first join with one set of allies – the bourgeoisie and peasant masses – to crush feudal autocracy; then straight away unite with a second set – the 'semi-proletarian' peasants, equally as dispossessed as the workers – in the struggle to overthrow the bourgeois regime.[37] *Unlike* the situation of the 'developed' countries, where the bourgeoisie is at the height of its powers, it is the Russia of February and October 1917 that offers the appropriate revolutionary model: it is here that we find concentration of industry, 'hideous' exploitation in the factories, 'political flabbiness' of the bourgeoisie, 'intolerable' conditions – including unlimited landlord power – in the countryside, stifling autocracy and a war which 'fused all these contradictions' into a profound revolutionary crisis.[38] These are the conditions under which Lenin's dual formula can be realised: revolution will triumph 'when the "lower classes" do not want the old way' and when the ruling classes 'cannot carry on in the old way'.

But there are two significant weaknesses in the universalist approach. The first is that Lenin's formula, as such, is merely another way of saying that revolutionary situations produce revolutions.[39] The more tautologous the formula, the truer it becomes, i.e. the less it can be disproved.[40] The more the formula is elaborated, on the other hand, to improve its *explanatory* powers, the more easily it can be refuted, simply by pointing to concrete exceptions. The second weakness is that the theory of the working out of the revolutionary process – either in the Third World or in the capitalist world – can only be confirmed, or disproved, 'in the long run'.[41] If the 'long run' is a matter of decades, or even centuries, in the future, then it is hardly a subject for precise scientific evaluation. Indeed, it is either an effort to 'save' the theory, by claiming that whatever the current situation of many countries 'ultimately' the revolutionary movement will prevail; or else it is an act of faith – that revolution will take place because it *must* take place. This act of faith is similar to that of Christian missionaries who were convinced that the conversion of the heathen was, if not imminent, inevitable.

The alternative, *empirical*, approach is reflected in the findings of a recent American symposium on peasants, land reform and revolutionary movements.[42] Three of the papers, discussed by Henry Landsberger, covered the entire range of methods of investigation. One author, using the single-case approach with all its subtlety and richness, was reluctant to generalise. The second attempted to generalise, but with certain qualifying conditions. Only the third looked for single-cause explanations of peasant behaviour. Landsberger's preferences lay between the first and second, but the third, he argued, could still be recommended for heuristic purposes. More significant is the matter of substance. The three papers showed 'considerable agreement at a high level of generalisation' on only two points: first, that the peasantry is a highly *differentiated* social category, a fact which should be taken into account in analysing peasant behaviour; and second, that the conditions which facilitate peasant revolt *include* population pressure, ecology and war. There was 'much less agreement' as to the nature of peasant differences and none on the question of which strata of the peasantry are most prone to rebellion. Both poor and middle peasants were hypothesised as being the driving force of rural revolution. But it was not clear what objective conditions and subjective reactions give rise to peasant revolt. A number of variables were suggested: rising expectations, an increase in peasant welfare or, alternatively, in economic misery. It is improbable, Landsberger concludes, that a single cause of peasant revolt can be identified. But it may be possible to isolate a small number of intervening variables so that unique explanations need not be employed for every case. [43]

Such is the approach taken in my study; one that is mid-way between universal laws and specific conditions. I have already indicated the important factors in the revolutionary process; these are necessary, but not sufficient, conditions. To get an idea of the latter, one must turn to individual cases.

Case studies: Philippines, Thailand, Vietnam

The Philippines: a revolution that failed

The Huk rebellion[44] in central Luzon came close to overthrowing the Philippine government in 1950–1. This was the high tide of peasant ·revolt, aided by urban intellectuals, which receded almost as rapidly as it had advanced. But the social conditions conducive to revolt, the motivation of the peasant forces and the formation of a rural-urban alliance are highly significant: and so are their local limitations.

The situation in the Philippines, as pointed out in the previous chapter, reveals extreme concentration of landownership, business wealth and political control in the hands of a tiny élite. The rest of the population is divided into a small urban element – 'middle classes', factory employees, petty traders, artisans, casual workers, 'marginals' – and a large majority of peasants: in the early post-war years some two-thirds of the peasants were tenant farmers (chiefly sharecroppers), or landless labourers. Their proportion had been increasing throughout the century: less than one-fifth of the rural population was composed of tenants in 1903; there were over twice as many, more than 37 per cent, in 1948; and up to 50 per cent in 1961. Conversely, two-fifths of the land was owned by just over one-third of 1 per cent of the population in the mid-1950s.[45]

Large estates were either rented or worked by hired labour in small parcels of land, with a minimum application of capital. The landlord's return was assured because the mounting pressure of population provided for a steady rise in land values and a highly favourable division of the product. Owing to the disproportionate amount of output transferred as rent to landowners, 'poverty and economic insecurity for the peasantry are inevitable'. The long history of agricultural dissidence reflects not so much aptitude for revolution, but 'chronic desperation'.[46] The densely-populated, wet-rice-growing, lowland plain of central and southern Luzon has an exceptionally high rate of tenancy, a small number of very large landowners, a high incidence of absentee ownership, and paucity of kinship bonds (only 16 per cent of tenants rented from their kinsmen in central Luzon, compared to a national average of one-third).[47]

There were three main areas of revolt. First south of Manila, where half the people were smallholders and the rest were labourers on large estates, sharecroppers and cottage industry workers – a region which had been 'systematically victimised' for 150 years by demagogues, unscrupulous politicians and land racketeers. Second, in Manila itself, where the communists had successfully infiltrated labour unions and appealed to intellectuals, students, the discontented and the un-employed. And finally in central Luzon.[48] Here the Huk movement, with an armed strength of some 12,000 in 1950, faced a corrupt, demoralised and lawless regime.[49] Although largely communist-led, the overwhelming majority of the rank-and-file were not communists. Their motives for fighting were chiefly to confiscate the lands of oppressive landlords and distribute them to tenants; to get rid of the corrupt men in government, who were deeply entrenched in power; and to drive out the foreigners who were draining the country's resources.[50]

As noted, there was a high rate of tenancy in central Luzon – affecting 60 per cent of the population in 1948 – and especially in the revolutionary province of Pampanga, where it amounted to 86 per cent. Population growth had reduced the average size of farm in Pampanga to under half an acre. Both factors combined to produce an acute sense of threat to peasant survival and of the social obstacles preventing a remedy. Peasant awareness was further sharpened in Pampanga by their higher than average literacy and by their proximity to Manila.[51] The disastrous impact of economic and demographic conditions combined with ready exposure to urban ideas and influences produced an explosive situation: all the more so as the result of a drastic change in the traditional relationship between landlord and tenant. Referring to the position in Pampanga, one scholar points out:[52]

> As absentee landlords, the caciques [chiefs, 'bosses'] were no longer
> familiar with the problems and needs of the tenants. Many of the
> landlords hired managers to operate the haciendas [estates]. The
> new owners had no interest in familial responsibilities and tended to
> run the estates according to strict business principles. Tenants were
> pressed for repayment of loans, charged for services rendered, and
> forced to perform extra labour without the compensation of a carefree
> siesta. Impersonal efficiency had replaced the old easy-going
> paternalism. . . . [The term] 'caciquism' became the expression
> for exploitation without a corresponding responsibility for assistance.

The accumulation of peasant economic and social grievances confronting a system which provided no legal means of redress – undelivered government promises, intimidation by the military and constabulary, over-loaded courts – exploded in rebellion. But even the potentially powerful combination of agrarian protest and urban intellectual dissent failed to spread beyond the Pampanga-speaking areas – until a new combination of peasant bitterness and student radicals, known as the 'New People's Army', sprang up in its place.[53]

Thailand: partial revolution

Effective intellectual or 'middle class' leadership with little or no peasant (mass) support represents a first phase of revolution. It may bring down a critically-weakened, incapable or detested regime without ensuring structural changes. It is more than a political coup but less than a social revolution. Here the experiences of student movements, which are either radical in intention or compelled by circumstances to act radically, are particularly instructive – both in industrialised countries and in the Third World. First, they reveal the gradual build-up of frustration and discontent among the 'opposition'. Second, they demonstrate the habitual, almost instinctive, reaction of the 'forces of order' to severe criticism and protest: the complacent expectation that repression will produce the desired results; and complacency turning to panic if this expectation is belied.

Consider the 1973 'October Revolution' in Thailand. Three factors were chiefly responsible for the extraordinary upheaval which took place in an apparently 'stable' society: student disillusionment amid a worsening economic environment; the role of the king; and the harshness, self-satisfaction and vacillation of the military leaders.

Student attitudes and activities in the two main universities – training ground for the future élite of the country – expressed both frustration and idealism. Students felt frustrated, personally, because they were aware of the growing difficulty in getting jobs in the bureaucracy – the traditional high-status career sought by Thai students – and, quite apart from their own ambitions, were frustrated by the regime's regression from even the most limited political advance: for in November 1971 the military leaders had abruptly put an end to the constitutional experiment inaugurated three years before, by abrogating the constitution, closing down parliament, banning political parties and reimposing martial law. The blatant and almost casual way in which this was done, in the absence of provocation or of an atmosphere of crisis, was an affront to the students' sense of what was 'proper' in Thailand and an insult to their idealism.

Student resentment burst out in various forms: first a boycott of Japanese firms late in 1972, an action which the government had evidently encouraged (unwisely as it turned out) to put pressure on the Japanese to rectify a trade imbalance; then a massive demonstration over a scandal involving the military, in June 1973, which quickly developed into a protest against 'law-breakers' accompanied by demands for action against corruption, for an end to severe rice shortages, for the proclamation of a new constitution, and for the withdrawal of US armed forces (symbol of American backing for the military regime); this was followed four months later by the largest student and popular demonstration ever to have taken place in Bangkok. A quarter of a million unarmed demonstrators, urging the release of a dozen students who had been arrested (for petitioning for a constitution, which the regime itself had been promising but continually postponing), were fired on by elements of the military and the police. Immediately a peaceful demonstration turned into a riot and a riot into a revolt. The army commander-in-chief rejected the deputy prime minister's order to crush the angry demonstrators by force. Disavowed by the king, who was appalled by the carnage, the prime minister and minister of defence, Field Marshal Thanom Kittikachorn, and his deputy, Field Marshal Prapat Charusathien, who was also minister of the interior, acting director-general of police and until recently army commander-in-chief, fled the country along with Colonel Narong Kittikachorn, son of Thanom and son-in-law of Prapat.[54]

It was the king who emerged from political obscurity to play the (momentarily) decisive role. A constitutional monarch, King Phumiphon Adunyadet was accustomed to acquiescing in military coups. A year after his accession, in 1974, the army forced the civilian prime minister into exile; in 1948 it removed from power the civilian government it had installed; in 1957 the army overthrew a government increasingly under the influence of the police, in which it had recently shared power; a year later the army leader, Field Marshal Sarit Thanarat, staged a 'revolution', the antecedent of 1971, in which he abrogated the constitution, closed down parliament, banned political parties and imposed martial law. During this entire period the king sought to moderate the excesses of the military, but could do little in public apart from taking a stand in support of student protests in one or two of the most outrageous instances. The immensity of the student-popular protest movement in October 1973 and the callous and characteristic reaction of Prapat, the 'strong man' of the regime, demanding 'suppression' of what he called 'communist-inspired' activities ('If I hear the word "Constitution",' he might have said, 'I reach for my revolver') was the moment of truth for the king. The moral and political bankruptcy of the regime revealed in glowing contrast, like a gem finally cleansed of the incrustation which had obscured it, the charismatic qualities of kingship; an object of great respect on the part of the urban élite, and of real devotion by the ordinary people of Thailand.

As for the Thanom–Prapat regime, it remained strong in its control of the means of coercion until the very end, but it was flawed in its composition, which reflected the jockeying for power of rival factions and cliques. As a result, its decisions were fumbling, confused and vacillating – in this it was at opposite extremes to the previous regime, dominated by the masterful Sarit. The two leaders had been in positions of power for twenty years. They and their associates were corrupted by power, or by the perquisites of power. They had become self-indulgent, soft, 'trading generals': especially Prapat and his allies, who were able to amass fortunes, legally and illegally, as chairmen or directors of banks, trading firms, manufacturing companies, state and semi-official enterprises, owners of construction concerns, recipients of contracts, commissions, kick-backs, pay-offs, protection money and bribes. They were 'soft' in the sense, or rather absence, of social discipline; but they were 'hard' in the pursuit of their own, if not the national, interest. They suppressed any attempt at effective criticism and they encouraged, or at least allowed to take place, certain activities by Colonel Narong, which all too easily recalled the sinister exploits of Sarit's rival, police chief Phao Sriyanon, two decades before. They were repressive, but also complacent. They had got away with so much in the past: the jailing of members of parliament and the banning of political parties, the perpetuation of martial law whether or not there was an 'emergency', the carefully-framed illiberal constitutions which would be petulantly scrapped if any of the provisions caused annoyance – all this had gone on for years almost without opposition. Even protest movements could be manipulated: manifestations were not permitted under martial law (no unauthorised grouping of more than five persons was allowed) but they were in evidence, when needed, for use against Sihanouk, communist puppet and national enemy when he was in power, and afterwards as leverage against Japan. Student demonstrations could be turned on, and turned off, as the occasion required. So when students 'turned on' in enormous numbers *without* permission in October 1973 the regime was more than surprised; it was seized by panic.

A comparison with the revolt by students and other urban elements in France and Cambodia reveals the same forces at work – during the 1968 'events' in Gaullist France and in the period leading to the downfall of Prince Sihanouk in 1970: frustrated and alienated students and other intellectuals; a complacent yet somewhat authoritarian regime, whose acts of violence precipitate the crisis (in the case of Cambodia, these acts were 'authorised' demonstrations against North Vietnamese encroachments, which got out of hand); the spontaneous upsurge of revolutionary demands; and the temporary paralysis of the chief instruments of coercion – the army and police.

If we take the university to be a microcosm of society then the events of May 1968, which nearly unseated the Gaullist regime, acquire a compelling significance in the drama that was played out – a drama of changing values, heightened awareness and spontaneous solidarity among the 'forces of opposition' confronting the traditionalist outlook, the customary reliance on the obedience or apathy of the masses, the readiness to suppress rather than accommodate any challenge to the system, of the forces of order.

Yet the 'revolutionary' events of 1968 in France, 1970 in Cambodia and 1973 in Thailand are all cases of arrested development. In the first place, the crisis of confidence in the regime affected chiefly the intellectuals, especially students (in Cambodia, also army officers and government officials); the crisis shook the capital, not the provinces; it was a political, rather than a social and economic, crisis, although France in 1968 may be an exception: the 'broad masses' were not involved. In Thailand the two field marshals were expelled, the military was for a time in a state of shock, but with its powers and privileges practically unimpaired it readily promoted the coup of October 1976 which ended the democratic experiment. In Cambodia students and intellectuals played a major part in the overthrow of Prince Sihanouk; but they soon found out that they had only exchanged one stifling, incompetent, arbitrary and corrupt regime for another, which was worse. In France the government recovered from its fright: it bought off the workers, successfully appealed to the conservative loyalties of the great mass of Frenchmen and, as the Cohn-Bendits anticipated, achieved 'economic expansion through social peace'.[55]

The intelligent self-interest of the Gaullist regime stands at opposite poles to the 'Bourbon' stupidity of, for example, the French previously in Indochina and Algeria, the Dutch in Indonesia, the Nationalist Chinese, and Diem and his successors in South Vietnam. De Gaulle and Pompidou had grasped the importance of bringing about that state of 'apathy' in ordinary people, of restoring their 'unreasoning trust' in authority, which Lenin had foreseen as a fundamental obstacle – not just to the development of a revolutionary situation, which could in certain circumstances be sparked off by a crisis (as in France, Thailand and Cambodia) – but above all to 'carrying it through to the end'.

Vietnam: complete revolution

The Vietnamese revolution marks the fusion of the Philippine-type rural-based rebellion with Thai-style urban dissidence. The worsening situation of the peasantry on the one hand and the national demand for independence from the French on the other created three basic revolutionary conditions: the formation of a broad united front against colonial rule; peasant mobilisation and the motive force of struggle; and popular determination and endurance to wear out and finally overcome a more powerful enemy.

As in Lenin's formulation, revolution triumphed in Vietnam because the mass of the people 'did not want the old way'; and the ruling élite 'could not carry on in the old way'. The traditional Confucian élite had failed to prevent the French conquest; it had no answer to the problems posed either by the victory of the French or by the 'modernising' consequences for Vietnamese society. Similarly French colonial rule, in spite of, or rather because of, its considerable material achievements – schools, hospitals, roads, modern administration, irrigation and vast expansion of exports – both created new social groupings and at the same time frustrated their national and their economic expectations:

> Vietnamese landowners who tried to get a foothold in industry and big business were generally kept out by the French colonial mono-polies. By and large, Vietnamese were excluded from both the control and the profits of the modern economic enterprises which the French brought to Indochina. . . . Rice cultivation remained the province of the Vietnamese; the rice trade was in the hands of the Chinese. But the great rubber plantations in the south and the mines and factories in the north were French-owned. The Indochinese economy was dominated by French banks, chief among them the powerful Bank of Indochina. The country was dominated by an alien minority – and, almost inevitably, in an alien interest.[56]

As for political expectations:

> the structure of the French administration in Indochina offered no channels through which popular discontent could be translated into constructive political activity. Political parties, under strict control in Cochinchina, were not permitted to exist at all in Tonkin and Annam. . . . By declaring political opposition illegal and subject to police reprisals, the administration left nationalists who desired action no alternative but to operate clandestinely, as revolutionaries.[57]

The economic transformation of the countryside, especially in the South, with the creation of large landed estates, development of cash-crop plantations, use of indentured labour, and dispossession of smallholders, was accompanied by rapid growth of population.[58] By the

1940s nearly one million smallholders, with an average holding of only just over one acre, owned 40 per cent of the cultivated area in the North (Tonkin); 180 landowners owned 20 per cent; and the rest was owned by middle farmers or was communal land. In the South (Cochinchina) three-quarters of the farmers owned only 15 per cent of the cultivated land; 2½ per cent – 6,500 landowners – owned 45 per cent of the land; more than half the rural population had become sharecroppers; and communal land had virtually disappeared.[59]

The beginnings of industrialisation and the spread of literacy wrought a similar transformation. Nearly 100,000 Vietnamese, mostly peasants, were sent to France in the First World War to become workers or to support the troops at the front; they learned to organise in unions and were readily influenced by socialist ideas.[60] The growth of national and social consciousness in Vietnam was reflected in an outpouring of 'inflammatory newspaper articles, speechmaking, processions and student strikes . . . strikes and clashes at mines, plantations and factories' culminating in the army mutiny at Yen Bay in 1930, the hunger marches of peasants and the formation of peasant 'Soviets' at Nghe An.[61]

As a French historian noted, it was the first time that a political movement (the newly formed Indochinese Communist Party) had been able to mobilise the rural population, which had hitherto been aloof from all political activities: 'The traditions of nationalism, the disappointed hopes of the humiliated intellectual élite, and the social aspirations of the proletariat had combined.'[62] Meanwhile hundreds of young activists made their way to Canton or Paris for technical study or revolutionary training. Union organising, workers' strikes, peasant protests against high taxes, land expropriation and usury, and urban demands for an end to government monopolies and administrative abuses – all gained in strength and legitimacy.[63]

This dual situation of frustrated urban nationalists and of peasants suffering from depressed prices for their crops, from eviction and indebtedness – all of whose attempts at organising for improvement had been suppressed by the French authorities – was dramatically altered by the effect of the Second World War. For the Japanese command in Indochina encouraged the formation of nationalist groups as a means of leverage against the French regime. Then, in March 1945 Japanese troops attacked, disarmed and ousted the French military forces and the colonial administration. Finally, in the confusion of the Japanese surrender in August 1945 the Vietminh 'Independence Front' – set up by Ho Chi Minh in southern China in 1941 – swept through

Vietnam 'like a miracle . . . almost without firing a shot, a whirlwind sweeping away Japanese, foreigners of all kinds, and even the national dynasty'. This was a classic revolutionary insurrection, a sudden and total change of authority, an unmistakable sign of the new 'Mandate of Heaven'. As the French scholar Paul Mus observed, the complete swing from the discredited French and the traditional mandarins and village 'notables' on the one hand to the Vietminh revolutionary nationalists on the other, 'proceeding not by compromise as in the West . . . but by a total replacement', is the way in which the Vietnamese people are accustomed to represent history and to anticipate it: 'At times of crisis, institutions, doctrines and the men in power change altogether, just as one season replaces another.'[64]

However, the 'Bourbon' attitude of the post-war French Government, its inflexible administration in Indochina and, above all, the pervasive influence of the 'separatist' French *colons* in Cochinchina, combined in refusal to concede to the Vietminh the independence and unity of Vietnam, and made conflict inevitable. 'In the face of an enemy as powerful as he is cruel', General Vo Nguyen Giap later wrote, 'victory is possible only by uniting the whole people within . . . a firm and wide national front.' Success would be achieved because: the struggle was a 'just war, waged for independence and reunification'; the revolutionaries were adopting the 'tactics and strategy of a people's war'. The Vietminh national front comprised 'all the revolutionary classes, all the nationalities'; 'people's power' had been established during the 'August [1945] Revolution' and was 'mobilising and organising the whole people for the Resistance'; and 'above all', the war was 'organised and led by the Party of the working class'.[65]

Vietminh agrarian policy played a decisive role, as Giap pointed out, in the building of rural bases, the reinforcement of rear areas and the 'impulse' given to the resistance: 'In a country where the national question is essentially the peasant question the consolidation of the resistance forces was possible only by a solution to the agrarian problem.'[66] The Vietminh reduced land rent and rates of interest, but it could not carry out a thorough-going programme of land reform for fear of alienating both landowners and better-off peasants who were sustaining the independence struggle. It was only with the mounting tempo of war and the need for the utmost support from the hard-pressed peasantry that the Vietminh leadership revived the campaign for land reform. 'The peasants', stated Ho Chi Minh himself, 'make the biggest contribution to the Resistance', providing soldiers, guerrillas, and paying taxes; 'nevertheless, they are the poorest people, because they have not enough land to till. . .'.[67] The goal of land reform, Ho reported in December 1953, is to 'distribute land to the tillers, liberate the productive forces in the countryside and speed up the Resistance war'; at the same time, 'it exerts an influence on and disintegrates the puppet [Bao Dai] army because the absolute majority of the puppet soldiers are peasants'.[68]

Precisely the same intense motivation on the one side and the lack of it on the other were to prove decisive in the revolutionary struggle in South Vietnam. As American intelligence analysts pointed out, the 'Nationalist appeal in Vietnam is so closely identified with Ho Chi Minh that, even in areas outside communist control, candidates and issues connected with "nationalism" and supported by the Vietminh would probably be supported by the majority of the people'.[69] Moreover, the Vietminh and its successor (the National Liberation Front) promised a social revolution to the people of the South; the Diem administration, creating a new bureaucratic structure on the wreckage of French rule, turned back to mandarin traditions.[70] Isolated and arrogant, ruthless yet incompetent, the Saigon government, despite overwhelming technical superiority and ever-increasing American economic and military assistance, was unable to make headway against a few thousand rural guerrillas. Once the insurgency had started in earnest in 1959 – actually in self-defence against the Diemist campaign of persecution and slaughter of former Vietminh supporters[71] – the regime was in serious trouble. In 1963, in an excess of folly, Diem turned against the Buddhists. All the fissiparous forces of South Vietnam, too long repressed, were now released: resulting in religious disputes, regional rivalries, army ambitions, political intrigues, student indiscipline, trade union unrest, tribal revolt – and, in the background, the rural-based liberation front, launching ambushes and attacks on an ever-wider scale. Thus by early 1965, according to American military reports, NLF units were advancing 'with total freedom' in central Vietnam and 'moving unimpeded' between their war zones north of Saigon and the 'critical delta areas'.[72]

South Vietnam was polarised between a network of peasant associations, organised and led by veteran revolutionaries, in a struggle based on immediate popular demands, and a government formed by, and in the interests of, a wealthy, educated, urban élite. The revolutionary leadership, as Jeffrey Race points out, had structured its forces so that they were inextricably bound into the social fabric of rural communities by ties of family, friendship and common interest. 'The [Communist] Party's demonstrated organisational superiority has come about not through attention to treatises on effective organisation, but rather through the development of social policies leading to superior motivation.'[73]

Bonds of loyalty between individuals and (NLF) local community leadership were based on the latter's ability 'to resolve concrete local issues of importance in the peasant's life: land, taxation, protection from impressment into the national army, or a personally satisfying role in the activities of the community'.[74] The land question was fundamental. In 1960–1 there were some 2 million landless peasants in the Mekong Delta, and about 6 million affected by tenancy – out of a total Delta population of 10 million.[75] 'Under communist practice land redistribution was essentially a local matter, decided by local people at the village level.' Government land redistribution, on the contrary, 'was carried out by cadres of the central government, on the basis of an inflexible law which made no provision for the differing needs of each locality'.[76] In terms of effective redistribution, Diem's land reform aided only about 10 per cent of the landless.[77] But from the peasant's point of view, communist land policies were 'for the vast majority, very effective'.[78]

Communist Party policies were, above all, aimed to redistribute power and status – again, contrary to traditional administrative practices. Under the Saigon government, as under the colonial regime, critical decisions were made at the lowest level by the district chief, or at higher levels by the province chief, regional delegate, etc., all of whom were appointees of the central government. These were initially civil servants, later military officers. Advancement to the appropriate administrative grade or entry into the officer corps required the French-style *baccalauréat* degree:

> Since the baccalaureate was effectively limited to the urban middle
> class and upper classes and the rural landlord and rich peasant
> classes, the overwhelming majority of the rural population was simply
> excluded from power over the decisions affecting their own lives.
> Power instead was exercised by those social elements least capable
> of empathising with the rural population and whose personal interests
> were in conflict with those whom they ruled.

Contrary to the communist policy of developing local initiative, the government suppressed local leadership, maintaining control instead by centralising power in the hands of officials appointed by Saigon to rule the countryside.[79]

The Saigon government, despite changes of personnel, survived for two decades – with American support. Saigon lived on massive transfusions of economic aid: a huge import surplus financed by the USA, bringing in a million motor bikes and scooters, 75,000 water pumps for irrigation, large amounts of subsidised fertiliser.[80] Saigon depended for its life on American military forces, airpower, training, money and equipment (over $5 billion worth of arms and facilities were captured in the 1975 campaign).[81] But once the artificial props were removed the entire structure collapsed.

3 * Structural context

The previous chapter first analysed the general conditions of rural instability, reflecting the impact of capitalism and demographic pressures on traditional systems, and then examined some specific cases, where these conditions culminated in protracted, rural-based resistance: i.e. a struggle to change the balance of forces, from initial weakness to strength. The significance of these cases is two-fold: contrary to Marx's suppositions, successful revolutions have broken out in the developing, rather than in the developed, countries; contrary to Leninist doctrines, the peasantry, rather than the proletariat, has been the motive force of revolution.

The present chapter begins by discussing yet another innovation in practice – and theory – which is in part an extension of Maoism and in part a return to Leninism. It starts from the fact that social instability in the developing countries makes possible protracted rural revolution; but goes on to argue that these same 'explosive' conditions can be 'detonated' – without the necessity either of peasant mobilisation or of protracted war. Just as the revolutionary theory of the 'weakest link' by-passes the industrialised nations, and as the Russian revolutionary model by-passes (or rather fuses) the hitherto obligatory two stages of bourgeois democracy and socialism, and as the Maoist revolution by-passes the proletariat, so the Cuban revolution by-passes all three – and the need for protracted struggle. In sheer economy of means the detonation theory can hardly be surpassed.

Cuba 'exploded'. But the very success of the Cuban revolution raises important questions for the theory and practice of revolutions. They can be divided into two main groups. First of all, is Cuba *exceptional*? Or are conditions in all or most parts of Latin America equally explosive – as the Cubans (used to) think? If they are, can they also be 'detonated'? Or, despite the Cuban experience, is it still unlikely that protracted struggle can be avoided? And second, does the Cuban revolution reflect the significance of *non-rural* factors in Latin America? If so, is urban insurgency more than a variant – in fact is it a substitute for rural revolt? Thus, given the *world-wide* trend towards rural displacement and urban growth, is the day of the peasant guerrilla over? Will urban insurrection be the model for revolutionaries throughout the Third World?

These specific factors must also be considered with regard to the voluntarist implications of 'detonation' and the structural implications of 'explosiveness', either within a rural or urban context. Last, whether the revolutionary struggle in a given country is professionally organised or is a spontaneous mass eruption, whether it is protracted or 'catalytic', rural or urban, the common aim is to bring about the 'revolutionary situation' expressed in Lenin's formula: i.e. the polarisation of society through awareness of their conditions by the poor and the repressed; and the disruption of the regime (its confidence and will to rule are shattered).

First of all, then, I shall discuss the specific features of the Cuban revolution and its projection on a 'continental' scale; second, examine the reasons for the failure of Latin American insurrections to develop according to the Cuban model; third, consider Algerian nationalism as an alternative model, with characteristics both of peasant resistance and urban struggle; fourth, point to the aims, experiences and consequences of urban insurgencies; and finally assess the efficacy, under present circumstances, of the Maoist strategy of rural encirclement.

Catalytic insurrection: Cuba

The key to the problem is suggested by Engels, in a letter written in 1885, when he states that there are 'exceptional cases where it is possible for a handful of people to *make* a revolution, i.e. with one little push to cause a whole system . . . to come crashing down and thus by an action in itself insignificant to release explosive forces that afterwards become uncontrollable.'[1] In Che Guevara's aphorism: 'It is not necessary to wait until all conditions for making revolution exist; the insurrection can create them.'[2]

The Cuban revolution is one of Engels's exceptional cases. It is a 'catalytic insurrection', as opposed to a protracted insurgency: a wide-ranging and rapid sequence of events, depending on an unusual configuration of circumstances for its success. According to Régis

Debray, its best-known theorist, the 'insurrectionary centre' (the *foco*), organised by professional revolutionaries, is set up as a 'detonator' precisely at the point where the regime is at its weakest; and it is designed to explode at the most favourable moment.[3] Debray claims that the insurrectionary process marks the 'growth of an isolated minority into a minority which is the nucleus of a popular movement, which in turn gathers force in a final tidal wave. . .'.[4] The myth of the *foco*, like that of Sorel's general strike,[5] electrifies the masses: it emits shock waves of energy and enlightenment, which galvanise the peasants and workers into awareness and action.

The tempestuous, elemental quality of 'unleashed' popular revolt puts the catalytic insurrection into a totally different category from that of the gradual, painstaking transformation of the balance of forces sought to be achieved by protracted insurgency. Insurrection is in the romantic, heroic tradition, the supreme expression of will; insurgency is calculating, realistic, the grim, stubborn determination to overcome formidable odds. The catalytic insurrection was the storming of the Winter Palace in the October Revolution of 1917; it succeeded 'as if by a miracle' in the Vietnam of August 1945; it was the aim of the Algerian revolutionaries, whose violent acts were intended as a psychological shock to awaken the masses from their disillusionment and apathy to hope and eventual action;[6] it was the 'Ghoshal Thesis' of the Burmese Communist Party to 'overthrow the government by force' in 1948;[7] it is the rationale for most forms of urban insurrection.

The catalytic insurgency offers a great attraction by the force of its logic and the economy of its means; yet it rarely succeeds outright. The Burmese communists are still fighting a protracted war; the Algerian nationalists were forced to take to urban terrorism, combined with guerrilla raids from mountain strongholds, and finally to the creation of an army in exile (across the borders in Tunisia and Morocco) before the French of the metropolis, sickened by the nature of the struggle and appalled by the danger of civil war, renounced the conflict. The Bolshevik Revolution itself could only be 'ratified' by the verdict of civil war, the Vietminh 'August Revolution' was only confirmed after eight years of guerrilla fighting against the intervening power, culminating in mobile operations and 'positional' war (the siege of Dien Bien Phu); the Mexican Revolution of 1910 only 'institutionalised' after a decade of bloody struggle, towards the end of which the leader of the southern peasant movement, Emiliano Zapata, was assassinated and Pancho Villa, northern peasant leader, made his peace with the forces of order.[8]

Two factors were responsible for the success of catalytic insurrection in Cuba: the unusually dependent, frustrating, 'transitional' character of the Cuban economy and society; and the abject failure of will of a corrupt and demoralised dictator, whose lawless methods had aroused nation-wide resistance.

Cuba's was a 'revolution of the rootless'.[9] Here the sugar industry, dominated by American capital, played an enormously important economic and psychological role. The whole economy 'fluctuated to the rhythm of the sugar harvest'. About one-third of the labour force was employed in the sugar industry: for five months the workers were comparatively well paid, but for the rest of the year they could expect to earn nothing.[10]

Cuban society had become increasingly stratified, but the country was far from impoverished by Latin American standards. Its relationship to the poverty of the Brazilian masses and the wretchedness of the 'banana republics' was like that of (Wolf's) middle peasants to subsistence farmers and landless labourers: increasingly drawn into the commercial world, hence vulnerable to external economic changes, but with the potential and the motivation for independence.[11] Indeed, Cuba was well on the road to modernisation, American-style. In 1956 its *per capita* income was the equivalent of $336, the second highest in Latin America. Its main industry, sugar, was highly mechanised, and the country possessed one of the three well-developed railway networks of the continent. One in five Cubans was a skilled worker; two-thirds of the people were literate.[12] Nearly a quarter of the economically active population was in 'middle-class' occupations: the third-highest proportion in Latin America, after Uruguay and Argentina, but before Chile.[13]

The price of modernisation was to live in the shadow of the economic power of the USA. In the 1950s, Americans owned 90 per cent of the telephone and electricity system, 50 per cent of the railways, 40 per cent of raw sugar, and banks holding a quarter of Cuban deposits. Over 70 per cent of Cuban exports went to the USA, over 75 per cent of imports came from the USA.[14] Yet nationalist reaction to this overwhelming alien presence was reflected in the outcome of the revolution rather than in the actual course of fighting. For Cuban attitudes to the USA resembled a love–hate relationship, similar to that observed in many colonial situations. There was an acceptance of dependence because of the material and cultural benefits that ensued but, at the same time, a rejection of what had been bought at the expense of national pride.

A 'frustrated' society, from the irregularity and insecurity of work and wages, the extreme fluctuations in world prices for sugar, the thwarting of Cuban aspirations for economic improvement ·and an end to corruption by the return of Batista to power in 1952, and the 'continuance of a cynical and short-sighted system': yet with an awareness of Cuban identity forged by generations of struggle against Spain (independence was achieved long after the liberation of other Spanish American colonies), the absence of regional-based obstacles to unity (because of the weakness of the Church, the disruption of the army, the subordination of trade unions), and finally a revolutionary tradition rooted in sixty years of 'almost perpetual crisis';[15] the fusion of patriotism and social aspirations produced the maximum unity of the revolutionary camp.[16]

The reason why Castro succeeded is evident. On 3 April 1961 the US 'White Paper' on Cuba summed up the position in two sentences:

> The Cuban Revolution . . . could not have succeeded on the basis of guerilla action alone. It succeeded because of the rejection of the [Batista] regime by thousands of civilians behind the lines – a rejection which undermined the morale of the superior military forces of Batista and caused them to collapse from within.[17]

In Cuba, Castro's heroic stand in the Sierra Maestra served to focus the individual strands of urban disgust with and resentment and fear of the Batista regime into one intense force which seared through the rigid, yet brittle, bonds of coercion. The revolutionaries themselves were predominantly young intellectuals, and the greatest sympathy with the movement was among the middle classes, observes a witness of the revolution.[18] Rául Castro underlined the role of the middle classes when he declared in June 1959 that 'twelve lonely men [the revolutionary vanguard], thanks to the support of the whole population, in collaboration with the workers, members of the liberal professions, intellectuals and businessmen, who loved their fatherland, destroyed an apparently invincible army'. Castro did not destroy the enemy, reported the French journalist Claude Julien, 'The latter collapsed because he was rotten to the core'.[19]

A valiant band of warriors, whose exploits seized the imagination of the people; the alienation of a significant part of the middle classes, who were appalled by Batista's counter-campaign of repression during which 'terror ruled the country. Torture became an everyday event'; a demoralised army, 'full of corruption and intrigues' which, after the failure of the 'final offensive' of mid-1958 was in a state of collapse.[20] These were the features of the Cuban revolution.

The irony is that the one outright success of catalytic insurrection in Latin America took place contrary to the original intentions of its promoters. The resort to rural guerrilla warfare did not occur out of any deliberate plan to use it. Castro 'backed into' it after all his other plans had failed. His first, abortive, attack on the Moncada barracks in 1953 was thought out in terms of 'a spectacular pronunciamento and heroic act to set off a popular uprising in Santiago de Cuba'.[21] Even the invasion of Cuba in December 1956 was a variant of the first plan. The landing was intended to coincide with a revolt in Santiago, to be followed by a country-wide campaign of sabotage and agitation culminating in a general strike – the so-called urban concept of struggle, later derided by Guevara and Debray. But, as one of the invaders put it, 'everything went wrong'. Of the 82 men who sailed in the *Granma* only a handful – not more than 12 or 15 – were able to strike out for the nearby Sierra Maestra to avoid capture.[22] Yet it was this audaciously improvised guerrilla warfare that was to become known as the Cuban model. The aim of the 'Sierra' – in contrast to that of the 'Plain' – as Guevara later rationalised it, was to 'carry out the guerrilla struggle, to spread it to other places and thus, from the countryside, to encircle the cities held by the dictatorship; by strangulation and attrition to provoke the break up of the regime'.[23]

Thus what was actually a catalytic insurrection in the form later publicised by Debray, which had been intended to be catalytic in the tradition of the *caudillo* or perhaps of Blanqui, was presented by Guevara as a protracted insurgency in the style of Mao. This was to have serious consequences for the understanding and still more the promotion of revolution in Latin America.

The extent of privation elsewhere in Latin America (with the exception of Europeanised Chile, Uruguay and Argentina) is far greater than it was in Cuba. The great majority of the people receive a disproportionately small share of the total product. The top 5 per cent of population own as much as one-third to two-fifths of total income in Colombia, two-fifths in Brazil, nearly one-third even in Argentina and 27 per cent in 'revolutionary' Mexico.[24] The depressed rural sectors, in particular, were (and basically still are) subjected to classic forms of exploitation by a small number of wealthy, little taxed, often absentee, landowners. About half the agricultural population in Latin America directly depend on large estates for employment. In Argentina more than one-third of rural families are landless, in Colombia almost one-quarter, in Brazil nearly 60 per cent. In seven countries, including the above, estate owners hold over three-quarters of the agricultural land: 'The state's police power is generally at the estate owners' disposal to protect their property and this may be supplemented by private strong-arm forces.'[25]

This was the explosive situation which the Rockefeller Report on Latin America seemed to confirm: 'The rising frustration throughout the Western hemisphere over poverty and political instability have led increasing numbers of people to pick the United States as a scapegoat and to seek out Marxist solutions to their socio-economic problems.'[26] However, the solution put forward by Fidel Castro was Cuba's *alternative* to 'institutionalised' communism – the way of armed struggle. 'The duty of every revolutionary', declared Havana, 'is to spread the revolution.'[27] For the 'objective conditions' for revolutionary struggle, claimed Castro, existed in the 'immense majority of Latin American countries'. And although 'the masses make history', they must be 'launched into battle by revolutionary leaders and organisations'.[28] With the formation of the 'guerrilla international' at the Havana Tri-Continental Conference of January 1966, which marked the high peak of revolutionary fervour, Castro clearly made a bid for the leadership of these insurgent forces.[29] A year later Che Guevara issued his famous call for 'one, two, many Vietnams'.

Guevara was convinced that 'a nucleus of 30 to 50 men' would be 'sufficient to initiate an armed fight in any country of the Americas with their conditions of favourable territory for operations, hunger for land, repeated attacks upon justice, etc.' The struggle, he wrote, 'will be bitter and long, reverses will be suffered; they [the guerrillas] can be at the brink of annihilation; only high morale, discipline, faith in final victory, and exceptional leadership can save them'. But, and this was the clinching argument, 'this was our Cuban experience'.[30] Both Castro and Guevara believed there were real possibilities of developing a continent-wide uprising. 'Everything indicates that this will go international from the start', Guevara told Castro at the beginning of his fatal Bolivian adventure.[31]

Why failure?

What falsified revolutionary expectations? Were Cuban conditions typical of other Latin American countries or was the downfall of the dictator exceptional? If conditions were typical, then why did insurgent movements elsewhere fail to maintain their 'promise'? For, as one analyst points out, most of the 'spate' of insurgencies in the 1960s were feeble and shortlived', even though some 'for a time seriously threatened either the stability of the government or its control over certain districts', particularly in Colombia, Guatemala and Venezuela, and later in Uruguay.[32] Yet by the end of the decade almost all the insurgencies had been contained: they were weakened, fragmented, and in many cases virtually decimated.[33]

Reasons for failure vary according to the level of analysis: first, that of personal qualities, including the unique characteristics of Castro and Batista; second, short-term changes, political, military and economic, in a number of countries; and finally structural factors: the immature and disorganised character of radical movements; loyalty of the armed forces; dependence of the peasantry; and the 'stabilising' role of the 'national bourgeoisie'.

First, leaders and personalities. Davis bluntly attributes the revolutionary failures in Latin America after Cuba to the fact that there has been no other insurgent chief with the political and military ability of a Castro, and no other ruler like Batista, 'both ineffective and unpopular, failing either to isolate the guerrillas politically or to bloody them militarily'.[34] Davis makes the further point that Latin America's presidents and generals have taken the lesson of Cuba very much to heart. Thus it is difficult to re-create the type of middle-class opposition to Batista, such as the 'Civic Resistance' formed in July 1957 in Havana, whose 'continual activity and courage . . . tied down police and soldiers and demoralised the government';[35] for everybody knows that the result in Cuba was the transformation of a middle-class revolt into a socialist revolution. As Debray puts it, the outcome of the Cuban revolution warned off elsewhere in Latin America precisely those sectors – the rich peasants, industrial middle class and petty bourgeoisie – which had been on the side of Castro's revolutionaries in 1958–9.[36]

Yet, in answer to Davis and Debray, it is possible to envisage a situation in which middle-class resentment and fear of a dictatorial and incapable regime are *greater* than their fear of the revolutionary potential of a united front formed with radicals to oppose that regime. Indeed, the situation in Nicaragua, and especially the upsurge in Iran, provide convincing examples.

In the second place, how correct is Davis's assumption that the extraordinary ability of the revolutionary leader confronting the uncommon weakness of government and crucial 'loss of nerve' of the Cuban dictator are circumstances that are unlikely to be repeated elsewhere? In contrast to the 'warning-off' effect referred to above, the significance of this assertion is its attempt to explain in terms of personality what are basically structural factors. It cannot, of course, be doubted that Castro's personal qualities markedly affected the outcome; but it is the latter part of the assertion that is misleading. Is a dictator's loss of nerve, as Davis implies, so very unusual?

In fact it is rather commonplace, and not only in Latin America. Ayub Khan of Pakistan was brought down by a few weeks of rioting in 1969 after nearly a decade of 'stable' rule, during which period his system of 'basic democracies' was seen as a model of enlightenment. Syngman Rhee, after fifteen years in control of South Korea, swiftly resigned once the army had refused to fire on student demonstrators. The Shah's 25-year authoritarian role in Iran, considered as the embodiment of stability in the West, collapsed in a matter of months in 1978. The 'panic' which seized Field Marshals Thanom and Prapat in Thailand, and the collapse of Prince Sihanouk of Cambodia, in spite of his vaunted popular support, have already been mentioned. As for Latin America, President Peron after a decade of power was ousted with almost contemptuous ease by the military in 1955; and President Arbenz of Guatemala showed conspicuous 'loss of nerve' in 1954, when the anti-communist exile, Castillo Armas, with a band of 500 to 1,000 men had only penetrated a few miles inshore.[37]

What is unusual about the Cuban situation is not the ruler's loss of nerve – but the fact that the leader who displaced him not only seized power and maintained power, but used it to carry out a social revolution. The purpose of Castro and his fellow 'radical nationalists' was to end the island's dependence on the USA. Otherwise even the overthrow of the dictator would have left the system unchanged, and the efforts of the revolutionaries would have been in vain. Yet the pursuit of economic independence – through land reform, expropriation of large estates, nationalisation of foreign-owned enterprises and utilities – by its assault on powerful American interests inevitably involved a confrontation with Cuban élite groups (especially landowners, exporters and owners of sugar mills) hitherto dominant in society, who supported those interests.[38]

The contrast with Bolivia is instructive. In 1952 an alliance of radical middle-class intellectuals and a group of young officers overthrew a discredited government – thanks to the timely defection of the militarised police. For the first time the mass of the population – over two-thirds Indian – had become politically and economically mobilised: peasants, organised in syndicates, seized the land of the big landowners (5 per cent of the population owned 70 per cent of the land); the workers formed their own armed militia; the regular army was disbanded; land reforms were proclaimed; and the major tin producers – including the three companies which dominated the modern sector of the economy, producing 80 per cent of the country's foreign exchange – were nationalised.[39]

The revolution was abortive. The party in power (MNR) failed to mould its disparate groups of supporters into one strong institutionalised party like the Mexican PRI, with its constituent organisations of peasants, workers, youth groups, co-operatives and others. Among the leaders of the MNR there were bitter personal rivalries. The miners' leader, Lechin, was alienated. Agrarian reform stagnated.[40] The army was reconstituted, with massive US assistance (the military budget doubled between 1960 and 1963), to act as a counterweight to the workers' militia. Severe inflation eroded middle-class support. To reorganise the mining industry President Paz Estenssoro sought large-scale foreign capital investment. This he received on condition that the government carried out a rigid economic stabilisation plan, with a wage freeze, that the miners were 'disciplined', and that he accept General Barrientos, Air Force Chief of Staff, as vice-president. That year, 1964, the army was employed to crush a miners' rising; teachers and other urban groups struck in protest against the policies of the regime; General Barrientos led a revolt against the president; and the MNR collapsed.[41] In Cuba a coup d'état had turned into a revolution; in Bolivia a revolution had turned into a coup d'état.

The second group of reasons for the failure to repeat the Cuban example centres on the political, military and economic changes that took place in a number of 'vulnerable' countries in the 1960s. These were chiefly:

1 Urbanisation – the massive migrations of the 1960s had reduced the revolutionary potential in the countryside, by removing the most active or discontented peasants.

2 A somewhat similar effect was achieved by land reforms, carried out with varying degrees of success and commitment, in Venezuela, Peru, Colombia and Chile.

3 'Pre-emptive nationalism' was at work among the various classes in Peru, Bolivia and Chile.

4 Counter-insurgency methods had greatly improved, in weaponry, techniques and doctrines, especially in Peru, Colombia and Guatemala. And finally

5 Debray's deviation from the insurgent norm, stressing the subjective element, contributed to defeat.[42]

Richard Gott, a partisan of the guerrillas, substantially accepts this verdict. Indeed the crucial question, in his view, is how to convert an apathetic, alienated peasantry into a revolutionary force.[43] Moreover, the internal migration of peasants to towns acts as a 'safety-valve', just as the overseas migration from Europe to the Americas was a substitute for revolution.[44] Debray and Gott also emphasise the 'extraordinary reinforcement of the repressive apparatuses' from 1960 on: 'Battalions of Colombian anti-guerrillas, Ecuadorian paratroopers, Peruvian commandos, Bolivian "rangers", Argentinian gendarmes (equipped with heavy armaments) and many other military formations are organised and trained by U.S. military missions.' The main effort of counter-insurgency has been organised at the United States Southern Command base in Panama, with a staff of 500 or 600 officers from the three services, which has trained since 1962 more than 20,000 officers from all Latin American countries.[45]

As for the role of Debray, and notably his controversial but highly influential treatise *Revolution in the Revolution?*, one can only agree with Huntington that Debray's emphasis on voluntarism and 'action', which is most evident in this particular work, and the uncritical enthusiasm with which the message was received, had a disastrous effect on those who tried to apply it. In effect, Debray overturned both Soviet concepts of political, and Chinese and Vietnamese concepts of military-political, action. The guerrilla *foco*, according to Debray, is 'organically separate from the civilian population', it rejects the 'fetish' of fixed base areas, and demands 'hegemony' not only over the urban bourgeoisie and proletariat, but also over political activities, the communist party organisation, and the broad national front. To Debray, the 'guerrilla *foco* is the party in embryo' – not the other way round. 'This is the staggering novelty introduced by the Cuban revolution.'[46] This was indeed the Cuban experience, or part of it: the *foco* detonated successfully. But what was exceptional for Latin America, Debray made into a rule.[47]

The third group of reasons for revolutionary failures is structural: the amateurish character of radical activities; military loyalty; peasant dependence; and the absorption of the middle classes into the 'system'.

All these factors apply to the rest of the Third World, with some qualifications: first, the far greater urbanisation and, with it, urban radicalism, in Latin America; second, peasant contentment rather than dependence in those countries of Africa and Asia where peasant small-holdings are extensive (but an equally desperate if dissimilar situation in densely-populated areas of India, Indonesia, Pakistan and Bangladesh); third, soldierly obedience to the officer corps, which has by and large survived the transformation from colonial to independent armies; finally, along with the latter, it is the 'national bourgeoisie' that has been the chief beneficiary of an end to colonial rule (in Latin America, more than a century before, it was the export-oriented, culturally European, landed aristocracy which benefited from independence).

These factors are 'structural' because each is a product of the social structure of underdeveloped countries. Radical amateurism flourishes as a direct result of the immaturity of workers' and peasants' organisations. Soldierly obedience, openly invoked for political purposes, and even ruthlessly exploited whenever troops shoot down people like themselves from the poorer classes, is a caricature of the military loyalty which has evolved in the 'developed' world. Peasant dependence, if not the function of an agrarian economy characterised by landlord–tenant (or even rich–poor peasant) relations, is certainly a product of it: although, like the obedience of peasant soldiers, which is taken for granted after years, decades or generations of unquestioned service, it can be pushed too far. Finally the 'national bourgeoisie' of the Third World, so far from representing the classic, innovating, thrusting, independent type of entrepreneurs who shaped Europe and America in their own image, is the epitome of dependence on the state. For the national bourgeoisie, 'nationalism' means industrialisation – the opposite of the old aristocratic cosmopolitanism, based on the export of agricultural products from large estates – which in turn means state encouragement and state protection, by subsidies and tariffs. Nationalist politicians need supporters, which means multiplying job opportunities, especially in the occupations most easily controlled by the party and government: the civil service, public utilities, nationalised industries.[48] The national bourgeoisie – in the armed forces and the bureaucracy – staff the modernising state.

(a) Radical amateurism

Student radicalism is a surrogate for proletarian revolution. It reflects the absence or insufficiency of an organised, militant, *autonomous* working-class movement. As in nineteenth-century Russia, Latin America's students play the part of populists, seeking to 'awaken' the masses to their destiny. As in nineteenth-century Russia, the masses hardly respond. For what is remarkable about the middle classes – their 'service' rather than productive character – applies equally to the 'working classes'. This is so whether the term refers to the small proportion of industrial workers[49] or the large and amorphous aggregate of casual labourers or marginals. Middle and working classes both depend – though to a varying degree – on the transfer mechanisms of the state: favourable fiscal policies for the one, social security and jobs for the other.[50]

Because of the dependent character and insufficient organisation of workers and peasants, students can and do claim to speak for the masses. 'In countries where education is a privilege, students behave like an elite entrusted with a definite social responsibility and are largely regarded as such by the masses.' Indeed, 'the active participation of students in political life in a revolutionary direction is so widespread in developing countries that it might be regarded as a reliable index of underdevelopment'.[51]

In Argentina and Uruguay, students were to form the backbone of what are (or were) the most effective urban guerrilla movements. In Cuba, students and ex-students provided both the guerrilla leadership and an important element – the 'student directorate' – of the urban resistance to Batista. In Peru, along with communists, Catholic reformers, peasants and the 'national bourgeoisie', students broadly supported the radical military regime in power from 1968 to 1975. In Venezuela the youth movement of the ruling Democratic Action party split off in 1960 to found the Movement of the Revolutionary Left (MIR) which, after the suppression of a general strike of students and workers, became one of several groups of guerrillas sporadically active in the 1960s and beyond.[52] These are all countries where the 'university democratisation' movement, starting in Latin America as early as 1918, was most successful. It provided the opportunity for student political training, and ensured – for a time – that the 'autonomous university' could operate like a state within the state.[53]

However, the notorious disunity of the Left, the 'confusion of revolutionary organisations, mutual ignorance and dispersal of forces' resulted in the failure of student radicalism: 'Several years of revolutionary action have now made it clear that heroism is not enough, and that ideological maturity and above all political sense, absence of sectarianism and seriousness in preparing armed struggle were lacking.'[54] Lenin's scathing comments on the amateurism of radical activities in late-nineteenth-century Russia is extraordinarily apt:

> The entire student youth of the period was absorbed in Marxism. . . . These new warriors,marched to battle with astonishingly primitive equipment and training. They marched to war like peasants from the plough armed only with clubs. A students' circle establishes contacts with workers and sets to work without any connection with the old members of the movement . . . without any organisation of the various divisions of revolutionary work, without any systematic plan of activity covering any length of time. The circle gradually expands its propaganda and agitation. . . . [They] establish contacts with other groups of revolutionaries, procure literature, set to work to publish a local newspaper, begin to talk of organising a demonstration, and finally turn to open warfare. . . .
>
> Usually the initiation of such actions ends in an immediate and complete fiasco . . . because, naturally, the police, in almost every case, knew the principal leaders of the local movement, since they had already 'gained a reputation' for themselves in their student days, and the police waited only for the right moment to make their raid. . . .
>
> The government, at first thrown into confusion and committing a number of blunders . . . very soon adapted itself to the new conditions of the struggle and managed to deploy well its perfectly equipped detachments of *agents provocateurs*, spies and gendarmes. Raids became so frequent, affected such a vast number of people, and cleared out the local study circles so thoroughly that . . . it became utterly impossible to establish continuity and coherence. The terrible dispersion of the local leaders; the fortuitous character of the study circle memberships; the lack of training in, and the narrow outlook on, theoretical, political, and organisational questions were all the inevitable result of the conditions described above.[55]

(b) Military loyalty

The development of a separate 'caste' loyalty by the armed forces – officers and men – is a second striking characteristic of Latin American societies: and this development, modified by the much shorter interlude of parliamentary or presidential regimes, is of course a feature of most African and many Asian countries. The officer corps normally considers itself to be the 'guardian of the constitution': this view was especially emphasised by the Brazilian armed forces (before 1964) and by those of Chile (before 1973). The guardianship concept stems from the belief that the armed forces are 'above' class interests, above political parties and their selfish manoeuvring and intrigues, and above purely economic considerations. The role of guardian implies that the armed forces 'watch over the essential values of the nation':[56] it is interpreted to mean that they act in the public interest when they remove an 'objectionable' ruler from power or discard an 'objectionable' political process. The military argue (often quite justifiably) that the ruler is perverting his office by favouring personal, family or sectional interests; and that political parties 'always turn out to be harmful to national interests'.[57] But these changes are in the form of coups, not revolutions: the prevailing social system usually remains intact.

There are exceptions to the rule of officers' loyalty to the existing social system, but they are most often to be found outside Latin America, for example the radical 'Nasserist' regimes in North Africa and the Middle East: and even these are more radical in name, and perhaps intention, than in policy. There are also instances of defection by officers and men: perhaps the most spectacular in Asia was the Nanchang uprising in 1927, when several thousand Kuomintang troops, led by Chu Teh, mutinied and joined Mao's guerrillas. In Latin America there have been numerous abortive military revolts, in some of which, for example in Cuba in 1957, Guatemala in 1960 and Venezuela in 1965, rebel officers became guerrilla commanders: but these are exceptional cases. In general the officer corps is faithful to the system, if not to the person chosen formally to be its head.[58]

As for the loyalty of the troops to their commanders this has rarely been breached. When soldiers refuse to fire on working-class, peasant or student demonstrators contrary to the orders of their officers this is indeed a revolutionary situation.

Conversely, no political organisation in a developing country can compare with the army in solidarity, discipline and centralised organisation – and in the means of coercion. Under certain conditions, this nation-wide capacity allied with a powerful 'corporate' interest permits the military to play a relatively independent role in society. It is not at all far-fetched to refer to the example of the Roman Empire where, as a result of the demoralisation of the plebs and the indifference of the villagers, the army became the only reliable consolidating force. It was Caesar who fashioned this new socio-political instrument – the army.[59]

For whatever the social class or ethnic origin of soldier or officer, the process of recruitment, training and operational work changes his attitudes and perceptions. Illiterate and unskilled peasants, often from remote villages, acquire new techniques when they join the armed forces; they become organised and disciplined, and are integrated into a powerful, hierarchical and, above all, national institution. Officers in Third World countries are frequently recruited from the provincial middle or lower middle classes or the better-off peasantry.[60] (The upper class, often educated abroad, prefers the traditionally higher status of employment in the civilian bureaucracy.) Officer cadets, often trained and educated in military schools and academies from an early age, imbued with *esprit de corps*, are formed as an integral part of an autonomous institution: in a more profound and enduring sense than students in the universities the military are a 'state within the state'.[61]

Yet whatever the degree of military autonomy and whatever the subjective intentions of its leaders, the military objectively facilitates, according to Mirskii, some course of social and economic development responding to the interests of a definite class or classes. This to Mirskii is either the capitalist or the 'non-capitalist' path – the latter depending on the conditions of society, the level of its development, the stage of maturity of the workers and the nation's ability to maintain its independence. However, the optimistic assumption that countries like Egypt, Syria, Algeria and Burma, under 'revolutionary-democratic' military leaders, are proceeding along the non-capitalist path[62] is hardly borne out by the evidence. Huntington's theory of military intervention is more appropriate. Where the issue is the displacement of an oligarchy and the accession of the middle classes to power, Huntington points out, the military is on the side of reform; but the greater the political demands of the masses, the more conservative, and even reactionary, the armed forces tend to become.[63]

(c) Peasant dependence

The archaic structure of land tenure throughout Latin America creates three critical problems: economic problems of inadequate production and wasteful use of resources; social problems of illiteracy, malnutrition and dependence; and political problems, notably the harmful effect on the political process of the continued isolation and backwardness of a substantial part of the population.[64]

Apart from the small, productive plantation sector (concentrating on export crops) the agrarian situation in Latin America is dominated by *latifundia* (large estates), family-sized holdings, and *minifundia* (uneconomic small plots).[65] More than 90 per cent of farm families in Colombia, Ecuador and Guatemala, for instance, were either in the last two categories or were landless farm workers on the big estates.[66] In Brazil 87 per cent of owner-cultivators, farming fragmented 'dwarf units', own less than 19 per cent of all non-public land; over 80 per cent of this land is owned by landlords whose estates range from 1,000 to 100,000 hectares.[67]

Excessively large estates, characteristic of the above countries and of Venezuela, Bolivia (until 1952), Peru (until 1968) and Chile (until 1970), monopolise land of which only a small part is farmed. Landlords can afford either to leave large areas uncultivated or use antiquated and unproductive methods, because they get more than sufficient returns from their limited use of capital. The excess land is usually leased to sharecroppers, who are obliged to work for fixed periods on the landlord's private farm for little or no pay: 'On the large estates all are dependents, be they paid workers, *colonos* [sharecroppers] or *peons* [day labourers].'[68]

This archaic society, which gives its subjects no incentive to improve their conditions:

> consists of a multitude of communities cut off from one another and from the nation as a whole. Problems are communal in scope and must be solved within each community. Since the communities are outside the market economy and outside the law in many respects, their members can expect very little from the national government and ask very little of it. A manorial society is a closed society, not only economically but politically as well.[69]

The effective isolation of a large part of the population has led to a form of political dualism: a trade-off between landowners and urban reformers, whereby each gets a free hand in his own sphere in return for non-interference in the other's. This compromise, which vitiated even the more 'progressive' governments that have since largely given way to authoritarian regimes, in effect sanctions rural stratification, inequality between town and countryside, and the stagnation of agricultural production.

Even when the peasant migrates to the city, to become a rootless 'marginal' element – marginal to the economy and to society – he does not escape dependence. Only a tiny percentage of urban workers is regularly employed in factories. The rest are semi-employed, lacking class consciousness, almost all of them dependent for their livelihood on the state; they expect improvements to come from their 'patrons', whether these are politicians, officials or trade union leaders. They dream of an independent, lower-middle-class existence.[70] Their natural concern is for 'immediate benefits in food, jobs and housing, which can only be secured by working through rather than against the existing system'.[71] The first generation of migrants are politically passive, content with minimal reforms, conservatively-inclined; but their children, growing up in an urban environment, with 'higher' aspirations, are likely to be radical and, if frustrated, violent.[72]

(d) Stabilising bourgeoisie

Finally there is the 'national bourgeoisie' which, in the course of the nineteenth century, succeeded either in displacing the traditional, cosmopolitan aristocracy from power or at least in sharing power with it. Its members are the civilian officials and technocrats, the newer army officers, members of the liberal professions, bankers, businessmen, politicians, trade union leaders and so on, who staff the organisations of the state, work with these organisations or depend on them for a living. But what is significant about the 'new men', who are sincerely anxious to modernise their country and perhaps to bring about genuine democracy, is that even the progressives among them have been obliged to compromise with the archaic rural sector when seeking to introduce reforms, at least into the modern sector. The Vargas regime in Brazil provides a good example of the way in which a division of labour was agreed upon, whereby the urban progressive forces and the lords of rural society left the other a free hand in their own area.

Vargas himself, returning to power after elections in 1950, established two parties – the Brazilian Labour Party (PTB), supported by the urban workers, and the Socialist Democrat Party (PSD) which, in spite of its title, appealed both to the national bourgeoisie and to the owners of large rural estates – of which he became president and honorary president respectively.[73] Yet although Vargas, when he first came to power in 1930, had called for progressive 'action to stamp out . . . the *latifundia*', in the first fifteen years of his rule, and in the years afterwards, he left the large estates untouched. 'The peasants, lacking their own organisation, remained isolated and at the mercy of the local political leaders. The popular movement was confined to the urban centres.'[74]

The failure to integrate the rural population into the mainstream of national society is the major defect of either reformist or populist regimes. The expedient 'alliance of progressive and conservative forces with opposite policies in urban and rural societies'[75] deprives the reformers of the mass (rural) support they need if they are to modernise their countries effectively against powerful vested interests; at the same time it perpetuates an inefficient and outmoded agrarian system, which acts like a deadweight on society as a whole. There are only two ways out of this impasse: revolution (Mexico, Cuba) or counter-revolution (Brazil). In Brazil, Vargas's heir Goulart realised at the end of 1963 that he could no longer evade the issue of land reforms. In order to force them through against the resistance of the feudal lords, Goulart 'organised or helped organise revolutionary demonstrations'.[76] But it was too late. Instead of launching a revolution he brought upon his country the counter-revolution.

An alternative: national resistance

The great struggles for national independence – in China against the Japanese invaders, in Vietnam and Algeria against the French, in Indonesia against the Dutch, in Angola and Mozambique against the Portuguese – united both the forces of nationalism and the forces of social revolution. This combined front, which also played a key role in the Cuban revolution, has not so far developed (for the reasons outlined above) in the rest of Latin America. The crucial question is this: now that independence has largely been achieved throughout the world, except in southern Africa, is nationalism no longer a revolutionary force? There is no simple answer to this question: for although the Cuban experience is exceptional, it none the less offers the possibility of being reproduced under similar conditions of overwhelmingly economic, if only indirectly political, external domination. Moreover, the drive for *ethnic* separation, by tribal and other minorities, remains a most potent force for revolution in Africa, the Middle East and in South and Southeast Asia. Finally the populist upsurge by middle-class elements, students, workers, and rural migrants in Iran represents still another form of nationalist struggle: i.e.

an anti-regime movement created by the very process of modernisation introduced by the regime itself, whose breakneck pace brought out – forced out – all the latent contradictions in society.

The national movement cannot be regarded as merely a political phenomenon: historically, it is a movement embracing the widest strata of society against *alien* – arbitrary, unaccountable, unresponsive – authority, typically military invaders or colonial rulers. But the perception of what is alien derives from the consciousness of alienation. For example, Japanese troops in French Indochina, the Netherlands East Indies and British Burma were regarded, initially at least, as liberators; it was only later that their acts of cruelty, repression and blatant exploitation (forced labour sent overseas, national resources drained for the use of the Japanese war machine, contempt for the local people) antagonised many Burmese and Indonesians – not to speak of the overseas Chinese. The fact that they were alienated from (racially different) Asians was important but incidental: what mattered was the way in which those Asians *behaved*. This is why the experience of the national movements is relevant today.

The Algerian revolution and the theories of Frantz Fanon (in large part derived from it) exemplify the relationship between the various components of a nation-wide resistance. These are: the combination of national and social aims; the alliance between urban and rural strata; the 'myth' of violence; and resistance to what is felt to be an illegitimate authority.

First of all, Fanon emphasised the combination of national aims (to overthrow alien rule) and social aims (e.g. the *women*, for the first time, participate in struggle: they throw off the veil).[77] Similarly, in China, Mao underlined the unity of political and social forces in the joint struggle against the domination by the state system (political authority), the clan system (clan authority), the supernatural system (religious authority) and of men over women: 'these four authorities are . . . the embodiment of the whole feudal-patriarchal system and ideology . . . binding the Chinese people.'[78]

The second factor, to Fanon, is the alliance of the rural strata, which he considered the repository of the nation's values, with the urban strata. For the leaders and the rank-and-file of a nationalist party are both urban: the latter are chiefly workers, artisans, primary school teachers and small shopkeepers. But their attitude is ambiguous, because even though opposed to colonial rule, they also profit by it; thus they take part in a dialogue – discussing improvements, debating reforms – which is never completely broken off.[79] It is only when nationalist parties are frustrated in achieving their aims (essentially to take the place of their masters), and when colonial repression intensifies, that the nationalist militants 'fall back towards the countryside and the mountains, towards the peasants'. They discover that the latter have never ceased to think of liberation except in terms of regaining the land from the foreigners, of national struggle and armed insurrection.[80] This 'sanctuary' offered by the peasants (and tribespeople) and by mountainous and remote areas has been of vital importance in all modern revolutions – from China and Vietnam to Cuba and Algeria.[81]

The third, and most remarkable, of Fanon's themes is concerned with the myth and the reality of violence. Similar to Sorel's 'heroic myth' of proletarian violence, symbolising and activating the primordial qualities of courage, audacity, determination and resistance (lost in the modern era of compromise), so Fanon's myth of violence is conceived as the necessary counterpart of the colonial myth of superiority and power. To Fanon, 'violence is a cleansing force. It frees the native from his inferiority complex and from his despair and inaction; it makes him fearless and restores his self-respect.'[82] As for the reality, it is seen in the response of Algerian nationalists to the French Government's capitulation to the *colons* in 1956: that colonialism only loosens its hold when the knife is at its throat. In Fanon's words: 'Colonialism is not a thinking machine, nor a body endowed with reasoning facilities. It is violence in its natural state, and it will only yield when confronted with greater violence.'[83] Nationalist violence, which is not the same as terrorism,[84] has three major purposes: it restores pride to the humiliated who stand up and fight back; it polarises society, by forcing people to face reality, to make their choice and to act on it; and it erodes the will of (alien) rulers to maintain their repressive regime.

Finally, the resistance of the alienated (violence in Fanon's and Sorel's terminology) is anti-colonial for historical reasons – the 300 years of Europe's dynamism and eventual world domination – but it is in essence directed against any 'illegitimate' authority. This is expressed in the well-known Chinese slogan: 'countries want independence, nations want liberation, people want revolution'. All three forms of struggle can be seen in the contemporary world: independence movements, as in southern Africa; would-be national movements, as in Eritrea, and Biafra; and popular movements against 'feudalism' or the 'parasitic' rule of the national bourgeoisie.[85]

All four strands of resistance were embodied in the Algerian revolution. This was a revolt of national consciousness, prepared and organised by young radical intellectuals – the 'Secret Organisation' formed by 'unknown' militants after the fraudulent elections of 1948 – whose patriotic uprising in November 1954 expressed the deepest feelings of the Algerian people: 'My religion, Islam; my language, Arabic; my country, Algeria.'[86] Barred from genuine assimilation by the stubborn opposition of the *colons*, Algerian intellectuals turned back to their origins, which had never been forgotten by the mass of illiterate peasants, workers, artisans, itinerant vendors and small shopkeepers. This consciousness, although it had inspired neither unity nor nationality in the past, differentiated Algerian Muslims from the French; both the misery of economic exploitation and the bitterness of ethnic discrimination kept the flame of opposition alive. Thus in spite of the losing military campaign, an organised, unified movement was built up from disparate social forces, capable of taking over from the French.

'Colonialism . . . is violence in its natural state, and it will only yield when confronted with greater violence': the French record only confirmed this bleak prophecy. The ferocious conquest of Algeria by Bugeaud in 1830, the harsh repression of feudal revolts over the next thirty years, the failure of the Blum-Violette reform proposals in 1936 because of the determined opposition of the *colons*, the Sétif massacre of 1945 – 1,500 Muslim victims against 200 Europeans[87] – and the rigged elections of 1948: all told the same story.

Finally, Fanon's characterisation of the despair of the rootless 'mass of humanity' leaving the villages to seek jobs in the towns, and the deception of the nationalists, is borne out, ironically enough, by the report of Jacques Soustelle, newly appointed Governor of Algeria, on 1 June 1955:

> The result of demographic pressure in an essentially agrarian country, with poor soil and a harsh climate, is chronic under-employment, abandonment of the countryside for life in shanty towns, and misery and despair among a growing number of individuals and families. While this sub-proletariat increases and becomes more embittered, a Muslim petty bourgeoisie, educated by contact with ourselves, seeks in vain not only economic, but above all administrative and political outlets. It does not find them. . . . Hence a double dissatis-faction: the social discontent of the masses, the political discontent of the élite. Joined together, these two forms of discontent have become an enormous explosive force.[88]

Another alternative: urban insurgency

Is urban insurgency the alternative to rural guerrilla warfare? Or is it an adjunct of guerrilla war, as the latter is an adjunct of conventional war – at least during the later stages of an effective insurgency? According to one revolutionary leader,

> in Venezuela it is just not possible to start a rural uprising that
> will end with the countryside encircling the towns. The rural areas are
> marginal to the life of the country. . . . A peasant revolt is impossible,
> in the last analysis, because we are not a peasant people.[89]

Although the great revolutions of this century have been the result of peasant mobilisation and urban leadership,[90] do recent environmental changes – notably the peasant drift to the towns, so marked in Latin America – require a change in revolutionary strategy? Is the only significant exception to the pattern of the past – the Cuban catalytic insurrection, in its urban as well as 'mountain' aspects – a precursor of a new model of armed struggle: that is, urban revolution without the need for peasant participation? Or is the Maoist strategy of the countryside encircling the towns (discussed in the final section) still valid, indeed indispensable, for Third World revolutionaries?

To answer these questions demands an examination, first, of the extent and character of environmental changes; then the aims and methods of urban insurgency in this context; the social forces motivated to rebel; and finally the experience of urban insurgency and the lessons to be drawn from this.

In the first place, the change in the balance of population between rural and urban elements is strikingly apparent. Already by 1960 half the total labour force in Latin America was urbanised, compared to one-third in 1920. And even though the urbanised work force in South and Southeast Asia in 1960 was only just over one-quarter of the total, and less than one-third in North Africa, the same trend is evident.[91] Taking the Third World as a whole, an urban population of 300 million in 1950 had doubled in 20 years – an increase from 16 per cent of the total population in 1950 to one-quarter in 1970. The projected total urban population by the end of the century is 2.2 billion people – not far short of the 2.9 billion estimated rural population.[92]

The vast increase in absolute numbers and the dislocation inherent in the shift from agricultural to industrial and especially service sectors pose enormous problems. The United Nations Conference on Human Settlements (Habitat) pointed out in June 1976:

> Symptoms of the crisis are visible everywhere. . . . Poverty and
> unemployment; the mass exodus from rural areas; urban slums and
> squatter settlements; a world-wide shortage of housing; air pollution;
> traffic jams; noise; ugliness; and the inability of governments to
> provide basic services.[93]

But however critical the problems of poverty and unemployment, which
can hardly be exaggerated, does such an amount of urban wretchedness,
affecting so many people, constitute a revolutionary situation? There are
two important qualifications to be noted. First, the tendency for the more
discontented and the more enterprising peasants to seek a new life in the
towns: this removes or reduces a potentially 'explosive' force in the
countryside. Second, the implications of the flow of 'rootless' rural
migrants – whether on a casual or permanent basis – to already swollen
urban conglomerations. This influx of people requires at least a
minimum of public services – health, housing, transport, education –
thus adding to the burden on the state; at the same time migrants are
dependent on these services and recognise their dependence. Moreover,
hard though it is to believe, the squalor and insecurity of existence in
shanty towns and slums is still better than a life of misery in the
countryside.[94]

To the new generation of revolutionaries, stale-mated by the apathy,
isolation and suspicion (of outsiders) of the peasants, this seething urban
environment does, however, seem to offer the explosive conditions that
acts of violence can detonate. Unlike the generation of Che Guevara, the
new vanguard of professional revolutionaries (Leninism brought up to
date) claim to have found capitalism's 'weakest link' in the very nerve-
centre of the state. Taking their cue from the October Revolution in
Russia – but ignoring the circumstances of Russia, torn by war, peasant
uprisings and government paralysis – they see themselves as the
inheritors of 'dual power', ready at one blow to storm the citadel of
autocracy.

  Their claim involves three fundamental assumptions: that a direct
assault will succeed because of the polarisation of society; that the latter
reflects a fatal split in society between the wealthy élite and the
struggling masses of the poor; and that dramatic action against the élite
will 'awaken' the masses, reveal their latent strength and the intensity of
their passions, on the one hand, and mercilessly expose the incompetence, corruption and blind repressiveness of a dying regime on the
other.

Urban guerrilla tactics, types of operation, the social composition of the movement, and its popular aims all flow from the 'catastrophic' situation envisaged above. Just as Sorel looked to that day when 'social peace', parliamentary reforms and 'resignation to routine' would no longer be possible, when every conflict is an incident in social war, 'when every strike begets the perspectives of a social catastrophe',[95] so urban revolutionaries seek salvation in the myth of polarising insurrection. The aim of the urban revolutionary is to compel the regime to reveal its 'true' repressive nature to those who have hitherto been indifferent to the authorities or have been obedient to them:

> It is necessary to turn political crisis into armed conflict by performing violent actions that will force those in power to transform the political situation of the country into a military situation. That will alienate the masses who, from then on, will revolt against the army and the police and thus blame them for this state of things.[96]

Revolt is inevitable because:

> As soon as a reasonable section of the population begins to take seriously the action of the urban guerrilla . . . the government has no alternative except to intensify repression. The police networks, house searches, arrest of innocent people and of suspects, closing off streets, make life in the city unbearable. The military dictatorship embarks on massive political persecution. Political assassinations and police terror become routine. In spite of all this, the police systematically fail. . . . The problems in the lives of the people become truly catastrophic. . . . These are the circumstances, disastrous for the dictatorship, which permit the revolutionaries to open rural guerrilla warfare in the midst of the uncontrollable expansion of urban rebellion.[97]

Yet this scenario did not take place either in Brazil, where the author of the *Minimanual of the Urban Guerrilla* was killed in 1969, or in Uruguay, where the gallant Tupamaros were suppressed in 1973, or even so far in Argentina, where wholesale intimidation of the Left by 'unofficial' military and police 'death squads' has hardly been offset by sporadic radical retaliation. Yet these countries seem to offer the most favourable conditions for urban insurgency, either in terms of absolute numbers of urban population (Brazil) or of the proportion of urban to rural population (Uruguay and Argentina). What went wrong?

Basically, what may in theory (or in potential) be the 'weakest link' is in fact the enemy stronghold. The urban insurgents *over*-estimated both the revolutionary consciousness and the 'tactical mobility' of the vast numbers of ever-increasing urban marginals; and they *under*-estimated the power, determination, capability and ruthlessness of an authoritarian élite.

First, let us consider the political disposition of urban marginals. Surveys indicate that the urban poor may be less disposed to blame the government for their conditions of life than may more privileged sections: in India, for example, it is the middle-class demonstrators who are most prone to violence. Moreover a great deal of discontent 'leaks' out of the system in apolitical responses.[98] The political apathy of the poor and least skilled stems from their preoccupation with survival. Their more modest and 'realistic' expectations are determined by their need for security and stability – similar to the norms of peasant behaviour, of those who are also on the margin of survival, noted by James Scott. Finally, the correlation between level of education and political interests and activities has been repeatedly demonstrated. But the essence of marginality is 'failure to gain access'. Hence the marginals' lack of exposure to urban institutions and processes: to education, adequate employment, services, housing, consumer goods and membership of organisations which are essential for the development of political influence.[99]

Second, the lack of tactical mobility. Because of the unreliability of marginals – as Fanon noted, the people of the shanty towns have both the strengths and weaknesses of spontaneity, capable either of struggling for liberation or serving the oppressor[100] – urban insurgents are deprived of a secure operational base among the people. This fundamental insecurity compounds their problems. The result, especially in periods when mass agitation has subsided, is the isolation – and not the expansion – of scattered clandestine networks, always in fear of betrayal, desperately seeking to survive on the proceeds of armed raids on banks, firms and public services. Staging these raids not only risks heavy casualties – the average life expectation of a Brazilian urban guerrilla is five months – but, above all, alienates the urban masses, who do not see their interests being defended by 'terrorist' activities.[101]

Third, dependent social structures. All the factors that were responsible for the failure of rural insurgencies played their part, to an even greater extent, in preventing urban insurgencies from reaching the take-off stage. Thus radical amateurism – spontaneity, lack of preparation, disorganisation and confusion – was the hallmark of guerrilla activities. 'Naturally the police, in almost every case, knew the principal leaders of the local movement, since they had already "gained a reputation" for themselves in their student days', as Lenin had warned. In Latin America, 'almost all [rural and urban *focos*] were destroyed by means of informers or the infiltration of police spies into the organisation'.[102] In the second place, peasant dependence on the system was carried over, in different forms, among the rural migrants; the urban 'marginals' proved to be unreliable and inconsistent supporters of revolution. Third, military obedience: the rank-and-file of the army and police had little in common with the student and ex-student middle-class intellectuals who were appealing to them in the name of proletarian solidarity; further, so far from the tactical initiative being with the guerrillas, the government's military force was more easily brought to bear within the confines of the city than was possible in dispersed rural operations. Finally, what was obviously effective repression prevented, rather than facilitated, the polarisation of society; to put it another way, polarisation, with the guerrillas in a minority, and an apathetic, cowed or even hostile majority, had the opposite effect intended.

Even the most daring, attractive and spectacular of all the urban guerrilla movements, the Tupamaros of Uruguay, finally overreached themselves when they directly challenged the military, in order to 'raise the level' of the struggle, in April 1972. After five years of brilliantly planned operations and widespread publicity, the Tupamaros felt they had reached an impasse: the regime, society itself, were 'getting accustomed' to their exploits. Accordingly, 'Plan 1972' called for a 'qualitative leap' to a higher level of armed struggle. 'Direct and systematic harassment of the repressive forces' would put the country in an evident state of civil war, when the people would have to choose between the Oligarchy and the Organisation (the Tupamaros). But the latter had unleashed forces they could not control. Compelled to act against the regime's 'Death Squad' the Tupamaros were caught off balance: they failed to foresee the rapidity and brutality of the regime's reaction.[103] The army took over internal security from the police (the police had in fact been infiltrated by the Tupamaros), and in an intensive campaign of repression rounded up hundreds of suspected guerrillas or sympathisers, eventually capturing the founder of the movement. Having tasted power in 1972, the army in a Brazilian-type coup in June 1973 virtually took over control of the country: the Congress was dissolved, the trade unions quelled and the university controlled.

Finally, one cannot ignore another model of urban insurgency – where, for ethnic, social or religious reasons, insurgents have operated with a certain basis of mass support. Significantly, the only effective cases are either in Europe and/or the Mediterranean, or where the metropolitan power has, for various reasons, been unable or unwilling to display the ruthless efficiency either of the French (*le style 'Para'*) in Algeria, or of the military and police torturers in Brazil, Chile, Uruguay, Argentina and elsewhere. Yet the examples are instructive in terms of aims (polarisation), methods (violence) and opponents (alien or illegitimate regimes).[104] Urban guerrillas tend to start with the belief that they can directly overthrow their enemy by armed revolt. Once the struggle is prolonged they are obliged to change their plans. Then the intention is so to harass government forces by bombing, sabotage and assassination (hence the far greater significance of terrorism for urban than for rural insurrections) as to compel the enemy to withdraw or cede for peace. In other words, urban insurgents seek to raise the costs either of military intervention from outside or of domestic military rule to the extent that the enemy finds it more advantageous to back down or get out rather than to stay and fight.

This was (and is) the situation in Palestine and Cyprus, and it is the aim of the provisional wing of the Irish Republican Army in Northern Ireland. The latter of course envisages, if its own activities (or those of Protestant extremists) should succeed in bringing this about, a struggle that is not confined to Ulster, where Catholics are outnumbered two to one, but an all-Ireland campaign, where the position is reversed.

As for the methods employed, urban guerrilla warfare, however justifiable its cause, almost invariably degenerates into terrorism, which is often indiscriminate and horrifying, for two main reasons. First, terrorism and sabotage are practically the only weapons guerrillas have in an area controlled by the 'enemy': in fact the headquarters of enemy activities. Second, guerrillas resort to this weapon both to demonstrate their own authority and to undermine that of the enemy. Use of force takes on different objectives, depending on the target: against the enemy, including rival organisations, to spread insecurity and panic; as the ultimate sanction to maintain order and discipline among guerrillas and their supporters; and to compel compliance by the 'neutrals', who are probably the majority of the urban population. Until the issue is decided, the latter find themselves ground between two millstones; the repressive power of the government to ensure 'business as usual' and the forcible acts of the guerrillas to demonstrate the opposite.

The Chinese way

What was Maoist strategy in China? And, is it applicable to other countries in the Third World? In answer to the first question, the Chinese revolution reveals three essential features: first, and as Fanon also emphasised, the combination of national resistance with social revolution; second, reliance on rural base areas to develop all the functions of a state within the state: 'In these base areas, we built the party, ran the organs of state power, built the people's armed forces and set up mass organisations . . . our base areas were in fact a state in miniature';[105] and finally, protracted struggle gradually to change the balance of forces in favour of the revolutionaries. The short answer to the second question posed above is that Third World conditions, despite the growth of urbanisation and the possibility of catalytic insurrection, do not basically detract from the importance of these features.[106]

Socio-economic conditions are the necessary cause of Chinese-style revolution; but the sufficient cause was the shock of the Japanese invasion provoking nation-wide awareness of an intolerable situation. Let us briefly consider these two aspects. First, the condition of China in the mid-1930s, which in fact or in potential is relevant to the Third World. Later, the polarising effects of the Japanese invasion, an exogenous factor combining military and economic elements. Writing in 1936, Mao emphasised China's main characteristics. The first is the 'uneven development' of a 'semi-colonial' country: 'a few modern industrial and commercial cities coexist with a vast stagnant countryside'. The second characteristic is a big and powerful enemy: 'The Kuomintang controls the key positions or lifelines in the politics, economy, communications and culture of China; its political power is nation-wide.' The third is the initial weakness of the revolutionary forces: 'The Red Army is small and weak. . . . Our political power exists in scattered and isolated mountainous or remote regions and receives no outside help whatsoever.' And the final factor, to Mao, is Communist Party leadership and the agrarian revolution:

> Thanks to this support [of the peasantry], our base areas, small though they are, are politically very powerful. . . . Small as it is, the Red Army has great fighting capacity, because its members, led by the Communist Party, are born of the agrarian revolution and are fighting for their own interests.

It followed from the first and fourth conditions, Mao argued, that

It is possible for the Chinese Red Army to grow and defeat its enemy. It follows from the second and third characteristics that it is impossible for the Chinese Red Army to grow very rapidly or defeat its enemy quickly; in other words, the war will be protracted and may even be lost if it is mishandled.

Such are the two aspects of revolutionary war which exist simultaneously.[107]

The fundamental change in the vital second and third characteristics came from outside. The Japanese invasion, starting in 1937, swept away, over large areas in the north and centre of China, both the army and the administration of the Kuomintang and its supporters. The Japanese themselves were not numerous enough to control all the territory they had conquered. The Chinese Communists 'filled the vacuum'. There are two main reasons why they could do so. First, only they (and not the Kuomintang) were experienced in and able to operate both the 'underground' methods needed to organise popular resistance in 'occupied' zones and the guerrilla warfare that was based on them. In the second place, the communists were received – and welcomed – by the villagers, because it was known that they had for years been defending peasant interests.[108]

The structural factors depressing revolutionary activities in most of Latin America and much of Africa and Asia simply did not operate in the China of the late 1930s and the 1940s. Chinese communist resistance to the Japanese enemy served as a magnet for patriotic students. But by joining the communists they joined an organisation which had been tempered and 'professionalised' by years of revolutionary endurance. Second, traditional peasant deference to authority, political apathy and economic dependence, were swept away in the urgent need for self-defence and an alliance with the communists against the invaders. In the third place, a strong, disciplined military force had been created in the communist zones, while on the other side the exhaustion of the Kuomintang by the war against Japan, and the utter incompetence and corruption revealed during the civil war, both undermined military morale and affected the loyalty of officers and men. Finally the urban middle classes were driven into opposition or despair by the unbridled speculation, hoarding, rice shortages and astronomical inflation, connived at or encouraged by the Kuomintang's ruling clique: a regime and a society at the end of its tether.

To conclude: the collapse of these structural supports for a 'modernising' regime acting in traditional ways ensured both the success of revolution and the reintegration of society: for it was the Chinese Communist Party which drew the 'backward' peasant masses into playing a positive, indeed decisive, role in the revolution. Elsewhere in the Third World these supports remain largely intact: unshaken by war (for the most part), impervious to coups, unaffected by riots and demonstrations, and either isolated from or absorbing the impact of economic changes in the modern sector. However, the magnitude and especially the *rapidity* of change in Iran makes it an exception: and this example may well be followed by others. Yet as long as these supports persist they will continue to be a major impediment to revolution; but they are also a serious obstacle to national integration and to social reform – the only constructive alternative to revolution.

Prospects

Repressive authoritarian regimes – now the norm in Latin America, Asia and Africa – may well endure without serious challenge for a decade or even a generation:[109] this lengthy duration is most probable in Latin America, where the cycle of repression is well under way, least likely in Southeast Asia (apart from Indonesia) where an alternative model (either China or Vietnam) is close at hand to act like a magnetic force on actual or latent fissiparous tendencies in society.

The endurance of most repressive authoritarian regimes can be attributed to three factors. First of all, the crushing of alternative political structures – either mass movements, like the Indonesian Communist Party (PKI) and its allies in 1965, or revolutionary organisations, as in Brazil in the later 1960s, and in Uruguay, Chile and Argentina in the early and mid-1970s. The second factor is popular readiness to acept 'a firm hand' for the sake of law and order – in reaction to the turmoil and uncertainty characteristic of democratic politics in oligarchical societies; and the final reason for endurance is the ruthless efficiency of the apparatus of repression – perfected methods of 'riot control', interrogation and torture of suspects, pervasive use of informers, detailed files on 'subversives', and so on. The importance of the third factor is apparent when it is noted that even democratically-elected governments in countries like India, Sri Lanka and Malaysia, which permit a 'loyal' opposition but suppress radical alternatives, make use of extensive police powers and draconian security regulations – taken over, virtually intact, from the colonial authorities. It is also instructive to observe that Colombia, one of the few remaining democracies in Latin America, has been under martial law for the last two years and that strikers and demonstrators expressing deeply-felt social and economic grievances – thus posing an obvious threat to law and order – are rigorously repressed.

Yet even these assets to longevity become eroded in time: for mass movements or revolutionary organisations find fertile soil in the existence of unresolved popular discontent, where no legitimate means of expression are allowed. Moreover, the arbitrariness of an unchallenged regime, its ignorance of popular attitudes (apart from the narrowly-conceived reports of the secret police) and the complacency that develops from years of easy access to wealth, privilege and power, all tend to dispel the regime's initial wariness and vigilance. The result is that all sorts of fissures and loopholes appear which an alert opposition can exploit.

Finally, repressive regimes are subject over time to cumulative social pressures: from the growing middle strata, the product of modernisation, demanding to take part in decisions that vitally affect their stake in society; from the pullulating mass of urban marginals, including the swelling numbers of slum-dwellers, casual workers, criminals or unemployed which are being continually recruited from an unending 'pool' of surplus labour in the countryside: this is a volatile and unpredictable force that can take an extreme direction either on the Left or the Right; and last from the polarisation of rural society resulting from the concentration of land ownership in the hands of the more affluent and technically-advanced, on the one hand, and the mass of dwarf-holders or dispossessed (small tenants or labourers) on the other.

Some, perhaps the majority, of these regimes will absorb these pressures, co-opt leaders of the new social forces and adapt in time to changing conditions. But, as history shows, there are numerous examples of rigid and unchanging regimes. For such as these, the longer their authoritarian structures endure, confronting social pressures which have no 'legitimate' outlet, the more devastating the explosion that will bring them to an end.

4 ★ *General theory of revolution?*

'I cannot . . . give praise or blame', Burke writes in his *Reflections on the Revolution in France*, 'to anything which relates to human actions, and human concerns, on a simple view of the object, as it stands stripped of every relation, in all the nakedness and solitude of metaphysical abstraction. Circumstances . . . give in reality to every political principle its distinguishing colour, and discriminating effect. The circumstances are what render every civil and political scheme beneficial or noxious to mankind.' Abstractly speaking, government as well as liberty is good. But, Burke continues, judgment should be suspended until one is informed how liberty is 'combined with government; with public force; with the discipline and obedience of armies; with the collection of an effective and well-distributed revenue; with morality . . . [with] property; with peace and order.'[1]

Now the great twentieth-century revolutionaries, however contrary their judgment of the 'stupendous wisdom' of the ages, place the same insistence on a 'detailed examination' of the circumstances. 'Absolutely hostile to all abstract formulas and to all doctrinaire recipes . . .', Lenin points out, 'Marxism demands an absolutely historical examination of the question of the forms of struggle. To treat the question apart from the concrete historical situation is to betray ignorance of the very rudiments of dialectical materialism.'[2]

In this chapter, then, I shall consider the problem of general theory and specific conditions; however, besides the universal-specific dichotomy, another distinction must be observed – that is, between objectivity and subjectivity. The latter refers here to voluntarism, or political choice. This distinction is an analytic one, for in practice will and environment are 'fused'. And I shall end by discussing four recent theories of revolution.

Universal theory, specific conditions

To put it crudely, there is no basic model of society in the sense that the economic system can be reduced to a simple model: Production equals Consumption plus Investment. The nearest political equivalent might be: Power equals Legitimacy plus Coercion, meaning that people act in accordance with the wishes of the power-holders because they believe the latter to be in authority over them and because the latter have sanctions at their disposal. However, this formula tells us nothing about the allocation of resources and values in society. A more comprehensive formula is that of Chalmers Johnson, derived from the work of Parsons and Weber: System Maintenance equals Value Structure plus Division of Labour, where values legitimise both the allocation of goods and services and the occupational stratification, and where this division of labour embodies society's values. Equilibrium is maintained so long as values are congruent with the division of labour. Where there is incongruity, 'disequilibrium' leads to 'power deflation' – meaning that more and more coercion is required – followed by 'loss of authority', perhaps to the extent of dissidence and open revolt.

The importance of this relationship between values and division of labour is strikingly indicated by the Negro question in America. When dominant White values – in this case the 'lower valuations', or prejudices, in Myrdal's construct[3] – postulated the Black as inferior, most Blacks accepted that they were inferior to Whites, which 'justified' their work as poorly-paid agricultural labourers or in other menial occupations. Only when Blacks rejected this valuation – as a result of various circumstances: war-time mobilisation, increased migration to towns (and to the north), run-down of cotton estates, greater employment in factories, changing legal conceptions, and so on – did their social and political inferiority seem intolerable. The similarity with the position of poor peasants and slum dwellers in many Third World countries is obvious.

Yet the social equilibrium model is not really comparable with the basic economic model for two reasons. First, the latter is quantifiable. Production, consumption and investment can readily be calculated in monetary terms. In the social model only division of labour can be assessed in any concrete form, certainly not the 'system equilibrium' and still less 'value structure', both of which concepts are vague, ambiguous and even contradictory: in a word, subjective. Second, further economic aspects – exports–imports, taxation–revenue, etc. – can be added to the basic economic model, making possible a sophisticated general theory. However, it is difficult to find similar complementary activities to add to both sides of the social equilibrium equation so as ultimately to account for the entirety of political experience.

Indeed there is widespread agreement among social scientists that there is no generally acceptable theory of social change in the sense of 'deductive theory, which explains and predicts empirical facts relating to violence and change from a few axioms. Theory, in this sense, is a set of propositions derived from the axioms and from which predictions are made . . . as in the physical sciences.'[4] The lack of such an achievement is either, in the traditional view, because 'we are faced in all decisions with decisive elements of uncertainty, contingency, and accident'; or, according to behaviourists, because we are still in an early 'pre-scientific' phase of understanding.[5] As Chalmers Johnson puts it:

> Revolution is a response to a particular crisis in a particular social system. . . . Revolutions are determined by an extremely numerous set of variables; and, given the present state of social science theory [the lack of firm agreement on the types of social systems and the varieties of 'disequilibrated' conditions that may arise], it is virtually impossible to isolate and recombine all of these variables into various abstract models.[6]

In this situation, where we cannot (yet) assume observed features of a society to be variants of a common form, we are obliged, practically speaking, to start the other way round: from the concrete aspects of the society under investigation to the generalisations that are possible. The revolutionary situation would indeed be 'determined' if we could reduce it to a model – but we cannot. Both specificity and voluntarism militate against it. This is relevant to Stanley Hoffmann's argument that freedom of choice in politics is bounded by objective conditions, since the latter dictate whether 'limit' of indeterminancy' is great or small; but it also depends on particular individuals or groups whether they seize or miss the opportunities that are available.[7] Now I would go further: individual or group action *may* (not necessarily *will*: Guevara's error) transform the objective conditions and thereby extend the boundaries of choice. The limit of what is determined and the power of the will are not mutually exclusive elements, as abstract analysis indicates, but each is affected and may be enlarged by the other in the process of interaction.

Gunnar Myrdal admirably expressed this point of view:

When a sudden and great opinion catharsis occurs in society, customs and social trends seem to the participants to be suspended or radically changed, as they actually are to a certain extent. In this sense history is undecided; it can take several courses.[8]

The question of voluntarism is discussed below. Here I want to underline the importance of specificity even for – particularly for – revolutionaries. On the one hand, as Lenin points out in *'Left-Wing' Communism*, there are the 'fundamental tasks' of the struggle; on the other, the specific features which this struggle assumes and must assume in each separate country in conformity with the peculiar features of its economics, politics, culture, national composition and so forth.

The immediate goal for all communist movements is the attainment of power; the means to attain that goal vary with the specific conditions in which these movements operate. To deviate from the 'fundamental task' for the sake of immediate but partial aims is right-wing opportunism; to seek to attain the revolutionary goal directly, without proper regard for practical conditions, is 'Left' doctrinairism. The former is all specificity; the latter an abstraction.

The problem of reconciling universal proposition with particular circumstances – theoretical rigour with practical scope – is especially acute at times of rapid social change when the patterns of regularity and the 'shared expectations' necessary to the functioning of society have largely broken down. Then we see the extremes of particularity. Voluntarism – the importance of will, personality, leadership — appears superior to the confining framework of conditions: man, not weapons, is the decisive factor; the force of violence sweeps away the obstacle of entrenched power; the insurrection creates the conditions for revolution; and so on. Yet, although voluntarism may be analytically distinguished from determinism – in this sense, objective laws of development believed to be common to all countries – in practice it is the fusion of man's will (embodied in organisation) and the environment that is the reality with which we are concerned.

For in a revolutionary situation, the distinction between the objective observer and the subjective actor cannot seriously be maintained. For Burke every particular of the French revolution is infused with the noble indignation of a man appalled by the prospects (and determined to prevent them happening, if at all possible) for France, for his own country, for mankind: to avoid the evils of inconstancy and versatility 'we have consecrated the state', that no man should dream of approaching but with pious awe and trembling solicitude'.[9] To Fanon the colonial state is so evil that it cannot be reformed, but must be purged through violence. Our attitude to particular states, or types of state, is inseparable from our values, norms, attitudes and information. Our understanding of revolution – the overthrow of the state – is a product of the fusion of intellect and emotion, the latter being to some extent socially determined. Similarly, the activity of revolutionaries and counter-revolutionaries is the product of a fusion of will and environment, which can also be considered in terms of the unique situation and what is common to (all or most) revolutions.

In other words, there is a fusion of generalising intellect – our effort to make sense of, to find patterns of behaviour in, the welter of discrete facts – with emotions that are to some extent peculiar to ourselves and that are derived from our own circumstances. This is evident in Mao's theory and practice, expressed in his search for the concrete link between the various levels of personal aspiration, mass organisation and universal ideology. For although the object of study is to discern the 'interconnection' between the particular and the universal, the problem, as Mao describes it, is that

> at certain times in the revolutionary struggle, the difficulties outweigh the favourable conditions and so constitute the principal aspect of the contradiction and the favourable conditions constitute the secondary aspect. But *through their efforts* the revolutionaries can overcome the difficulties step by step and open up a favourable new situation; thus a difficult situation yields place to a favourable one. . . . Conversely, favourable conditions can be transformed into difficulty if the revolutionaries make mistakes.[10]

This is sensible, but what has it to do with contradictions? The fact that revolutionaries may make mistakes, as Guevara did in Bolivia, and that this may prove disastrous (as it did on that occasion) may be considered a 'contradiction' between inexperienced but valiant guerrillas and their formidably well-armed and mobile adversaries. But it is clearly a different order of contradiction to that between the Chinese peasant and the landlord, or between the Chinese people and the Japanese militarist, or even between one imperialist power and another.

The latter kinds of 'contradiction' are instances of a general theory: the contradictions between landlord and peasant, or the people and the foreign invader, determine the revolutionary situation in a 'semi-colonial' country like China. The former 'contradictions' express both voluntarism and particularity: in an optimistic sense, 'the will of man triumphs over fate', according to the Vietnamese revolutionary leader, Truong Chinh.[11] How can we take into account these *subjective* qualities of will, morale, courage and endurance that may tip the scales in an 'objectively' unfavourable war or civil war? Even if we can assess the intensity or salience of emotional attitudes or political doctrines from personal interviews or by developing appropriate survey techniques, by content analysis of doctrinal appeals or evaluation of support for the regime,[12] how can we predict whether or not these will be sufficient to tip the scales – as Castro's few hundred men tipped the scales against Batista's 40,000?

> We see, therefore, how from the commencement, the absolute, the mathematic as it is called, nowhere finds any sure basis in the calculations in the art of War; and that from the outset there is a play of possibilities, probabilities, good and bad luck, which spreads about with all the coarse and fine threads of its web, and makes War of all branches of human activity the most like a gambling game . . . [War not only] changes its colour in some degree in each particular case, but it is also . . . composed of the original violence of its elements, hatred and animosity, which may be looked upon as blind instinct; of the play of probabilities and chance, which makes it a free activity of the soul; and of the subordinate nature of a political instrument [a continuation of politics . . . by other means], by which it belongs purely to the reason.[13]

Although Clausewitz often speaks of certain 'principles' to be followed (Bernard Brodie points out), he specifically rejects the notion that there can be any well-defined body of rules or principles that universally dictate one form of behaviour. Units such as battalions look uniform on paper; but they are made up of and led by men, variously subject to fears, hunger and exhaustion. 'What we get from Clausewitz is a deepening of sensibility or insight rather than a body of rules', because in so far as he offers rules he shows the qualifications and historical exceptions to them. Yet, Brodie adds, 'there has been no one to match him since'.[14]

The problem of applying general principles to varying political situations and, still more so, to wars and revolutions, where the unique factors and the effect of chance play so important a role, is aptly illustrated by the domino theory. It is not unfair to select this theory if only because it is directed at the 'grey area' between outright aggression and customary diplomacy: the area of infiltration, insurgency and subversion. In its simple form the domino theory asserts that a communist take-over of country A will be speedily followed by the collapse of country B, and then of country C, and so on 'like a row of falling dominoes', to quote its best-known exponent, President Eisenhower.

Eisenhower's presentation is typical. If South Vietnam were 'lost', reported Secretaries Rusk and McNamara to President Kennedy in November 1961, 'we would have to face a near certainty that the remainder of Southeast Asia and Indonesia would move to a complete accommodation with communism, if not formal incorporation with the communist bloc'.[15] Again, as McNamara reported to President Johnson in March 1964, 'unless we can achieve this objective in South Vietnam almost all of Southeast Asia will probably fall under Communist dominance, . . . Even the Philippines would become shaky, and the threat to India to the West, Australia and New Zealand to the South and Taiwan, Korea and Japan to the North and East would be greatly increased.'[16]

What strikes the reader is, first, the imprecision of the terms used, and second, and related to the first, the failure to differentiate between the 'dominoes'. What does 'complete accommodation' with communism mean? Is it renunciation of military or economic ties with the West, a policy of neutrality, a foreign policy in agreement with that of communist countries (and which countries?), an internal policy favourable to communist interests, a coalition government including communists, or one dominated by communists? 'Complete accommodation' would seem to be nearer the end of the spectrum than the beginning, but the earlier alternatives – had they been stated – are more realistic. What is the nature of the 'threat' to India, Australia, Japan and so on? Is it the same threat to each of them? Is it the threat of invasion, of infiltration, or of diplomatic pressure to conform? The reader can take his choice.

To make a sensible choice, the reader must possess certain information. He must have some knowledge of the capacity as well as the intention of the domino-activating power – belief in 'world domination' is not really enough to go on – and the same applies to each of the dominoes: the strength and weaknesses, the state of morale or indecision, of government, organisations and people. This is largely a matter of empirical evidence. But the weakness of the domino theory is that it is a general theory – if an over-simple one – unaware of or unconcerned with particular situations and events. This is also, in a practical sense, its strength. The theory makes its psychological impact precisely because it is undifferentiated, formless, alarming.

Thus, to those who tend to judge revolutions in terms of universally valid propositions, the parallel between Thailand and Vietnam, two countries often nominated for a domino relationship, seems evident. But this is to ignore the differences in the *internal situation* of the two states. For the internal situation determines the face of the nation, *not* external events – always excluding the use of force by a bigger power. The internal situation in Thailand after the October 1976 military coup is far more uncertain than it has been for years, but it is still very different from the previous internal situation of South Vietnam. There are a number of factors to which the success of insurgency in Vietnam can be attributed, and not one of them operates to anything like the same extent in Thailand.[17]

The National Liberation Front of South Vietnam was largely a peasant-based movement: its local guerrillas were peasants by day and soldiers by night. Its appeal, as previously mentioned, was to the great mass of tenant farmers and landless labourers. In Thailand, by contrast, the great majority of farmers own their land. The proportion is actually higher in the north-east, where an insurgency has broken out, but there the land is poor and largely unirrigated: as a result, the average income of villagers in the north-east is about half the national average.

Much of Vietnam is mountainous and densely forested, providing excellent cover for guerrillas: Ho Chi Minh himself hid out most of the war against the French in caves only 80 miles from Hanoi; and for years the NLF command headquarters (COSVN) was said to be located in the forest of Tay Ninh province, about the same distance from Saigon. Yet most of Thailand is flat, and the low hills in part of the north-east – the Phu Phan range where the guerrillas live – bear no resemblance to the mountains of Laos, Burma or Vietnam, where insurgencies have flourished. The north-east region is remote from Bangkok, and internal communications, in spite of the rapid construction of strategic highways, are still insufficient. For many years revolutionary cadres, fostering regional resentment and seeking support from impoverished villagers, have been active; but only in the last decade, and then only sporadically, have they turned to armed struggle.

Nationalism – the struggle for independence – is not an issue in Thailand, as it was for the Vietminh. The latter's prestige in the 'Resistance' remained with those of its members who continued to live in the south after 1954. The Vietminh, too, endowed the NLF with an organisational network throughout South Vietnam. This was decimated during the Diemist repression, but because of the reservoir of rural support — from peasants whose right to land, granted by the Vietminh, has been annulled by Diem – it could be revived. There is no such extensive, motivated, thorough organisation in Thailand; nor is there the experienced, skilful and nationally-known leadership that there is in Vietnam. Moreover, respect for monarchy and the Buddhist religion are far from outdated in Thai villages. There is *as yet* no effective radical alternative either to traditional beliefs or to the present 'mixed' parliamentary-bureaucratic system of rule.

There is, of course, a similar division between rich and poor, urban and rural, official and peasant in Thailand as formerly in Vietnam, and as elsewhere in the Third World, but it is not so blatant as it was in Vietnam, exposed to the stress of war. Nor, of course, have village or city Thais suffered the traumatic overthrow or subjection of their sovereigns, as happened in colonial Burma and Vietnam. In fact the continuity of administration in Thailand – coups at various intervals only changed the leadership at the top – marks the greatest contrast between it and Vietnam, which fell successively under French, Japanese, Vietminh and again French rule, before independence.

Nevertheless the October 1976 coup has speeded up the process of polarisation in Thailand, which had become evident after 1973. The 'assets' of the system are increasingly being eroded: royalty has become politically involved with conservative politics; the military leaders are factionalised, disunited, unable to act constructively; the administration is immobilised (inhibited from carrying out the changes required); the modern intellectual-professional element has been alienated by the suppression of democracy; and, above all, many radical student leaders have rallied to the insurgents, providing them (for the first time) with the educated cadres they need.

Among students of insurgencies and revolutions, it is natural that the historian should emphasise particular cases, while the political scientist seeks to conceptualise (quantifying those, hopefully relevant, factors that can be quantified) and the activist postulates his 'theory of victory'.[18] The paradox is that the empirical historian, peering into the past, is able to discern a pattern of events (because the outcome is evident), while the conceptualising political scientist, concerned with the contemporary situation, stands in the midst of apparent confusion and uncertainty, which is the normal state of affairs. The political scientist requires a conceptual model to 'order' the overwhelming diversity of facts: for the historian, history itself is the model.

Imagine being back in the period of the first Indochina War in 1946–7.

Who, at this time, when the French had driven the Vietminh out of their capital and had seized the populated areas of Vietnam, could have foretold the way the struggle was to end, eight years later, and to revive another five years after that? Here the historian has an inestimable advantage. Knowing the outcome he can ignore the turns that history did not take, the tendencies that failed to materialise, the broad avenues of opportunity that became blind alleys.

Yet, regarded historically, even the common factors in the Chinese and (first) Vietnamese revolutions – and the reasons for the failure of the contemporary insurgencies in Malaya and the Philippines – hardly provide the basis for a systematic theory of universal validity. They are more like blocks of stone of varying size, which can be put together in different shapes, each of which then forms a building. At the beginning we cannot tell what type of building will emerge. It is doubtful, if the stones are faultily arranged, that the building will stand securely. And if the builders are incompetent and pressures to complete the work prove too much for them, the stones may never form a coherent shape at all. For the stones also exist as natural features of the landscape and they may remain that way.

Thus there were 'natural features' in the China of the early twentieth century which predisposed people to turbulence, organised and unorganised violence and revolution. But even if we consider peasant support to be the first condition of effective insurgency, then it varied not only in area (from south-east to north-west China) but also in motivation, as the struggle shifted from socialist to nationalist objectives; consequently the social composition of the revolutionary movement changed from an organisation mainly of tenants and landless labourers desiring land to a wide coalition ranging from poor peasants to 'patriotic landlords'. The second condition of rural revolution – ability to sustain protracted war – was not originally conceived of in this way at all. The revolutionaries fell back on it – as Castro did on guerrilla warfare – because of the total failure of the Soviet-style vanguard revolt of the urban proletariat to seize power by immediate, direct action – the general strike culminating in insurrection.

The Vietminh, by contrast, seized the psychological moment – presented by the surrender first of French forces in Indochina and then of the Japanese – and spread outwards from the cities to the countryside. Only from 1946–7 did the 'war of resistance' follow the Chinese pattern of rural-based insurgency and protracted war. As for the Algerian revolutionaries in the 1950s, they put more emphasis than either the

Chinese or Vietnamese on the support of middle-class nationalists in the towns; but they, too, were driven by the strength of official repression to seek refuge in the countryside and to rely on the 'backward' peasant masses.

Apart from, or as a result of, the 'detailed examination' of particular cases, what conclusions can we come to about the political, economic, social or psychological conditions that are conducive to effective political violence? These are discussed in the final section. Meanwhile a homely analogy is not out of place.

Flying over a country the observer notices with extraordinary clarity the neat clusters of towns and villages below, the distinct lines of roads and rivers, the shape and colour of mountains, the pattern of fields. It is only when he has landed at the airport and is being driven to his destination that he finds himself among the blurred images, the rapid changes of scene, the confusion of direction and the altered perspectives of a different sort of reality. The rarefied, clear, rational observation of the strategist has given way to the immediate, emotional, impressionistic feelings of the man on the ground – the insurgent in the trackless jungle, the soldier patrolling the tree-lined fields and villages. The conceptualist perceives the essence of the situation, displayed like a map before him, with its universally recognised symbols, its definite boundaries and obvious relationships, while the man in the street hardly looks beyond his own town or village, in which every house or tree is known to him like the back of his hand.

The first type of observation, in its deceptive clarity and lack of detail, gives rise at one extreme to 'universal' theories such as that of the dominoes collapsing one after the other in the shock waves emitted by the 'fall' of the first. The second type, from its inability to see the wood for the trees, yields at the other extreme to a description or chronicle of the 'facts'; in the absence of perspective, it is rapidly overtaken by events. Theorists of political violence or social change are ranged somewhere between the two. Another analogy may suit them better.

A mountain overlooks the capital city. At the summit of the mountain are reputed to be the tables of the law; but no one has yet climbed to the top. Some theorists, treading a well-worn path, are sceptical of the very existence of the tables. Their aim is to keep a close watch on the activities of the city but, by rising a little above it, they maintain an air of detachment. Others are beating out a separate path through the dense thickets that grow around the base of the mountain. From the point they have reached they have quite a different view of the city. Instead of the old administrative and ceremonial centre, with its orderly squares and dignified buildings, they find they are looking down on sprawling modern residential suburbs, which have extended far beyond the original confines of the city; they are also dimly aware, further in the distance, of the mean twisting streets with the hovels, blackened by grime and half-obscured by fumes, of the poor. Still others, mounting the precipitate crags which are the most formidable obstacle to the direct ascent to the summit, find themselves at times cut off by rugged natural features from any sight of the city; at other times they are presented with superb glimpses, although from peculiar angles, of the city below. Some of them, as a result of their very strenuous exertions, believe they have climbed much higher than is really the case. This is because almost as much of their time is spent going backwards or sideways, traversing the treacherous slopes concealing dangerous crevasses, as well as descending and ascending the deep gullies, as it is in clambering upwards. Finally there are those who have pushed beyond the tree line and can make out distinctly the icy peak of their endeavours etched against a brilliant sky. The prospects are so exhilarating that they ignore the scattered bones of the pioneers, who have passed this way before, mute reminders of the fate that awaits the imprudent or the unlucky. By now they hardly remember the city left so far behind. Indeed, while the network of streets, the blobs of factories and the patterns of the surrounding countryside are still visible to the naked eye, it requires powerful glasses to make out the tiny dots that are people, deprived of all individuality. Sometimes their gestures can be observed, but what they are indicating to each other certainly cannot be discerned from this distance; it can only be presumed.

Political, psychological, systemic theories

The four theories I shall discuss – by Charles Tilly, Ted Gurr, Samuel Huntington and Chalmers Johnson – provide a wide range of interpretations.[19] Tilly and Huntington focus on political power and political institutions; Gurr on psychological dispositions; Johnson on the social system. Each writer reveals considerable, but partial, insights into the problem of revolution, tending to be deficient in those factors held to be important by the others. The common problems facing them all are: (1) questions of methods; the integration of theory and the social reality under study; (2) questions of diagnosis: how adequate are the various explanations of reality? and (3), questions of prediction: it is significant for the nature of the subject that in spite of the predictive assumptions underlying these writers' basic conceptions, these assumptions are neither explicitly stated nor confirmed.

Each of these problems stems from 'partiality' of insight. Tilly, Huntington and Gurr enlarge on the forms of political violence – with insufficient *social* content. Johnson's approach to the 'disequilibrated' social system – the discrepancy between legitimating value structure and the changing environment – has insufficient *political* content. Although the following brief analysis of the four theories cannot do justice to the positive character and the valuable insights evident in all these works, it does, I believe, substantiate the points made above. I start with Tilly's 'contenders' for power, then discuss Gurr's 'relative deprivation' thesis, followed by Huntington's 'explosion' of political consciousness out-pacing institutional capacity, and finally consider Johnson's 'power deflation' in a disequilibrated system.

Charles Tilly is concerned with the 'polity' – not society. His group-conflict theory presents in modern guise the naked power struggle: that 'general inclination of mankind, the perpetual and restless desire of power after power, that ceaseth only in death'.[20] For Tilly, revolutions and collective violence tend to flow directly out of the 'central political process'.[21] The power struggle (a phrase he does not use) is the result of specific claims or counter-claims made on the existing government by various mobilised groups. These claims for established places within the structure of power, rather than, in Gurr's view, the generalised discontent or satisfaction of groups, are crucial. 'Resources' – land, labour, information, arms, money – and morality are alike subordinate to the struggle for power. A group gains the capacity to 'contend' for power by mobilising and acquiring collective control over resources; while challengers whose claims are denied tend to define themselves as 'deprived of rights' due to them on more general grounds. On the other hand, Tilly goes on, groups in power which are *losing* their 'membership' tend to accentuate tradition, usage and particular agreements in support of their claims to threaten privileges and resources. Thus both those claiming or losing positions of power have a special propensity to articulate 'strongly moral definitions' of their situation.[22]

The three necessary conditions for revolution, according to Tilly, are: (1) appearance of contenders, or coalitions of contenders, advancing 'exclusively alternative claims' to control of government; (2)

commitment to these claims by a 'significant segment' of the subject population, and (3) the unwillingness or incapacity of the agents of government to suppress the alternative coalition or the commitment to its claims. However, the crucial contenders are 'disaffected members' of the polity rather than newcomers to power. A further qualification: 'contraction of resources' is very likely to increase the probabilities of new groups, or new kinds of groups, coming into being as the result of structural changes. The efficiency of government coercion, a highly important element of the third condition, Tilly adds, is likely to decline where the character, organisation and daily routine of the population to be controlled changes rapidly: 'This appears to be one of the most direct effects of large-scale structural change on the likelihood of revolution.'[23]

In other words structural change, which Tilly proposes only as a 'strongly facilitating' and not as a 'necessary' condition of revolution, now appears to have a 'direct effect' on one of the crucial conditions (the third, coercion). Further, the commitment to contending claims by a 'significant segment' of the population (the second revolutionary condition) is said to increase, for example, when the government fails to meet established obligations, or greatly increases its demands on the population, when the 'coercive resources' of the opposition increase, and when claims are cast within a 'moral framework' which is 'already employed by many members of the population'. The latter point, as well as the emphasis on 'established obligations', suggest that morality is more than (in Tilly's view) merely an ideological justification used by ins and outs; in fact it corresponds to Johnson's 'legitimating' value structure, reflecting the norms, beliefs and attitudes of members of a community. A third problem for Tilly's political model is that the nature of the 'demands' on the subject population is not specified. If a 'significant segment' of the latter (second condition) is affected, then it would seem likely that the demands on the people go far beyond the confines of political rivalries. As for the increased 'coercive resources' of the 'alternative bloc' these, too, would seem to depend on something more than the claims of mobilised groups for 'established places within the structure of power', but are more likely to be the result of a broader 'popular' appeal: for example, demands by new groups brought into being or old groups affected by 'structural changes'.

In spite of these qualifications, Tilly's dominant political focus enables him so to narrow the field of enquiry that his power-contending model appears to offer a comprehensive explanation of reality. Having arbitrarily restricted the field he can then plausibly claim that his

conception 'exhausts' the common distinction between success and
failure, proletariat and bourgeoisie, colonialist and neo-colonialist,
centre and periphery, and so forth.[24] He asserts a further advantage of
his model, in that it avoids using the 'ill-defined entity' called society as a
basic analytic unit. (His unit is the polity, defined as the 'set of
contenders which routinely and successfully lays claim on the
government'.) It is not surprising that having done away with society he
can throw social classes (bourgeois and proletariat) and socio-economic
factors (neo-colonialism, centre and periphery) out of the window. The
third advantage of his theory, he claims, is that it puts forward 'well-
defined connections among mobilisation, contention, and conflict'; but
again this is so because Tilly has chosen to make it so: that is, by the
narrowly political interpretation put upon 'mobilisation, contention and
conflict', which omits or relegates to the sidelines those socio-economic
factors that cannot simply be subsumed under the notion of power
struggle.

Tilly is evading problems of substance by concentrating on the 'forms'
of struggle. Yet he himself notes that a group gains the capacity to
contend by mobilising and acquiring collective control over resources; it
is the resources that give them the *capacity* to confront the existing
power-holders. But *how* are they able to control these essential
'resources'? Tilly is not concerned with this problem, because if he were
he would have to answer questions about the specific relationship
between economic resources and political power. (This is also a problem
for Gurr.) It is this 'connection', not at all 'well-defined', that Tilly needs
to investigate.

Even study of the *process* of conflict requires investigation, as Tilly
agrees it does, of the 'precise way' in which urbanisation and political
centralisation – the examples he gives – affects the 'mobilisation' and
'demobilisation' of different segments of the people. Urbanisation,
which is in part the result of migration from rural areas (for what
reasons: pressure of population, system of land tenure, crop failures?),
and political centralisation (central control over what: the 'periphery',
groups formerly under 'local' control, and which groups and under
whose control?) are not just 'political' but are surely also social and
economic matters. On the one hand, Tilly insists that 'large-scale
structural change' only 'indirectly' affects the power struggle, concepts
of justice, organisation or coercion, formation of coalitions and the
legitimacy of the state – the 'traditional concerns of political thought'.
On the other, he admits that socio-economic factors 'transform' the

identities and structures of potential aspirants for power within the population, affect their opportunities for mobilisation, and 'govern' the resources available to the government and through it to the main holders of power. Is there any need to say more?

Why Men Rebel by Ted Gurr is an admirably systematic, wide-ranging, intelligent and fair-minded survey and analysis of the psychological and sociological literature of violence in its political setting.[25] Yet although profusely illustrated with examples of revolutionary behaviour from Vietnam to Cuba,[26] Gurr's 'psychologising' (an approach which Tilly tends to dismiss along with the 'sociologising' of revolution) is too broad and too general to apply satisfactorily to specific cases: the abundance of revolutionary instances 'illustrates' but does not validate the theory.[27] Yet, as Gurr acknowledges, it is the possibility of revolutions in particular countries that matters: 'the compelling need in the real world [is] to be able to anticipate political violence and the consequence of various responses to it.'[28]

It is a tribute to Gurr's realism and open-mindedness that he is so clearly aware of the problem of integrating theory with social reality. Thus on the crucial question of what attributes of a political system contribute to its adjustive capacity (to demands for political participation) and hence to its ability to minimise violence, he observes that a comprehensive review of the literature suggests one answer: 'almost anything' – ranging from constitutional structure to high levels of economic development, to élite ideologies of mobilisation, élite incumbent skills, national resources, consensus on solving problems co-operatively, and so forth.[29]

Yet Gurr points out that the usefulness of his basic causal model for synthesising information and facilitating explanation depends on 'precise specification' of the psychological and societal conditions that determine the intensity of 'relative deprivation' (RD) and the balance of institutional support for regime and dissidents.[30] But this is the problem. One method of assessing the psychological variables – intensity of RD, intensity of normative and utilitarian justifications for violence, legitimacy of the regime, identification, sense of community and so on – is to employ 'expensive and infrequently practicable' survey techniques; another is systematic inference from narrative and aggregate statistical data; while an alternative or supplementary approach to studying particular societies or cases is the analysis of class or group configuration. Groups or classes can be distinguished – 'analytically, structurally or

subjectively' – and their likely degree of RD inferred from such conditions as 'the total goods available for distribution in the society,
changes in each group's means for obtaining those goods, and their
changing levels of value attainment – *vis-à-vis* their own past and the
experience of other classes'.[31]

But this method, designed to elicit the 'specific' determinants of RD,
evidently requires a 'total' investigation of a society: that is, the 'total
goods', economic and political, 'available for distribution', presumably
by economic processes, governmental decisions and habitual
arrangements; the 'changes in means' to obtain those goods, which
require at least an historical analysis; and the changing values and
attainments, which require a psychological and sociological one as well.
This is not to condemn: merely to point out the difference between a
'guide to analysis', which is indeed well and thoughtfully formulated,
and the analysis itself, which we still await.

The second problem stems from the first. Gurr admits the wide range
of factors that contribute either to the state's adjustive capacity or to the
relative deprivation of its citizens. But he does not establish the precise
connection between (a) the diffuse psychological orientation – the
'disposition to collective violence', (b) the specifically 'depriving'
conditions, which are chiefly economic, and (c) the resulting *political*
activity, whether in the form of 'conspiracy', 'turmoil' or 'internal
war'.[32]

Gurr's explanation is that the impetus to collective violence (whether
this is justified normatively or for utilitarian reasons: i.e. it 'worked'
before) is focused politically when political actors are held 'responsible'
for depriving conditions. Attribution of such responsibility is possible
partly because of the 'ambiguous origins' of many deprivations in
modern complex societies; partly because of the greater scope for
government intervention in resolving 'value-distribution conflicts'. In
Gurr's view, most discontents in the modern world are not political, but
are politicised.[33] This is certainly correct, as far as it goes; but it does not
go far enough. First, by concentrating on the form of political struggles
(as does Tilly) Gurr does not pay sufficient attention to the content.
Second, by perpetuating a distinction between politics and economics,
he fails to see the nature of the connection.

Thus Gurr's explanation for the indubitably political form and objectives of much collective violence sidesteps the main issue: how can
revolutionary struggle be carried on against powerful political actors
without a substantial socio-economic or nationalist basis of support? The

latter not only motivate and make possible revolution in the first place, but they are an *integral part* of political action. Conversely, to attribute the reasons for politicisation of socio-economic discontent to the conspicuousness of government, its salience in certain roles or indeed its primacy (in the democratic theory of sovereignty), is also to underestimate the societal factors: what is the connection between governmental roles and economic structure? What is it that makes government 'responsible' for deprivation? It is not a scatter of examples, but only detailed study of individual countries, preferably over a lengthy period of development, that can provide the answers.

Samuel Huntington's *Political Order in Changing Societies* not only approaches the range of Gurr's work but at the same time his theories of modernisation, 'praetorianism' and revolution are effectively integrated into the social reality he is studying. Violence and instability, he writes, are largely the 'product of rapid social change and the rapid mobilisation of new groups into politics coupled with the slow development of political institutions'. This is his basic thesis:

> Social and economic change – urbanisation, increases in literacy
> and education, industrialisation, mass media expansion – extend
> political consciousness, multiply political demands, broaden political
> participation. These changes undermine traditional sources of
> political authority and traditional political institutions; they
> enormously complicate the problems of creating new bases of political
> association and new political institutions combining legitimacy and
> effectiveness. The rates of social mobilisation and the expansion of
> political participation are high; the rates of political organisation
> and institutionalisation are low. The result is political instability and
> disorder.[34]

The absence of opportunities for social and economic mobility and the low level of political institutionalisation in most modernising countries produce a correlation between social frustration and political instability.[35] There are three main ways of dealing with this situation. The first is 'praetorianism', defining 'political systems with low levels of institutionalisation and high levels of [popular] participation': these are mass societies, 'unclassifiable in terms of any particular governmental form because their distinguishing characteristic is the fragility and fleetingness of all forms of authority. Charismatic leader, military junta, parliamentary regime, populistic dictator follow each other in seemingly unpredictable and bewildering array.'[36]

Conversely, 'political systems with a high ratio of institutionalisation to participation may be termed civic polities'; these are the politically modernised states, characterised by rational authority (traditional authorities are replaced by a single, secular, national political authority), the differentiation of new political functions, and increased participation in politics by social groups throughout society:[37] included are Western democracies and communist countries alike.

The third possible outcome is revolution:

> The political essence of revolution is the rapid expansion of political consciousness and the rapid mobilisation of new groups into politics at a speed which makes it impossible for existing political groups to assimilate them. Revolution is the extreme case of the explosion of political participation. . . .
>
> To be more precise, the probability of revolution in a modernising country depends upon: (a) the extent to which the urban middle class – intellectuals, professionals, bourgeoisie – are alienated from the existing order; (b) the extent to which the peasants are alienated from the existing order; and (c) the extent to which the urban middle class and peasants join together not only in fighting against 'the same enemy' but also in fighting for the same cause. This cause is usually nationalism.[38]

The alienation of the middle classes allied to peasant discontent (land hunger), especially where narrowly centralised (traditional, military or colonial) regimes prevented the political participation of new groups, brought about the great revolutions in France, Russia and China, and indeed in Mexico, Algeria and Vietnam.

Yet although 'old regimes' are continually collapsing, Huntington points out, only rarely is this collapse followed by revolution: the fall of the Habsburg, Hohenzollern, Ottoman and Qajar (Persian) dynasties did not lead to major social upheavals. In these cases Huntington suggests that 'if a new social force (as in Egypt in 1952) or combination of social forces (as in Germany in 1918–19) can quickly secure control of the state machinery and particularly the instruments of coercion' it may well be able to stem the revolutionary tide. 'The crucial factor is the concentration or dispersion of power which follows the collapse of the old regime.'[39] The less traditional the society and the more groups that are able and available to participate in politics, the more revolutionary the situation. If no group is able and ready to establish effective rule, however, 'many cliques and social forces' struggle for power. The most notable among these are the moderates, like Kerensky, who are unable to cope with political mobilisation, the counter-revolutionaries (especially the military), and the 'radical revolutionaries' seeking to mobilise and organise the peasantry.[40]

Now Huntington has significantly shifted his ground. The crucial question for the realisation or prevention of revolution is who controls power. Already the focus has been narrowed – away from socio-economic changes producing an explosion of political consciousness – to concentration on the 'instruments of coercion'. From here it is but a short step to perceive the conditions for or against revolution in terms of the effectiveness or incompetence of governments. Indeed this is Huntington's position. Since the key variable is political institutionalisation, then regardless of whether the state concerned is 'communist totalitarian' or 'Western liberal', both 'belong generally in the category of effective rather than debile political systems. The United States, Great Britain, and the Soviet Union have different forms of government, but in all three systems the government governs.' Governs: but for what purpose? And in whose interests? These questions seem to be of no concern to Huntington.

Concentration on political power at the expense of social factors leads to dubious assertions. First, is it really the case (as he suggests) that the 'less traditional' society, with more groups contending, is more prone to revolution? The Bourbons and the Romanovs, whose overthrow was accompanied or followed by revolution, were highly traditional; but so were the Habsburgs, Hohenzollerns and Ottomans, whose overthrow was not. To understand the problem we must look at the social forces involved: obviously of great importance was the alienation of the peasantry in France and Russia, resulting from the systems of land tenure, with the additional burden, in Russia, of the heavy casualties inflicted on peasant soldiers in a senseless war. Conversely, in Imperial Germany, Austria-Hungary and Turkey, the peasantry was less important in the more developed economy of the first, the nationalism of subject peoples was the most striking feature of the second, and traditional attitudes of rural deference and passivity had not yet been overcome in the third.

The second dubious assertion is that the Leninist-type revolution is basically a political struggle. Lenin, contrary to Marx, who 'had no recognition of politics as an autonomous field of activity', gets Huntington's approval for elevating a 'political institution, the party, over social class and social forces'. But presumably this party was struggling in the interests (as the party conceived them) of the poor peasantry and proletariat and with their *support* – which no amount of conception, or elevation or even 'manipulation' could by itself have achieved. Huntington continues: 'The decisive factor is the nature of political organisation, not the stage of social development.'[41] That a political organisation, however brilliantly led, could carry out a revolution without much regard for the stage of social development, I find hard to believe. Certainly the men who made revolutions, Lenin with the slogan 'Bread, Peace and the Land' and Mao emphasising the 'uneven development' of China and the importance of the agrarian revolution, did not believe it. The revolutionary to whom 'political autonomy' is most appropriate is, of course, Fidel Castro: but the Cuban revolution, as is generally acknowledged, is exceptional.

Yet it is by reducing social factors essentially to political factors that Huntington was able to claim that there is little evidence that the revolutionary appeal of the NLF in South Vietnam, for example, derived from material poverty or could be countered by material and social benefits – rural development, land reform, education, official honesty, etc. 'The appeal of revolutionaries depends not on economic deprivation but on political deprivation, that is on the absence of an effective structure of authority.'[42] Yet Huntington overstates his case. Certainly the attitude to authority is crucial: but this attitude, in turn, depends on such 'material' factors as peasant resentment against landlords over insecure tenure, high rents, usury, and so on; their desire to own the land they farm; and their dislike of corrupt and oppressive officials. Race also asserts that 'development' itself is not an issue in the struggle – it goes on whoever wins. But he emphasises what Huntington overlooks:

> Government programs [in South Vietnam] were focused largely on providing a general *increment* of wealth or income, whereas what attracted people to the revolutionary movement was that it represented a new society in which there would be an individual *redistribution* of values, including power and status as well as material possessions.[43]

As Huntington (initially) attributes violence and instability to the fact that political development tends to lag behind social change, so Chalmers Johnson bases his theory of revolution on the discrepancy between values and environment, as a result of internal or external change.[44] The 'disequilibrated social system' is marked by what Talcott Parsons calls 'power deflation'; that is, in a situation of increasing demands on the system, the leadership attempts to maintain control by relying increasingly on force instead of confidence: excessive use of force is the 'end of the line'.[45] For it is contrary to the basic values of society which, when adhered to, legitimise authority. 'Loss of authority', when force is no longer considered legitimate, is a necessary condition of revolution. The immediate cause of revolution, however, is the result of what Johnson calls 'accelerators', which are often fortuitous factors preventing the regime from being able to employ its chief instruments of coercion effectively.[46]

Leadership responses to the development of such a crisis range from 'conservative change', introducing new rules of practical conduct based on existing values (i.e. reforms to avert revolution), to 'élite intransigence', which is a 'wilful reaction' still further violating the norms of society.[47] But Johnson fails to indicate what it is that determines the élite response in one direction or another.[48] Moreover, to consider the disloyalty or ineffectiveness of the armed forces (the latter most commonly caused by defeat in war) to be merely an 'accelerator' or catalyst of revolution is inconsistent with the general tenor of his discussion. Such 'disloyalty' or ineffectiveness is inseparable from the political or social factors that brought it about; these are almost certainly the *same* factors that have brought about popular 'loss of confidence' in the regime, which Johnson correctly states to be a determinant of revolution.

'The time is out of joint.' These four theories deal with the different levels of disequilibrium. For Huntington, social change has outrun the capacity for political institutionalisation. Johnson goes one stage back: he examines the incongruence between the value structure of society, which legitimises political authority, and the changed environment. Gurr goes two stages back: from the political, and the societal, to the psychological. Relative deprivation produced by the discrepancy between value expectations and capabilities is expressed in 'frustration–anger–aggression' behaviour. The form and magnitude of collective violence, however, depend on the balance of coercive control and institutional support between regime and dissidents (i.e. a return to the first stage: Huntington, Johnson, Tilly concur). Each theory – Tilly's is restricted to the first stage – contains valuable, if partial, insights. It is the integration of theory and 'social reality' that remains to be achieved.

My own preference is for a structural model, but one that explains (i.e. what has happened or is happening under certain circumstances, and why) and does not attempt to predict. The four factors I have outlined in the previous chapter reflect the 'underdeveloped' social structure: peasant dependence, radical 'rootlessness', military caste loyalties and either bourgeois absorption in the system or management of the system. To recapitulate: these are *pivotal* strata of society. Peasant conservatism may be transformed into radicalism when peasants (that is, a substantial number of them) become aware of their situation and of the possibility of change; the amateurism of workers and intellectuals may develop into 'professionalism' by dint of experience in coping with repression, in working with other strata and in organising an appropriate response; soldiers may mutiny or desert; the national bourgeoisie may be alienated by the refusal of the 'intransigent' forces of order to provide a genuine opportunity for political participation, by economic crisis, and so on.

There are both societal and psychological factors at work:[49] peasant deference to authority, radical militancy and spontaneity, military obedience and patriotism, bourgeois reformism (when it is in a position of assured superiority) and acquisitiveness. But I give priority to explanation rather than prediction, because voluntarism and hence particularity will break through the best-constructed conceptual frame: 'The will of man triumphs over fate.' Thus Clausewitz emphasises the importance of 'chance', not in the sense that there are no laws of regularities (if we know enough we can trace the causal links), but because events so often occur as 'chance' to men at war. Conditions change too rapidly and, at the time (and even afterwards), too many factors are unknown.

Psychological dispositions (Gurr), social system (Johnson), political processes (Huntington and Tilly) – and the effect of will (the detonator): only then is the equation complete. One half of the equation – the necessary conditions – permits either conflict or co-operation in society; the other half – will, personality and chance: the sufficient conditions – decides which trend will in fact be realised. Both halves combine, and can only combine, in concrete cases: 'revolution is a response to a particular crisis in a particular social system'.[50] But the multiplicity and complexity of factors determining the revolutionary process (emphasised by all the authors, except Tilly) and the inherent difficulty of reducing voluntarism to order (i.e. within the limits of indeterminacy)[51] are against the formation of a universally valid model of revolution.

Part two
⋆ INTERVENTION ⋆

Introduction

The various models of revolution discussed in the previous chapter state the *likelihood* of revolution given certain broad social conditions (such as peasant unrest, urban alliance with the peasantry, severe split in the governing apparatus). The *form* it takes (or does not take) depends on specific conditions. These are two sides of the revolutionary equation.

The same applies to the global strategic model of American super-power whether from the pluralist or neo-Marxist perspective. Broad socio-political conditions create global involvement which leads, under further conditions, to political penetration or military intervention. But the form intervention takes (or does not take) depends on *specific* conditions.

The two sides of the equation are the structural (or 'necessary') conditions and the 'contingent' (or sufficient) conditions: both have to be taken into account. This is evident if we further analyse US foreign policy. Super-power status is the *necessary* condition and global involvement flows from that necessity; but the form involvement (or intervention) takes in any specific case cannot with certainty be deduced from the structure of super-power, because of the operation of contingent factors – i.e. elements that are not determined by (outside the control of) that structure. These contingent factors and their relative importance can only be established by empirical investigation; they are *not* deducible from the super-power model.

This is evident from an examination of American intervention in Vietnam. Given the global 'structure' of US military and economic power facing an 'unacceptable' challenge (rebellion in Vietnam), in a relatively low-risk environment, then a *disposition* to intervene – to restore order – was predictable. But whether intervention would or would not take place, and the consequences of action or inactivity, were not predictable – because of the role of contingent factors – from the model. To put it another way: it could be deduced from the model that events in Vietnam affected the security of the USA. (This *was* the US Government's deduction.) But the form of the ensuing intervention – in its magnitude, intensity and effects – was not predicted, and could not have been predicted, from the *originating* circumstances.

To repeat: the necessary conditions for American intervention were present. But the form of intervention, and its eventual failure, were the result of contingent factors – the power of resistance of Vietnamese revolutionaries, the fatal flaws in the Saigon regime, the pressures of the Russians and Chinese, and overall international constraints (the need to avoid nuclear war). American failure and its obverse, Vietnamese revolutionary success, were contingent, not necessary. Just as the effectiveness of US intervention could not be predicted (although it was assumed) neither could its failure. The same applies to the Vietnamese: i.e. the model of victory through people's war. For it was well within the bounds of possibility for the USA and its allies, at various stages of the war, to have crushed the revolutionary challenge – just as the majority of Latin American regimes have crushed their revolutionary opponents.

In terms of predictive theory, the problem is this. Neither of the models – global-strategic on the one hand, people's war on the other – *adequately* relates the contingent to the necessary factors. This we have seen in the case of Latin America, where many countries, according to Marxist theory, were 'objectively' ripe for revolution, but where revolutionary movements apart from Cuba have (so far) failed. The persuasive strength and explanatory weakness of global models lie in their simplicity. But for this very reason they cannot cope with the multiplicity of factors that have to be taken into account; nor can they establish which among these factors will prove to be significant at the time they were beginning, perhaps obscurely, to operate.

Nevertheless, the structural factors are basic – the contingent are qualifiers. The position can be re-formulated in this way: (a) The structural characteristics of most Third World countries create the likelihood – not the certainty – of rebelliousness and the possibility of revolution. (b) The structural characteristics of world-wide super-power create the likelihood – not the certainty – of significant American involvement in a given Third World country and the possibility of intervention – i.e. the change from a collaborative to a determining role.

Whatever the 'contingent' qualifications, the structural characteristics of American super-power resemble the world-wide economic, political and military power of European nations in the nineteenth century. The main difference – the extent of direct colonial rule – is not as substantial as it may appear. The colonial power could, at least from its own standpoint, 'legitimately' suppress internal challenges, while a super-power requires the authorisation of the 'sovereign' government concerned; but as this suppressive action (in the positive form of economic aid intended to remove grievances, or in the negative form of counter-insurgency) is in the interest of both parties, this is not usually difficult to obtain. As for economic development, it may meet material needs, but at the same time it usually increases disparities between rich and poor – thereby creating new *social* demands, which an élitist ruling system is unlikely to concede. That is why US aid (for development) and counter-insurgency so often go hand-in-hand.

The consequences that flow from the structure of super-power are as follows:

The projection abroad of America's vast internally-derived power, as it 'meshes' with indigenous power structures in a variety of forms, provides the essential security framework within which American foreign policy operates. There are two points to note: first, US power abroad is not subject to those domestic constraints which, apart from Watergate, normally apply; and second, the ultimate determinants of security operate regardless of the personal preferences of individual policy-makers.

Security considerations, especially at times of crisis, prevail over more 'idealistic' concerns, e.g. home-based pluralist values: see the following chapter. (US policy toward Thailand is just one example. US aid in the 1950s contributed significantly to economic development; by the early 1960s it was actually being phased out. But by the critical mid-1960s, *three-quarters* of the revived US aid was directly related to security: equipping para-military police, building 'strategic highways', concentrating on 'sensitive' communist-affected provinces, etc.) Crises, which for a world power are likely to break out quite frequently, are not atypical phenomena – but rather the reverse. Crises are the *test* of 'world order', i.e. the system of interlocking US–Third World–élite military, political and economic power. The latter has to be 'geared' to meet crises at all times – inevitably affecting even the 'normal' operations of the system – if mutual security is not to be at risk.

The normal situation is one of American 'involvement' in Third

World countries. But involvement tends to escalate to 'intervention' at times of crisis. Crises are usually the result of changes in the status of a client regime – either voluntarily, by a shift in allegiance, or involuntarily through internal instability or external pressure – which are deemed to pose an unacceptable threat to the global system (at a minimum, by adversely affecting the overall balance of power). Involvement and intervention form a continuum: from US economic interest in a Third World country to direct military engagement (see Table 3, chapter 6).

Intervention takes the form of 'limited war' (chapter 7), counter-insurgency (chapter 8) or 'destabilising' measures, including intervention by proxy (chapter 9). Although the post-Vietnam doctrine, or rather presumption, of 'self-reliance' for allies and friends has to a certain extent changed American policy, it has not changed the *conditions* under which that policy operates (see the 'Conclusion'). These are the conditions – outlined in Part One of this study – conducive to acts of dissidence, revolt or revolution that are considered a threat to world order.

5 ∗ US foreign policy: two perspectives

This chapter is designed to test the assumption, outlined in the Introduction to Part Two, that security is ultimately the determining factor in the operation of US foreign policy. I do this by considering at the outset an alternative thesis – the pluralist or developmental approach. As in the first chapter of this book, I use the adversary procedure, presenting first the case for pluralism, then the neo-Marxist structural-dependency thesis, and ending with my conclusions.

I shall begin by examining the proposition that the way in which a society is organised politically and economically ('domestic structure') affects its foreign policy. In the case of the USA, the domestic structure reflects the prevalent values – ideas, beliefs, customs, attitudes, historical experiences, etc. – of a pluralist society, expressed in competitive party politics, regular elections, a free press, autonomous interest groups, and so on. It follows that pluralist values, influencing the domestic structure, are 'carried through' into American foreign policy. Analytically, however, there are two distinct aspects of this process: first, the policy-makers' *perceptions* of the external environment (here, the countries of the Third World); second, their *formulation* of policy, designed both to further the 'interests' of the domestic structure and to fit the perceptions of the environment to which that policy relates. While I accept the general proposition and the particular statement about American values and domestic structure, it is the deduction – that pluralist values significantly affect the conduct of American foreign policy – that I seek to test. This is to be done in the context of the *environment* to which US foreign policy relates and which, through its feedback effects, is crucial to foreign policy performance. Analysis of the Third World environment is therefore essential to this study.

As regards the formulation of American foreign policy, pluralism is not only a valid object of investigation in logic, it is important in practice.

To judge by the declared aims of policy – support for the democratic as opposed to the totalitarian model, the notion of the 'free world', collective security of sovereign states, and so on – it is reasonable to assume that pluralist values are of major significance. I wish to test this assumption on these grounds: if the 'pluralist effect' should prove to be only a marginal one in times of crisis (the issue I am basically concerned with) then other factors are clearly of overriding importance. The question then is, what are these other factors?

As for the perceptions of American policy-makers, they determine the *type* of pluralism that is most appropriate to my study. This is what may be called 'developmental' pluralism, i.e. that associated with and widely diffused by the Committee on Comparative Politics of the US Social Science Research Council. It is appropriate for two main reasons: first, along with other forms of pluralism, it specifically reflects the liberal-democratic values of American society (the reason for choosing pluralism in the first place), while non-pluralist conceptions of the Third World, regardless of their possibly greater significance, do not do so; second, developmental pluralism is specifically intended to explain the Third World environment, while other forms of pluralism (regardless of whether or not they are more illuminating in their own particular contexts) do *not* have this objective. Therefore on both counts – reflection of American values and reference to the Third World – developmental pluralism is the appropriate choice (see Table 1).

Table 1   Characteristics of developmental pluralism

---

1   Developmental pluralism, as sponsored by the SSRC's Committee on Comparative Politics, reflects *American* experience: Harry Eckstein notes that 'many of the concepts, methods and interests now being applied in comparative politics came out of the intensive study of American politics'; Gabriel A. Almond, founding chairman of the Co,nmittee, affirmed at its first research session in 1957 that 'our present theories of interest groups, political parties and public opinion are based on American and to a lesser extent European experience.' (Eckstein, 'A Perspective of Comparative Politics, Past and Present', in Harry Eckstein and David E. Apter (eds), *Comparative Politics: A Reader*, Chicago, Free Press, 1963, p. 25; Almond, 'A Comparative Study of Interest Groups and the Political Process', in Eckstein and Apter, *Comparative Politics: A Reader*, p. 397.)

2   *Relevance* of developmental pluralism to American foreign policy: the Committee's first major research project, *The Politics of the Developing Areas*, edited by Gabriel A. Almond and James S. Coleman (Princeton University Press, 1960), was acclaimed as 'far and away the most influential recent work' in the rapidly growing field of analysis of political systems, particularly that undertaken in the USA, 'whose emergence as a

Table 1 contd

---

world power has suddenly confronted scholars and policy-makers with the urgent need to find answers' to questions of stability and change (Robert A. Dahl, *Modern Political Analysis*, Englewood Cliffs, N.J., Prentice-Hall, 1963, p. 112).

3 *Development* of developmental pluralism: it has gone through three stages. Stage one is represented by *The Politics of the Developing Areas* (1960): Third World countries are classified in terms of their development towards the goal of the democratic 'Anglo-American model' of competitive party systems, autonomous interest groups, bargaining culture, etc. Stage two is represented by Gabriel A. Almond and G. Bingham Powell Jr, *Comparative Politics: A Developmental Approach* (Boston, Little, Brown, 1966); it marks a shift from the Anglo-American model to 'effectiveness' of the system as the main criterion of development; political development is defined as an increase in the differentiation and specialisation of political structures and increased secularisation of political culture: in general, increased effectiveness of performance (p. 105). Stage three, the present stage, is represented by Gabriel A. Almond (ed.), *Comparative Politics Today: A World View* (Boston, Little, Brown, 1974): it reveals disillusionment with the Third World; goal-less empiricism; in effect, support for the status quo (Almond, 'Introduction').

4 *Plausibility* of developmental pluralism: the body of work in this field cannot account for the entire range of pluralist or comparative-political studies in the USA, but it is in the mainstream of those theories of development which have been most influential in shaping American conceptions of the Third World. It should be pointed out that it is not necessarily (indeed not usually) the most sophisticated or most penetrating approaches that are the most widely diffused and most influential in a given society – but those that are most plausible under the circumstances. Developmental pluralism fulfilled this role, both in formulating American concepts and in reflecting the actual experiences – evident in the three stages noted above – of American foreign policy.

I argue, however, that the liberal-democratic values of a pluralist society do *not* have an appreciable effect on American foreign policy, for two main reasons. The first is the overriding importance of security in a world of uncertainty, turbulence and danger, both for the preservation of the American domestic system and the maintenance abroad of a climate favourable to American corporate activities. (I leave aside, for the present, the question whether strategic or economic motivation is the dominant factor.) The second is the way in which societies in the Third World are organised, politically and economically, that is, for the most part in élitist and authoritarian structures. Whatever the personal preferences of American policy-makers for liberal or democratic solutions, they are obliged to act, first, in terms of necessity (national security) rather than ethical choice, and thus second, within the framework of the *given* situation in Third World countries rather than of 'hypothetical' ideals.

Security and pluralism

The link between the concept of developmental pluralism and American foreign policy stems, ironically for the pluralist thesis, not from the autonomy of the development process, but from its *dependence* on security. In the long term, as former US Defense Secretary Robert McNamara put it, development provides security; but in the immediate situation of stress, 'security means development': 'the irreducible fact remains that our [US] security is related directly to the security of the newly developing world.'[1] How did this relationship come about?

The explanation lies in the developmental-pluralist theory of 'transition' from traditionalism to modernisation. There are four main processes involved. First, 'state building', the penetration and integration of the polity by the centralised bureaucracy; second, 'nation building', the cultural diffusion of loyalty and commitment (in Ivan Illich's words, 'schools rationalise the divine origin of social stratification with much more rigour than churches have ever done');[2] third, participation, the result of pressure by groups in society to take part in decisions affecting them, and fourth, distribution, such as social welfare, redistribution of income and so on.[3]

All these changes – and particularly economic change, which does not appear except indirectly in the last item – have a disturbing impact on traditional attitudes, beliefs and behaviour. Formerly isolated, subsistence-level villagers are drawn into a monetary economy characterised by contractual rather than personal ties. Growing numbers of people are exposed to new ideas and new ways of life through mass communications, many are physically relocated in cities and towns, adopting an entirely different mode of employment (wage labour), and they are constantly (rather than intermittently) made aware of the power and scope of the bureaucracy in the form of official regulations, police controls, taxation and so on. It is hardly surprising that the negative, disorienting effects of social and economic change at first outweigh the benefits; for postponement of gratification (voluntarily for the entrepreneurs, compulsorily for the masses) is the essence of the process. The work ethic requires toil and sacrifice, in austere conditions, before the years of labour bear fruit. This is precisely the period of greatest danger for the system, when opposition to the harsh effects of 'penetration' and 'integration' is most likely to be felt *before* the material benefits of production 'trickle down' by way of 'participation' and 'distribution'. It is in this transitional period, moreover, that internal 'deviance' is likely to be stimulated, aided and 'directed' by external 'subversion' to the detriment of nation building and to the detriment of international stability and security as well.[4]

The perceived connection between internal and external security provides the link between American domestic pluralism and its global foreign policy. Pluralist development requires security; and the domestic security of each is the international security of all. To complete the circle, 'world order' is identified with American national interests: 'We are struggling to maintain an environment on the world scene which will permit our [U.S.] open society to survive and flourish.'[5]

Dominance and dependence

The 'dominance-dependence' thesis starts from the same premise: that it is in America's interests to 'struggle to maintain' a world order of stable states. But it stands the pluralist assumption of autonomous internal development on its head. In one of the most cogent and lucid presentations of this thesis, Susanne Bodenheimer argues as follows.[6]

The underdevelopment of the Third World is not the reflection of each country's autonomous growth, nor is it a transitional stage on the way to modernity, but it is structurally conditioned by imperialism: the more advanced the process (as in Latin America) the less the autonomy. For 'growth' occurs as the reflex of the expansion of the dominant nations and is geared to the needs of the dominant economies. It is precisely in the 'most dynamic and strategic' industrialised sectors of a nation's economy that foreign control is most marked, whether by direct ownership of enterprises or by control of the distribution of products. The result: outflow of capital (profits) abroad; adaptation of the economic structure to the needs of foreign investors; and the introduction of labour-saving technology which aggravates unemployment.

Besides shaping the economy in the interests of foreign capital, the international system generates and reinforces in underdeveloped countries an 'infrastructure of dependency': certain institutions, social classes, processes (industrialisation, activities of socio-economic élites, urbanisation, etc.) respond to the interests or needs of the dominant foreign powers, not to national needs. These 'clientele social classes', with a vested interest in the international system, attain an increasingly privileged and hegemonic position in their countries; they are both 'junior partners of metropolitan interests' and 'dominant élites in their own societies'.

The 'infrastructure of dependency', through which foreign interests operate, is the functional equivalent in nominally independent countries of the former colonial apparatus. Efforts to create 'bourgeois national' or 'state capitalist' solutions ['nation building'] must fail in the end because the social classes on which these attempts rely are limited by their role in the international system. Similarly, nationalist advocacy of an 'independent' foreign policy (such as in Brazil before the 1964 coup) or the expropriation of foreign holdings (as in Peru) lacks substance when the infrastructure still depends on foreign investment and the élites still compromise with foreign interests.

Dependence on imperialism is not created by occasional acts of military intervention, but is a 'chronic condition' maintained by the 'subtler mechanisms', referred to above, in day-to-day, usually peaceful relations. 'Isolated' military or political acts, such as the Cuban missile crisis, must be understood in their overall context – the preservation of capitalism as an economic order. Coercion is only the ultimate resort, when the subtler mechanisms prove ineffective.

The activities of the US government abroad and the socio-economic structure of the American system are integrally related. Private corporate operations abroad require protection by the imperialist state, while the interests of the state come to overlap with those of the multinationals. Imperialism is a stage in the development of capitalism as a world system. The concentration of capital and resources in multinational corporations marks a progressive shift from rivalry among capitalist powers to the integration of the capitalist world order under US hegemony. Similarly, capitalist reliance on immediate returns of profit from foreign investment is shifting to long-range planning, avoidance of risk, and 'maximum political stability' to preserve a favourable climate for the perpetuation of corporate operations. Nor does corporate capitalism exclude limited measures of development and social reform in the Third World – 'welfare imperialism' has the dual aim of rendering the system more palatable to the dependent population and of expanding the domestic market for corporate products.

Dependency and imperialism are two sides of the same coin. But dependency is not a stabilising condition. On the contrary. First of all, capital-intensive industrialisation, by generating increased unemployment and 'marginalisation', limits the expansion of the domestic market and thus the expansion of foreign investment. In the second place, the 'industrial bourgeoisie', increasingly dependent on the international system, lacks the potential to mobilise national support and thereby forfeits its 'ideological hegemony' over the popular forces. The consequence, thirdly, is that underdevelopment is aggravated, new sectors become radicalised, state repression intensifies: the repression-resistance cycle becomes chronic.

Perspectives compared

The neo-Marxist thesis provides a systematic and comprehensive explanation of the roles of social, political and economic forces and, above all, their interaction both in national and international perspective. Pluralist developmentalism lacks ˙this systematic and comprehensive character. It cannot but look to the autonomy of groups, classes, institutions and processes within a country and the autonomy of 'sovereign states' within the international system. Democratic pluralism may be the *outcome* (as in the West) of increasing specialisation and differentiation of functions, reflected in the growth and influence of 'middle classes'; but in the contemporary circumstances of the Third World there is little evidence as yet to support this thesis. To the contrary, middle-class professionals, technocrats and bureaucrats have generally either approved of or acquiesced in the subordination of constitutional liberties to the goals of economic development, administrative efficiency and national (élite) security pursued by the 'new autocracies'.

The weakness of the pluralist model, as previously pointed out, is that there is no necessary connection between the existence of Western pluralist institutions and the perceived tendencies towards pluralism in the Third World. The former are the product of specific historical conditions – conditions which are unlikely to be repeated in the Third World. Indeed, circumstances are against the latter following the democratic path, for three main reasons: the intensive and growing population pressures, the sheer rapidity of change (telescoped into a matter of decades) and, above all, the fact that the developing countries operate in the context of a mature, global, economic system, in which they play a dependent role: this is vastly different from the advantageous position of Western Europe and America in their era of modernisation.[7]

Developmental pluralists are aware of the discrepancy between the model and the reality of most developing countries. But they consider this discrepancy to reflect the stage of *transition* from traditional attitudes and activities to 'modernisation' on Western lines.[8] When this assumption is challenged by the actual trend *away* from democratic pluralism and towards authoritarianism, the developmentalists fall back on indiscriminate empiricism: preoccupied with the classification of existing structures and functions, regardless of what they are 'developing' into, they earn Kissinger's reproach (in his academic days) to the 'bureaucratic-pragmatists'; they are more concerned with where they are than where they are going, with method than with judgment; they seek to reduce judgment to methodology and value to knowledge.[9]

Both Marxist and, in a more limited way, patron–client analyses offer more realistic explanations. There are, however, significant weaknesses in the neo-Marxist thesis. But I shall first consider its strengths. It seems to me broadly correct in emphasising four basic features of the contemporary world: the state of underdevelopment of most countries of the Third World; the dependence of their economies on the dominant global economies, the patron–client relationship whereby the 'junior partners' of metropolitan interests maintain themselves as dominant social élites in their own societies; finally, the operation of the system normally without the use of direct external force; the latter occurs chiefly when the 'local' components, for one reason or another, fail to carry out the first two functions.

Now, the evidence of poverty and inequality associated with underdevelopment is amply documented from official sources: for example, the previously cited growth of tenancy in the Philippines. To give some further examples. The characteristic situation in Latin America is one of widespread urban and rural poverty, considerable unemployment or underemployment, uneven industrialisation and marked inequality of incomes and living standards. Half the population in the region in 1969 had an average income per head of $120, while the top 5 per cent had an average of $2,600.[10] In India, with a *rural* population larger than the total population of Latin America (or Africa), nearly one-third of village households, owning an average of one-tenth of an acre, owned only 0.54 per cent of the total cultivated area: the top 3.2 per cent of households owned nearly one-fifth of the total area.[11] The President of the World Bank reported that 'among 40 developing countries for which data are available, the upper 20 per cent of the population receives 55 per cent of the national income in the typical country, while the lowest 20 per cent of the population receives 5 per cent'. Nearly 800 million people, or some 40 per cent of the total of two billion people in the developing countries (i.e. excluding China), survive on incomes estimated at 30 cents a day in conditions of malnutrition, illiteracy and squalor. 'They are suffering poverty in the absolute sense.'[12]

This is not to ignore the 'success stories' of countries like South Korea and Taiwan and the city states of Hong Kong and Singapore. But even in these cases, two sets of rather unusual circumstances are required if the benefits of free enterprise, export-based 'strategies of development' are to reach all strata of society, including rural society, and not be monopolised by the élite. First, the existence of skilled manpower or material resources, external demand for products, and a favourable man/land ratio: this is the factor of growth. Second, and on the basis of the first, is the distributive factor. This requires the development of intensive 'egalitarian' farming by peasant cultivators who own their land (as, for example, in Korea and Taiwan after land reforms) and are given appropriate incentives and opportunities to raise yields. Conversely, the existence of a large population with a very unequal share in the land does not preclude growth in the modern sector of the economy, by means of technological improvements. But the benefits of growth not only do not go to the large majority of the people but are actually at its expense. It is to check, or reverse, this process of concentration of wealth and power that *institutional* changes – even in favoured countries: above all in the less-favoured – are essential.

The state of poverty and inequality *within* Third World countries is equally characteristic of the wider international system, i.e. the dependence of what has been called the 'periphery' (developing countries) on the 'centre' (the industrialised countries). Particularly in their 'modern' sectors, Third World economies (with few exceptions) are dependent on the dominant economies. The USA alone, as McNamara points out, with 6 per cent of world population consumes about 35 per cent of the world's total resources. This is the achievement of American corporate enterprise, which is highly concentrated. Eighty per cent of direct private American investment abroad is the property of 187 transnational corporations, with over 10,000 subsidiaries in the capitalist world. The estimated value of all these foreign affiliates of US corporations amounted in 1968 to $130 billion – or four times the value of US exports. In Latin America, US subsidiaries accounted for over one-third of all Latin America's imports and more than two-fifths of all exports of manufactured goods.[13] The impact of enormous – and increasing – American economic power, in addition to that of Western European countries and Japan, at one end of the scale, and the small, and decreasing, power of the great majority of developing countries (with the exception of the oil-producers and a few owners of important mineral resources), at the other end, is reflected in their respective 'shares' in the global product. The countries of the developing 'periphery', with nearly 70 per cent of the world's population, owned 17 per cent of the global product in 1963, a share which was reduced to 15 per cent by the end of the 1960s. The share of the periphery in world trade similarly was reduced from 32 to only 21 per cent in the two decades up to 1968. Even this small share is largely confined to 'traditional' exports of primary products.[14]

A similar relationship between centre (big business and the power élite) and periphery (the masses) characterises internal conditions in most Third World countries. Just as most developing countries are increasingly dependent on, and yet marginal to, the developed countries so most people in the developing countries – whether as smallholders, tenant farmers or landless labourers in low-productivity agriculture or as rural migrants seeking work in the towns – become increasingly dependent on, and marginal to, the political and economic structures of power in their own societies. The attempt to reduce this dependence and with it the crushing burden of poverty, especially in rural areas, as recommended by the World Bank, illustrates the extent of the problem. The main aim is greatly to increase production on small farms, which at present maintain a bare level of subsistence for some 700 million people in the developing countries. To achieve this aim six measures are essential: accelerated land and tenancy reforms; better access to credit; assured availability of water; expanded extension and research facilities; greater access to public services; and new forms of rural organisations and institutions 'that will give as much attention to promoting the inherent potential and productivity of the poor as is generally given to protecting the power of the privileged'. Yet the pervasive obstacle to these measures – and the case of land reform will serve as an example for the others – 'is that land reform is not exclusively about land. It is about the uses, and abuses, of power – and the social structure through which it is exercised.'[15]

The other side of the coin is the high income enjoyed by the powerful and wealthy élites in these societies, described as an 'international community of the affluent and influential'.[16] As Sunkel notes, there are four sources of high income. First, profits from high-productivity primary export sectors or from the protected manufacturing industry. Second, where there is some transfer of income to social groups not linked to the above, usually through the mechanism of the state: for example those members of the middle or organised working class who benefit from a certain amount of income redistribution. Third, where there is a high degree of concentration of ownership or control of the means of production, and where there are imperfect markets, especially in primitive or traditional activities, such as agriculture, handicrafts, small industry and many service activities. Salaries can be kept low because there is an abundant supply of unskilled labour, while markets for goods and services are imperfect because of institutional power arrangements. Finally, through income transfers from abroad, or from foreign or international organisations. 'The low productivity of the larger part of the productive structure . . . must be organised on an exploitative basis in order to provide minority groups with high incomes.'[17]

This is a compelling indictment. Yet there are also serious weaknesses in the neo-Marxist thesis.[18] It is not the 'facts' – i.e. the conditions of Third World countries, as revealed by the investigations of Marxists, 'structuralists' like Sunkel and Myrdal, and others – that are in question, but the *relationship* between the facts. There *is* underdevelopment and extensive poverty in most countries of the Third World; they *are* dependent economically; and the relative affluence of the privileged élite is in glaring contrast to the wretchedness of large sections of the rural and urban population. But is the first condition, underdevelopment, essentially caused by the second and third, that is, international dependence and élite structures? And if it is, why should the second (the international economic system) rather than the third (national élites) be considered the dominant factor?

Similarly, there is need to qualify Bodenheimer's fourth point – the normal and 'critical' operation of the global system. First, how closely integrated in fact are the political and economic instruments of American imperialism; and how closely integrated are the other leading capitalist powers under the umbrella of US hegemony? Second, what is the evidence for the thesis that the political arm (spheres of influence, military strategy) is subordinate to the economic arm (expanding corporate investment, overseas trade and profits)? Third, why must national or international élites always, or even usually, be expected to act out of economic self-interest? Why should not one or the other act 'irrationally' (in economic terms) for reasons of national pride or national security[19] – even to the extent of jeopardising the economic foundation? (My own, rather different interpretation of the US role in its external environment is set out in the next chapter.)

The very persuasiveness, clarity and coherence of the neo-Marxist imperialism-dependence thesis owes much to the *reluctance to qualify* its basic premises, which are tantamount to economic determinism. In fact the issue comes down again to the question of autonomy – and with it the problem of prediction. The Marxist prediction of chronic instability, the repression-resistance cycle and ultimate revolution is predicated on the *absence* of any genuine autonomy either of classes within society or of states within the international system. On the issue of autonomy, the Marxist denial that it is possible – at least to any substantial degree – is as much open to question as the pluralist insistence on its overriding importance. The primacy, implied by the autonomy, of politics[20] at one extreme gives way to the primacy of economics at the other.

Finally, prediction. Whether the Marxist prediction is confirmed or is invalidated, neither case, it seems to me, provides ground for optimism. On the one hand, there will be a situation of intensified repression in the Third World, as mass-élite conflicts gather force, aggravated by the coercive power available to one side (or perhaps both) as a result of technological innovation and the growth of the international arms market. Only the most dogmatic Marxist can rest assured that most of these conflicts, except in the very long term, will be won by revolutionaries. On the other hand, should the pluralist model prevail, the autonomy of political and economic structures – nationally as well as internationally – provides no guarantee that interest groups, however complex and differentiated, will harmonise either at the state or the state-system level. What evidence, in the latter case, leads us to suppose that the national rivalries leading to the First and Second World Wars will no longer play a role in an era of nuclear proliferation, population pressures, and conflicts over scarce resources?

Conclusion

This final section examines the conduct of US foreign policy towards the Third World, first in terms of the pluralist and Marxist criteria outlined above, and second in the context of the American goal of world order. Three issues are common to both sets of criteria, though the interpretation differs widely: security, co-operation with governments of allied and 'friendly' nations, and 'system-maintenance'.

First, security. In the pluralist view security is essential for the development of autonomous interest groups in the modernising process.

In the Marxist view, however, 'security' reflects the coercive power of the state machine maintaining a system of exploitation in the interests of the dominant class. Second, the issue of co-operation. Official American co-operation with Third World governments is, according to the pluralist thesis, merely one of several autonomous functions in international relations – others being trade, investment, communications, cultural ties, tourism, etc. – pursued by the various interest groups concerned. Marxists, on the contrary, perceive American co-operation with élitist regimes as the link between domestic and international systems of exploitation; for Third World élites function both as 'junior partners' of capitalist powers and as dominant classes in their own societies. Third, system maintenance. According to pluralists, the system operates in the domestic arena by harmonising various interests to mutual advantage, through the input-output conversion process; internationally, such harmony is achieved through the diffusion of 'modernity' – via trade, investment, technology transfers, aid,[21] security, information and the like – from the advanced and industrialised to the transitional and developing countries. This interlocking network of domestic and international exploitation, as perceived by Marxists (i.e. precisely the diffusion effect so favourably viewed by the pluralists), is not normally kept in being by direct imperialist intervention, but by 'subtler' methods of indirect rule through the subordinate 'infrastructures of dependence'.

These differing interpretations of America's relations with the Third World must also be considered in the overall context of US foreign policy. America's overriding objective, ever since the Second World War transformed the country from an economic power to a military, economic and political super-power, is expressed in the Carter–Brzezinski formulation of 'world over politics' as in the Nixon–Kissinger 'stable structure of peace'.[22] Under current conditions of nuclear parity, Sino-Soviet rivalry, and Japanese and West European restiveness, this is most easily accomplished by maintaining a balance of power among super and great powers (i.e. a mixture of 'partnership', conciliation and strength) rather than by the undifferentiated and outmoded containment strategy of the Cold War era. Then and now, however, the creation of a stable international milieu is considered most conducive to the operation inside America and the sustenance and expansion outside it of 'liberal capitalist' values, institutions and interests. Since the overall objective is common to all the major interest groups in America, the debate revolves around the question of *methods*:

how best to create and maintain a stable structure of peace? The 'strategic realism' of Nixon and Kissinger is one method, the 'cold war liberalism' of Kennedy and Johnson another. Even if Carter's 'constructive global involvement' in principle represents a strikingly different alternative either to massive Dullesian threats or Eisenhower-type immobilism, on the one hand, or to Nixon–Kissinger *realpolitik*, on the other, in practice the results are much the same.[23] The reason for this similarity is evident – the global requirements of order determine the methods. Policies, whether reformist or otherwise, and whether of a political or economic nature, conform to these requirements.[24]

The dictates of order are one thing, the environmental obstacles to realising them another. How does America deal with the threat (in pluralist terms) or the challenge (viewed by Marxism) to 'the kind of world order our own well-being requires' caused by structural instability and violent change? The global strategist insists that 'security is indivisible'; that a threat to one is a threat, directly or indirectly, to all. The problem is that even if the 'autonomy' of revolutionary situations is accepted (and this is far from being the case) – i.e. that they are basically a response to 'local' conditions, not instigated from outside – then 'local' upheavals must still affect global processes, from both pluralist and Marxist points of view. The security-pluralist is convinced that overall stability is the prerequisite of liberty, that world order is the condition of pluralist diversity (*not* the other way round). The Marxist in turn sees revolution as an act of world-historical significance designed to end the 'infrastructure of dependence' that links the national and international systems of exploitation and without which the latter cannot survive. Security/exploitation is indivisible: reaction to the threat by the 'subtler mechanisms' or, if they fail, by external intervention is inevitable; the repression-resistance cycle becomes chronic. . . .

Is this the only outcome: global power confronting global challenge until one ultimately prevails? From both pluralist and Marxist perspectives this is indeed the catastrophic outcome. Pluralism, at first reflecting a 'naive' faith in evolutionary progress, has become disillusioned at the failure to realise democracy and liberty in the Third World,[25] and ends up advocating a goal-less indeterminacy: this is in itself a rationalisation of the practice of American foreign policy: to maintain, irrespective of internal conditions in the countries concerned, a global 'structure of peace' advantageous to American interests. Marxism, on the contrary, sceptical (not without reason) of liberal-democratic professions of faith, denies the very possibility of groups, classes and nations 'stepping out of' their historic roles and transcending the structural limitations on behaviour.

Between the two extremes of determinism – for the apparent indeterminacy of 'comparative' pluralism masks the determining role of security – what possibility is there of independent action? Paradoxically, both the 'true' pluralist, welcoming diversity, and the undaunted revolutionary – 'the will of man triumphs over fate'[26] – have shown, each in his own way, a solution to the predicament: the predicament that is the perpetually varying and unresolved conflict between unique conditions and global processes, between autonomy and dependence, freedom and necessity.

6 ⋆ America and the Third World: from involvement to intervention

Succinctly stated, America throughout its history has had three basic objectives: 'security against attack'; maintenance of an 'international environment in which the United States can survive and prosper'; and, finally, the idealistic attempt to ensure that 'the United States should, by example, or action, or both, exert influence toward the spread of more representative and responsive governments in the world'.[1]

Security and a favourable international environment correspond to the first two propositions advanced in the Preface to this study. The desirability of spreading 'more representative and responsive governments' corresponds to the 'developmental pluralist' approach examined and substantially eliminated as a significant factor in the previous chapter. My third proposition is derived from the first (security) and second (favourable environment): i.e. the common interests of US decision-makers and Third World regimes. It is in three parts: (1) the global system – a network of political, military and economic relations – normally operates peacefully; however (2) Third World regimes, if confronted by internal instability or dissidence, tend to suppress the challenge to their authority by force – and their use of force escalates as the threat increases; moreover (3), if indigenous coercion fails to remove the threat, then external intervention is necessary to maintain an 'environment in which the United States can survive and prosper'.

This third proposition is essentially borne out by Bundy's own analysis of the foreign policies of successive US administrations, i.e. their preference for 'stable' authoritarian regimes over unstable democratic ones, and their readiness to intervene, if necessary, in order to 'maintain' the system. Even one of the architects of US policy notes that these occurred under every single post-war President. Truman: 'in its worldwide effort to organise the so-called free world to hold a line against

122

communist expansion [after Korea], the United States found itself in the 1950s drawn into the full depth of the ambiguities implicit in the old Wilsonian formulations': a world 'safe for democracy' and for 'self-determination'. The ambiguity for Bundy is whether, in addition to freedom from imperial or colonial control, the 'popular will' should also express itself in governance. If the latter is the case, then in terms of America's moral responsibilities, 'are nations worth saving if they fall under dictators?'

Eisenhower: 'In Iran and Guatemala, the real or fancied threat of communist political action led to decisive covert interventions. . . . One after another of our "free world" allies came under governments of an increasingly repressive and dictatorial character.'

Kennedy: 'Genuinely sensitive' to the issue of democracy and freedom, but 'unable to avoid many of the persistent ambiguities of the American posture.'

Johnson: 'Misguided apogee of the cold war' in Indochina, but its decline elsewhere as a result of détente.

Nixon: 'On strained terms' with 'almost every democratic government in the world, while condoning and cultivating dictatorial regimes both in great and lesser powers . . . [setting] new records in making a vice out of necessity.'[2]

Bundy's presentation, however, omits a further important ambiguity. This stems from the fact that while rivalry between the super-powers demands priority for security rather than morality in foreign policy, yet the prospect of mutual annihilation, if such rivalry gets out of hand, requires détente (efforts to prevent or resolve tension). Further, the risk of nuclear annihilation sets limits to intervention by the super-powers – at least in those cases where the action of one power would adversely affect the 'vital interests' of the other.

Bearing this qualification in mind, I shall discuss in this chapter: first, the nature of America's involvement in the Third World; second, the question of strategic or economic motivation; third, America's desire to avoid direct intervention, if possible, both for reasons of prudence and economy – but the urge to intervene where 'necessary'; and consequently America's 'bind', whereby the 'pull' of internal dissidence within Third World countries tends to reinforce the 'push' of compulsive globalism.

I shall reserve for the last three chapters the special problems posed by 'limited war', counter-insurgency and the Nixon Doctrine, each of which can be seen as a form of 'preventive' globalism. In reverse order, US military and economic 'assistance' to Third World regimes is designed to prevent internal instability turning into dissidence; counter-insurgency, where 'self-reliance' is in doubt, is designed to prevent dissidence turning into revolution; and limited war, where counter-insurgency has failed, is to prevent the revolution from succeeding.

I must point out that much of the information in this chapter, covering such a vast field, has been severely compressed.

Global involvement

The nature of American involvement is conditioned by the two basic features of the environment in which it operates: the marginality of the masses, and the mutual, though unequal, benefit of client (élitist regime) and imperial patron: these are the characteristics of the global system – with consequences for American policy, which will be discussed below.

The great majority of people in Third World countries – in the traditional rural sector and among migrants and casual workers in the towns – are marginal to the modern economic sector. They are marginal to the élite groups in power, whether these are military, bureaucratic, business or political, who either manage the modern sector or co-operate with it for mutual advantage. The marginality of the masses is revealed in their minute share of the national product. To recapitulate the World Bank's report, 'among 40 developing countries for which data are available, the upper 20 per cent of the population receives 55 per cent of the national income in the typical country, while the lowest 20 per cent of the population receives 5 per cent'. Two-fifths of all the people in the developing countries live in malnutrition, illiteracy and squalor.[3]

Similarly, the great majority of Third World countries are marginal to the developed industrial nations. The developing countries, with over two-thirds of the world's population, own only 15 per cent of the global product.[4] Apart from a few producers of urgently needed commodities, these countries 'lack effective demand'. As Myrdal points out,

if the whole Indian subcontinent with what will soon be a population of one billion people should sink into the ocean tomorrow, this would cause only minor disturbances to the curves of international trade, production and consumption, wages and other incomes, values of financial stocks, etc., in the developed countries. . . . The developed countries need so little of what is produced in [Bangladesh,] Pakistan and India, while these countries need so much from them.[5]

It is this situation, rather than the 'exploitation' of countries more fully integrated into the world market system, that marks the extremity of dependence.

Although a majority of the population of these countries is or is becoming 'superfluous',[6] a small, educated, largely urban, élite derives its wealth from primary export production and protected manufacturing industry, from its control of the state mechanism, and from 'joint ventures' with foreign corporations and foreign governments. The typical situation, at least in the early stage of development, is a division of labour between these domestic élites and foreign business: the 'élite aspired to control the government apparatus' rather than become modern businessmen, technicians and managers; and they considered foreign investment to be 'more supportive than threatening to their objectives'.[7]

This, as Vernon points out, was the initial pattern in Mexico ('large loans to government; huge investment in the country's railroads, power plants, and mines . . . appreciable amount of technical assistance'), Argentina, Brazil, Chile, Peru; after achieving independence, in Sierra Leone, the Ivory Coast, Zaïre and other francophone countries in Africa; in Malaysia, Taiwan and South Korea; and 'after the traumatic departures of Sukarno from Indonesia and of Nkrumah from Ghana, these countries also began to adopt such a point of view'.[8]

This provides an interesting parallel with the colonial system. It was the colonial regimes which educated, trained and recruited the 'new men' required for a centralised administration – clerks, professionals, junior officials, soldiers – as well as created the modern infrastructure of trade, communications, urbanisation and education. This in turn indirectly permitted other groups to emerge – businessmen, lawyers, engineers and politicians – i.e. the nationalist élite which would in time replace the colonial rulers politically, but would also co-operate with them economically.[9] In the same way, the initial stage of 'permissive' foreign investment in developing countries created its own rival and reactive forces:

> the government bureaucrat, as he sought to maintain power and
> control over an expanding local economy; the local businessman, as he
> aspired to shift from the role of supplier, provisioner and customer
> of the foreign enterprise to the status of competitor; and the
> intellectual outside the local establishment, as he sought to develop
> and promote a competing ideology.[10]

The second stage of development, then, sees the transformation of those who were formerly ancillaries of foreign entrepreneurs, if not to the status of equals, at least to that of associates or rivals aspiring to a more equal share. The result is 'international patron–client relations': no longer what was basically exploitation by the massive foreign corporation (or domination by the imperial power) but compromise – admittedly wrested by struggle, and still requiring struggle. For the balance between patron and client is a shifting and precarious one, weighted as it is by enormous economic and military power, heavily in favour of the patron.

The nature of the patron–client relationship is functional, rather than formal. It does not require specific political recognition, or treaty relations, though this is often the case. The function is two-fold: to derive mutual (though not equal) material benefit; and to ensure the security of the joint enterprise. This is effected by a new division of labour. The client (Third World regime) provides the facilities: notably a suitable 'investment climate', with appropriate legislation, tax concessions and so forth, accompanied, in the case of authoritarian regimes, by bans or curbs on labour unions, prohibition of strikes, and suppression of 'overly' nationalistic or left-wing movements. The patron (imperial power) provides protection against external enemies and 'assistance' in dealing with internal opposition.

There is a similar division of labour with regard to the economic and political aspects of patronage. The state – the various agencies of the US government – performs certain services that are indispensable to the overseas activities of the US multinationals, chiefly by reinforcing the power of local élites, through and with whom these corporations operate. Such tacit or implicit co-operation between economic and political entities is taken for granted. Common to both are the global positivist assumptions of order permitting enterprise, and enterprise validating order.[11]

In addition to the bilateral relationships between imperial power and individual regimes there is an entire hierarchy of patron–client relations spreading downwards from international super-power to the indigenous power of local élites. Within the hierarchy there is an intermediate range of great and middle powers – patrons in their own right, with their subordinate following, but (in at least one essential respect: strategic or economic) clients in relation to the supreme patron. Similarly, every client, however lowly in international terms, is also the 'lord' of his own *domestic* hierarchy. This 'patron' – whether in the form of authoritarian leader, or members of a military clique, or military-bureaucratic establishment – has his own dependent clients in a subsidiary system of mutual benefit: such as businessmen, technocrats, politicians, lawyers, middle-level officers and officials, better-off farmers, and so on down the scale.[12]

The profitable functioning of the *international* hierarchy of patron–client relations depends on the proper functioning of all these subordinate patronage systems. This applies to super-powers (the Soviet Union of course has its own, though less extensive, patronage network); to other great powers such as Japan, Germany, France and Britain, with military, political or economic dependencies; and to the intermediate range of middle powers acting as regional patrons: Brazil in South America, Iran (until 1978) in the Persian Gulf, the combination of Egypt and Saudi Arabia (influence and finance) in the Arab world, Zaïre for a time in Black Africa, and Indonesia in much of Southeast Asia. By assisting intermediate patrons and backing regional associations, the USA seeks to share the 'responsibilities' of patronage with its 'partners'. The 'primary purpose' is to 'invoke greater efforts by others – not so much to lighten our [US] burdens as to increase their commitment' to maintaining an 'ordered world'.[13]

The important role of regional patrons is officially acknowledged: 'The outlook in Asia is brightened by the emergence of a stable Indonesia . . . whose enlightened economic policies [i.e. through co-operation with the West] and active diplomacy promise benefits to its neighbours as well as its own people.'[14] The 'special relationship' with Brazil accorded by Kissinger has shifted, under Carter, to a more autonomous regional stance. (The implications of the growing autonomy of regional patrons for 'world order' are discussed in chapter 9, 'Prospects'.) Yet this still forms a relationship whose significance for the USA had been underlined earlier – the role of military forces in the Western Hemisphere:

> These forces represent a key element in almost all Latin American societies, and in many they have assumed national leadership. Because we have recognised their various roles and because of our mutual security interests, we have developed over the years close ties of cooperation and friendship with many of the military leaders of Latin America.[15]

As for Black Africa, a 'high State Department official' suggested late in 1974 that the USA viewed the position of Zaïre as roughly similar to that of Brazil in South America. Both were large countries with untapped resources. Both were relatively stable in parts of the world where stability of any kind was scarce. Both maintained this stability through force. Both occupied strategic geographic positions. There was 'a thrust' within the State Department 'to bolster Zaïre' in the hope it could extend its hegemony throughout the continent.[16] Although President Carter limited US assistance to Zaïre in the 1977 and 1978 Shaba (Katanga) crisis, this was more than made up by the prompt action of intermediate patrons – notably France, Egypt and Morocco and the tacit support of the Organisation of African Unity.[17] In fact the Zaïre case illustrates how readily alliances can shift. For many years, imperial Ethiopia was America's favoured client in Black Africa; then Zaïre became prominent; and it is quite possible that Nigeria will assume this role in future.

The next case is Iran, which President Nixon in 1972 agreed to supply with 'anything it wanted' on the assumption that, in the wake of Britain's withdrawal from the Persian (Arab) Gulf, Iran would take over the task of security. 'We concluded', the State Department argued, 'that only the regional countries, particularly Iran and Saudi Arabia, could take on the responsibilities for regional security, and that the perception of the threat they face and their judgment of what they needed to do the job must be given serious weight in responding to their arms request' – for the most modern destroyers, fighters, air defence missiles and, in Iran alone, over 4,000 American advisers and technicians.[18] To this shopping list, President Carter himself (despite his intention of reducing America's trade in arms) has added new sophisticated weapons, notably the airborne warning and control system, which has obvious regional as well as internal counter-insurgency potential. Indeed the Shah, in an interview with *Newsweek* of 14 November 1977, in which he reported exchanges of intelligence with the Arab gulf states, concluded that 'Iran must be prepared to do the job [provide security to the gulf] alone if necessary'.

The 1978 crisis in Iran has exposed the weaknesses of America's regional strategy, which was attempting, as it were, to build a 'stable structure' on shifting sands. First it reveals the danger of blindly supporting an autocrat and his regime (as late as 12 December 1978 President Carter informed a news conference that the 'Shah has our support and certainly has our confidence') ignoring the evidence of massive corruption, social dislocation, and repression. The Shah himself belatedly admitted, on 6 November 1978: 'I promise that the past mistakes and illegalities, cruelty and corruption, will not be repeated.' In the second place, the crisis has demonstrated anew the unpredictable and often unmanageable impact of *internal* changes on regional or international 'order'. On this occasion, at least, a broadly-based, religiously-inspired movement can hardly be branded, and hence challenged, as one of 'communist subversion' instigated from outside. And finally the example of what has happened to one autocratic, modernising, oil-rich regime casts a shadow on the future of the others.

President Carter, too, has moved still further than his predecessors towards a 'balanced' relationship in the Middle East between Israel and conservative Arab states, culminating in the 1978 Camp David agreements between Israel and Egypt. 'Egypt's economic and political stability is of paramount importance to the entire region', observed officials accompanying Treasury Secretary Blumenthal to Cairo in October 1977. The USA from 1977 has been providing $1 billion a year to aid in this objective. Moreover, the Carter administration announced in February 1978 its plan to sell Egypt its first US jet fighters (50 F5Es) – along with more fighters for Israel and 60 F15s for Saudi Arabia. Then Washington's informal alliance with Saudi Arabia, Egypt's most prominent paymaster, was developing nicely. As informed commentators have noted, Saudi Arabia depends on US technological and managerial expertise to build up its economy, and it also relies on the USA for military help to protect its oil fields and to ensure stability in the region. In return, the Saudis have 'quietly brought about a decrease in Soviet influence in South Yemen [although this proved only temporary] and helped persuade Somalia, across the Red Sea, to end its dependence on the Russians' (Somalia's expulsion of Soviet and Cuban experts in November 1977 followed the ill-fated occupation of the Ogaden, from which Somali forces were repulsed by the Cuban-led and Soviet-equipped Ethiopians in March 1978). 'The Saudis also are believed ready to help the Sudan buy arms abroad to fight the communist-backed threat it perceives coming from Ethiopia' (the Sudanese government had expelled its Soviet military experts in May 1977). 'The Saudis also have pledged a billion dollars to black Africa, clearly an effort to support nonradical regimes there and they have been active all along the Persian Gulf to limit the chances for leftist movements.'[19]

The vital link between local 'stability' and international security is provided for by a web of formal and informal military connections. As President Johnson put it, success in fighting 'subversion' rests ultimately on the skill of the soldiers of the threatened country. That is why 'we' –

the USA – 'now have 344 teams at work in 49 countries to train the local military in the most advanced techniques of internal defence'.[20] (US military aid groups now operate in 54 countries. See Table 2.) In fiscal year 1974 the USA first became heavily involved in the sale of arms to clients, especially in the Middle East, with $4 billion worth to Iran, $1 billion to Israel, and $700 million to Saudi Arabia.[21] By 1976, total sales to Iran amounted to over $10 billion, to Saudi Arabia $6 billion; and the then deputy Defense Secretary announced that the Defense Department would be engaged in a 'high priority' mission of developing foreign military sales for the next 15 years. The present level of sales to all

Table 2 Selected US military aid recipients (fiscal year 1977; $ million)

East and Southeast Asia	
*South Korea	286
Indonesia	46
Malaysia, *Philippines, *Taiwan, *Thailand (altogether)	168
Middle East, South Asia and North Africa	
Egypt	750
Israel	1,785
Jordan	224
Syria	90
Morocco, Lebanon, Afghanistan, Nepal, Sri Lanka, Bahrain, India, Pakistan, Tunisia (altogether)	53
Latin America	
*Brazil ⎫ renounced in 1977	61
*Argentina ⎭	49
*Bolivia	15
*All other countries (except Cuba and *Chile: military aid to Chile banned by Congress in 1975)	83
Black Africa	
Ethiopia	23
Zaïre	31
Kenya, Ghana, Liberia, Senegal (altogether)	6

*US defence treaties, bilateral or multilateral.

Source: US Department of Defense, *Security Assistance Program, Congressional Presentation, Fiscal Year 1977*; reported in *International Bulletin* (North American Congress on Latin America), 7 May 1976.

Note: The significance of US military aid relations is three-fold: (1) recipients include aligned and non-aligned nations; (2) in the non-aligned category there is some overlap with Soviet military aid recipients; (3) Britain and France have substantial military aid programmes, especially in the Middle East and Africa, which in terms of providing security may be said to supplement US objectives. See *The Military Balance 1977–1978*, International Institute of Strategic Studies, September 1977, and subsequent issues.

countries is between 9 and 10 billion dollars a year.[22] Significantly, the Carter administration, despite guidelines intended to curtail these sales, decided to fulfil the $32 billion in arms orders for the next six years already approved by the Nixon and Ford administrations.

Such are the military, political and economic components of international patron–client relations. Not all the components may be involved, at any one time, in any one country. But these are exceptional cases. India, for example, has been the recipient of some $9 billion in US economic aid in the two decades since 1954, compared to $2 billion from the Soviet Union, but its political and military orientation, especially since 1971, is towards Russia. Egypt has oscillated from a position of substantial military and economic ties with the Soviet bloc from 1955 to similarly substantial ties, after 1973, with the West. Syria has received massive Soviet military aid but, under President Assad, has also co-operated economically with the conservative Arab states. Libya has veered even more dramatically from militant anti-communism to support for revolutionary movements, often in line with Soviet policies. And Algeria combines a radical foreign policy with dependence on Western aid and investment to build up its industrial infrastructure. Meanwhile in 1978 Iraq shifted away from the Soviet Union and South Yemen and Ethiopia moved still closer.

Apart from these exceptions (which can more properly be regarded as clients or ex-clients of the adversary) the significance of the interlocking patron–client relationship, and the way it operates, is most clearly brought out in a crisis, when the client's ability to carry out his functions is endangered. The success of the revolutionary movement in South Vietnam presented just such a crisis – though, as I shall argue, it was perceived as a threat to the *strategic* rather than the economic role of the patron. An influential former US Foreign Service official emphasised precisely the 'mixture' of components involved:

The outcome in Vietnam is directly linked to the region as a whole and cannot be treated separately, even though Vietnam has become the arena of decision. The resolution of conflict and new approaches to regional order will require a skilful meshing of [US] political and military actions and the use of diplomacy and force in tandem. Military containment alone is not enough. Only a mixture of political, social, economic, and defensive measures, particularly in Vietnam, can give us any hope for some stabilisation. Vietnam is the crux of this challenge and the keystone for peace or war.[23]

Strategic-economic nexus

Only a 'mixture of political, social, economic and defensive measures . . . can give us any hope for some stabilisation'. Awareness of the connection between strategic and economic objectives – 'an international environment in which the United States can survive and prosper'[24] – has been a consistent feature of American (and indeed all countries') foreign policy. Similarly, the 'global' range of components at risk has been repeatedly emphasised from President Truman onwards:

> Much of Asia at this moment [1952] is under communist attack. The free nations are holding the line against aggression in Korea and Indochina and are battling communist-inspired disorders in Burma, Malaya and the Philippines. The loss of any of these countries would mean the loss of *freedom* for millions of people, the loss of *vital raw materials*, the loss of points of *critical strategic importance* to the free world.[25]

There are two important issues to note. First, the characteristic misconception implicit in linking the very different situations in Korea and Indochina – the former arising from a military invasion, the latter from revolutionary unrest. Significantly in view of what was to follow, the Truman administration's unawareness, under-estimation or 'suppression' of *indigenous* factors in Indochina resulted from the projection on to a particular area of its generalised fear of communist aggression and subversion – i.e. the undifferentiated global approach. Second, and following from the first, is the way in which humanitarian, economic and strategic considerations are blended, so that each reinforces the others. This is aptly expressed in President Carter's own words, previously referred to in his address of 17 March 1978, which represent his response to Soviet initiatives: 'We will match, together with our allies and friends, any threatening power through a combination of military forces, political efforts and economic programs. . . . We shall use our great economic, technological and diplomatic advantages to defend our interests and to promote American values.'

The problem of 'globalism' will be considered in the next section and in the following chapters; here I shall try to disentangle the differences and assess what is common to economic and strategic roles. Contrary to the dogmatic 'profit maximisation-imperialist expansion' thesis, I suggest a more qualified blend of profits plus security *combined* with power plus security, in corporate and governmental enterprise respectively. These, as I see it, are twin operative factors in American global activities. The initial phase is one of a 'dominant' drive for profits, and its political counterpart is the drive for power. These are qualified, in the consolidating stage, by readiness to accept a share with others (rather than fight for sole control) as regards markets; the political counterpart is sharing power (by balance of power policies) and separating power, through spheres of influence. The final qualification, in the 'mature' stage, is preference for risk-reduction rather than high-risk high-profit activities; in Vernon's words, 'reducing the unpredictable elements in their business environments'. This is the equivalent, in foreign policy, of reducing areas of uncertainty in the political-strategic environment; e.g. by clarifying interests and commitments, drawing up specific rules of conduct, and acting on them: the politics of détente.[26]

There are four ways of analysing these three components and their relationships: first, in terms of their compatibility or incompatibility; second, as cyclical trends, with the emphasis on one or the other (power or security); third, the question of priorities in times of crisis; and finally, the balance between strategic and economic goals in 'normal' times.

First, power (the drive for profit) and security: either, taken to extremes, is incompatible with the other; but a judicious blend, according to circumstances, can be mutually reinforcing. The problem arises when personalities, institutions and environment combine to 'dictate' extremes of behaviour; such as the concentration of *economic* power in the hands of multinationals and the rapacious exploitation of natural and human resources, at the expense of good security relations with allies and friends, on the one hand; concentration of *military* power and the 'military approach' to political problems, at the expense of established or potential investment, on the other. Conversely, emphasis on 'security at any price' – risk-reducing behaviour – inhibits the dynamics of economic growth and of political self-confidence: it thus prepares the ground for the situation – stagnation leading to vulnerability – it is designed to prevent.

Second, cyclical trends. It can be argued that, at any one time, there will be either a dominant drive for power (or profit) or a search for security. They go in successive stages. The first stage is characterised by an 'aggressive' expansionist 'strategy': 'seizing' markets, 'eliminating' competitors – the military metaphor is matched by appropriate action. The aggressive phase is followed by the 'mature' stage of consolidating the advance, of safeguarding the status quo: the watchword is now market-sharing and risk-reducing; or détente, balance of power, principles of peaceful coexistence, as the case may be. These stages alternate, although the leading power may change: the first stage is followed by the second and – after a respite (peace) – the cycle begins anew.

Third, priorities in times of crisis. Evidently the threat to 'order', underlying prosperity, determines the strategic priority. In an emergency the entire economy is subordinated to the military machine, to the need for victory – or survival. Just as the routine of 'diplomacy' is the normal run of foreign policy, while the vital substance is tension, crisis and war, so economic interest is a country's norm, but security is the necessity. Yet there have been mixed feelings throughout history concerning the ambiguous relationship between force (war or 'internal war') and order: force needed to maintain or restore order; or order which is undermined by the use of force? These ambiguities are reflected, externally, in the glorification of war combined with dread of its effects; internally in the cult of violence, justified as 'firmness' by the partisans of law and order, or as a 'necessary response' to provocations, by extremists of the Right or Left. These combined with fear of turmoil, lie inter-mingled at the heart of politics. Both cult and glorification arise from the supreme sense of mastery of or over violence. But fear and insecurity arise from the belief that, on the contrary, events are 'out of control'.[27] It was this apocalyptic fear of the surging forces of turmoil and revolution in the world that inspired the Kennedy administration and its successors in their attitudes to wars of national liberation and their belief in the domino effect: hence the 'special war' in Vietnam (Kennedy), the military take-over (Johnson) and the 'special commitment' to Saigon maintained by massive military aid (Nixon and Kissinger) even at grave economic cost.

Fourth, the balance between strategic and economic factors in 'normal' times. Evidently the 'proper' functioning of the global system allows for separate paths towards the common objective: a satisfactory international environment. Thus large corporations may and often do 'hold the U.S. government at arm's length'[28] on specifically economic matters – markets, competition, investment, production – which are of no direct political concern. However, certain qualifications must be noted. First of all, governments are obliged to act in cases where corporate operations lead to political instability in the 'host' country – e.g. by provoking nationalist reactions to economic 'domination' or 'exploitation'; or by creating unfavourable publicity as a result of extensive bribery and corruption. Similarly the multinationals may not be overly concerned with specifically political-military issues – such as alignment or non-alignment – which do not affect economic interests. But corporations cannot remain uninvolved if an unpopular treaty commitment (e.g. Thailand under the dictatorship) spills over into attacks on American enterprise; or where a politically non-aligned regime chooses economic independence as well. On the other hand, there is considerable, if usually informal, co-operation aimed at reinforcing a common 'stake' in developing countries: thus the 'strategic' relationship between the oil companies and the US government has often been cited.[29]

Genuine divergence stems either from a 'partial' economic crisis – e.g. expropriation of a US-owned subsidiary – which does not pose a threat to political stability or to America's political influence; or from a partial political crisis – such as the fall of a domino – which does not credibly curtail economic opportunities: consider American efforts to trade with China in the 1960s. However, the two partners are readily brought together again when a partial crisis – economic or political – is *perceived* as a total crisis: for example, where 'radical nationalist' economic measures affect the political structure (Chile), or where falling dominoes threaten 'world order' (Vietnam).

Since the exceptions are so important, it is worth considering two of these *politico-economic* issues – American intervention in Vietnam; and access to crucial raw materials – in more detail. In doing so, I shall examine the thesis of 'economic imperialism'.

For the 'revisionist' critics, US intervention in Vietnam, 'the most important single embodiment of the power and purposes of American foreign policy since the second world war', has dual significance: first, for the survival of the American domestic system of 'liberal corporate capitalism'; second, to guarantee its global economic role.[30] Kolko directly relates US strategic expansion to the 'domestic backlogged economic and social problems and weaknesses [the US] has deferred confronting for two decades'. He adjudges that, without an activist foreign policy, America's 'disappearing strength in a global context would soon open the door to the internal dynamics which might jeopardise the very existence of liberal corporate capitalism at home'.[31] This is, of course, a variant of the Leninist thesis that imperialist countries 'exported' class conflict from the metropolitan area to their colonies (where it was transformed into a national struggle) because colonialism enabled the metropolitan proletariat to emerge as an expioiting class – on the backs of the colonial peoples.

On the second point, Kolko concedes that Vietnam itself is of relatively little value to the USA, but this renders it 'all the more significant as an example of America's determination to hold the line as a matter of principle against revolutionary movements. What is at stake, according to the "domino theory" with which Washington accurately perceives the world, is the control of Vietnam's neighbours, Southeast Asia and, ultimately, Latin America.'[32]

However, just as late-nineteenth-century imperialism of the European powers 'may best be seen as the extension into the periphery of the political struggle in Europe',[33] so I suggest it is essentially *political* control for reasons of *security* that is 'at stake', whichever the power concerned, America, Russia, Britain, China or France, whether or not its leaders' fear of loss of control is well-grounded, and whatever the area involved: global, Eastern Europe, Suez, and so on. Kolko, on the contrary, insists on one country – America; one role – imperial; and one basic purpose – economic exploitation:

> The existing global political and economic structure . . . has made possible, after all, a vast power that required total world economic integration not on the basis of equality but of domination. And to preserve this form of world is vital to the men who run the American economy and politics at the highest levels. [For] when the day arrives that the United States cannot create or threaten further Vietnams [this will plunge both America and the world into a period of profound crises] as the allocation of the earth's economic power is increasingly removed from American control.[34]

I consider this image of the USA single-mindedly undertaking world-wide military and political intervention for purposes of economic exploitation – 'imperialism' in Lenin's sense – to be misleading, for three reasons. First, like the domino theory itself, it is indiscriminately global in character. Second, American economic expansion is more often and more efficiently carried out by indirect means rather than by direct political (or military) conquest, annexation or control. And third, most developing countries do not have a decisive role in supplying the needs of the American economy.

Thus, for Kolko to state that control of Vietnam is necessary for the control of Southeast Asia and ultimately of Latin America is to confuse the discriminating process of economic expansion, guided by the search for profits, with 'indiscriminate' strategic globalism. The latter did 'require' intervention in Vietnam to suppress a war of national liberation which, if unchecked, so it was believed, would have undermined the stability and threatened the viability of other states to the detriment of US security. American economic interests, on the other hand, were comparatively little involved in Indochina, which was a French preserve, and were only drawn in (in the form of arms supplies, technological equipment, and especially consumer goods) as an adjunct to the military-political process. It is a supreme irony that major oil discoveries along the Southeast Asian and Chinese coastal shelves only later attracted American economic enterprise to that area – long after the original rationale for military intervention has disappeared.

Second, Kolko's contention that the domino theory represents Washington's 'accurate' perception of the world, only holds good for that particular phase of policy. In spite of Nixon's own fundamentalist belief in the dominoes, his 'Doctrine' with its emphasis on self-reliance and the rapprochement with China (the chief beneficiary, it used to be said, of the domino process) demonstrates that the 'Kolko' type of globalism that required *direct* intervention is *not* essential politically.

Again, how necessary for the American economy is control of the Third World's resources – control which requires, according to the neo-imperialist theory, the type of intervention that culminates in a 'Vietnam'? Now it is evident that, just as Lenin's enormously influential thesis in *Imperialism, The Highest Stage of Capitalism* assumed incorrectly that 'the principal sphere of investment of British capital is the British colonies', when over half of Britain's foreign assets in the decades before 1914 were held outside the Empire, especially in the advanced economy of the USA and in Argentina (while within the Empire there was more investment in Australia and New Zealand than in India and the whole of Africa);[35] so the present-day 'revisionists' are equally mistaken when they assert the vital importance for the American economy of trade with and investment in the developing countries.

On the contrary, it is 'the developed countries like Canada, Great Britain, France, Germany and Australia [which] together account for about one-half of all direct American foreign investment'. Even at a time when rates of return on foreign investment in the Persian Gulf were as high as 20 per cent, compared to 11 per cent in Latin America and 8 per cent in Canada, the Gulf attracted less than one-tenth of American foreign investment. The preference for investment in relatively developed and culturally familiar economies is hard to fit into Leninist theory.[36] Altogether, income received from direct private American investment in Third World countries from 1960 to 1968 (three-quarters of which was in the petroleum industry, manufacturing and mining) amounted to $3.3 billion on a total of $20 billion invested. This can be compared with the $2 billion income received from nearly $48 billion invested in the developed countries.[37] Clearly, the sheer *profitability* of the former cannot be overlooked; equally clearly, *security* of investment must also be taken into account.

Further, the American economy has enormous capabilities for domestic development and therefore does not require a surplus for export to prevent the system collapsing: in fact, US exports and imports amount to less than 7 per cent of gross national product, a much smaller proportion than in the case of trading nations like France and Japan, 10 to 12 per cent, and Britain and Germany, as much as 16 to 17 per cent.[38] Nor does America 'need' wars like Vietnam as some critics allege, simply to keep the economy going. Production of military equipment and recruitment to the armed forces certainly provide employment (substantially in certain areas where the economic situation therefore has a direct political impact); it is an important source of profits and is useful for exports – but it is not essential to economic survival.

Finally, there is the problem of access to crucial raw materials. Kolko is on firmer ground when he points, not to America's need for a dominant world-wide economic role, but to the importance to the American economy of *specific* items – oil, minerals, other raw materials – which are produced in a small number of countries. Imports of five critical metals had increased to 32 per cent of the total amount used in the case of iron ore, 98 per cent of bauxite, 35 per cent of lead, 60 per cent of zinc, and only in the case of copper had declined to 46 per cent. Only zinc and lead, among the major metals, are found in 'politically stable' regions; over half America's imports of iron ore come from Venezuela and three 'equally precarious' Latin American countries (Brazil, Chile, Peru); Jamaica, Guyana and Surinam produce about half the world production of bauxite; while Chile, Rhodesia, Zaïre and Peru account for over two-thirds of foreign copper reserves.[39] But even if the producing countries are 'precarious' they are also few and 'manageable' by the normal economic processes of the world market – the same processes which were the substance of the 'informal' British empire of the past[40] and which are no less evident in the imperial role of a super-power today.[41]

The brutal fact is that while the developing countries as a whole need American (and Japanese and West European) aid, investment and exports, America and other capitalist countries do not need, apart from a few specific items, the products of the developing world. Nine-tenths of manufacturing industry and nine-tenths of power generation are concentrated in the advanced capitalist countries and only one-tenth in the developing countries (leaving out the communist world). More than two-thirds of the extractive industry is controlled by the advanced countries. The post-war scientific-technological revolution has greatly increased the productive capacity of the latter and at the same time has reduced their demand for many raw materials, the staple product of developing countries. This, along with the big expansion of international trade, which is also chiefly carried out among the advanced countries, has still further widened the gap between them and the developing world – with the exception of a few 'privileged' states, notably the special case of the oil-producers, and efficient exporters like Korea and Taiwan.[42]

Stages of intervention

Whereas the revisionists argue that imperialist domination is a function of the primordial drive for *economic* exploitation, my own view is that US intervention in the Third World (see Table 3 below) stems rather from considerations of *security*, whether misplaced or not. For although the underlying aims of economic corporations and US government agencies are essentially the same – the safety and welfare of the global enterprise – yet the way in which a particular problem is perceived – whether in political or economic terms – undoubtedly affects the type of decision that is made.

Threats to American business operations overseas, such as those posed by nationalisation of banking, insurance, manufacturing or extractive industry in a given country, are naturally taken seriously by the US government. But they are not usually seen as matters of the very highest level of importance to the USA. In this respect they are unlike, for example, either a marked increase in communist subversion, or electoral successes by communist parties, or the rise of powerful revolutionary movements, in key areas – the 'key' denoting their strategic rather than their economic importance to the USA.

The significance of politics, rather than economics, can be seen in the entire range of circumstances with which the USA is confronted, from the normal situation to the extreme. The 'norm' of a politically unchallenged, or 'stable', relationship – i.e. where there is a properly functioning partnership between local élites and their US counterparts – is one that does not require direct US intervention in its support. Conversely, the critical cases, where such acts of intervention do occur – because local élites are either unable or unwilling to play their allotted parts – indicates that the system has broken down.

Table 3 US military intervention and non-intervention (outcome for intervening power: F = Failure; S = Success)

Area	Circumstances	
(i) *Direct US intervention*		
Southeast Asia		
Vietnam (1965–73)	Civil War	F
Laos (1964–73)	Civil War	F
Cambodia (1970)	Civil War	F
Middle East		
Lebanon (1958)	Civil Conflict	S
Latin America		
Dominican Republic (1965)	Civil Conflict	S
(ii) *US military intervention by proxy*		
Southeast Asia		
Burma (1950–61)	Kuomintang (Taiwan) against Nu Govt	F
Indonesia (1958)	Separatists against Sukarno Govt	F
Middle East		
Iran (1953)	Shah (in exile) against Mossadegh Govt	S
Latin America		
Guatemala (1954)	Military Exiles against Arbenz Govt	S
Cuba (1961)	Exiles against Castro Govt	F
Chile (1973)	Armed Forces against Allende Govt	S
Africa		
Congo (1960)	President Kasavubu against Lumumba Govt	S
Angola (1976)	South Africa against Cubans: 'National Liberation' against 'Popular Movement'	F
(iii) *US military involvement with regimes engaged in civil conflict*		
South Asia		
Philippines (1947–52)	Huk Revolt	S
Thailand (1965–75)	Communist, Ethnic Insurgencies	?
S. Vietnam (1959–65, 1973–5)		F
Laos (1959–61, 1973–5)		F
Cambodia (1970–5)		F

Table 3 contd

Area	Circumstances	
Middle East		
Jordan (1970)	Palestinians	S
Iran (1978–)	Populist upsurge	?
Latin America		
Argentina Nicaragua	Guerrilla movements in 1960s:[a]	
Bolivia Panama	substantial in Colombia,	
Brazil Paraguay	Guatemala, Peru, Uruguay,	
Colombia Peru	Venezuela	S
Ecuador Uruguay	Argentina,	?
Guatemala Venezuela	Nicaragua	?
Haiti		
Africa		
Congo (1961–4)	Leftists, Secessionists	S
Portuguese Mozambique (1964–75)	Nationalists	F
Portuguese Angola (1950–75)	Nationalists	F
Ethiopia (1960–)[b]	Ethnic – Secessionist	?
East Asia		
China (1945–9)	Communists	F

(iv) *US involvement or connivance in coups*

Area	Circumstances	
Southeast Asia		
Thailand (1958, 1971)	Sarit; Thanom-Prapat	S
Cambodia (1970)	Lon Nol	S
Vietnam (1963)	Armed Forces	S
Philippines (1972)	Marcos, Martial Law	S
Latin America		
Brazil (1964)[c]	Armed Forces:	S
Uruguay (1973)	two major examples	S
East Asia		
South Korea (1972)	Park, Martial Law	S

(v) *Successful revolutions: US non-intervention*[d]

Area	Circumstances
Southeast Asia	
Indonesia (1945–9)	Independence struggle
Middle East	
Iraq (1958)	Overthrow of monarchy and 'feudalism'
Africa	
Egypt (1952)	Overthrow of monarchy and 'feudalism'
Algeria (1954–62)	Independence
Ethiopia (1974)	Overthrow of monarchy and 'feudalism'
South Asia	
Bangladesh (1971)	Independence
Afghanistan (1978)	Power struggle

Table 3 contd

Area	Circumstances
(vi) *Unsuccessful revolutionary struggles (civil wars): US not involved*	
Southeast Asia	
Malaya (1948–60)	British suppression of communist 'emergency'
Indonesia (1965)	Military suppression of communists
Middle East	
Lebanon (1976)	Christians, Syrians suppress Left, Palestinians
Oman (1956–75)	British troops, Sultan against Left, ethnic–secessionists
Africa	
Nigeria (1976–70)	British outbid Russians to help Lagos against Biafra
Sudan (1958–72)	Ethnic, religious conflict in south
Chad (1969–)	Ethnic, religious conflict in north
Rwanda-Burundi (endemic)	Ethnic conflicts
South Asia	
Sri Lanka (1971)	Leftist (student) revolt

a 'The US government engaged itself deeply in the domestic affairs of countries as diverse as Venezuela and Chile, Peru and Brazil, Bolivia and Panama, Cuba and the Dominican Republic, Guatemala and Honduras. US pressures forced elections to be held, and sometimes determined the results. US influence caused civic action programmes to be started, planning boards to be established, and currencies to be devalued. US troops were used only in Santo Domingo in 1965, but the USA also influenced Latin American politics by granting or withholding diplomatic recognition or "aid"; by providing technical assistance and advice; by training military and police units and supplying them with sundry types of equipment; and by all the techniques illustrated in the Chilean and the Cuban cases' (Abraham F. Lowenthal, 'The United States and Latin America', *Foreign Affairs*, October 1976).

For a recent report on the situation in Argentina, see Philippe Labreveux, 'Meanwhile in Argentina: Repression Grinds Silently On', *Le Monde*, trans. *Guardian Weekly*, 6 November 1977.

b Ethiopia switched sides in 1977, opting for Soviet and Cuban support; its adversary, Somalia, backing ethnic rebels, correspondingly reversed its pro-Soviet stance.

c Five days before the coup, the US Ambassador cabled Secretary Rusk naming the probable leader of the military who intended to take power. A US naval task force was ordered into position off the Brazilian coast as part of a contingency plan: 'We feared the possibility of a civil war . . . and one side might need some outside help', the Ambassador stated (declassified US official documents, quoted by Lewis Diuguid, 'Brother Sam and the Brazilian Coup', *Washington Post*, reprinted *Guardian Weekly*, 9 January 1977).

d Reasons for non-intervention: (a) risk of super-power conflict, where important adversary interests at stake: Iraq; (b) anti-colonial revolutions acceptable: Indonesia, Algeria; anti-feudalism acceptable: Egypt. (US 'tilted' in favour of Pakistan, but accepted the outcome in Bangladesh.)

(The outcome of the Black armed struggle against the white regime in Rhodesia is undecided: the USA backs the British approach of seeking to negotiate Black majority rule, but the 'Patriotic Front' guerrillas oppose the 'internal settlement' accepted by the constitutionalists.)

Note: I am not concerned here with the US attitude to 'conventional interstate conflicts', such as the North Korean invasion, Arab–Israeli wars, Indo-Pakistan campaigns, Algeria–Morocco border wars, and Indonesia's 'confrontation' of Malaysia: see Lincoln Bloomfield and Amelia C. Leiss, *Controlling Small Wars: A Strategy for the 1970s*, New York, Knopf, 1969. Apart from Korea (discussed in the next chapter), the USA has not directly intervened in these conflicts – even if it has usually been involved, in the sense of arming one or both parties – either (a) because the result, whoever wins, is unlikely to disturb the global balance; or (b) because the result could be destabilising, but the risk of intervention, provoking counter-intervention by the Soviet Union, is considered too great. In the latter case, both patrons have generally sought to restrain their clients (see also the next section).

From an empirical examination of the evidence, it is clear that major acts of intervention have taken place for three main reasons: where an allied or friendly regime is *endangered* (Dominican Republic, Lebanon, Indochina), even though this is largely the result of internal opposition; in a successful attempt to *reinstate* a dispossessed allied regime (Iran); and to *overthrow* a communist or suspected-communist regime within the American sphere of influence, failing in Cuba, succeeding in Guatemala and Chile. The covert US attempt to oust Sukarno by backing the 'separatist' revolt of 1957–8 in Indonesia failed as a result of the rapid collapse of the main group of rebels. Note that all these cases occurred either because communist movements were involved to a greater (e.g. Vietnam) or lesser extent (e.g. the 53 communists in the Dominican Republic)[43] or because 'international communism' either was (Iran in 1945)[44] or was believed to be (the Lebanon in 1958,[45] Angola in 1975–6[46]) in a position to benefit.

As noted above, there have been two main restraints on American intervention in revolutionary situations: positively, where 'nationalist' revolutionaries have endangered allied regimes, for example the Indonesian struggle against the Dutch[47] and the Algerian revolution; negatively, where the risk of conflict with the Soviet Union and, to a lesser extent, China outweighed the expected political advantages. Thus the USA did not intervene to reinstate an ally, for example in Iraq in 1958, where covert means were insufficient and where international circumstances – including the likelihood of counter-measures by the Soviet Union – posed too great a risk. In this case, 'containment', by bolstering the governments of neighbouring or rival states, was the policy adopted.

I have called the first form of restraint 'positive' because US policy 'tilted' in favour of such nationalist revolutionaries, for three reasons: because they were anti-colonial; because it was felt that American sympathy for them would improve its image in the Third World; and because a victory for non-communist nationalists offered the best guarantee of an acceptable form of stability in those areas. The last point is crucial to the question of US intervention or non-intervention.

How otherwise could the USA have taken such a different attitude towards the independence struggle in Indonesia compared to that in Vietnam? In regard to the former, the American government correctly pointed out that

> the use of force [by the Dutch] in this situation makes the solution far more complex and difficult. . . . The Republic of Indonesia [led by Sukarno] represents the largest single political factor. . . . The Republic has a two-fold nature. First it is a political entity; secondly, it is the heart of Indonesian nationalism. This latter attribute cannot be eliminated by any amount of military force. . . . Real peace in Indonesia can be expected *only if there is a settlement of the political issues*.[48]

The same conditions were characteristic of the struggle in Vietnam. The nationalist movement, the Vietminh, 'represented the largest single political factor'; it was the 'heart of Vietnamese nationalism' which could not be 'eliminated by any amount of military force'. And *yet* by 1952 the Truman administration was supporting the use of military force by the French colonialists and their traditionalist allies – notably the unrepresentative and ineffective Bao Dai regime in Vietnam – as an 'integral part of the world-wide resistance by the Free Nations to communist attempts at conquest and subversion'.[49]

It is evident from the record that the USA has *not* intervened (it usually had no need to) in certain types of civil conflicts: where *others* could do the job – the British in Malaya, the French and their allies in parts of Africa, the military, up to a point, in Latin America; where *non*-communist nationalists offer internal stability and scope for foreign enterprise, such as Indonesia in the 1950s and after 1965; or where the prospect of success is minimal and/or the risk of Soviet counter-intervention is too great, e.g. the Chinese civil war.[50]

Conversely, the USA has intervened where these three conditions were negative: the 'stage' of intervention depending on the degree of negativity. Thus, in an escalatory progression: the first stage is one of US military and economic *assistance* to allied or 'friendly' regimes which cannot on their own withstand or suppress the dissident movements that their policies or lack of policies provoke: as in Table 3, section (iii). The second stage is intervention '*by proxy*' where the policies of nationalist regimes bring about internal 'instability' (reforms disturbing powerful interests) or endanger foreign property, or both, to the presumed advantage of international communism: as in Iran,[51] Chile,[52] and Guatemala;[53] and the final stage is one of *direct* military intervention where the 'assisted' regime is unable to cope with the threat,[54] and where there is little or no risk of substantial adversary reaction.

But *why* should so costly an American enterprise – in terms of money, casualties and material destruction, or international reputation, or both – be undertaken to 'rescue' what in most cases are patently unsatisfactory regimes? The answer lies in the circumstances of the Second World War and its aftermath, which made intervention both 'necessary' and possible. The power of the Soviet Union and the ideological appeal of communism to the poor and frustrated (victims of the status quo) *had* to be contained if the alternative 'free world' system could survive. However, the brutality of Stalinism and its obvious threat to liberal-democratic values made it possible to perceive the Cold War conflict – and to project it world-wide – in terms of a crusade for freedom against despotism. In this 'life or death' struggle, in an 'all or nothing' situation (the 'loss' of any one area to one side being seen as the automatic gain of the other), in conditions of rapid and perhaps uncontrollable change (the sheer momentum of one loss following another, if unchecked, leading to disaster), intervention was 'necessary'.[55] But under these circumstances it was also 'possible', because in the 'free world' there was no alternative policy, such as tolerance of diversity or of neutralism, and no alternative power (apart from America's allies, who of course shared the same ideology and in any case were weakened by war), that could stand in its way.

The necessity and the possibility of intervention are clearly brought out in Herbert Tillema's admirable study of American military intervention in the era of containment. In Tillema's view, the 'operational code' of US policy-makers defines what constitutes a serious threat to America's security and the appropriate response. These threats are perceived on a graduated scale: (1) imminent peril to US territory; (2) threat that a communist government will come to power in countries of 'special interest' to America; (3) the same possibility in 'communist-threatened' regions; (4) the same in 'just another country'; (5) in a 'disputed territory at the margins of communist states'; (6) threat of something other than a new communist government; and (7) developments in communist states. The first threat is obvious. But the second, concerning a 'special interest' for America, includes long ties of interest and affection or paternalism, as well as repeated statements that the area will be defended as if it were American territory: thus the Caribbean on the one hand, the NATO zone on the other. 'Communist-threatened' areas are those where the existence of a communist government signifies its increasing power and the likely establishment of other communist governments: thus mainland Southeast Asia and the Fertile Crescent plus Iran; and presumably the Kissingerist view of Chile and Angola. 'Just another' country was Korea when it was placed outside the Acheson perimeter. And 'disputed at the margins' includes West Berlin [?], Nepal, northern India, Tibet and Taiwan.[56]

A major restraint on US intervention, particularly of course in the last category (developments in communist states), is the need to avoid armed conflict with a major communist power, as already indicated. A second restraint is the US administration's reliance on 'incremental' decisions: taking a number of small steps rather than one giant stride or, as Roger Hilsman puts it, the 'tendency to decide as little as possible' at any one moment. The 'first step' may be a show of force, as in the Berlin airlift crisis, or it may take the form of increased military assistance programmes for threatened countries. Such limited moves may themselves help to resolve the crisis, or other actors may do so; for instance, United Nations' intervention in the first Cyprus crisis, British counter-insurgency in Malaya, and the effective action of local governments, such as in Bolivia in 1967. A further restraint on US intervention is the need for broad Congressional support, often depending on the support of major allies, which was lacking in the 1954 Indochina crisis and was confined to America's intervention in the Lebanon – and not Jordan or Iraq – in 1958. A final restraint is the requirement of a 'just cause', that is, either a 'request' from a government calling for help or evidence of external interference which can be publicly condemned.[57]

The drawback to Tillema's conception is that although it offers reasons why the USA intervened with military force and why, often in rather similar circumstances, it did not, the scheme itself does not differentiate between one instance of intervention and another (for example, between the Dominican Republic and Vietnam) in terms of scope, duration and intensity of intervention. There is a world of difference between the 22,000 troops (reduced within a year to 90) who hardly fired a shot in the process of quelling disturbances in a small island and the half-million armed forces who fought such savage battles at such vast expense in Vietnam. (It is this 'difference' that I discuss in the following chapters.)

America in a 'bind'[58]

Evidently there is no sharp discontinuity between the upper level of American 'involvement' (i.e. military and economic assistance to a wide range of developing countries) and the lower level of 'intervention': stepped-up assistance, including ever greater use of military advisers, police specialists and counter-insurgency methods, to regimes struggling to suppress challenges to their own domestic systems – challenges (as shown in Part 1 of this study) that have resulted from the operation of these systems. There is thus no effective 'threshold' inhibiting the transformation from involvement to intervention: in fact the reverse. For the issue is not so much one of *initiative* by the United States (i.e. whether or not to intervene) as *reaction* by the latter to certain extrinsic changes: in effect, the deterioration in the internal situation of a client, which it is beyond America's capacity to prevent at the involvement stage. These are the circumstances requiring counter-action by the United States merely to maintain the status quo. In a deteriorating situation, 'more of the same' (US military and economic assistance) is *not* the same: it is qualitatively different. Involvement has *become* intervention.

Nevertheless, the highest stage of direct military intervention and the penultimate stage of intervention by proxy are basically aimed at 'correcting' two different situations. Direct military intervention is to rescue a beleaguered client regime. Intervention by proxy, as in Guatemala, Chile and Angola, is aimed against a former client, where the regime (or change of regime) has demonstrated its 'undesirability' by actions adversely affecting US interests, political, strategic or economic. Undesirability can be measured in terms of (a) the importance of the particular country and hence of its 'loss' to the global system; or (b) its demonstration of defiance of the system (or some aspects of it) which indicate to *other* clients a way out of dependency. Intervention in each case is 'necessary', but whether it is 'possible' depends on relations with the adversary power.

To recapitulate: when the undesirable ex-client is within the American orbit and peripheral to Soviet or Chinese interests, then US intervention is both necessary and possible. But with regard to an undesirable ex-client in an area of obvious strategic importance to the Soviet Union, such as south Asia or parts of the Middle East, it is not possible. Now American intervention, where it is both necessary and possible, may or may not succeed. Where it succeeds (Guatemala, Chile) then the adversary, despite the loss of a client, accepts the *fait accompli*, for the loss is not central to his system. Where it fails (Cuba) the intervening power dare not escalate to the direct stage because the risk of counter-intervention by the adversary on behalf of an ally (rather than merely a client) is too great: the trade-off, in 1962, was America's pledge of non-intervention in Cuba in return for the withdrawal of Soviet missiles. America's fallback position is containment: to prevent the spread of revolutionary infection by bolstering the encircling environment.

Where there is great instability in America's global system, i.e. where internal dissidence in a subsidiary client 'boils over', there is great pressure on the patron to intervene even in an area peripheral to both super-powers. Such was the case in Indochina, where the credibility of each patron, with regard to support for clients in South and North Vietnam respectively, was equally involved. Of course, the area was not peripheral to China; but the Chinese, lacking comparable military strength, had to be content with an unsatisfactory trade-off: America's pledge not to overthrow the government of North Vietnam in return for Chinese 'acquiescence' in US efforts to induce Hanoi to 'desist' from aiding revolutionaries in the South. In the very complex situation of the Vietnam war – a civil war in the South, continuation of the struggle for reunification in Vietnam as a whole – the USA intervened directly in the South and by all means short of this in the North. However, as in the case of Cuba, the USA dared not escalate to the highest stage against the North because of the certainty of Soviet and Chinese retaliation in defence of an ally.

The USA is in a bind, because such challenges to subsidiary client systems (believed to affect the entire network) are bound to arise, in one country or another, 'from natural causes'; similarly the challenge by the adversary in terms both of expanding global power and of the appeal of an alternative system is also on the increase: both types of adversary challenges, of course, are made possible as a result of the first, i.e. 'destabilising' changes in the American global network. The bind takes two partly-simultaneous, partly-consecutive forms, reflecting both 'push' and 'pull' factors.

(1) Push factor. This is the *compulsive* ideology of intervention, shaped by zero-sum attitudes, domino fears, need to demonstrate a 'reputation for action', and the demands of global credibility: it is expressed, paradoxically, in the doctrine of *containment*. Even the conservative Raymond Aron observes that

the concept of containment was in fact expanded into a doctrine of international order, and this doctrine was calculated to lead to imperial, or even imperialist, intervention, or to put it another way, intervention in order to uphold a government favorable to the institutions and ideologies of the United States, even against its people's aspirations.[59]

(2) Pull factor. Here, too, America's interest in maintaining the patron–client system comes up against the problem of domestic *instability*: élitist structures, arousing mass opposition, enmesh the patron ever more tightly in defence of the client's survival. The 'realist' solution to the pull factor is to promote 'self-reliance' among clients: however, assistance for this purpose to a 'deteriorating' client is liable to end up as intervention. The obverse solution is to put pressure on the adversary to prevent him from achieving 'unilateral gains' (as a result of the erosion of the American system) either through internal challenges or external 'probes':[60] both aims are envisioned in the *balance of power* strategy.

Now even if particular administrations have emphasised one or the other factor – containment from Truman to Johnson, balance of power from Nixon to Carter – post-war American policy is essentially a combination of both. The practice of containment never quite matched the crusading ideology of the Truman or Eisenhower Doctrines.[61] Conversely, the 'realism' of the Nixon–Kissinger and Carter–Brzezinski balance of power strategy has been marred by compulsive fears both of the domino variety (reminiscent of Kennedy and Johnson) and of America's lack of credibility should it remain 'inactive' in the face of subversive 'threats'.[62] The result was – and is – an *unstable* combination, oscillating unpredictably in times of crisis between compulsion and realism: a state of affairs which is *not* conducive to the administration's goal of a 'stable structure of peace' or 'world order'.

The two attempts by the USA to *resolve* the problem of instability inherent in the global system – briefly indicated already – reflect the operation of the same factors. Thus first, at the international level, there is what may be called *manipulation from above* as an integral part of the balance of power concept. This objective is formulated in the doctrine of strength of the USA; partnership with allies and friends; and negotiation with the adversary, to reduce sources of tension.[63] The doctrine thus seeks to impose a 'world order' which reflects both the rivalry and the collaboration of the super-powers and other big powers. To achieve this objective requires, on the one hand, continuing demonstration of

American power and resolve; on the other, negotiation of differences with the adversary which otherwise might escalate to the level of global confrontation. The policy, in other words, is to prevent the two super-power systems colliding over interlocking client disputes: thus each patron, while generally fostering the interest of his client, also tries to manage and restrain any of the latter's 'destabilising' ambitions. The corollary is that where internal problems clearly occur in one or other power's sphere of interest, by tacit agreement each permits the other to 'maintain order' in that sphere.[64]

Second, at the national level, American policy amounts to *manipulation from below* (the equivalent of containment). The objective is to prevent or reduce internal challenges to client regimes, which if successful could adversely affect the overall balance. The methods are either *suppressive* – assisting regimes to put down by force any significant movements of opposition; or *reformist* – to improve the regime's image and performance to the extent that dissident movements either do not arise or are easily contained; or, usually, a combination of both. Clearly the reformist policy is both more compatible with American values and more economical. Again this notion is reflected in the policies of various administrations: the Truman Point IV programme, Eisenhower's reference to 'performance' in 'undertaking needed reforms' as the criterion for US support for Diem, the 'Alliance for Progress', and so on.

The undoubted desire for liberal and economical (preventive) solutions, however, confronts the reality of Third World regimes: for in few cases do élitist structures permit the 'luxury' of genuinely liberal or democratic reforms; from their point of view, a more open, participatory system poses a threat to their possession, or control, of power, wealth and prestige. Thus it is hardly surprising that the most illiberal regimes are likely to provoke (in time) the greatest resistance. In spite of this, reformist Americans remain victims of the illusion that even the most repressive regime is ready to evolve, under conditions of 'stability', towards a more representative, or at least more responsive, form of rule.

Thus both attempts to resolve problems of global instability – by manipulation from above, and from below – face contradictions that are inherent in the system: that is, opposition by clients to being manipulated by patrons in the interest of 'world order'; and opposition by the *subjects* of clients to that type of domestic order which best suits the requirements of world order. It is in the latter case that the 'pull' of internal dissidence tends to reinforce and confirm the 'push' of compulsive globalism – in the direction of intervention. This is certainly the implication of Carter's major address of 17 March 1978:

> 'We have important historical responsibilities to enhance peace in East Asia, in the Middle East, in the Persian Gulf, and throughout our own hemisphere. Our preference in all these areas is to turn first to international agreements that . . . minimise the threat of conflict. But we have the will, and we will also maintain the capacity, to honor our commitments and to protect our interests in those critical areas. . . . In all these situations, the primary responsibility for preserving peace and military stability rests with the countries of the region. We shall continue to work with our friends and allies to strengthen their ability to prevent threats to their interests and to ours. In addition, however, we will maintain forces of our own which can be called upon, if necessary, to support mutual defense efforts. The Secretary of Defense at my direction is improving and will maintain quickly deployable forces – air, land and sea – to defend our interests throughout the world.'

How can the USA and the Soviet Union, for its part, get out of this bind? For if they do not, the very process of involvement leading to intervention (in its various forms) results in the use of methods – as we shall see in the chapters on limited war and counter-insurgency – that, first of all, are morally repugnant to a humane society; second, have proved, in one major instance, to be unrealistic and ineffective; and finally even if they have temporarily succeeded in suppressing resistance, are incapable in the long term of assuring stability.

7 * Limited war

We are at war with a system, which, by its essence, is inimical to all other governments and which makes peace or war, as peace and war may best contribute to their subversion. It is with an *armed doctrine* that we are at war.

Edmund Burke, *First Letter on a Regicide Peace*.[1]

There is today in Communist China a government whose leadership is dedicated to the promotion of communism by violent revolution. . . . To accept mainland Chinese domination in Asia would be to look forward to conditions of external domination and probably totalitarian control, not merely for twenty years, but quite possibly for generations.

William Bundy, Speech at Pomona College, 12 February 1966.[2]

The contrast between Burke's day and Bundy's is not in the degree of militancy aroused, or in fear of the threat, but in the over-riding need in the nuclear age to avoid an all-out war. Hence the ambiguity of 'limited war': when the methods of war against an 'armed doctrine' are limited by necessity; but the ends remain unchanged.

'Limited wars are won or lost within definite frameworks (theatre of operations, types of weapons used, volume of resources, resolution or patience of the population) *which the strategists cannot extend at will*', writes Raymond Aron, admittedly after the event – Vietnam – had proved his contention.[3] A similar point was made by Morton Kaplan some years before. He was referring to the difficulty of applying the American criterion of 'limited strategic retaliation' to an adversary attempting to undermine by military force the status quo. Some kinds of 'quasi-military' measures to overturn the status quo, he argued, may not justify the risks of nuclear reprisals. The importance of the area must be considered; so must the problem whether defeat in this particular instance – say the Taiwan Straits – is likely to affect expectations of the actual decision-makers in ways that induce them to surrender, or to leave an alliance system, or to attack. 'These questions are empirical rather than theoretical. Whether the postulated consequences are likely or unlikely to happen depends upon the state of the world and not upon theoretical propositions concerning international politics.'[4]

Education in the Cold War

The purpose of this chapter is to relate the theories of limited war, which flowered brilliantly in America during the later 1950s and early 1960s, to the practice of intervention. The theories were developed, on the basis of the containment policy, to overcome the strategic dilemma facing the USA. The latter's nuclear armoury could deter total war but, as one leading strategist observed, 'unless the nation can also wage limited war successfully, communist aggression may force the United States to choose between total war, non-resistance or ineffective resistance. Such a three-pronged dilemma would be disastrous for America's military security and her diplomatic position.'[5]

Without having recourse to the methods of limited war, Osgood insists, in the event of 'limited communist aggression' or the 'threat' of it, that the USA would find itself in danger of 'acquiescence in a series of piecemeal conquests'. These would 'so weaken America's relative power position and so undermine its prestige' as to leave little to choose between 'gradual paralysis' and the sudden disaster of all-out war.[6] Note, first, the universalist approach; it is not a question of where the 'threat' may be felt, or what form it is likely to take; but if there is a threat it must be met to avoid the extreme consequences either of not meeting it or of over-reacting to it. Second, the blanket assumption of 'communist aggression': in retrospect, it is odd that a pluralist society should have taken so monolithic an attitude. However, this assumption, 'confirmed in practice',[7] was what underlay the containment policy. In the first two decades after the war this was basically directed against the Soviet Union; in the later 1960s against China; and in the 1970s back to the containment of Soviet 'expansionism'.

George Kennan, in his famous 'X' article in *Foreign Affairs*, had advocated in 1947 a 'long-term, patient but firm and vigilant containment of Russian expansive tendencies'. Soviet pressure against the free institutions of the Western world, he continued, 'can be contained by the adroit and vigilant application of counter-force at a series of constantly shifting geographical and political points'.[8] As Osgood analysed the 'nature of the threat to U.S. security' requiring containment – an analysis that was generally accepted at that time – it consisted of two decisive political and military considerations. The military condition was the development of incredibly destructive weapons, which if used in total war would be a catastrophe. 'The political condition is the existence of a powerful communist bloc of nations, which is bent upon seizing every opportunity to extend its sphere of control.' The communist leaders, he wrote, 'retain their expansionist ambitions, in direct conflict with American security'.[9]

Now the purpose of Osgood's book was to educate the American administration and public in the realities of the Cold War, including the way to handle limited war. For the risk of total war was too dangerous to allow the traditional American all-or-nothing attitude to prevail; as indeed it had done under the Dulles strategy of threatening 'massive retaliation' if local deterrents failed. According to the traditional view, peace was the normal state of affairs, quite distinct from war, but once involved in war the USA must achieve a clear-cut military victory as rapidly as possible. As Osgood points out, wars fought by Americans were 'always impassioned, always tinged with outrage, moral fervour or sheer animal exuberance': these emotional qualities tended to override the rational control of force for limited ends.[10] The continuing effect of this attitude can be seen in popular frustration at the limitations on objectives, weapons – and indeed 'success' – revealed in the Laos crisis and in the wars in Korea and Vietnam.

This was a new situation, bounded by the need to avoid recourse to total war. Americans had to understand that the 'rational control of force' implied 'co-operating' with the enemy to make sure that both sides knew what was involved in any 'local' confrontation and thus would not push matters too far – in other words, would keep their tactical objectives limited. At the same time, and this was where the element of ambiguity was so significant, such 'co-operation' was incidental to the world-wide struggle for power between the two rivals, a struggle not only initiated as a result of powerful emotional drives on both sides but one in which the course of action continually fostered those same emotions. The more rational the methods of control – the techniques of 'signals', 'demonstrations', 'bargains', 'reputations', 'manipulation of risk' and 'power to hurt', evolved by the strategic theorists[11] – the more irrational became the perception of the threat, as it materialised under certain circumstances, to which these methods were to be applied.

Military solutions preferred

Adam Yarmolinsky puts the matter in a more technical perspective, looking back in 1970 as a former principal Deputy Assistant Secretary of Defense during the latter part of the McNamara era:

> Perhaps the greater efficiencies we tried to build into the system in the Kennedy years had the perverse consequences of strengthening America's military options at the expense of her diplomatic and political flexibility. Theories of limited war and programs to widen the President's range of choice made military solutions to our foreign problems more available and even more attractive.[12]

In the 1940s and 1950s, Yarmolinsky recalls, there was only a limited range of alternatives offered:

> In the 1960s, on the other hand, with almost 10 per cent of the Gross National Product being spent on military capabilities, including 'flexible response', Presidents Kennedy and Johnson would be presented with a variety of alternative military moves suited to defending Berlin, reacting to the placement of Soviet missiles in Cuba, coping with a revolution in the Dominican Republic, or supporting Saigon against the Vietcong . . . a different prescription for each imaginable situation and for each of its phases.

In practice, the heavy investment in military forces and the strategy of flexible response 'probably has increased the likelihood that a President in a crisis will consider military options above other possible options'. Thus, 'political problems, if thought about primarily in military terms, become military problems'.

Why were military solutions 'more attractive'? There are three main reasons: the *perception* of the threat; the *experience* of intervention; culminating in the *generalised* power-asserting approach.

'National liberation war' threat

The perception of the communist threat varied from 'overt' to what was still seen in quasi-military terms as 'indirect aggression'. Now, in regard to the former, the USA maintained a satisfactory position at the nuclear level (one at that time of superiority) and an unsatisfactory position, particularly in Europe, with regard to conventional forces – but it was one that could be lived with. However, 'wars of national liberation', believed to be 'inspired' or promoted by the Soviet Union and China, were seen to be undermining the structure of US strategic security at its weakest link. In time this would change the balance of world forces to America's disadvantage. Maxwell Taylor, President Kennedy's military adviser and later Chairman of the Joint Chiefs of Staff, conveyed this sense of alarm when he reported from Vietnam in 1961. The USA 'must decide how it will cope with Khrushchev's "wars of liberation" . . . a new and dangerous technique which by-passes our traditional political and military responses.'[13] Speaking before the Senate Foreign Relations Committee on 17 February 1966, General Taylor still insisted that the administration's intention was to 'show that the war of liberation . . . is costly, dangerous and doomed to failure. We must destroy the myth of its invincibility in order to protect the independence of many weak nations which are vulnerable targets for subversive aggression.'

Khrushchev's emphatic approval of 'national-liberation wars', proclaimed on 6 January 1961, had indeed 'made a conspicuous impression on the new President, who took it as an authoritative exposition of Soviet intentions', states Kennedy's biographer, Arthur Schlesinger Jr. 'The declared faith in victory through rebellion, subversion and guerrilla warfare alarmed Kennedy more than Moscow's amiable signals [that it would not press revolution to the point of nuclear war] assuaged him.' Referring to Russia and China in his State of the Union message, Kennedy declared: 'We must never be lulled into believing that either power has yielded its ambitions for world domination.'[14]

Khrushchev had defined national-liberation wars as those which 'began as uprisings of colonial peoples against their oppressors [and] developed into guerrilla wars'; he gave Cuba, Vietnam and Algeria as examples. Now, first of all, it is obvious that this is a rather mixed bag and that Khrushchev was clearly out to claim as much credit as he could for the turmoil in the world, which at that time also included rebellion in the Congo and civil war in Laos, practically none of which could be attributed to Soviet direction, but almost all to local conditions.

Second, the anti-colonial potential for national-liberation wars, stressed by Khrushchev in 1961, had already been greatly diminished by de Gaulle's grant of independence to France's African colonies in July 1960, and by the virtual completion of British de-colonisation, starting with India and Pakistan in 1947 and ending with Kenya in 1963. Finally, Khrushchev's speech and the Moscow Declaration of Communist Parties of 6 December 1960, to which it referred, certainly foresaw (with misplaced optimism) 'peoples rising with growing determination in the struggle against imperialism' and a 'gigantic battle between labour and capital'; but it also notably reaffirmed the possibility of 'peaceful transition to socialism'. This, indeed, was one of Khrushchev's major innovations: the other was his denial of the 'inevitability' of war between capitalist and socialist systems.

Had it not been for the prevailing sense of Cold War anxiety and the obvious fear of the potential of Khrushchev's and Mao's new weapon, then what the Americans called 'indirect aggression' – which incidentally ranged from armed insurgency to political subversion – would have been recognised either as civil war, stemming from severe internal conflicts, or as legitimate political activity of the sort that is practised in democratic countries. The fact that such activity may be *effective* in its appeal to depressed or unrepresented sectors of society is all the more reason for insecure ruling élites to outlaw and suppress it. (Note, as a current example, the Indonesian 'New Order's' so-called 'floating mass' directive of 1971 banning political activities in the villages.)

American policy-makers and strategists, however, were not so much concerned with the internal, political aspect of civil conflict or insurgency, as with the external or strategic aspect: that is, the fear that upsetting the status quo in any 'sensitive' area would be to the detriment of American security. Thus Morton Halperin, in his synthesis of the vast corpus of limited war literature (he annotates 343 books and articles), recommended that 'although the United States cannot have adequate forces in every possible conflict area, the value of prepositioning American troops should not be overlooked'. No communist aggression has been 'unleashed', he declared, where such troops have been stationed. More important still, US troops are a symbol of an 'American commitment to intervene against aggression'. Halperin continued:

A dominant American objective in any local war [one in which
the United States and the Soviet Union saw themselves on opposite
sides but in which the homelands of the two major powers did not
come under attack] is likely to be to demonstrate to communist
nations as well as to allies and neutrals a *willingness to fight*, when
necessary, to prevent communist expansion by force.[15]

Experience of intervention: Greece and Korea

The second factor in making military solutions more attractive was the experience of US intervention in Greece and Korea,[16] although the latter also had unfavourable effects. Greece supplied the element of large-scale military and economic assistance to and close political support of a strategically-placed but repressive and unrepresentative regime: a policy which paid off, by laying the foundations for parliamentary rule, for nearly two decades, until the Colonels seized power.

Korea provided the element of heavy military intervention by ground combat troops in the context of external aggression. The Korean War also saw the USA raising its objectives when the conflict took a favourable turn – from repelling aggression in the South to insisting on the reunification of Korea – which brought an appropriate response from the other side. However, Korea represented a 'frustrating and bewildering' experience to Americans – to be repeated to some extent in Laos and especially in Vietnam – of a war which cost a heavy price but brought no decisive victory. Indeed, the opinion of the US Joint Chiefs of Staff during the early Laos crisis was that the USA ought never again to fight (as in Korea) a limited war in Asia: rather than getting bogged down in the jungles, if force were to be used, it should be all-out, striking at the source of enemy power.[17] As for Vietnam, the advice of US commanders was succinctly put: 'There are only two ways to fight this war without increasing American casualties. One is to go all-out . . . the other is to go home.'[18] Indeed, fighting a limited war in Korea, with one hand tied behind its back, the USA was forced to acquiesce in a stalemate. Yet it could have won, 'persuasive voices' reasoned, had US forces been freed of 'political restraints'.[19]

'Limited war' was obviously, and correctly, marked by political restraint. But the *impetus* to engage on a global policy, which clearly involved the possibility of military intervention (to say the least), stemmed from political-*cum*-strategic considerations. Thus the commitment to Greece and Turkey by President Truman in 1947 'was a direct reflection of a general view in the government that the whole Middle Eastern and Mediterranean area was a strategic unity, no part of which could be allowed to fall to Russian imperialism if the United States were to preserve the geopolitical bases of its security'.[20] This view is amply confirmed by Dean Acheson, who as Secretary of State told Congressional leaders in February 1947 that in the past eighteen months,

Soviet pressure on the Straits [of Bosphorus], on Iran, and on northern Greece, had brought the Balkans to the point where a highly possible Soviet breakthrough might *open three continents* to Soviet penetration. Like apples in a barrel infected by one rotten one, the corruption of Greece would infect Iran and all to the east. It would also carry infection to Africa through Asia Minor and Egypt, and to Europe through Italy and France. . . . The Soviet Union was playing one of its greatest gambles in history at minimal cost.[21]

The USA, Acheson recalled, was alone in a position to 'break up the play'. These were the 'stakes'. The commitment to Greece and Turkey was immeasurably extended as a result of the Korean War and the French struggle in Indochina to include virtually the whole of 'free' Asia, from the Middle East to Japan.

Power-assertion

The crux of the matter is that America's purposes, now global in scope, still had to be applied to specific conditions. But where conditions were unfavourable to these purposes, there arose the divergence between global conception and empirical reality – the 'credibility gap'.

In Vietnam US aims lost contact with reality.[22] The Johnson administration believed that American bombing of North Vietnam, its 'military presence' in the South and 'political and economic carrots' could be used as 'bargaining trade-offs' for an end to Hanoi's infiltration of men and supplies, its removal of cadres *'and a dissolution of the organised Viet Cong military and political forces'*:[23] in other words, the total collapse of any organised resistance to the Saigon regime. What sort of 'bargain' was this? Inevitably, when the'deal' was rejected, America's bargaining 'cards' had to be used: i.e. policies had to be *enforced*.

Thus 'military potential' came, not merely to be held in reserve, but to be utilised as an integral part of American foreign policy. The rationale for power-assertion or 'coercive diplomacy' is set out in Thomas Schelling's authoritative work, *Arms and Influence*:

To inflict suffering gains nothing and saves nothing directly; it can only make people behave to avoid it. The only purpose . . . must be to influence somebody's behaviour, to coerce his decision or choice. . . . The power to hurt is bargaining power. To exploit it is diplomacy.[24]

Indeed, *control of behaviour*, rather than attempting to win people's loyalty, is the criterion of the 'revisionist' counter-insurgency school.[25] 'It is the threat of damage, or of more damage to come', Schelling writes, 'that can make someone yield or comply.'[26]

'Compellence' (coercive diplomacy) backed up by 'competition in risk-taking' and the importance of maintaining, on a world scale, a 'reputation for action' became essential components, of the American strategy of 'limited war'. The result, in a 'losing' situation, however, was that the need for more effective 'war' increasingly came to prevail over the need for 'limitation' – i.e. the 'rules of the game' accepted by both sides. Indeed the more 'compellence' was employed, and resisted, the more important to the strategists was the 'need' to take greater risks and demonstrate 'effectiveness' by *escalating* the conflict – to the detriment of the rules they had established (see Table 4).

Table 4   Limited war in Vietnam

---

1   *Rationale*: 'The choice is not simply whether to continue our efforts to keep South Vietnam free and independent but, rather, whether to continue our struggle to halt communist expansion in Asia. If the choice is the latter, as I believe it should be, we will be far better off facing the issue in South Vietnam' (statement by Defense Secretary McNamara of 18 February 1965 before the Armed Services Committee of the House of Representatives).

2   *Reputation*: 'It is essential – however badly SEA [Southeast Asia] may go over the next 1–3 years – that U.S. emerge as a "good doctor". We must have kept promises, been tough, taken risks, gotten blooded, and hurt the enemy very badly. We must avoid harmful appearances which will affect judgments by and provide pretexts to, other nations regarding how the U.S. will behave in future cases of particular interest to those nations – regarding U.S. policy, power, resolve and competence to deal with their problems.' Specifically, 'U.S. aims: 70% – To avoid a humiliating U.S. defeat (to our reputation as a guarantor). 20% – To keep SVN [South Vietnam] (and the adjacent) territory from Chinese hands. 10% – To permit the people of SVN to enjoy a better, freer way of life' (Draft Memorandum by Assistant Secretary of Defense McNaughton for Secretary McNamara, 24 March 1965).

3   *Rules of the game*: 'We should be developing a posture of maximum readiness for a deliberate escalation of pressure against North Vietnam. . . . By means of these actions, Hanoi will get the word that the operational rules with respect to the DRV [Democratic Republic of Vietnam] are changing' (US Mission in Saigon to State Department, 18 August 1964). 'If, as the evidence shows, we are playing a losing game in South Vietnam, it is high time we change and find a better way. . . . In bringing military pressure to bear on North Vietnam . . . [at] the bottom of the ladder of escalation, we have the initiation of intensified covert operations, anti-infiltration attacks in Laos, and reprisal bombings. . . . From this level of operations we could begin to escalate progressively' (briefing by Ambassador Maxwell Taylor, 'The Current Situation in South Vietnam – November 1964', 27 November 1964).

4   *Commitments*: 'Why are we in South Vietnam? We are there because we have a promise to keep. . . . We are also there to strengthen world order. Around the globe – from

Table 4 contd

Berlin to Thailand – are people whose well-being rests, in part, on the belief they can count on us if they are attacked. To leave Vietnam would shake the confidence of all these people in the value of American commitment. . . . We are also there because there are great stakes in the balance. Let no-one think that retreat from Vietnam would bring an end to conflict. The battle would be renewed in one country and then another . . . the appetite of aggression is never satisfied' (President Johnson, address at Johns Hopkins University, 17 April 1965). [Comment: the 'confidence of all these people' was indeed shaken, but their doubts were not so much about the US maintaining the commitment as about America's judgment in entering into it. In fact the Vietnam commitment was so misguided that the greater the efforts made to sustain it the more evident became the unwisdom of the choice, and all the more drastic the eventual policy reversal. . . .]

To sum up: the contradiction in the limited war strategy is between the 'requirements' of *globalism* – coercion, risk-taking and world-wide 'reputation for acting' in defence of commitments – and the reality of a *specific* environment. The resulting failure of strategy in Indochina could have been lessened, or perhaps avoided altogether, *only* by a sense of discrimination, which the dictates of globalism did not permit.

8 ★ Counter-insurgency: analysts and operators

The contrast between the analyst – aware of the external environment – and the operator – executing global policies – and the dilemma this poses for each of them, are even more characteristic of counter-insurgency than of limited war. For two 'profoundly different' views of insurgency in the celebrated 'National Security Study Memorandum No. 1' on Vietnam, prepared for the Nixon administration in February 1969, are ascribed in the document to the gap largely 'between the policy-makers [i.e. in the bureaucracy], the analysts and the intelligence community on the one hand, and the civilian and military operators on the other'. The analysts envisaged political compromise; the operators recommended 'wholehearted' support for Saigon.[1]

To put it crudely, the analysts *know*, but the operators *do*: this is the law of power. To overlook this law is to live in a world of illusion. Paradoxically, for the analyst, particularly the academic, the illusion takes two mutually exclusive forms: first that *because* he understands a political or social problem he can, and indeed should, shape or influence the way in which it is tackled; second that *although* he understands and clearly states the problem he has no further responsibility for seeing how it is tackled., The first form is the *folie de grandeur* to which intellectuals are especially prone; the second is the *trahison des clercs* – but in a diametrically opposite sense to that used by Julien Benda – and the same comment applies.

Underlying both forms of illusion is the fact that the analyst is free – to draw conclusions 'purely' on the basis of intellect, judgment and experience – but he is 'irresponsible', he is not in a position of power. The analyst, let us say the social scientist, can usually live with this contradiction. Nevertheless, the implication of 'right judgment' is a heightened sense of moral responsibility, backed often enough by the personal desire, that is the ambition, to put that judgment into practical effect. This duty and this desire are immeasurably strengthened in times of crisis.

The contrary emphasis on the analyst's lack of power (or if serving in the bureaucracy, his lack of substantive power), however, absolves him from any further responsibility in following up his conclusions. His task is to diagnose – not to carry out the treatment: to mix the two is to imperil the 'purity' of his original diagnosis. Whichever form of attitude or behaviour the analyst adopts his position is radically different from that of the operator. The latter is not free as the analyst is free: whether bureaucrat or politician in office he is subject to the restraints of governmental policy on the one hand, of the external environment on the other. Yet he is actually responsible for influencing or making decisions, which gives gravity to his behaviour, and this renders it different in kind from the 'participation' of the activist type of analyst, *as* an analyst, whether this is the result of duty or ambition.

The dilemma facing both analysts and operators stems from incongruity between the values they attempt to live by – often clearly marked in the domestic context – and the environment, especially a foreign environment, in which a particular policy operates. When this incongruity is most evident, that is *at times of crisis*, analysts according to their type take up two main positions. Those who insist on purity of diagnosis affect a 'value-free' stance with conservative implications; for the conservative assumes 'naturally' either that his findings are value-free, that is, he is not aware that they are influenced by his opinions, or if he is, that his opinions are common to all right-minded people, which comes to the same thing. Such analysts, if they have become critical of an established policy, because the 'credibility gap' simply cannot be ignored, are at stage one: their aim is to correct or improve policy within the accepted framework. The activists, on the other hand, who may have been at stage one, when the crisis was in its early phases, are now at stage two: they question the very premises of policy. Both, however, are concerned with matters of fact and with matters of value. Does, or will, the policy work? And is the policy right: does it apply appropriate means to achieve worthwhile ends?

Those at stage one, because of their conservative bent, are actually reinforcing the operators: they help to maintain the system. They are analysts-as-technicians, who are not operators but, paradoxically in view of their assumptions of 'purity' and value-free research, act as if they were. Those at stage two are not operators, but because they are activists would like to be operators (that is, be both analysts and operators); in some cases they think they are operators, for they believe in the power of persuasion; in a few cases they actually become operators, by taking action against the system.

Somewhere in between these two stages – uneasy about stage one but not ready for stage two – are the operators who are conscious of their values, the unconventional men, military or political, who have often played an important part in shaping policy. They are unconventional because they are very much aware of values[2] and consciously seek to embody them in practical policy. Where the environment is 'receptive' they have had marked success.

Their opposite numbers among the operators are the 'professional' officers and officials, many of whom have not even reached stage one. Such are the conventional administrators, who devise 'standard operating procedures' and who show a greater concern with where one is rather than where one is going: they tend to divert attention, Kissinger acidly remarks, from the act of choice – the ultimate test of statesmanship – to the accumulation of facts.[3] Then there are the professional soldiers whose devotion to duty and loyalty to their service have become second nature. 'Command is the word,' Brodie observes from years of experience, 'and within sharply ordained limits, tough aggressiveness is the desired style.' Such training as the military get in international and political affairs is 'too brief, too casual and comes too late in life' to be able to change the basic attitudes of military men. Consequently, at the top of the military profession and as the adviser to Presidents, 'our Chief of Staff is one who shares with his colleagues a great belief in the efficacy of force in dealing with recalcitrant peoples or regimes abroad'.[4]

Clearly the external environment and the perception of that environment are crucial. For both the existence and the threat of insurgency have dominated American policy towards the Third World – from Indochina and Cuba to Angola and Palestine. The fear that even 'indigenous' insurgency could be manipulated – first by 'international communism', then either by Moscow or Peking – in a chain reaction that would endanger America's security, led to world-wide US counter-measures . . . and the end of that process is not in sight.

In this chapter, therefore, I seek to relate the two types of analyst and operator and the two stages of analysis to the critical problems of 'recalcitrant peoples or regimes'. In the first section I consider the official justification for academic research on counter-insurgency; in the second, 'the neutrality of technicians' and its implications (stage one); in the third, 'suppression', the dilemma of unconventional operators and the attitude of the critics (stage two); and finally, 'hardware' versus 'software' as a counter to insurgency. Now American research, according to the Defense Department,

> has ranged from such software efforts as analyses of the insurgencies in Malaya, Philippines and Thailand, and lessons learned in Vietnam, to such hardware efforts as development of unattended ground sensors, foliage penetrating radar, radio propagation in jungles, assistance [to allies] in the development of a military Research Development, Test and Evaluation capability.[5]

But it is hardware that will determine the character of 'ground warfare in the future':

> Concentration of firepower will reach new levels of intensity. Electronic warfare will be robust and sophisticated. Precision weapons and new techniques for target acquisition and control *will change the way the battle is fought and the way it can be won.*[6]

Contract research

The issue of 'contract' research for counter-insurgency purposes forced itself into academic awareness by the disclosure early in 1965 – around the time of American intervention in the Dominican Republic – of the US Army's ill-starred Project Camelot. The following official description of the project had been issued in December 1964 to scholars presumed to be interested in the study of 'internal war potentials':

> Project Camelot is a study whose object is to determine the feasibility of determining a general social systems model which would make it possible to predict and influence politically significant aspects of social change in the developing nations of the world. Somewhat more specifically, its objectives are:
> *First*, to devise procedures for assessing the potential for internal war within national societies;
> *Second*, to identify with increased degrees of confidence those actions which a government might take to relieve conditions which are assessed as giving rise to a potential for internal war; and
> *Finally*, to assess the feasibility of prescribing the characteristics

of a system for obtaining and using the essential information needed
for doing the above two things. . . .
[Further] The U.S. Army has an important mission in the positive
and constructive aspects of nation building; as well as a responsibility to assist friendly governments in dealing with active
insurgency problems.[7]

This seems quite clear and above-board. American scholars would be
asked to assist their government in its task of alleviating discontent and
promoting 'nation building' in developing countries, just as they might
be asked to carry out social surveys of depressed areas and to recommend
economic improvements back home. But the situation of many of the
Third World countries is not similar to that 'back home'. In such
countries, and it is these that are usually affected by insurgency or other
forms of internal conflict, US agencies may be helping governments to
suppress what, in democratic nations, would be regarded as legitimate
movements of 'interest articulation and aggregation'. Even the well-
intentioned promotion of nation building may in practice be confined –
given the difficulty of persuading these governments to carry out needed
reforms – to improving the capacities of the indigenous administration,
regardless of what these improved capacities will be used to achieve:
perhaps better allocation of resources, perhaps more effective methods of
suppression. To put it bluntly – and this has been borne out in Southeast
Asia and Latin America – US aid and technical assistance helps not only
to enlarge overall economic performance, it also specifically reinforces
the coercive capacity of the armed forces, the para-military units, and
the police.

Project Camelot rose and fell in a matter of months in 1964–5. A
decade later the debate over the project may seem something of a storm
in a tea cup. But Camelot is significant for three reasons. First of all, it
made explicit the rationale for US intervention in Third World countries
–'the US Mission' of counter-insurgency to maintain the status quo.
Second, it marked the end of the attempt to recruit from a broad
spectrum of the 'social science community'. And finally, official
recruitment and projects did not cease: they were increasingly diverted
from theoretical to practical and from open to closed studies.

US agency-determined research has powerful inducements to offer,
notably the opportunities for extensive field research and the large sums
needed to finance them. The directors of Camelot expected to spend $1
million to $1½ million a year over four years. This would have

represented only a fraction of the $30 million spent annually by the US Government in the behavioural and social sciences, according to Dean Rusk's testimony at the time.[8] In 1965 more than 90 per cent of expenditure ($27.3 million) was provided by the Defense Department, of which about one-sixth ($4.86 million) went to finance 'software' studies of foreign countries, counter-insurgency and unconventional warfare.[9]

Neutrality of technicians

Camelot was the exposed tip of the iceberg of war-related studies; the great bulk remained, especially in the heyday of direct intervention (1965–8), largely undisturbed and unseen. The rationale for the vast expansion of area studies, to which counter-insurgency attached itself, was disclosed in 1968 by the Director of Defense Research and Engineering of the US Defense Department: 'If we are better informed . . . about the cultural, political and economic aspects of a nation we are in a better position to determine what effects, if any, the introduction of military force would have on the particular problem of concern.'[10]

The annual report of the RAND Corporation emphasised two years later: 'We are looking closely at current and past insurgencies for insights to guide U.S. policy in the future. During 1969 we concentrated on the Philippines, Vietnam, Northeast Thailand, and Communist China.'[11] In regard to Vietnam, RAND stated that 'enormous dividends could have accrued from more knowledge, and more effective use of knowledge, about the social and political institutions'. What 'use' this knowledge would be put to is not stated. Indeed the inference is that this is no concern of RAND's. For it is evident that the underlying assumptions of the sponsors of war-related studies are not to challenge official policy decisions, but to make them more effective. As Johan Galtung observes, not a single word in the many documents of Camelot ruled out the possibility of maintaining a Batista in power: 'the idea seems only to be that it should happen with more graceful means than U.S. military missions or direct military intervention'.[12]

The former President of RAND, Henry Rowen, after pointing out that most of RAND's research projects were now on subjects of domestic concern, such as housing and health, admitted in 1972 that he had been powerfully impressed by the 1967 report of Joseph Zasloff, *Origins of the Insurgency in South Vietnam, 1954–1960.*[13] A preliminary RAND report on 'Vietcong motivation and morale' had appeared as early as March 1965, showing that recruits to the Vietcong had joined for a 'mix of motives including protest against social injustice at the village level, lack of educational and career opportunity on the Government of Vietnam (GVN) side, antipathy to being drafted by the Army of the Republic of Vietnam'; they did not see themselves as being involved in a struggle of North against South, or communist against anti-communist, but in a 'struggle between the legitimate leaders of an independent Vietnam and usurpers protected by a foreign power'. This report was given as a briefing to Ambassador Maxwell Taylor and General Westmoreland in Saigon, John McNaughton and officials of Defense and the State Departments in Washington.[14]

Yet although Rowen had thus recognised both the intensity of revolutionary motivation and the ugly conditions of Diemist repression, Zasloff's report, he said, had had no effect on subsequent policy.[15] It does not seem to have occurred to him that since Zasloff's and other people's research had shown official American assumptions about Vietnam to be misguided therefore he should have exercised what influence he had in trying to get these assumptions – and hence policies – changed. It is as if his views on Vietnam and on the policies of the administration were kept in two quite separate compartments: rationally, he could understand the nature of the conflict in Vietnam; but this understanding did not impinge on the assumptions in the higher compartment, which consisted in accepting US policies as given, and as therefore needing to be carried out in the most efficient, best informed and technically most appropriate manner.

As the 1960 Report by the Committee on University and World Affairs, organised by the Ford, Rockefeller and Carnegie Foundations, put it (Dean Rusk, then President of the Rockefeller Foundation, was a member of the Committee): 'If our understanding and our capacity to act in such areas as Asia, Africa and Latin America are to be illuminated by a critical appraisal, greatly expanded opportunities are needed for scholarly studies of those countries.'[16] The scholars were to provide the understanding, the government the capacity to act.

The neutral quality of the academic technicians – their job is to keep the machine running, not to see where it goes – is well adapted to the revisionist theories of behaviour-control of insurgencies. (As they would put it: there is no point in getting emotional about dictators like Stroessner of Paraguay, who controls the behaviour of his people rather well, because this presents few problems to the USA.) The revisionists take their cue from the counter-insurgency specialists *par excellence*, the

French majors and colonels of the Indochina and Algeria campaigns, who had learned their concepts of revolutionary war (not always correctly) from Mao and Giap. If, as one of them (Roger Trinquier) insists, the 'essential weapon which allows our enemies to fight effectively with a few means' is terrorism – a widely-shared belief which has the advantage of avoiding research into the roots of the problem – then it is vital for the 'forces of order' to provide security by strict means of control. 'Supervision of the masses by a strict hierarchy and often even by several parallel hierarchies is the master weapon of modern war.'[17]

Trinquier, who was on the staff of General Massu, the paratroop commander notorious for his use of torture in Algeria,[18] urges the authorities to turn away from the illusory aim of 'rapid and spectacular success' through conventional military operations and pursue instead the 'essential, though less noble, task of working on the people in depth' and of destroying the insurgent political and military organisation.[19] Centres must be set up to turn out great numbers of government information agents: 'Then we will disperse them throughout all the branches of human activity.'[20] Backing up this operation are police measures of village control: each inhabitant is individually and secretly interrogated to reveal the members of the clandestine organisation. 'Constant police operations are necessary to prevent the organisation re-forming; only by methodical work can progressive supervision over the village be established.'[21] Tactically, the population is subdued. Depriving the guerrilla of his support, however, can be attained only 'by a long-term policy based on comprehensive reforms capable of rallying the population'. This, Trinquier adds, is the responsibility of the government and goes beyond the range of this study.[22]

Under the inspiration of these methods – they were applied with grim effectiveness in Algeria – American counter-insurgency specialists got down to the 'task of working on the people in depth'. They were enthusiastic, if undiscriminating, borrowers – for there were many examples to choose from: the *style-para* in Algeria, Magsaysay's 'all-out force and all-out friendship' in the Philippines, Templer's control measures in Malaya, Japanese repression in China, Nazi reprisals in occupied Europe – all were grist to their mill. The Center for Research into Social Systems (CRESS), which took over, until 1970, from Camelot's Special Operations Research Office (SORO), meticulously listed various population control techniques. They include measures of collective responsibility (such as German Army reprisals against Polish civilians for acts of sabotage by the resistance – 'a forceful deterrent'), resettlement and relocation (Malaya and Algeria), legal controls, registration, censuses, food control and counter-insurgency intelligence, focusing on 'individuals and their behaviour patterns'.[23]

The problem is political: the response is technical, which has political implications. R. W. Komer, director of the pacification programme in Vietnam during the last years of the Johnson administration, still insists on the 'managerial key' to the control of insurgency.[24] Komer's report for RAND is 'one of several studies on the organisation and management of "counter-insurgency" responses in Southeast Asia funded by the Advanced Research Projects Agency [of the US Defense Department] in an effort to learn what practical lessons they can teach'.[25]

In his analysis of the problem of South Vietnam, Komer asks 'Why Did We Do So Badly?' at such an enormous cost in lives, destruction and money (the war cost the USA $150 billion). 'Most of what we did turned out to be futile, wasted and even irrelevant.'[26] He answers:

> Politically, we failed to give due weight to the revolutionary dynamics of the situation, the popular appeal of the Vietcong, the feebleness of the Diem regime or the depth of factionalism among traditional Vietnamese elites. . . . In retrospect, perhaps the greatest single restraint on the United States' ability to achieve its aims in Vietnam was the sheer incapacity of the regimes we backed. . . . The lack of a sufficiently viable, functioning government was a crucial handicap.[27]

One would have thought that this comprehension of a government in the last throes of defeat would have prompted Komer to explain (now at least) that the 'lesson' of Vietnam for the USA was 'never again' to intervene in such a hopeless situation. But not a bit of it. First of all, Komer merely argues in traditional terms, as if the Nixon Doctrine had never been announced and the Nixon visit to Peking had never taken place, that the US administration failed to realise in time 'the extent of the threat'. Second, that too much emphasis was on 'search and destroy' operations, and not enough on pacification: in fiscal year 1968 the USA spent nearly $4 billion on bombing and offensive operations; only $850 million on pacification and socio-economic programmes.[28] Third, that insufficient effort was made to change the 'behaviour patterns of the GVN and U.S. institutions involved in the struggle'.[29]

At one stage in the Vietnam war the pacification programme was entitled 'Revolutionary Development', as if to take over the energy and inspiration – the 'dynamic' – of the insurgents along with their terminology; but 'Managerial Revolution' would seem a more fitting reminder of its paternity.

'Suppression'

While strategic studies had flourished in the late 1950s and early 1960s, area studies and studies of counter-insurgency took off towards the end of that period. Area studies, as one of its practitioners puts it, developed in the USA from the accumulation of disparate information about individual societies to an attempt to establish an 'orderly, structured global pattern, on the basis of which systematic analysis and policy-making could go forward'. The latter was notable, first, for its addiction to functionalism; it presented a mechanical model applicable to all societies regardless of their histories and was admirably adapted to social engineering; and second, by its aversion to nationalism, partly because nationalism in concrete terms is 'irreducibly particular' and hence fits uneasily into the universalist, functional scheme.[30]

Counter-insurgency studies, which are a legitimate offspring of strategic studies but an illegitimate one of area studies, are equally dominated by the social engineering approach. Extremes of ingenuity have been applied to devising appropriate techniques of behaviour control, but the question – *techniques for what purpose?* – has been studiously avoided. The analyst's dilemma faces those who seek an answer to this question.

For counter-insurgency is a cumulative process. It starts with the physical and 'social' engineering approach toward 'problem-solving', rather than an attempt to understand complex situations for which there may be no 'acceptable' solution. This leads to increasing pressure to achieve what, under the above circumstances, are 'inappropriate' aims – i.e. those dictated by *global* considerations, contrary to local conditions. Finally the *combination* of the engineering drive and the contradiction between policy and environment results in efforts to eliminate the source of frustration (of desired ends) by technically-innovative but morally unacceptable means; indeed as an integral part of this effort, within the overall engineering approach, technological science (hardware) gradually drives out social science (software).[31]

By 'morally unacceptable' means, I refer to those involving destructiveness out of all proportion to the importance of the end-purpose and to what was actually achieved. In the category of excessive use of force I would include: the Second World War bombing of German and Japanese cities by the Allies (despite hundreds of thousands of civilian casualties, it did not 'paralyse' the enemy war effort); Britain's Suez 'adventure' (so much reputation lost, for so little that could, realistically, be gained); Soviet suppression of 'national liberation' in Hungary and Czechoslovakia (which speaks for itself); France's colonial wars in Indochina and Algeria; and American intervention in Vietnam.

Consider the latter case. Whatever the importance attached to the aim (to prevent a communist takeover or, more remotely, to guarantee US credibility) it could not justify the mass slaughter of Vietnamese, the disruption of their society, the pervasive corruption – in fact the wholesale degradation of a nation that was to be 'saved'. Moreover, both the French and the American counter-revolutionary wars in Vietnam were 'worse than a crime, they are a blunder'.[32] The blunder is indiscriminate globalism: for the French too believed that to yield in Vietnam would be to undermine the French presence throughout the world. Thus they were 'compelled' to fight in an unpopular cause (first that of the *colons*, then of Bao Dai) under adverse conditions: and the greater their frustration, the more violent their acts of repression.

Similarly, in Algeria, the French mustered some 800,000 troops (including half a million regulars) against a guerrilla force of 35,000 which by 1961 had been reduced to some 5,000. More than two million Algerians were moved into 'regroupment centres'; torture, and napalming of villages, were widely practised. Even so, the Algerians endured the bitter struggle out of a 'determination to end injustice and humiliation', which they associated irrevocably with the alien presence.[33]

In Vietnam the same contradiction – between the aims of a 'civilising mission' and conditions which no longer made it possible – was ironically revealed by one of America's most publicised participants in the conflict: John Paul Vann, 'hero' of David Halberstam's *The Making of a Quagmire*, later co-ordinator of field operations for the US Operations Mission in Vietnam, who died in a helicopter crash in the Central Highlands in June 1972. 'The understandable concern of the U.S. with the communist involvement in this revolution', Vann officially reported in 1965, 'has obscured the fact that most of the objectives of the revolution are identical with those for which Americans have long fought and died' – that is, the 'American creed' of liberty, equality, justice and fair opportunity. Yet Vann was not prepared to leave it at that. 'The major challenge facing the U.S. in Vietnam', he wrote, 'is to stimulate such an alternative [to the NLF] to be offered by GVN, and to ensure that its achievement is both possible and compatible with our own objectives.'[34] But what if the 'alternative' is either not possible or if possible not compatible?

This is the operators' dilemma. From their experience and professional competence they realise that official policy is not effective; from their attachment to values they know that it is wrong. But out of loyalty to their government and country (here the two are identified) they cannot bring themselves to admit the implications of what they both know and believe. To suppress the contradiction they resort to (usually unconscious) subterfuge: first, they aim their criticism all the more strongly at the methods, while thus avoiding the premises, of official policy; second, the outrage suffered by their sense of values is redirected to the 'real' enemy − normally the communists, but in Algeria the 'nationalists', whose resistance is made responsible for all that has gone wrong.

Let us examine the contradiction more closely. These operators are aware of the conditions which give rise to dissidence and revolt. As John Pustay, author of *Counterinsurgency Warfare*, explains, the 'general problem of instability' includes poverty, over-population, absentee landlordship, nationalism, dissident groups, deficient civil administration, and 'selfish, tyrannical elites' accompanied by 'corruption and police brutality'.[35]

On the other hand, these operators acknowledge the many *positive* features of the 'Maoist type' of insurgency. First, the close relationship between the guerrillas and the people: 'It is obvious that Mao holds military salvation, ideologically speaking, as a direct concomitant of the political conversion of the masses.' Second, the 'politicisation' of insurgent military forces − that is, the subordination of military to political goals. Third, the care taken not to launch reckless offensives: 'the very price of survival is caution'. Fourth, self-discipline: 'Mao . . . contends that the peculiarities of guerrilla warfare dictate that discipline have a democratic basis and that it be imposed from within, not a product of external compulsion.' Fifth, propaganda, which can assist the guerrillas' aim − undermining the enemy will to resist and achieving an aura of success for insurgent forces − and so 'hearten' the populace in its resistance to the incumbents. Finally, recruitment and operations: in principle only volunteers are acceptable for guerrilla service and they operate only in their home area. This ensures two great advantages over the enemy: superior knowledge of the terrain and superior claim to intelligence from the populace.[36]

Now any political analyst, worthy of the name, will then come up with the question: whose side should we be on – or, more discreetly, whose side should we *not* be on? But this is the one question the operator dare not pose. To the latter, 'it is obviously imperative that the USA, and the West in general, design and employ appropriate doctrine and instrumentalities to aid in the prevention of insurgency warfare in the developing areas'. For in the very process of modernisation it is evident that 'the [indigenous] military will be called upon to back the civil police in providing stability during this period of civil turmoil'.[37] Reactionary élites are the *lesser* evil given that communism is the 'real' enemy of all good patriots.[38]

The problem of the irresistible object (American anti-communism in its global scope) meeting an immovable mass (popular support for insurgency) is obviously acute. It is depicted in Clark Clifford's memorandum on the conference when President Eisenhower handed over to President-elect Kennedy on 19 January 1961:

> President Eisenhower opened the discussion on Laos by saying that the United States was determined to preserve the independence of Laos. . . . President Eisenhower said with considerable emotion that Laos was the key to the entire area of Southeast Asia. He said that if we permitted Laos to fall, then we would have to write off all the area. He stated that we must not permit a communist take-over. . . .
>
> President Eisenhower [concluded this phase of discussion] in commenting philosophically upon the fact that the morale existing in the democratic forces [i.e. the Right wing under General Phoumi Nosavan] in Laos appeared to be disappointing. He wondered aloud why, in interventions of this kind, we always seem to find that the morale of the communist forces was better than that of the democratic forces. His explanation was that the communist philosophy appeared to produce a sense of dedication on the part of its adherents, while there was not the same sense of dedication on the part of those supporting the free forces. He stated that the entire problem of morale was a serious one and would have to be taken into consideration as we became more deeply involved.[39]

Eisenhower's 'philosophy' was indeed a prophetic one. But to reconcile an American world order with elementary justice the 'idealist' operator could only take refuge in illusions: above all the pathetic illusion that in a country like Laos or South Vietnam he will find another

'Magsaysay', who will save the security situation, who will not stoop to 'tainted' measures and in whose personality and policy there is a generous fusion of interests and ideals.

The career of Major General Edward Lansdale, confidant of both Magsaysay and Diem, reputedly the hero of *The Ugly American* ('Hillandale'), provides an apt illustration. According to Lansdale, the Filipino trust in Americans at the time of the Japanese invasion 'depicted the ideal relationship which should exist between peoples who share the same principled beliefs' – a relationship he was to find as friend and adviser to Magsaysay. At the end of his first tour of duty in Vietnam, after his service in the Philippines, he recalled:

> I was convinced, more than ever, that the most pragmatic course for Americans serving in Asia was to heed the idealism of our country's political tenets and make them the basis for our acts. . . . But I was dismayed by what many of my fellow Americans looked upon as strength. We said 'in God we trust' and then put our main trust in material things – money, machines, goods and battalions – to win this struggle. . . . We couldn't afford just to be *against* the communists. We had to be *for* something ourselves.[40]

The trouble is that Lansdale's *practice* – as opposed to his precepts – was to prove just as subversive of 'our country's idealism'. In 1954–5 he headed 'a "cold war" combat team' undertaking paramilitary operations *after* the Geneva Conference, such as 'contaminating the oil supply of the bus company [in Hanoi] . . . taking the first actions for delayed sabotage of the railroad . . . and in writing detailed notes of potential targets for future paramilitary operations'.[41] Meanwhile in South Vietnam, Lansdale refers in his memoirs to the arrival of Filipino volunteers from 'Operation Brotherhood', whose 'one aim' was to 'ease the suffering of their fellow Asians'.[42] In a confidential memorandum to General Maxwell Taylor in July 1961, however, Lansdale revealed that Operation Brotherhood was 'capable of considerable expansion in socio-medical operations to support counter-guerrilla actions. . . . It has a measure of CIA control. Their work was closely coordinated with Vietnamese army operations which cleaned up Vietminh stay-behinds and started stabilising rural areas.'[43] A similar dual role was played by another 'nonprofit, public service corporation', the Freedom Company of the Philippines, which appeared (in the memoirs) 'vividly dedicated to the principle of man's liberty'. In his 1961 memorandum, however, Lansdale explained that this organisation (by then re-named the

Eastern Construction Company) had 'almost untapped potential for unconventional warfare (which was its original mission)'.

In such an atmosphere of deception, black propaganda, sabotage and 'unconventional' warfare, it may seem surprising that Lansdale could also be genuinely concerned about social injustice, bullying by military or police, and 'entrenched corruption'. These, he writes, are grave weaknesses in a country 'that can lead to its downfall'. But Lansdale had 'few illusions' that Washington would adopt the 'attainable ideal' of countering these weaknesses by stressing the need for government to uphold 'the spirit of the country's laws . . . [and] giving social justice to the people'.[44] However, Lansdale's criticism surely applies as much to his *own* activities in helping (by dubious methods) to maintain the Diem regime in power. Although he was actually referring, in another memorandum, to the attitude of US Ambassador Durbrow, the accusation rebounds against him: 'I cannot truly sympathise with Americans who help promote a fascistic state and then get angry when it doesn't act like a democracy.'[45]

The way the operators try to resolve the contradiction between ideal and practice is by reiterating that 'Americans must understand that these [counter-insurgency] struggles are composed of the means that shape the ideological end'[46] of a world made safe for democracy. Yet the more the Americans in Vietnam (and the French in Algeria) met resistance to their 'means', i.e. their efforts to maintain 'fascistic' regimes in power, the more they turned to force to attain their goal. They relied on the expedient solution, the power politics and the 'brute usages of our physical and material means':[47] in effect, torture, brutality and indiscriminate violence in Algeria; massive and ruthless destruction in Vietnam.

From the beginning of 1965, the USA dropped over seven and a half million tons of bombs in Indochina (more under Nixon than under the Johnson administration), compared with two million tons dropped by all the allies in the Second World War.[48] About six million South Vietnamese are thought to have become refugees mainly as a result of artillery and air bombardment.[49] To 'pacify' one NLF-dominated province in the Mekong Delta in 1968 perhaps 5,000 civilians – out of nearly 11,000 'enemy' – were killed in the course of a single operation.[50] These are among the activities which Komer had in mind, when he reported 'more optimistic than ever before' after nearly a year in Vietnam: 'Few of our programmes – civil or military – are very efficient, but we are grinding the enemy down by sheer weight and mass.'[51]

According to a report by the International Peace Research Institute, Stockholm, more than ten times the quantity of napalm employed in the Korean War was used in Indochina, accounting for about 10 per cent of deaths attributable to fighter-bomber attacks. The Institute called in October 1972 for an international conference to draw up rules for air warfare, prohibiting the use of incendiary weapons as 'an appropriate first step towards reasserting the primacy of humanitarian constraint over the demands of military convenience'. A statement prepared for the UN Secretary-General on 17 October 1972 recommended that the General Assembly work out measures to prohibit the 'use, production, development and stockpiling of napalm and other incendiary weapons'. According to the report: 'A clear line must be drawn between what is permissible in time of war and what is not permissible.'[52]

The use of napalm as a 'conventional' weapon by the armed forces of France (in Indochina), Israel (against Egyptians), Egypt (against Yemenis) and numerous Latin American and some Southeast Asian governments (against guerrillas) marks a step back into barbarism compared with the situation at the turn of the century when the Hague Convention outlawed the dum-dum bullet. Yet, as Sir Robert Thompson has emphasised, writing on Vietnam, 'the war must be won in an acceptable way' and the use of napalm or weapons of mass destruction is utterly to be condemned.[53] Britain indeed showed the way by abandoning the use of incendiary weapons after the start of the Malayan campaign and 'forgoing them altogether – in spite of alleged military pleas – in the Aden fighting'.[54] Napalm is not in itself a decisive weapon: it is a weapon of terror, a symbol of the frightfulness of modern war. Yet if there is to be some restraint on objectives, implicit in the notion of limited war, there must surely be some restraint on methods of waging war.

SMASH

The US Army's 'Southeast Asia Multiple Sensor Armament System Helicopter' (SMASH) is one of the 'advanced research projects' spawned by the war in Vietnam – an area singled out by Maxwell Taylor himself as early as 1963 for its 'importance . . . as a laboratory'.[55] Under the SMASH programme, infra-red detectors are installed in attack helicopters. These are among the mechanical systems – 'sensors' – developed by researchers under contract to the US Defense Department

for the detection and surveillance of guerrilla forces in Southeast Asia –
and elsewhere. The Department's 'Defense Special Projects Group',
according to its then Director, General Deane, 'is authorised use of the
highest industrial priority to expedite its development'. This was
disclosed at the 1970 Senate Hearings, entitled 'Investigation into the
Electronic Battlefield Program'.[56]

What are the policy implications of the enormous sums of money –
over one and a half billion dollars, according to official figures – devoted
to the 'research, procurement and emplacement' of electronic sensors
and anti-personnel munitions? How does the 'software' approach –
social science research into counter-insurgency – compare in
effectiveness? And what of the other countries involved in the
'experiments'?[57]

The rationale for the technological approach was set out by the then
Director of the Advanced Research Projects Agency, Charles Herzfield,
in 1968:

> The ARPA reconnaissance system and detector programmes are
> now concentrated on the problem of detecting and locating insurgent
> forces, and their basing and logistic systems. The guerrilla tech-
> niques characteristic of insurgent operations require a comple-
> mentary mix of ground-based and air-borne equipment which will
> allow our forces to find and fix small groups of personnel at night and
> in the jungle environment typical of Southeast Asia.[58]

The Deputy Director of Defense Research and Engineering of the
Defense Department, Leonard Sullivan, Jr, explained:

> Almost all of these new equipments have operational utility beyond
> Southeast Asia and will become part of our post-war standard. Hence
> our efforts [in Vietnam] contribute not only to our combat capabilities
> in Southeast Asia, but to the combat potential of our future tactical
> forces.[59]

The 'exciting' possibilities for 'instrumentation of the entire battlefield'
(Sullivan again)[60] were a major objective of research under 'project
Agile', which included both soft and hardware methods; after the demise
of 'Agile' in 1974 the technological projects were taken over by another of
ARPA's main divisions.[61] Agile, according to the official memorandum
of 1967, was responsible for research and development 'supporting the
DoD's [Department of Defense] operations in remote areas, associated

with the problems of *actual* or *potential* limited or subversive wars involving allied or friendly nations in such areas'. The project, according to Klare, had field offices in Vietnam, Korea, Thailand and Iran, with an annual operating budget of some $30 million prior to 1969, and afterwards, as a result of Congressional cuts, of about $20 million.[62] Project Agile is better known for its role in electronic 'counter-infiltration' and interdiction operations along the Ho Chi Minh Trail. (These surveillance facilities became an object of contention in Thailand after the end of the Vietnam War; the facilities were closed down, and American personnel withdrawn, by July 1976.)

Next to Vietnam, Thailand was the main 'laboratory' for counter-insurgency theory and practice. From January 1973 until the surrender of Saigon in April 1975, Thailand replaced Vietnam as headquarters for all US air operations in Southeast Asia. However, after July 1976 only 270 US military advisers remain – compared with a total, at the height of the Vietnam War, of over 47,000 US military personnel.

Thailand has ceased to be the US counter-insurgency laboratory: but the *products* tested there are available for use elsewhere.[63] Thailand's role over the past decade, which other 'suitable' candidates in the Third World can now be expected to take over,[64] therefore amply repays study. The relative value of Thailand and Vietnam for the USA has been nicely put: Vietnam was the 'quick-fix' area, where research was on an immediate basis and solely for use in that country; 'Thailand is used to define and proof-test longer-term projects, not only for this country, but for others which are located near the electro-magnetic equator'.[65]

But this was not merely a one-way process, providing little in the form of benefits for the 'host country'. For the 'laboratory' was developing social characteristics of its own, which made it suitable, not just for product-testing but for applying the duly perfected products in a home-grown environment. Dr Herzfield, then Director of ARPA, testified before Congress in 1967 on what were then regarded as stimulating prospects for software research:

Last year ARPA initiated major R & D programmes to assist the Royal Thai Government and the U.S. Mission in Thailand in their effort to suppress the growing communist insurgency in that country's northeast provinces. Under the rural security program, ARPA will marshal the R & D community to (a) gather and collate critical information on the local geography, the way of life of the local people, and on their attitudes towards the Government; (b) to set up and help maintain current data files on insurgency incidents and operations, and on the many Government programs and activities undertaken for counter-insurgency purposes in the northeast; and (c) provide assistance in analysing the effectiveness of various counter-insurgency programs. . . . This program will mark the first time that R & D has been given a major role in supporting a counter insurgency in a comprehensive way, from the earliest stages of the conflict.[66]

An 'exciting' prospect indeed.

Subsequent measures to counter-insurgency include, as US Ambassador Unger revealed in 1969,

the design and establishment, as a pilot project, of Thailand's first continuously up-dated storage and retrieval system for counter-insurgency intelligence data keyed to the country's 39,000 villages; a manual concerning the Meo, a non-Thai [hill-tribe] ethnic minority presently being infiltrated by the communists; and development within the Royal Thai Air Force of a capability to perform [deleted] reconnaissance.[67]

In addition, the so-called Academic Advisory Council for Thailand (AACT), composed of American scholars and officials, was established 'to support and strengthen the operations of the U.S. aid program in Thailand' – an aid programme 75 per cent of whose effort (as in Laos and South Vietnam) was devoted to counter-insurgency, particularly to strengthening police and para-military forces.[68]

One of the most exciting software projects was the 'Village Security Pilot Study' in northeast Thailand, to provide information on the location, size, economy, leadership, population characteristics, and proximity to police posts and military bases, of every village.[69] Stanford Research Institute (SRI) was given the contract to develop a 'Computerised Village Information System (VIST)'. VIST would collect, store and retrieve information 'in a form usable by the Royal Thai Government' on 'conditions and events in the villages and towns of Thailand'. As SRI's President, Charles Anderson, stated in 1969, VIST would assist the Thai Government to deal with 'civil disorders' and 'subversive activity' and 'other problems peculiar to a peasant society'.[70]

But, confessed the then ARPA Director, Dr Eberhardt Rechtin, in 1970 – later promoted to Assistant Secretary of Defense (Telecommunications) – the 'results of past research have been mixed'.

Projects like border security, which rely on instrumentation, are paying off well, while others, notably village security, are 'not being implemented for a variety of non-technical reasons'. 'The "core of the problem" is the relationship between the Thai Government and the people – so "political" a relationship', Dr Rechtin concluded in a burst of Pentagonese, that 'it has proven generally impractical as a field of ARPA research producing implemented results.'

Rechtin went on to tell the House Appropriations Committee that ARPA's 'greatest single problem area' was 'unquestionably overseas research in counter-insurgency'; as a result of reduced expenditure (from a peak of $16 million in 1969 to under $7 million in 1971) 'R & D on the relationship of the host country's government or military organisation to the population will be minimised'. Besides financing RAND's analytical studies of insurgency, Project Agile would henceforth concentrate on 'small independent action forces', equipped with portable laser and infra-red devices, and 'intrusion detection sensors and subsystems'.[71]

This is a revealing statement. The software counter-insurgency programme cannot be carried out properly in the existing political environment. So it is necessary to switch to hardware, which hardly depends on the vagaries of politics: indeed 'laser technology', as Rechtin's successor, Dr Lukasik, explained, 'offers prospects of an entirely new type of military capability'. With 'primary emphasis' on 'technological superiority', research and development are concentrated on sensors, computerised intelligence, lightweight weapons and such achievements as remotely-piloted vehicles, which 'will carry television and night thermal imaging sensors to acquire targets, missiles and cannon-launched guided projectiles to attack hard targets with small warheads'.[72]

With such an Orwellian vision of the near future – for sensors, we are told, can replace tasks that are 'error-prone and extremely tedious for humans' – what need is there for the painstaking, uncertain and often disillusioning methods of social science research? For ARPA's village surveys and investigations of rural attitudes had indeed come up with a problem: villagers suspected, feared or disliked 'their' government – or rather, the agents of government – as much as, if not more than, they distrusted the insurgents. Why should this be so? Puey Ungphakorn, former Governor of the Bank of Thailand and a man of indisputable integrity, has suggested the answer. Instead of a policy of repression, he urged a truce with the insurgents, whom he said it was foolish to brand entirely as 'communists': some are communist, some Muslims (in the south), some tribal (in the north), and some are citizens seeking revenge on oppressive officials.[73]

Consider the northern revolt. It stems largely from a clash of cultures – the Meo, Yao, Karen and other hill peoples on the one hand, the lowland Thais on the other – and from growing competition for land. One of the first incidents between the Meo and the Thai authorities occurred in 1967 when a Meo village was burned down by the police. It arose out of 'a series of extortion attempts' by Thai officials. In efforts to maintain security the Thai army carried out a sweep of border areas in October 1967; but the situation was 'aggravated by the army's preferred tactic of napalming entire villages suspected of harbouring enemy personnel'.[74]

The insurgency in northeast Thailand is particularly significant because of the size of the region – about one-third of Thailand – its historic and cultural links with Laos and its depressed economic condition: earnings per head are about one-half the national average. Here villager–official, rural–urban, regional–centre relations are peculiarly ambivalent. Consider just two factors – the role of the police, and of other government officials.

First, when the police are present they provide rural security; but it can be at the cost of harassment, corruption and exactions, which figure frequently in villagers' complaints. For the police are poorly paid and so have an interest in seeing that laws and regulations – such as control of tree cutting and pig slaughter, prohibition of home stills, etc. – are enforced, unless they (the police) are bribed to desist. Police powers of investigation and arrest of alleged suspects are widely distrusted.

Second, effective official leadership is needed to carry out development projects but it is generally lacking. What leadership there is, according to villagers, is often of the wrong kind: the power, arrogance and arbitrary behaviour of the traditional 'boss' or overlord. Thus although government officials start with an apparent advantage – the villagers' customary respect for authority and their passivity or compliance even in the face of mistreatment – this outward show of acceptance may conceal strong feelings of resentment, which can break out in non-co-operation, mute obstruction or violence.[75]

Social science research can discover these problems, but it cannot solve them. This is the business of politics, which in Thailand still means the politics of business, broadly speaking: this ranges from minor official corruption which may still have serious consequences in 'sensitive areas' (as we have seen) to massive extortion by 'trading generals'; among these, Field Marshal Prapat, former deputy Prime Minister, had amassed the equivalent of over $18 million in assets uncovered by the end of 1973.

This is why Dr Rechtin recommended that counter-insurgency, instead of getting embroiled in intractable 'problem areas', where nothing is clear-cut, or if it is, has disturbing implications, should rely instead on the dead certainties of hardware: the sensors will detect, the bombs explode, regardless of what people think, or how governments (mis)behave.

RAND's studies of insurgency, according to Dr Rechtin, show the right spirit. Their purpose is to 'analyse insurgent conflicts as you would analyse nuclear conflicts', concerned only with the 'pluses' and 'minuses', and 'endeavouring as best as you can to get the morality out of the equation because there have been good revolutions put down by bad governments and bad revolutions brought down by good governments, and all kinds of combinations'; so the concentration is on 'what are the tactics'.[76]

Neanderthal Man lives. Air Force Neanderthal advocates 'bombing North Vietnam back to the stone age', which is itself stone-age behaviour (apologies to the stone age). Scientist-operator Neanderthal finds it painful or puzzling to think, impossible to re-think, about the complexities of politics and civil war. It is not surprising that George Kennan should 'sometimes wonder' whether American 'democracy is not uncomfortably similar to one of those prehistoric monsters with a body as long as this room and a brain the size of a pin. . . . Once he grasps [that his interests are being disturbed] he lays about him with such blind determination that he not only destroys his adversary but largely wrecks his native habitat.'[77]

Dr Rechtin does not seem to realise that whether a revolution is 'good' or 'bad' is not simply a moral evaluation; it is also a question of political judgment. Now there are certain criteria, generally well known – awareness of the evidence, analytical skills, consistency and so forth – which must be met in the social as in the physical sciences to permit an informed judgment to be made. Further, what Dr Rechtin says about revolution naturally applies to any political phenomenon, American foreign policy, for example, or even Dr Rechtin himself. Because it is hard to 'know the whole story', because it is difficult to judge correctly, without disagreement, or controversy, or even different shades of interpretation, this is *no reason* to abdicate from both political and moral responsibility and to fall back instead on the use of force.

To the Dr Rechtins of the world, the neutral technicians in charge of enormous resources, the situation is given: policy is no concern of theirs. But carrying out that policy – to help our (designated) friends; to destroy our (designated) enemies – that they will do, as efficiently and inventively as time and money (the Defense R & D Budget for fiscal year 1979 amounted to $12 billion)[78] will allow. The 'concentration is on the tactics', the research and development of an infernal paraphernalia of seismic, magnetic, acoustic and olfactory devices, the spherical bomblets and gravel mines, the incendiary cluster bombs, the perfected products of 'limited war laboratories', of Corporations ('Atlantic Research'), Institutes (of Science and Technology) and the Lincoln Laboratory (all worthy of their name), of years of painstaking research on 'environmental extremes' (deserts, high altitudes, dense evergreen forests, the 'humid tropics . . . are about twenty per cent of the world's land area'), of devoted work on the 'instant airbases', prepackaged for use on newly cleared or abandoned airstrips; 'almost all these equipments have operational utility beyond Southeast Asia', the rapid deployment of airborne units and 'hunter-killer' teams, ready to act with lethal efficiency 'through the use of data links, computer-assisted intelligence evaluation and automatic fire control', opening up all these 'very exciting horizons as to what we can do five or ten years from now . . . instrumentation of the entire battlefield . . . a "Year 2000" vision. . .'.[79] SMASH!

9 ⋆ *Implications of involvement*

America's military withdrawal from mainland Southeast Asia is widely considered to mark a turning point in American foreign policy – that is, away from intervention in the internal affairs of Third World countries. This is how the Nixon administration's policy of détente with Russia and rapprochement with China – following Johnson's reversal in Vietnam – is customarily represented.[1] This and the policies of subsequent administrations seem to denote an end to the ideological fervour and practical excesses of the era of containment, which had resulted in over-commitment to 'unsound' causes; and to mark the beginning of – in Europe terms, a return to – the 'realistic' management of balance of power. Yet the implications of *managing* the global balance need to be explored. They are by no means as reassuring as its advocates believe.

The basic features of America's global policy have been admirably set out by Kissinger, in a way that clearly commands the support of the Carter administration, whatever the differences in style and tactics. Just as Carter refers (in his address of 10 May 1977) to the ambiguous situation of co-operation and competition with the Soviet Union and plans to 'manage this dual relationship properly . . . leading to an increasingly stable relationship', so Kissinger explains:

> We must balance off Soviet power around the world through a combination of political, military and economic means. In the Far East, the PRC [People's Republic of China] must be part of our political calculations. . . . We must contain the Soviets and prevent their expansion either through Western weakness or through the application of military force. To do this we must achieve domestic support for a long-term conception of our national interest. We must [also] draw the Soviet Union into relationships which are both concrete and practical and we must create the maximum incentives for a moderate Soviet course.[2]

This is a 'delicate and complex' policy: striving for an equilibrium of power on the one hand, for 'habits of mutual restraint, coexistence and ultimately cooperation' on the other.[3] Now all the indications are that this balance – between major allies and with adversaries – requires 'manipulation from above': the great powers seek to impose 'world order' on the lesser breeds below. But the 'order' is inherently unstable, because it reflects both the rivalry and co-operation of the imposing powers. To restrain the 'destabilising' tendencies of America's rivals, therefore, also calls for US 'manipulation from below': to prevent or reduce internal or external challenges to client regimes, which if successful could adversely affect the overall balance.[4] This prophylactic policy is most prudently and economically served by aiming at 'self-reliance' for Third World regimes, so that the internal stability of each contributes to the external stability of all.

Such are the implications of the post-Vietnam doctrine. But the practice is more problematic. For the global objective of a super-power remains what it was: an international environment satisfactory to American political and economic enterprise. It is the *means* to attain this goal, 'adjusting' to changing realities, that have altered. In effect, the intention is *involvement without intervention*: to maintain the essentials of the global system without recourse to the domestically (and internationally) unacceptable costs of direct military action.

Even the problem of Vietnam in the early 1970s fitted conceptually into the new scheme of things. It required a dual strategy: on the one hand, carefully graduated withdrawals of US troops; not too much at a time, which would upset the confidence of Saigon; not too little which would deprive the adversary of an 'incentive' to negotiate. On the other hand, 'Vietnamisation' phasing in as the Americans phased out. The planned process: to complete the US-sponsored 'military modernisation' programme (*before* negotiations were brought to a conclusion) underpinned by massive military and economic aid. The intended result: the establishment of a self-reliant Thieu regime, not only to vindicate American efforts (if not judgment) in the past, but to present a model of stability for the future.

Involvement without intervention – assistance without combat forces – did not work in Vietnam, Cambodia or Laos. It did not work in Angola. What are its prospects, even under more 'normal' conditions, elsewhere? This chapter is an attempt to answer this question. I shall first examine the ambiguities of the 'Nixon Doctrine' with regard to interests and commitments in the global balance. Second, I shall analyse

US 'involvement' in the Third World in terms of the 'push' factor, i.e. global compulsions, whether these are old strains persisting from the era of containment or new varieties generated by the balance of power; and then the 'pull' factor: the way in which the requirements of the global system *engage* American patronage in the domestic processes of Third World clients. Third, I shall assess the combination of push and pull, the outcome of which takes two main forms: the normal form of 'preventive' involvement; and the 'pathological' form of crisis involvement. Finally, in a separate 'Conclusion', I shall discuss the contrary arguments in favour of, on the one hand, US strategic withdrawal and, on the other, a 'strong' American global presence to deter communist expansion; and put forward my own suggestions.

Nixon Doctrine: two views[5]

The 'key elements' of the Nixon Doctrine are:

> The United States will keep all its treaty commitments. We shall provide a shield if a nuclear power threatens. . . . In cases involving other types of aggression we shall furnish military and economic assistance when requested and as appropriate. But we shall look to the nation directly threatened to assume the primary responsibility of providing the manpower for its defence.[6]

The 'doctrine' is plausible in the abstract. The question, in practice, however, is whether it does or does not provide adequate guidance to *distinguish* between 'unsound' and 'essential' commitments, to *extricate* from the former without damaging the latter, and to *reconcile* what I call 'manipulation from below' (US involvement with Third World regimes) with 'manipulation from above' (maintaining a balance among the powers).

Three factors must be considered. First, the distinction between national 'interests' and commitments. Second, their relationship to stable or unstable environments: in other words, where there is muted or ineffective adversary reaction, on the one hand, or determined and effective opposition, on the other. And finally the doctrine must be considered from the perspective of global policy: where the emphasis is on the political aspects (contributing to détente) or on the strategic aspects – i.e. maintaining the alliance system and involvement in the internal security of allies and 'friends'.

The official view, as regards the first two factors, is that 'our interests must shape our commitments, rather than the other way around'; it tends to assume the existence of a stable environment. The critical view, however, stems from the belief that priority is still given to the preservation of existing assets (that is, US backing for commitments regardless of 'interests', discriminatingly defined by area and circumstance) often in an unstable environment.

This relates to the third factor. Under conditions of stability and 'realism' (where interests shape commitments) the official interpretation emphasises the tactical role of the doctrine in the strategy of higher policy: détente between the super-powers, in an era of negotiation, leading to the creation of a 'stable structure of peace'. But the critical interpretation – viewing 'assets' as 'liabilities' – is concerned with the damaging effect of open-ended commitments to insecure allies, possibly in regions of low strategic importance, on the overall balance.

Now the official interpretation takes the doctrine seriously both as a profession of faith (in the future world order) and as a statement of intent (how the USA will act with regard to its commitments so as to help bring about that world order). The critical interpretation takes political behaviour seriously – noting that vested interests, bureaucratic inertia and long-established commitments inhibit or contradict the proposed changes – and it considers the doctrine sceptically, if not cynically, either as a facile attempt to have it both ways (extensive commitments *and* a structure of peace) or as a dignified façade hiding the ugly reality of 'tilting', expediency and *realpolitik*.

Although it is beyond the power of the USA to 'have it both ways', it is still possible, from an optimistic point of view, to reconcile carefully-defined national interests with a stable balance of power. Indeed the Nixon Doctrine, in its self-reliant aspect, proposes a discriminating approach to potentially critical areas: 'In contemplating new commitments' – old ones that are 'unsound' will *in time* be liquidated – 'we will apply rigorous yardsticks: What precisely is our national concern? What precisely is the threat? What would be the efficacy of our involvement?' The more US foreign policy is based on a 'realistic assessment' of our own and other interests, the presidential report goes on, 'the more effective our role in the world can be'.[7]

Yet it is not so much the question of new as of *old* commitments that is the flaw in the doctrine. Unsound commitments – i.e. backing *unstable* regimes in areas not of major strategic importance to America – should be ended, according to the Doctrine, for this very reason.[8] But it is argued that this cannot be done quickly for fear of undermining the 'confidence' of other allies in US readiness to come to their assistance. 'Phasing out' gradually, on the other hand, means continuing to underwrite an unstable ally for a dangerously open-ended period.[9] For as long as the ally remains unstable it cannot be 'abandoned' – at least without loss of prestige. As Kissinger points out: 'Given our central role, a loss in our credibility invites international chaos.'[10] Thus the guarantor ends up with precisely the risk of being 'obliged' to intervene (in order to retain credibility), which it is the aim of the doctrine to avoid. Here in all its ambiguity is the desire, but not necessarily the ability to see the USA extricated from rash and ill-thought-out commitments, undertaken for reasons of outmoded global strategy, to governments whose inability to cope with domestic difficulties lays an unnecessarily heavy burden on the intervening world power.

For this reason, the *official* interpretation of the Nixon Doctrine suggests a return to the 'indirect approach', characteristic of British imperial policy during much of the nineteenth century; this was also characteristic of American policy, apart from Central America and the Caribbean – i.e. economic expansion free of political entanglements – up to the outbreak of the Second World War. *But* America's current international responsibilities cannot be assured merely by maintaining the network of political and economic ties involved in the system of 'bargains' with Third World élites.

As Gallagher and Robinson point out with reference to nineteenth-century Britain, where informal means failed to provide security for its enterprises, then it was necessary to resort to direct rule. Both were intertwined aspects of expansion overseas. Political action aided the growth of commercial supremacy which, in turn, strengthened political influence. The latter varied with the economic value of the territory, the strength of the political structure, the readiness of rulers to collaborate with the metropolitan power's commercial or strategic purposes, the ability of the native society to undergo economic changes without external control, the extent to which domestic and foreign policy situations permitted external intervention, and how far foreign rivals allowed a free hand. 'Stable governments' were encouraged as 'good investment risks', while weaker or unsatisfactory states were liable to be coerced into a more co-operative attitude.[11]

The inescapable problem of what methods are to be employed by a super-power to maintain 'supremacy' in an international system of states with such diversity of capability and authority *cannot* be resolved according to uniform principles – but only by a process of discrimination which establishes concrete priorities.

Given the immense power of the USA, the variety of forms in which it can be used (military, political or economic) and the many opportunities available in the Third World for using it, the question whether priority is to be given to commitments *or* interests (including the enlightened self-interest implicit in a stable structure of peace), to a 'global' *or* a discriminating policy towards friends and allies (according to the calibre of their regimes and their strategic importance to the USA or lack of it) and to taking due account of the reasons for instability *or* acting on the mere presumption of internal subversion or external manipulation – this question is of vital importance. The doctrine is plausible: but what of the performance?

Push and pull: global alarms

Despite the intention of the Nixon Doctrine to discriminate between one commitment and another, universalised fears continue to dominate American policy. As recent administrations perceive the situation even after Vietnam, the threat to the global balance remains; it is the nature of the threat that has changed. To the Cold War ideologists, *subversion* leading to insurgency was primarily the threat – 'sweeping' through the developing world – which the adversary could then turn to his advantage. To the post-Vietnam 'realists', reverting to a more traditional stance, the power of the (rival) *state* is the threat: subversion is not so much the instrument as the opportunity.

Yet if the focus has altered, the end result is much the same. For, as Roger Hilsman noted in a period of intense Cold War anxiety, the threat of insurgency is not because it may mean the coming to power of indigenous revolutionaries in a particular country; but because it can be exploited by Soviet leaders, who consider it 'the best way of using force to expand the communist empire with the least risk'. The theory of wars of national liberation 'enables Moscow and Peiping [*sic*] to manipulate for their own purposes the political, economic and social revolutionary fervor that is now sweeping much of the underdeveloped world'.[12] The idea, still more succinctly put, is that revolutionary movements are puppets, without autonomous existence: thus the Pathet Lao in Laos, according to a senior State Department official in 1961, 'can be turned on and off from long range'.[13]

In the era of containment, subversion was (subjectively) strong, while the military might of the adversary – apart from Europe – was comparatively weak. Now, with greater experience of the Third World, fear of subversion has lost some of its emotional force; but the growing power of the adversary has taken its place:

> [The Soviets] now possess the capability to project great power at great distances; they continue to improve their ability to operate naval units, aircraft and re-supply forces far from their shores. Their command, control and communications capabilities are already global. This is a striking transformation for a nation historically preoccupied with defense of the homeland. . . .[14] *The Soviet Union can achieve dominance in deployed military technology in the 1980s.*[15]

'For the first time in history', Kissinger explains, 'the Soviet Union can threaten distant places beyond the Eurasian landmass – including the United States.' With no part of the world outside the range of its military forces, 'the USSR has begun to define its interests and objectives in global terms. Soviet diplomacy has thrust into the Middle East, Africa and Asia. This evolution is now rooted in real power.'[16] These are 'pressures' the USA must resist.[17]

Carter, too, in his address of 17 March 1978, points to the 'ominous inclination on the part of the Soviet Union to use its military power – to intervene in local conflicts with advisors, with equipment, and with full logistical support and encouragement for mercenaries from other communist countries'; while the CIA Director, Admiral Turner, refers to the 'imperialist thrust' of the Soviet Union 'pushing their opportunities wherever they develop', but not to the point 'where it involves a major commitment' (interview with *U.S. News & World Report*, 16 May 1977).

These official US perceptions of the Soviet attempt 'to convert military power into political advantage' (Turner) are, unfortunately, both correct and exaggerated. In so far as they are correct – in the assessment of current *capabilities* – they reflect the actual environment of super-power rivalry and suspicion that continues to promote tension and conflict. In so far as they are exaggerated – by imputing more sinister *intentions* – they encourage an excessive reaction which tends to create the very situation that has been predicted.

To repeat: such fears are not groundless; but the way in which they are interpreted, including the perceived consequences of 'not acting' in response to the threat – 'we will surely soon find ourselves in a period of chaos and peril that will dwarf all previous experience'[18] – prompts *over-reaction* by the USA in precisely that arena of super-power rivalry in which it believes itself most vulnerable, but where its presence can be most felt: the countries of the Third World.

Manipulation from below

'Manipulation from above' – the American strategy of balance of power – has, as we have seen, the dual but ambiguous aim of 'sharing' the responsibility for world order (with major allies, with major adversaries), but at the same time of preventing adversaries from 'usurping' too great a share. 'Manipulation from below' – action with, through, and sometimes in spite of Third World regimes – is an integral part of the 'above' strategy. It is designed to prevent America's rivals from taking advantage of unstable conditions in the Third World to advance their power or to strengthen their ideological influence, either of which, from the American standpoint, would adversely affect the overall balance.

US methods of checking or eliminating internal challenges to client regimes (causing 'instability') are, to recapitulate, either suppressive or reformist. Suppression is to assist regimes to put down by force any significant movements of opposition. Reformism is to improve the regime's image and performance – its legitimacy – to the extent that dissident movements either do not arise or, if they do, are easily contained. Reformism is both more compatible with American domestic values and more 'economical'; but reformist policies which, for one reason or another, fail to achieve their aims tend to give way to suppression. This, like it or not, is the *political* environment in which American policy (whether directly aimed at the Third World, or indirectly at the global balance) is engaged. This political environment is intimately linked with the military and economic environments discussed below.

The *military* environment can be considered under three heads: US militarisation of allies and 'friends' as an essential component of 'self-reliance'; the technological interdependence between arms-selling patron and receptive client in the use of increasingly sophisticated weaponry;[19] and the problem of nuclear proliferation, which the US has contributed to, but also tried to prevent, with regard either to rival or potentially rival regional clients – such as Brazil and Argentina; Egypt, Israel and Iran; Pakistan and India – or to clients in a hostile or insecure environment – such as South Africa, Taiwan and South Korea.

Here I shall only briefly discuss the first point: the militarisation of allies and friends. Now the logic of self-reliance is that Third World regimes are in a position to defend themselves (and thus not require direct US military intervention in their defence) both against conventional external threats and against internal dissidence. American assistance – military, political or economic – is directed toward that end. For, as Kissinger correctly observes, all foreign policy begins with security.[20] Geared to security requirements, the Nixon Doctrine of 'assistance' to allied and friendly regimes inevitably engenders an increasingly repressive Third World: first, because the USA, in its basic pursuit of stability, is not overly concerned with the fact that internal discontent may well be justified and hence should be conciliated rather than suppressed; second because US policy is precisely to *hand over* the military and economic wherewithal (i.e. the power to enforce decisions) to its clients – so that they, and not the USA, can do the job. If the client, facing domestic troubles, prefers coercion to persuasion there is not a great deal that even a more enlightened, or more far-sighted, patron can do about it. This is because the patron's fear of creating 'instability' (as a result of pressing for reforms) tends to prevail over imperial distaste at clients' methods or anxiety over their long-term consequences: as we have seen from Guatemala to Chile, and from South Vietnam to South Korea.

Now the implications of militarised and repressive Third World regimes are highly disturbing, for three reasons. First, because of the ensuing *incongruity* between US foreign policy (assisting militarisation and hence repression) and American domestic democratic values: this makes it more difficult for the administration to achieve that 'domestic consensus' which it rightly sees as essential to an effective foreign policy (see also the next section, below). Second, because US co-operation with repressive regimes involves co-operation, above all, with *particular elements* of the ruling class – the hard-line military, security police, conservative bureaucrats, right-wing parties or movements (where they exist) and the venal press; moreover, the *form* of co-operation – counter-insurgency, intelligence, interrogations, propaganda and 'law and order' – tends to 'pervert' those who co-operate, and this perversion feeds back into US domestic society (see also, below). The final disturbing factor, to those who believe in peaceful change, is that repression may more effectively eliminate dissidence (consider Chiang Kai-shek's massacre of Chinese communists in 1927) than conciliation may do; but it may also result in the long-term build-up of an organised and determined revolutionary movement (China after 1937).

The *economic* environment is also one of 'partnership': between American corporate enterprise and Third World regime. Its *open* aspect is revealed, on the 'host' side, by investment promotion policies, tax holidays, tariff laws, labour regulations and so on; on the corporate side by loan raising and repatriation of profits and by the introduction of scientific management, modern technology, labour training and product marketing. An example of the 'open' way in which the system operates to maintain or (in this case) restore a favourable climate for business enterprise is that of the collapse of Peruvian radical-nationalism in 1975–6.

Peru, one of the poorest countries in South America, had been 'hard hit by sharply rising import prices for oil and food, declining copper prices, a small anchovy catch [a major export], an oil boom that fizzled out and economic mismanagement by the "revolutionary" military regime' (i.e. the attempt to carry out land reforms – 82 per cent of all farm land had been occupied by large estates – nationalisation of foreign enterprises, worker participation, social welfare and a heavy arms bill). Peru's international current account deficit soared and international reserves fell below zero. President Velasco, leader of the 1968 revolution, was ousted in August 1975. In March 1976 World Bank President McNamara 'lectured' the new Peruvian Cabinet on financial discipline; American banks, approached for loans, insisted that strong remedial measures were necessary if Peru were to qualify as credit-worthy. Austerity measures were announced in June. The currency was devalued in August. By September 1976 a group of the largest US banks decided to approve a new loan to Peru, 'following a conservative swing in that country's economic policies'.[21]

The *covert* aspect is also illustrated by a recent news item:

> The biggest producer of aluminium, Alcoa, voluntarily disclosed to SEC [US Securities and Exchange Commission] that in 1971 the US Ambassador to Jamaica had solicited, and Alcoa had paid, a contribu- tion of at least $25,000 to the ruling party in that country. The purpose: financing an 'educational program' to sell Jamaican citizens on the advantages of permitting huge investments like Alcoa's in Jamaican bauxite.[22]

Note the 'economical' engagement of the various elements: the US government (through its representative) taps the US corporation for a tiny fraction of its wealth (extracted from operations in the host country and elsewhere) to 'promote' the then ruling party so as to continue the favourable conditions for the production of more wealth and the assurance of more stability . . . and, crowning achievement, to persuade the victims of the manoeuvre (Jamaica's unwitting citizens) that they are actually its beneficiaries. As William Colby, former Director of the CIA, explains: 'Isn't it easier [to do it this way] than to defend ourselves with bombs and soldiers? Isn't it easier to help some political group?'[23]

This combination of strategic, political and economic aims – the mirror image of the adversaries' designs on vital raw materials, human resources and strategic areas[24] – may realistically be termed 'subversion from above': i.e. it is normally undertaken in *collaboration* with Third World regimes, or important sections of them. This distinguishes it from the adversaries' 'subversion from below', which is normally in opposition to those regimes. (Of course, the position is reversed in the case of a regime considered 'unfriendly' to American political, economic or strategic interests: but this is exceptional.) Subversion from above is aimed at the preservation or enhancement of the patron–client relationship – in all relevant fields, political, military and economic, and whether the activities are covert, 'undisclosed' or overt. Covert activities, in other words, are merely one aspect of the total relationship and their role is determined by that relationship.[25]

The same situation applies, as I have pointed out, to the adversary – but in reverse. Indeed action by the one tends to provoke counter-action by the other.[26] What I am concerned with here, however, is not so much that such activities (overt or covert) exist as their *implications* for American policy and 'performance'. This requires a brief summary of the main facets of covert political action, given in Table 5.

Table 5   Congressional reports on US covert operations

1   *History*. Post-Second World War covert political activities started in the late 1940s. These were mainly to finance and support labour unions, political parties and other groups in Western Europe in their efforts to resist a communist takeover. During and after the Korean War, paramilitary operations received priority (Report of the Senate Select Committee to study Governmental Operations with Respect to Intelligence activities – hereafter the Church Committee – of April 1976; 'Foreign and Military Intelligence', Report No. 94-755, 26 April 1976, pp. 22–4).

2   *Directives*. In 1955, National Security Council directive NSC 5412/2 instructed the CIA to counter, reduce and discredit 'international communism' throughout the world – not merely in areas contiguous to the Soviet Union or China. Covert operations were

Table 5 contd

---

defined as any covert activities related to propaganda, economic warfare, political action (including sabotage, demolition and assistance to resistance movements) and all activities compatible with the directive. NSC 5412/2 was superseded by National Security Decision Memorandum 40, dated 17 February 1970, which authorised secret activities to further official US programmes and policies abroad – without reference to communism. The CIA was considered responsible for devising its own programmes. As CIA General Counsel Memorandum 4/6/62 puts it: 'The average person, both in government and outside, is thinking along normal lines and to develop clandestine cold war activities properly [requires] persons knowing both the capabilities and limitations of clandestine action' (Interim Report of the Church Committee, No. 94-465, 'Alleged Assassination Plots Involving Foreign Leaders' – hereafter 'Alleged Assassinations' – dated 20 November 1967, p. 9).

3 *Action Categories*: Covert activities since 1965, according to the Pike Committee, fall into three main categories: (i) electoral support; (ii) media and propaganda; (iii) paramilitary. Those projects involving heavy expenditure of funds or classified as 'politically sensitive' required the approval of the '40 Committtee', chaired by the Presidential Assistant for National Security Affairs.

(i) Electoral Support. Nearly one-third of approved projects took the form of 'financial election support to foreign parties and individuals', chiefly in developing countries. In one case examined in detail by the Pike Committee (Italy) $65 million had been spent for this purpose in twenty years; during the 1972 election campaign alone nearly $10 million went chiefly to 'a major political party' and to 'a political organisation created and supported by CIA' (Pike Committee, as cited, pp. 35–6).

(ii) Media and Propaganda. Nearly one-third of approved projects. They included 'support of friendly media . . . insertion of articles into the local press, and distribution of books and leaflets'. The CIA acknowledged that free-lance journalists and 'stringers' with whom 'the Agency has a relationship are often directed to insert Agency-composed "news" articles into foreign publications and wire services'. From time to time 'planted' stories may (unintentionally) find their way into the American press. To ensure that official Washington is not deceived, the CIA 'maintains high-level liaison with the Department of State and the U.S. Information Agency to identify spurious stories' (Pike Committee, pp. 40, 43). Such fabricated stories were also apparently planted during the Angola affair (*Newsweek*, 'New Book of Revelations', 22 May 1978).

(iii) Paramilitary Operations. Nearly one quarter of approved projects, but 'by far the most expensive' category. They include 'secret armies; financial support to groups engaged in hostilities; paramilitary training and advisers; and shipment of arms, ammunition and other military equipment'. The great majority of these projects were proposed by parties outside the CIA (often over CIA objections or misgivings), such as a foreign head of state, Departments of Defense and State, the Presidential Assistant for National Security Affairs, and the President. One case investigated by the Committee: to please the Shah of Iran, Nixon and Kissinger agreed to arm Kurdish dissidents fighting for autonomy in Iraq; the US–Iranian intention was not that they should win, but merely 'continue a level of hostilities sufficient to sap the resources' of Iran's hostile neighbour, Iraq. When this had achieved its aim – i.e. pressure on Iraq to compromise over a border dispute with Iran – the Kurds were abandoned to their fate. 'Their adversaries [Iraqis], knowing of the impending aid cut-off, launched an all-out search-and-destroy campaign the day after the agreement [with Iran] was signed' (Pike Committee, p. 37).

Politics and morals: the linkage

Such activities involve two forms of 'linkage': political and moral, and domestic and external. These are connected. For as Kissinger has aptly put it in his address on 'Moral Purposes and Political Choices': 'A Nation's values define what is just. Its strength determines what is possible.'[27] Both forms of linkage are evident in statements by supporters and critics of covert operations – over 900 major operations around the world since 1961, according to the Church Committee. On the one hand, a former Attorney-General and Under-Secretary at the State Department, Nicholas Katzenbach, came out with the proposal:

> We should abandon publicly all covert operations designed to influence political results in foreign countries. Specifically, there should be no secret subsidies of police or counter-insurgency forces, no efforts to influence elections, no secret monetary subsidies of groups sympathetic to the United States, whether governmental, non-governmental, or revolutionary. We should confine our covert activities overseas to the gathering of intelligence information.[28]

That an 'establishment' figure like Katzenbach, a man who still sees no alternative to US intervention in Vietnam (it is the methods he disapproves of), should speak out so decisively for an end to covert operations indicates the seriousness of the problem. Katzenbach's concern is that the administration's 'manipulation of facts' and its covert activities abroad, undertaken on the grounds of national security, tempts the President to let the end justify the means – 'even if the means requires dissembling or misleading the Congress and the American people'. Thus he directly relates the 'excesses' of American policy in Indochina, oriented to Cold War concepts of national security, to the Watergate affair. As Katzenbach puts it to restore the domestic consensus in support of US foreign initiatives, by encouraging candour and openness in decision making, is also to safeguard the democratic process at home.

To Katzenbach, the foreign–domestic, moral–political linkage is one in which US covert activities result in the perversion of American democracy. To William Colby (the veteran CIA operator and recently Director) it is the other way around: the defence of American democracy sanctions external subversion (i.e. those covert 'political or paramilitary activities' which amounted to 30 per cent of the CIA budget in the 1950s, compared to 5 per cent now. But, Colby warns, 'in the 1980s, if the world goes on facing totalitarian developments, we might go back to that 30 per cent or more').[29] Such activities are justified, according to Colby, because 'we decided that we would go any distance to fight for freedom' – meaning, essentially, the preservation of the American way of life. For 'freedom' to Colby, as we shall see, does not refer to *internal* freedom so far as America's Third World allies and friends are concerned: it refers to freedom from external threats or internal subversion, i.e. security.

This significant, if confusing, use of 'freedom' is evident throughout Colby's interview with Fallaci. (When he was questioned about the discrepancy between 'our [CIA] right to protect freedom in the world' and America's role before and after the military coup in Chile, he answered in two different ways. First, this was a matter of official policy and 'it is up to the government to decide it'; second, he argued that the Chilean military were no threat (unlike the Russians): 'Pinochet is not going to conquer the world. Nobody is worried about Pinochet.' On the one hand, Colby insists on *realpolitik*: the end, defence against communism, justifies the means. On the other hand, and this is more revealing, he believes in America's moral purpose: 'Maybe our morals are not perfect but they are better than others'. American policy is regarded all through the world as a pillar of freedom.'[30]

What is so disturbing is this combination of self-righteousness and ideological fervour which blinds people like Colby to their wrong-doings – plotting assassinations,[31] bribing politicians, falsifying evidence;[32] acts of corruption and degradation on an immense scale – and to the *implications* of their motivations and decisions: that is, especially under conditions of 'instability', the ever more intimate engagement of US agencies and agents, not only in the domestic processes of the 'protected' nation – political and electoral (where they exist), military and security, labour and management, mass communications – but with the most 'dependable', tough and often most reactionary elements within those processes:[33] those who share with the US administration the perception of the same threat to 'national security' (i.e. communism or other forms of internal dissidence) and would 'go to any distance' to fight it.

It is this state of mind, alluded to by Katzenbach, which permitted the recruitment of thugs and criminals to carry out some of the more wayward projects. Among such recruits, according to testimony before the Church Committee, was a 'soldier of fortune' code-named WI/ROGUE. The CIA's Africa Division characterised him as a man who 'learns quickly and carries out any assignment without regard for danger'. Further, 'he is indeed aware of the precepts of right and wrong, but if he is given an assignment which may *be morally wrong in the eyes of the world*, but necessary because his case officer ordered him to carry it out, then it is right, and he will dutifully undertake appropriate action.'[34] What essential difference is there between this attitude and that of Kissinger obeying superior orders by carrying on a brutal and senseless war in Cambodia,[35] or Nixon (responding to the higher call of national security) killing the people of Hanoi?

Deep involvement

Katzenbach's remedy is insufficient. Secrecy and covert activities are the symptom, not the problem. The problem is involvement. As Colby said of the Greek colonels, the US government did not support them: 'We just worked with them.'[36] It is instructive to consider two well-documented examples of such involvement ('working' with regimes) leading to intervention: Chile and Vietnam. The first reveals the 'enmeshing' of military, political and economic processes in the context of a friendly regime transformed into an 'unacceptable' one. It shows the way in which the patron–client system tends to operate in a crisis: in this case, intervention by proxy. (It is a crisis that brings out the latent or undisclosed relationships that are normally concealed.) The second case is one in which 'assistance' to a deteriorating client involves direct military intervention by the patron: as a result of its symbiotic relationship with the Saigon regime, the USA found itself obliged to take over more and more of the functions of government from its ailing partner. (The supreme instance of what was virtually a colonial relationship is Laos, where the USA was operating a parallel government, with its own military, administrative and economic branches – to which the Royal Lao Government deferred.)

Now the normal state of US involvement ranges from advocacy of liberal reforms to support for repression, from economic to paramilitary aid, and from open to covert operations. The more self-reliant the regime, the more important the open involvement. Conversely, the more dependent the regime on external assistance, in a deteriorating situation, the greater the covert involvement: and the more this covert involvement – starting with a nucleus of the military, the security police, Ministry of the Interior, conservative political parties, and perhaps social and religious movements – widens and deepens, through an expanding network of patronage relations, until even the 'normal' political, economic and administrative functions are interwoven with the indispensable external presence: as in Cambodia, Laos and Vietnam.[37]

In realistic terms there is nothing to object to in America 'choosing sides' – the anti-communist side – in this manner, *provided* (a) that the choice is not declared or believed to be a moral one (the cause of freedom, etc.) if this is not the case; and (b) that the strength, effectiveness and authority of the chosen side – and of its adversaries – is accurately assessed. The problem with deep involvement, however, is that it tends to be both perceived and acclaimed in moral terms: to some extent, for domestic reasons. Partly as a result of this and partly because of the nature and extent of the commitment (resulting in the tendency to empathise with, or share, the client's viewpoint) the assessment of strengths and weaknesses is often unduly subjective.

Vietnam

America's attitudes toward Vietnam were ambiguous. US objectives were mainly conceived in realistic terms (defence of territory, 'reputation for action') but more often presented as a moral crusade: for self-determination, defence against aggression, freedom. When the shortcomings of Saigon came increasingly to light (see Table 6), the divergence between morality and policy became obvious. Even more serious, from a realistic viewpoint, was the discrepancy between US objectives and the Vietnamese environment: as a result, not only was morality not being served, but policy, too, was unlikely to be achieved.

The crucial point is that, despite these glimpses of accuracy, the extent of America's involvement in Vietnam *prejudged* the issue. Thus America's aim: 'The creation of an effective national organisation is the major change needed to provide the GVN [Government of (South) Vietnam] with a dependable, enduring political base'[38] and the South Vietnamese reality: 'In order to function effectively, such an organisation must have real political power. The conflict that would ensue between it and the army, which currently is the real, if not the constitutional power base, is only too obvious.'[39] In reality, the USA had first decided to 'sink or swim with Ngo Dinh Diem' – beginning the process of involvement to intervention – then connived at the military coup against him (1963),[40] vainly propped up a succession of fleeting military or civilian governments (1964–5), turned to the 'authority' of Air Vice Marshal Ky (1966) and finally backed the 'winner', General Thieu (1967): so tightly interwoven a relationship could not be disentangled – only severed by defeat.

Table 6 US assessments of the situation in South Vietnam

---

1 'Enemy main force activities have in the past relied on active assistance from the population in the countryside for intelligence, food, money and manpower. This has enabled the enemy to use the countryside as a springboard' (*U.S. Foreign Policy for the 1970's*, 1970, p. 70).

2 'Are the Vietnamese [Saigon regime] developing the leadership, logistic capabilities, tactical know-how and sensitivity to the needs of their own people which are indispensable to continued success? . . . Most important, what are the attitudes of the Vietnamese people? . . . Are they truly being disaffected from the Viet Cong or are they indifferent to both sides?' (ibid., pp. 75–6).

3 'Military considerations are likely to dominate the time of officials, the content of programs, and the freedom of political life. . . . [Yet] ultimately the fate of Vietnam will turn on political factors – the motivation of the people during the conflict; the cohesion of non-communist political forces . . . the solidity of the political institutions during and after the war' (*U.S. Foreign Policy for the 1970's*, 1971, p. 25).

4 'Vietnamisation [is] encouraging . . . [but] substantial problems remain . . . improving the leadership . . . rooting out the Viet Cong infrastructure . . . assuring political stability . . . managing the strains of the Vietnamese economy . . . and moving against corruption which not only poisons the moral atmosphere but also carries potential political impact' [an interesting observation, coming from Nixon] (ibid., pp. 26–7).

Chile

Finally, US involvement in Chile. The details of the covert activities revealed by the Church Committee are almost incredible. Yet we should realise that from the Eisenhower administration onward, in planning and executing covert operations the US Government was advised to forget 'hitherto acceptable norms of human conduct'.[41] Even so, Chile was no banana republic, but a country with a large and diversified middle class, a sophisticated political system, and a proud record of constitutional government. However, as in Italy, the prospect of communist or left-wing electoral gains was all that was needed for the US government to undertake 'large-scale political action programs', including bribery of politicians, subsidies for the media and incitement of a military coup.

Covert electoral support by the CIA began in 1964 when $2.5 million in campaign funds were provided for the successful Christian Democrat Presidential candidate, Eduardo Frei, though without his knowledge. In 1965 the USA gave financial support to twenty-two Congressional candidates, selected by the US Ambassador and the CIA station chief. Altogether some $13 million was spent between 1963 and the overthrow of Allende in 1973 – $8 million allocated for propaganda and support of political parties, and $4.3 million to influence the mass media. The pattern of covert financing, according to the Church Committee's interim report, spread through the entire political and economic sector of Chile, encompassing labour unions, business organisations and right-wing extremist groups.[42] These operations were 'in the best interests of the people of Chile', explained President Ford in September 1974, 'and certainly in our best interests'.

The critical period for the USA was the presidential campaign of September–October 1970, won by the Socialist candidate, Salvador Allende, at his third attempt. Already in March 1970 the '40 Committee' had approved a joint US Embassy/CIA proposal for 'spoiling operations' against Allende. Despite this move, and the increased funds requested by the US Ambassador in June, Allende won by a plurality of votes over his right-wing and Christian Democrat opponents. Allende's election plurality on 4 September had to be ratified by the Chilean Congress, meeting on 24 October.

The American intelligence assessment of the situation on 7 September was that the 'U.S. has no vital national interests within Chile' – though it would suffer 'tangible economic losses' – and the world balance of power would not be significantly altered by Allende's accession.[43] Nevertheless, as the Church Committee records,

> on September 15, 1970, President Nixon informed CIA Director Richard Helms that an Allende regime in Chile would not be acceptable to the United States. The CIA was instructed by President Nixon to play a direct role in organising a military coup d'etat in Chile to prevent Allende's accession to the presidency.[44]

According to Helms's notes on the 15 September meeting, which was attended also by National Security Adviser Kissinger and Attorney-General John Mitchell, the participants agreed:

> One in 10 chance perhaps, but save Chile! . . .
> not concerned risks involved . . .
> $10,000,000 available, more if necessary . . .
> game plan
> make the economy scream.[45]

The following day Kissinger explained in a background briefing:

[It is] fairly easy to predict that if Allende wins, there is a good chance that he will establish over a period of years some sort of communist government. . . . In a major Latin American country you would have a communist government, joining, for example, Argentina, which is already deeply divided, along a long frontier, joining Peru, which has already been heading in directions that are difficult to deal with, and joining Bolivia, which has also gone in a more Leftist, anti-U.S. direction. . . . So I don't think we should delude ourselves that an Allende takeover in Chile would not present massive problems for us, and for democratic forces and for pro-U.S. forces in Latin America, and indeed to the whole Western hemisphere.[46]

On 21 September the US Ambassador reported that he had informed the outgoing President Frei (through his Minister of Defense) that

Frei should know that not a nut or bolt will be allowed to reach Chile under Allende. Once Allende comes to power we shall do all within our power to condemn Chile and the Chileans to utmost deprivation and poverty, a policy designed for a long time to come to accelerate the hard features of a communist society in Chile.[47]

That same day, CIA headquarters cabled its station chief in Chile: 'Purpose of exercise is to prevent Allende assumption of power. Parliamentary legerdemain has been discarded. Military solution is objective.'[48] Between 5 October and 20 October, CIA agents in Chile made 21 contacts with 'key military and Carabinero [police] officials in Chile'. Those who were inclined to support a military coup were given 'assurances of strong support at the highest levels of the US Government, both before and after a coup'. The major obstacle was the Commander-in-Chief, General Schneider, who insisted that constitutional processes be followed. It was therefore understood that the general might have to be 'neutralised', if necessary by 'displacement'.[49]

The US Embassy and the CIA in Chile realised that the Chilean military, at this time, were incapable of seizing power and unwilling to do so.[50] To carry out President Nixon's directive, therefore, it was essential, first, to '*create a coup climate* by propaganda, disinformation, and terrorist activities intended to provoke the left to give a pretext for a coup'.[51] Second, to justify a military coup claiming to save Chile from communism, CIA headquarters suggested the use of such 'themes' as 'firm intel. [intelligence] that Cubans plan reorganise all intelligence services along Soviet-Cuban mold thus creating structure for police state'. A 'report' should also be prepared 'based on some well-known facts and some fiction to justify coup, split opposition and gain adherents for military group'. Such a report 'could even be planted during raids planned by carabiniers.'[52]

The coup did not take place – in 1970 – although General Schneider was assassinated in a kidnap attempt unconnected with the CIA. But, as the then CIA Deputy Director for Plans, Thomas Karamessines, told the Church Committee, 'I am sure that the seeds that were laid in that effort in 1970 had their impact in 1973.'[53]

The point is not that the USA instigated the military coup of September 1973, or even participated in the planning, but that it 'worked with' important elements in Chilean society that were either opposed to, obstructing, or doing their best to bring about the downfall of the Allende regime. First, the branches of multinational[54] as well as Chilean business and professional organisations, which deliberately exacerbated the economic problems of the Allende regime by encouraging or supporting 'middle-class', truck-owners', and housewives' strikes;[55] second, political parties, from the far Right National Party to the Right wing of the Christian Democrat party, headed by Frei, which sought confrontation rather than conciliation; and finally senior officers in the armed services (apart from the 'constitutionalist' minority in the Army) who were won over to the idea of a coup by June 1973.[56]

The situation in Chile was so uneasily balanced[57] – and became so quickly polarised by the campaign, on *either* side, to raise class consciousness[58] – that American involvement, open and covert, had a major impact both in 'creating a coup climate' and in supporting those groups and personalities that were either urging or preparing a military coup. (Of course, the Centrist and Right-wing politicians later regretted their role of encouraging military intervention. They had assumed – as had indeed been part of the US plan in 1970[59] – that the military would oust the Allende government and then hand power back to its 'rightful' possessors, the non-socialist parliamentarians.)

The effect of American interference and the connivance at or encouragement of intervention by the Chilian armed forces is that a sophisticated political society has been plunged into barbarism: the very openness of the political context – the years during which communist and socialist party branches, party agents, officials, members and sympathisers, were known and their activities publicised – made the work of repression all the easier. The insistence on legality by Allende and most of his supporters was their undoing: it prevented recourse to the only method, organising and arming a workers' militia, which could have saved them. Ironically, those who refused to abide by the constitutional system, the extremists of the Left (as also those of the Right), were the ones most likely to escape the dragnet, because they were already working underground. Perhaps the most disturbing implication of the military takeover in Chile is precisely its brutal rejection of 'peaceful transition to socialism' in a continent where violence is all too readily employed either to advance or to obstruct political and social change.[60]

To conclude: even after the downfall of Richard Nixon and the return to a more discriminating assessment of the external environment, the problem of American behaviour in a crisis persists. Admittedly, mainland Southeast Asia has at last been removed from the 'active' list of plans for US intervention on behalf of precarious clients; but there is no shortage of other clients whose salvation, in periods of danger, is likely to be deemed essential to US security. Consider, for example, the probable new candidates emerging from internal conflict or regional hostility in such vital areas (not to speak of Western Europe or the Mediterranean) as the Middle East, Northeast Asia (Korea and Japan), Africa (the south, centre and Horn of Africa) and central America.

Certainly, Washington's interpretation of which areas are of critical importance varies from time to time: thus Black Africa and southern Africa in the 1960s and early 1970s – apart from the Congo crisis – were comparatively unimportant; while South America in the 'revolutionary' 1960s was critical, and so was Southeast Asia. Yet the former is relatively quiescent at the moment and the latter, if hardly free of turmoil, is no longer considered of strategic significance. The point, however, is that at any given time there are 'vital' areas of instability in the world where the situation of US involvement may trigger intervention.

Prospects

The logic of the Nixon Doctrine, flowing from the change in international conditions – Soviet attainment of nuclear parity, emergence of communist pluralism, the US failure in Vietnam, the impact of OPEC – dictates greater American reliance on intermediate patrons. For the purpose of the doctrine, as pointed out above, is to reduce the US 'burden' of maintaining global security. This can be achieved in three ways. First, by sharing the burden with America's 'partners'; second, by a more discriminating assessment of America's security stake, as between one country or region and another; and finally by redefining US commitments – i.e. the conditions under which America would intervene and the forms intervention could take. Regional patrons, like Saudi Arabia and Iran, are accordingly being assisted and encouraged to play a greater role – both in their own interest and that of the USA – in maintaining regional stability and in countering moves by the common adversary and his allies.

But the greater the build-up of regional patrons, the more these patrons are empowered to pursue policies of their own, which may either clash one with another (say between Saudi Arabia and Iran) or may no longer coincide with those of the imperial patron. Moreover the future leadership of such heavily armed powers is, to say the least, problematic. Thus the long-term prospects of great powers, like Germany and Japan, and even of regional patrons, like Brazil and Iran, lie in ever greater autonomy of action.[61] For in a world where the nuclear monopoly of a few states has been broken, and where the post-war economic rules of the game have been so drastically changed, an increasing number of great and middle powers is likely to pull out of the orbit of common interests with the USA, not only in the economic, but also in the political and conceivably in the military, sphere as well. Such divergence will eventually spell the end of the post-war American patronage system, with its relatively well-defined adversaries and its clearly marked division of labour between patron and client serving common ends. Extreme divergence of interests and perceptions could even fragment the global system into rival and conflicting blocs, operating in an increasingly chaotic environment – marked by population pressures, unemployment, famine and rebellion in one 'developing' country after another[62] – culminating in international anarchy.

For the international process of growing autonomy of great and middle powers — in communist and non-communist spheres alike — runs parallel to the domestic process in many Third World regimes of an explosive build-up of social pressures, as pointed out in the first part of this study. To these socio-political pressures (of the have-nots) must also be added the potential for disintegration posed by ethnic fragmentation (due to the awakening consciousness of minorities increasingly exposed and subjected to the power-holders of an alien state) especially in Southeast and South Asia, the Middle East and Africa.

This combination of international and internal fragmentation suggests a world of instability, which even the 'global strategies' of the multinational corporations may be unable to overcome. For the management, financial controls and research activities of these corporations are concentrated in the hands of nationals of the advanced industrialised countries and they have complemented, rather than contradicted, national objectives. The experience of the German cartels and the Japanese Zaibatsu before the Second World War is a chilling reminder of this fact. It thus seems unlikely, in future, that multinationals will go contrary to 'national interests' even when divergence between nations is an obvious source of instability, or that they will be able to hold together by economic means 'host' countries that are falling apart. (The working relationship of the multinationals is with the élites of those countries and it is precisely the élites that will be facing and perhaps unable to cope with growing social and/or ethnic pressures.)

This world of instability will provide greater – and not less – opportunity and 'necessity' for patrons to intervene in the troubled affairs of clients in order to safeguard their (the patrons') interests from the threat of a takeover by rival interests. And there will be more rising patrons – not less – with both the capacity and the will to intervene.

10 ⋆ *Conclusion: the global condition*

The problem, as we have seen, is the nature of American involvement in Third World societies which leads, under certain conditions, to intervention. It has both political and moral dimensions. The political dimension is the involvement of a super-power seeking to maintain 'world order': at each level of the patron–client international hierarchy – national, regional and global; and through the various forms of power, military, political and economic: to influence, induce or compel 'satisfactory' behaviour by others.

The moral dimension (noted in the previous chapter) is underlined both by advocates and critics of involvement:[1] the former regard America's involvement as necessary for the preservation and enhancement of a valued way of life against the challenge of an 'unacceptable' alternative; the latter point to the 'perverse' forms that involvement, and especially intervention, have taken – perverting both the society that uses such methods and the societies subjected to them. The critical view accepts that perverse aspects are only part of a 'total' involvement with Third World societies, much of which may indeed be beneficial; but it argues that under crisis conditions (the result of 'alternative' challenges either directly to Third World regimes or indirectly to the balance of power) the perverse element develops disproportionately to the beneficial; and it becomes excessive as involvement leads to intervention.

What is the solution to this predicament? Broadly there are two 'feasible' alternatives, i.e. those that are possible, if not probable, under existing circumstances. (Outside the scope of this inquiry, therefore, are alternatives that may well be more desirable, involving a radical reconstruction of American and Third World societies, and their mutual relationship, whether envisioned under the 'World Order Models Project'[2] on the one hand or by neo-Marxists on the other. But, at least in the case of America as a super-power, these are most unlikely in the foreseeable future.)

One alternative, stemming from the critical view of involvement, is 'strategic disengagement'; the other, projected from an opposing standpoint, may be defined as 'total engagement': the use of decisive strength in the initial stages of the involvement-intervention process to avoid the frustrations of protracted conflict or even defeat. Within this framework of alternatives extends the current range of intermediate policies. These vary from containment (tending toward total engagement) to balance of power policies, but discriminating with regard to commitments; the latter policy tends toward, but is still far from, disengagement.

Strategic disengagement

The 'case for strategic disengagement' envisages 'a pluralism of unaligned states':

> a . . . dispersion of nation-states, great, large and medium in size and 'weight' with relative power a less critical factor in assessing and constructing relationships; agnostic about maintaining the shape and tone of the system as a whole, and not bound to restrain other – especially distant – nations for the sake of their own security or the integrity of the system.[3]

In the view expressed here, 'general unalignment' is the only present alternative to the contemporary balance of power system (discussed in section 3 below). The latter is made up of 'a limited constellation of powerful nations or blocs, all fully engaged and all with a stake in preserving the system, even at the cost of occasional forcible exercises; differing politically and contending economically, but observing certain "mutual restraints" or rules of engagement'. But the balance of power system is unlikely to 'adjust' effectively (i.e. without ruinous conflict) to 'six critical conditions' of our expected future. These are:

> i. Instability: 'high probability of troubles, such as embargoes, expropriations, coups, revolutions, externally supported subversions, thrusts by impatient irredentist states, and calculated probes of defense perimeters'.
> ii. Interdependence: 'a set of functional linkages of nations' con-

cerning resources (raw materials, energy and food), access routes
(commercial and strategic), economic activities (trade, monetary and
investment), populations, and physical environment; all contain
problems which, if aggravated, could become threats to security.
iii. No Supranational Authority: the absence of an 'ultimate adjustment mechanism' that can authoritatively dispense justice and grant
relief, 'especially in those extreme cases that threaten to unhinge
the system'. Even tacit 'rules' of balance of power will break down
precisely when they are most needed.
iv. Unilateral Intervention – rather than a collaborative world order,
in the search for stabilisation: this is the 'interim conclusion' of the
above factors.
v. Unmanageable Diffusion of Power: by any measure of power,
military (nuclear or conventional), economic or political, there may
be 15 or 20 powerful, 'salient' states in a Gaullist world.
vi. Lack of Domestic Consensus: most evidently lacking when most
needed.[4]

The keynote of strategic disengagement, in contrast to balance of
power, is 'adjustment' to these present and 'expected future' conditions.
'It is a prescription for an orderly [US] withdrawal from our political-
military commitments to other nations and from our military positions
overseas': a measured withdrawal, unilaterally determined, but
'responsive to opportune circumstances and to the sensibilities of our
allies and the conduct of our adversaries', possibly taking one or two
decades.[5] The essentials of strategic disengagement are therefore (a)
dissolution of alliances, rehabilitation of neutrality, and respect for
international law, and (b) 'a strict but limited definition of national
security [including] acceptance of revolutionary change in the world,
acquiescence even in the forcible rearrangement of other countries'.[6]
Ravenal then considers the obvious objection that the USA would put
itself in jeopardy by 'opting out of the international system'. Can the
USA defend what it must unavoidably defend – its own existence and
integrity – if it allows 'ancillary strategic assets' to go by the board? Can
it credibly deter 'central threats to its existence' if it declines to deter
lesser threats? His response is the 'concept of equanimity' – an *acceptance*
of situations and consequences: a sense of the limits of foreign policy in a
world largely 'given'.[7] Thus Ravenal proposes, above all, an alternative
definition of security, one which requires the American decision-making
system to adjust its most fundamental presumptions: about the

relevance of threats, the calculus of risks, and the nature of national interest.

Ravenal's proposition is that the 'loss of territory to communism' syndrome – which motivates unilateral intervention for the sake of 'stability' – will disappear if America's 'stake' is redefined: the 'loss' will be no loss once it is accepted with equanimity. This solves the subjective part of the problem (the push factor of compulsive globalism). But it 'wishes away' the objective part: the 'pull' of the international environment of partly-competing, partly-co-operative super- and great powers; and the Third World arena in which they play out these roles. For it is only reasonable to assume, first, that the element of rivalry (on the part of adversaries) will develop at the expense of co-operation if the restraints of opposing powers are withdrawn; second, that client states, disillusioned by the indifference of their patron, will switch to an alternative patron. The dual consequence could indeed be momentous.

Ravenal rightly draws attention to the importance of subjectivity; but taken in isolation it raises serious problems. Consider the analogy with European religious conflict, which in time was superseded by tolerance and (eventually?) co-operation. Ravenal does not suggest this analogy, but it is an appropriate one. For tolerance depends on changed perceptions of what religion meant: i.e. that religious differences were no longer 'vital' (worth dying for); in this way the religious stake (no pun intended) was redefined and the loss of territory (population) to a rival religion accepted with equanimity. But the point is that religious differences *were* no longer vital: a different religion no longer represented an 'unacceptable', alternative *way of life*; to put it bluntly, a proselytising religious movement, like that of the Huguenots in France, was no longer seen as a challenge, because it *was* no longer a challenge, to the existing social order. Conversely a 'reactionary' movement, like that aiming at the restoration of Catholicism in England, ceased to be a threat once Catholics were accepted as loyal citizens – because that is what they had become.

Such an evolution may, and hopefully will, take place in Europe and the Third World with regard to the secular religion of our time, communism (leading to Eurocommunism, and other forms of national communism) and its rival, capitalism (the spread of welfarism, social democracy); but so far it is no more than a trend that is not irreversible. To act on the *assumption* that the desired situation already exists ('reflected' in disengagement and indifference) is actually to 'unbalance' an essential element of the conditions (the rivalry-co-operation duality of coexistence) of its emergence. The objective, surely, is to work primarily to assure the desired evolutionary process, which then provides the setting in which tolerance – equanimity – can survive.

Total engagement

The strategy of total engagement, or decisive intervention, previously noted in chapter 7 ('Limited war') can be summarily stated. The underlying philosophy is one of 'strong American forces [which], by making a vital contribution to international stability, provide us with the influence and leverage we need in negotiating with both our allies and our potential enemies'.[8] The specific application is envisioned in the use of tactical nuclear weapons, for example, in the case of a second Korean War.[9] Allusions to 'forceful intervention' in the Middle East in the event of another Arab oil embargo or instability in the Persian Gulf are also part of the scenario.[10]

The rationale for decisive intervention was set out by James Schlesinger, then Defense Secretary, in 1975. One of the lessons of Vietnam, he claims, is that 'rather than simply counter your opponent's thrusts, it is necessary to go for the heart of your opponent's power: destroy his military forces rather than simply being involved in endless ancillary military operations'.[11] As Samuel Huntington states the position:

> In the future, the United States is likely to respond to challenges to its 'hard' commitments (i.e. commitments reflecting its interests and moral purposes and backed by both branches of government) in ways quite different from those which it might have used in the past. During the 1950s and 1960s, gradual response, flexible response, and limited war came to be the prevailing policy and doctrine. In the future, however, no President will wish to run the political risks of any sustained overseas limited engagement . . . [the] failure of the 'compellence' strategies in Vietnam has reoriented U.S. military doctrine towards the more decisive use of force including a renewed emphasis on the potential of tactical nuclear weapons. All these factors – legal [the War Powers Act], political and military – mean that the U.S. response to a challenge to a 'hard' commitment is likely to be immediate, overwhelming and potentially devastating to the aggressor.[12]

There are three flaws in this approach. First, the military orientation to political problems. Schlesinger's 'lesson' of Vietnam is that of the political illiterates of the hardware school, discussed in chapter 8. Second, even Huntington's more sober appraisal – challenges to 'hard' commitments are 'likely to be met by a massive military response' – overlooks the fact that Vietnam, for example, fully met the requirements of being 'hard' *at the time* that US involvement was being transformed into intervention: i.e. it reflected US interests ('vital' ones) and moral purposes (self-determination, freedom from aggression, etc.); and it was backed by both branches of government. Third, and related to the above, is the fact that decisive intervention, whatever its relevance to conventional war, is usually inapplicable to an insurgency. For insurgency by definition is a protracted process. In its incipient stages the revolutionary 'threat' to the existing regime may not even be realised; by the time it is apparent – and the insurgents and their supporters have 'enmeshed' themselves in the very society they are preparing to take over – it would be difficult to justify a 'massive military response' either by Huntington's standards or by customary military rules of engagement. Finally, in an insurgency the client regime may not permit the USA to take over the war (this was Diem's attitude during the crucial formative period of the insurgency); or it may object to the ruinous costs of massive intervention on its behalf, epitomised in the comment: 'It became necessary to destroy the town to save it.'[13]

Intermediate strategy

Contrary to the alternative futures outlined above, US administrations, even in periods of crisis, have tended to pursue an intermediate course: they have neither accepted the 'humiliating' role of disengagement[14] – Laos in 1960–2 being a partial exception – nor faced the global risk of all-out war. The present balance of power strategy is no exception. The complex (but 'on balance' advantageous) equilibrium between détente and a show of strength rests (for its advantage) on the stability of US allies and friends and their confidence in America's protective role. It also requires the backing of Congress and the American public – demonstrating support, where necessary, for US resolution, strength and action.

The balance of power strategists share the underlying apprehensions of the 'total interventionists': i.e. the fear particularly of Soviet global expansionism, military and political, in the 'vacuum' created both by American 'inactivity' (as a result of Congressional obstruction) and Third World instability. But they reject (or modify) the interventionists' unbalanced attitude toward détente[15] and they are opposed to the risks of 'total' intervention. Conversely, balance of power strategists accept the premises of the strategic disengagers – the 'high probability of troubles', political, subversive and economic (energy, access, resources) – but they reject the conclusions.

The implications of an 'intermediate' policy, from the official viewpoint, are set out in Table 7.

Table 7 America's balance of power

---

1 *Strength.* 'The kind of forces we will have will determine the kind of diplomacy we are able to conduct. . . . While we cannot prevent the growth of Soviet military strength, we can and must maintain the strength to balance it and ensure that it will not be used for political expansion.'

2 *Area threats.* 'Under conditions of nuclear parity, world peace is more likely to be threatened by shifts in local or regional balances – in Europe, the Middle East, Asia, Latin America, or Africa – than by strategic nuclear attack.'

3 *Confidence.* Adversary 'probes' at the regional level must be discouraged: 'If leaders around the world came to assume that the United States lacks either the forces or the will to resist while others intervene to impose solutions, they will accommodate themselves to what they will regard as the dominant trend.'

4 *Imbalance.* 'An unopposed super-power may draw dangerous conclusions when the next opportunity for intervention beckons. Over time, the global balance of power and influence will inevitably shift [to America's disadvantage].'

5 *Inaction.* 'The danger was – and is – that our inaction – our legislatively imposed failure . . . – will lead to further [adversary] pressures on the mistaken assumption that America has lost the will to counter adventurism or even to help others do so.'

6 *Action.* 'It is time that the world be reminded that America remains capable of forthright and decisive action.'

Source: Henry Kissinger, 'Foreign Policy and National Security', Dallas, 22 March 1976.

What difference has the advent of the Carter administration made? Its foreign policy is evidently well within the bounds of intermediacy. Although it tends toward disengagement (less alarm about Euro-communism, 'guidelines' on arms sales, more consultation and less unilateral action) rather than toward intervention, it still represents a shift in emphasis rather than a change of direction.

Consider the 'five cardinal premises' of the Carter–Brzezinski foreign policy of 'constructive global involvement' announced in the President's speech of 22 May 1977. These are: (1) 'Promote the cause of human rights.' (2) 'Close cooperation among the industrial democracies' because 'we share the same values.' (3) 'Based on a strong defense capacity . . . to improve relations with the Soviet Union and China. . . . We must reach accommodations that reduce the risk of war.' (4) Attention to the developing nations 'to reduce the chasm between the world's rich and poor'. And (5) to work with all countries 'to solve such formidable global problems as the threat of nuclear war, racial hatred, the arms race, environmental damage, hunger and disease'.

Four out of the five premises are squarely in line with the proposals of the previous administration. It is the first premise – human rights – that marks the most interesting and significant departure from Nixon–Kissinger 'realism', and the return to 'democratic' idealism. Concern for human rights is important in Carter's foreign policy; it is not mere rhetoric, but neither is it the decisive factor. It has no priority over security. The administration may reduce military aid to Uruguay, Argentina and Ethiopia – this is in any case more symbolic than effective – but, as Secretary Vance puts it, it is not prepared to pressure governments like those of South Korea and the Philippines, where America's strategic interests are involved. (This is one of the reasons why the administration disclaims the 'linkage' concept: human rights are considered on their own merits, not 'linked' with the progress of détente, on the one hand, nor with the military build-up of important allies on the other.)

The real innovation of Carter's policy (in contrast to the Nixon–Kissinger era) is not so much the promotion of American values abroad – a rather selective process, as we have seen – but *their reassertion at home*. This inspirational campaign, with which Carter personally identifies, is designed to draw public strength from the well-spring of private morality – the 'American Creed', as Gunnar Myrdal calls it, of liberty, equality, justice and fair opportunity for all.

The purpose, in terms of Carter's foreign policy, is this: with the assurance of American confidence in its own values the USA itself can play a more effective world role. As Carter points out, *because* 'we are confident of our own strength' we can seek substantial mutual reductions in the nuclear arms race; 'being confident of our own future, we are now free of that inordinate fear of communism' which led to reliance on dictatorships; finally, 'a foreign policy . . . based on our fundamental values' is one that 'the American people both support and understand'.

The last point, in view of the difficulties facing previous administrations, is crucial. For it was precisely the *lack* of public backing for US foreign policy – in certain important aspects – that Kissinger himself warned against, and sought to rectify. What he failed to admit, however, was that the administration's own policies – the secret bombing of Cambodia, the efforts to prop up Saigon in a continuing war, the urge to intervene in Angola, the support of the Greek Colonels, the involvement in the Chile coup – had created the very situation of public and Congressional 'obstruction' that Kissinger was criticising.

Carter's attempt to 'reintegrate' public opinion – through the affirmation of common values – with foreign policy has important implications. His objective is to free foreign policy from the 'crippling' procedures which thwarted the unilateral initiatives of former administrations – procedures which of course reflect the constitutional operation of checks and balances. Thus if on important strategic issues there is renewed congruity of purpose among all three elements – executive, legislature, and public opinion – then under an activist President it is 'all systems go'.

Such are Carter's intentions. But they have not worked out that way, for several reasons. The first and most obvious reason is the legacy of suspicion and distrust created in Congress and among the public by the Vietnam War and the machinations of the imperial Presidency. The second, and currently much publicised, reason is the failure of the Carter administration to put over its policies persuasively and cohesively, owing to the President's apparent indecisiveness and his absorption in detail, and the discordant voices of prominent decision-makers. It is these weaknesses that have become the target of much critical comment.[16]

The final reason, however, goes deeper than Carter's specific troubles or personal foibles. This is the predicament to which neither Carter nor his predecessors have found, and his immediate successors are not likely to find, a solution: that is, the change in the 'management' of the international environment – from Cold War and containment to living with détente. This is an uncertain posture, reflecting an unstable environment, in which it is far more difficult to achieve consensus, compared with the days of overwhelming fear of communism which helped create solidarity against the common threat. Instead, the present situation is one which still gives scope to national rivalries – witness the opportunities afforded by the growing tensions and instabilities in Africa and the Middle East – but which must be kept within a framework of super-power co-operation to prevent such rivalries escalating to the stage of mutual suicide.

This is the new environment in which Kissinger himself, for all his conceptual skill and tactical brilliance, was also floundering; and it is certainly one in which Carter, rightly rejecting the darker side of his predecessors' designs, has no obvious signposts to guide him through the many and treacherous uncertainties so characteristic of the current era. The Cold War is being wound down, but it is great power antagonism – preventing the global scientific and economic co-operation needed to solve issues vital to humanity – that has taken its place.

As Carter views the international situation, in his speech of 22 May 1977, 'we cannot have accommodation in one part of the world and the aggravation of conflicts in another. . . . We hope to persuade the Soviet Union that one country cannot impose its own social system upon another, either through direct military intervention or through the use of a client state's military force.'

Yet the danger of 'aggravation of conflicts' lies precisely in the instability of much of the international environment – including the possible upheavals, in an era of transition, from 'one social system' (e.g. white rule in Rhodesia, apartheid in South Africa, the 'occupied' or 'liberated' territories in Israel, the territorial integrity or ethnic independence of regions in Africa, upheavals in Iran, Southeast Asia and elsewhere) to another system. These among others are critical situations which each super-power may seek to defuse (both in the spirit of co-operation and from fear of a wider conflict) but at the same time either may be unable to pass up the opportunity to gain a major advantage over the other. The world situation, then, affords little assurance of non-intervention of the great powers – rather the reverse.

For there are four major flaws in the global approach – whether in the form of balance of power, 'world order politics', or total engagement.

1 *Global syndrome.* The requirements of global policy constantly override sensitivity to or concern with regional or local characteristics, sometimes with disastrous results ('You may be right about Africa, but I'm thinking globally').[17] During the 1975–6 Angola crisis, for example, a majority of members of a task force of experts on Africa (from the State Department, Defense Department, CIA and other agencies) 'recommended diplomatic efforts to encourage a political settlement rather than intervention'. The experts were informed by National Security Council aides that it was improper for them to make a recommendation

on policy.[18]

Ironically, in view of Carter's disavowal of Kissinger's 'linkage' concept, a similiar struggle between global strategists and 'Africanists' over how the USA should respond to the growing Soviet–Cuban involvement in various conflicts throughout Africa is reportedly taking place within the present administration. Andrew Young at first set the pace by supporting 'African solutions for African problems' in the belief that the force of African nationalism would best check the spread of communism and of Soviet influence. Recently, however, Zbigniew Brzezinski seems to have gained the upper hand. He deliberately links Soviet expansion in Africa with overall super-power relations, arguing that the USA should react to the Soviet-Cuban build-up in the Horn (and potentially in Rhodesia) or face a destabilising situation.[19] In this he has clearly gained the support of President Carter, who in March 1978 denounced the 'ominous inclination' of the Soviet Union to intervene in local conflicts, as in Africa, and called for a 'matching' response, combining military, political, and economic means.

2 *Fear of instability*. An integral part of the 'global syndrome' is the fear that instability in the Third World can and will be 'manipulated' by adversaries to America's fatal disadvantage. However, as indicated in the case of Angola, the compulsive nature of the belief in and urge to act against 'instability' *confuses* the concrete processes and consequences of unrest, subversion or dissidence, which vary country by country, with the generalised threat to US national security. This failure to distinguish between the particular and the global is a major cause of interventionism. Admittedly, it could reasonably be argued that the tensions and strains of modernisation in Third World countries do give rise to political and social disorder. But the question to be asked is whether it is external communist powers, or even local communists, who gain from this disorder. The answer surely is that military or authoritarian-civilian leaders rather than communists (or democrats) are those who have come to power in one country after another. Even where radicals have come to power, e.g. the Marxist leaders in Angola and Mozambique, and the few remaining radical rulers elsewhere, they are evidently nationalists first, ideologues second.

3 *Credibility*. The overriding theme of 'confidence' (that is, the credibility of US commitments 'from Berlin to Thailand') is precisely the 'undifferentiated globalism' Kissinger criticised before he came to office. There are two major inconsistencies involved. The first arises from the fact that the marked differences in *circumstances* – the stability or

instability of allied or friendly regimes and their strategic importance to the USA or lack of it – rules out any undifferentiated approach. The second is that in spite of the universality of the theme, if applied universally it is self-defeating. Thus credibility – the demonstration of the will to back up commitments and possess the desired 'reputation for action' – although promoted by American politicians and strategists and intended to apply to American policy, is evidently a universal mode of behaviour (not the only one, fortunately). What applies to American conduct, with the aim of reassuring 'wavering' allies, must also apply to every other power in similar circumstances, including the adversary. But if one country will not yield in a crisis for fear of 'losing face', neither can its enemy – for the same reason. Carried to its logical conclusion, 'credibility' or 'reputation' becomes mutually suicidal.

4 *Domestic dissension.* As the administration argued, 'We have gone through a difficult decade not because we were weak, but because we were divided.'[20] The world sees 'our policies in Africa, the eastern Mediterranean, in Latin America, in East–West relations, undermined by arbitrary congressional actions that may take decades to undo.' Such obstruction 'will end by wrecking the nation's ability to conduct a strong, creative, moderate, and prudent foreign policy. The result will be paralysis.'[21] Ironically, however, it was when Congress was *not* 'obstructive', when it went all the way with the Executive, that the USA entered its most difficult decade; it was Congress, after all, that approved, by overwhelming majorities, the Tonkin Gulf resolution. What was the reason for *subsequent* Congressional obstruction? It was the discrepancy between global expectations and local conditions. Or, to put it another way, the 'credibility gap' between what the administration stated was happening and what it said it was doing (or not doing), above all in Indochina, and the growing awareness by the American public of what it meant to be engaged in a brutal and 'unwinnable' war. Congressman Pike, bluntly if belatedly, spoke for many when he declared: 'The average Senator, the average Congressman . . . only believed what the government said. . . . It took this investigation [the Pike Committee] to convince me that I had always been told lies.'[22]

Solution?

Neither 'involvement' – subsuming both the intermediate policies and those of total engagement – nor strategic withdrawal get to the root of the problem. The problem is this: Globalism is more than a policy: it is a condition.

Thus the 'subjective' changes considered above – whether in the form of decisive action or masterly inaction – are insufficient to escape the global predicament. The environment conducive to global involvement (and its perverse consequences) must also change.

What kind of 'objective' changes in the Third World are likely to limit both the capacity and the *opportunity* to intervene by super- or great powers? The most hopeful sign is the intention of Third World regimes to work for a 'new economic order'. Substantial economic collaboration by weak states, particularly among producers of commodities much in demand, provides the type of leverage for the weak that great powers understand. Admittedly the benefits to be gained by effective pressure will accrue largely if not entirely to the élites (their plea for 'justice' is made in the name of the people, but it is justice for themselves that is intended).

Yet the re-ordering of the international economic system is a step in the right direction. Once a fairer distribution of the *global* product takes place it can only strengthen the claim for a more just distribution of the domestic product. However, this process (analogous to the international process) is more likely to result from the pressure of the 'weak' elements in society – when organisations of workers, farmers, even marginals, conscious of their 'interests', *combine* to put forward their demands – than it is from the subjective initiatives, the 'good will', of the élites.

The transformation of the international economic structure *may* bring about the transformation of a sufficient number of domestic structures to neutralise the perverse forms of US–Third World involvement and encourage the more constructive aspects – a type of behaviour hitherto largely reserved for the developed, or 'equal', nations.

It is in *interaction* with this process of objective change[23] that the subjective changes (from the standpoint of great powers) are most likely to be productive. Subjective changes, which are both cause and consequence of objective changes, include:

1 facilitating the economic evolution described above;
2 extricating from perverse forms of involvement;
3 recognising that popular unrest in the Third World is a cry for justice: to give some weight to justice in calculations of policy that are almost invariably biased in favour of expediency;
4 acting with tolerance and restraint; appreciation of the diversity of

situations in the world: hence discrimination instead of global determinism.

This is a possible 'reformist' scenario. In the abstract, there are many solutions – including some of the alternatives already discussed. (For a more pessimistic scenario, pointing to the anarchic international tendencies coinciding with explosive domestic situations, see the previous chapter, 'Prospects'.) In practice there is no easy way out. There is no assurance that the requisite subjective–objective transformation will take place. For America and its global 'condition' *there may be no solution* – until either America loses its grip over its clients and a new world power, or combination of powers, emerges on the scene *or* the environment conducive to the exercise of global power by one or more states (whether in rivalry or co-operation) is radically changed.

Notes

Preface

1 This is a general tendency: the qualifications are discussed in chapter 6. These stem chiefly from the risk of reaction by the main adversary, the Soviet Union, in an area considered 'vital' by the latter: e.g. south Asia, parts of the Middle East. Thus the USA made a 'show of force' in the Bay of Bengal during the Indo-Pakistan-Bangladesh war in 1971; but it did not intervene. In Vietnam it did intervene. In eastern Europe the situation is reversed: the Soviet Union is the imperial patron, the governments clients. 'Instability' in this region, whether the effect of internal challenges to east European regimes or changes of attitude by the regimes, similarly results in intervention.

2 My use of 'pluralist' and 'Marxist' concepts is selective, on the basis of their relevance to this study and their heuristic properties. On pluralism see the opening paragraphs of chapter 1 and chapter 5 in part 2. In regard to Marxist conceptions, I select those I consider to be appropriate to the context, leaving aside such important, if questionable, tenets as the leading revolutionary role of the proletariat (the *organised* working class in the Third World is either small or else largely co-opted into the system), class struggle as the motive force of history (in many countries class consciousness is either not apparent or the process of class formation is only under way), the thesis of 'increasing misery' in industrialising countries leading to catastrophic revolution (which fails to take account of the countervailing power of organised labour, of welfare reforms and the mixed economy), the declining rate of profit, labour theory of value, and so on. For the most part I have relied on neo-Marxist modifications of Marxism; and I have modified the modifications.

3 Preface to *Capital*, Chicago, Kerr, 1906, vol. I, p. 13: Maurice Meisner, 'Utopian Socialist Themes in Maoism', in John Wilson Lewis (ed.), *Peasant Rebellion and Communist Revolution in Asia*, Stanford University Press, 1974, p. 214.

4 The Ayatollah Khomeini's drive to create an Islamic-fundamentalist society is a form of 'cultural revolution'. Islam – the cutting edge of the revolution against the Shah – assures both the legitimacy of the successor regime and the means to prevent backsliding into 'Westernisation'. But the more Islamic fervour is mobilised against 'revisionist' tendencies, through incessant mass campaigns, the more difficult it is to institutionalise the system, in order to assure its continuity. This was precisely the dilemma facing the leaders of the *Chinese* cultural revolution. In the event, the Left-extremism of the Chinese revolution

resulted in the isolation and outflanking of the Gang of Four by the moderates and, perhaps later, the Right. The Right-extremism of the Iranian revolution, on the other hand, may thus lead to the outflanking of Khomeini by the moderates – or the Left.

5 The attempt to reverse the conditions of Soviet strategic inferiority, so evident in the 1962 Cuban missile crisis, began as early as 1962–3, according to a recent statement by US Defense Secretary Brown. It was then that the Soviets embarked on their 'policy of building forces for a pre-emptive attack on US intercontinental ballistic missiles': address at Annapolis, 30 May 1979.

1 Perspectives on the Third World

1 While Marxism is 'universally' applicable to social situations in space and time, pluralism as used here is limited to 'modern' and 'modernising' countries, i.e., to a small number of countries for some two centuries and a large number for one or two decades. However, as this discussion is of contemporary circumstances, both theories are relevant.

2 T. Dos Santos, 'The Crisis of Development Theory and the Problem of Dependence in Latin America', in Henry Bernstein (ed.), *Underdevelopment and Development: The Third World Today*, Harmondsworth, Penguin Books, 1973, p. 72.

3 Rather than being bound by 'conventional security interests', the aim of America's global policy is the 'maintenance under American leadership of a stable world order that would ensure the triumph of liberal-capitalist values and institutions' (Robert W. Tucker and William Watts (eds), 'Introduction', *Beyond Containment: U.S. Foreign Policy in Transition* (Washington, DC, Potomac Associates with *Foreign Policy*, 1973, p. xxv). A similar view is held by Robert Gilpin: 'The international economic order over the past several decades has rested on a pax Americana. . . . Upon this economic and military foundation, the United States created the political superstructure' (Gilpin, 'The Multinational Corporation and American Foreign Policy', in Richard Rosecrance (ed.), *America as an Ordinary Country: U.S. Foreign Policy and the Future*, Ithaca, Cornell University Press, 1976, p. 180).

4 Susanne Bodenheimer, 'Dependence and Imperialism: The Roots of Latin American Underdevelopment', in K. T. Fann and Donald C. Hodges (eds), *Readings in U.S. Imperialism*, Boston, Porter, Sargent, 1971.

5 James S. Coleman, 'Conclusion: The Political Systems of the Developing Areas', and Gabriel A. Almond, 'Introduction: a Functional Approach to Comparative Politics', in Almond and Coleman (eds), *The Politics of the Developing Areas*, Princeton University Press, 1960.

6 Coleman, 'Conclusion', pp. 566–8.

7 Lucian W. Pye, quoted by Coleman, 'Conclusion', p. 567. While Pye's contribution, 'The Politics of Southeast Asia', notes that 'The Philippine parties, for all their historical continuity, still represent primarily the network of personal ties and obligations of the Filipino politicians of the moment' (p. 115), it also states that it 'seems quite probable that Philippine politics is moving in the direction of highly articulate interest-group politics *along the lines of the* American model' (pp. 123–4, italics added).

8 Amado Guerrero, *Philippine Society and Revolution*, Hong Kong, Ta Kung Pao,

1971, p. 3. Amado Guerrero, Chairman of the Central Committee of the Communist Party of the Philippines, is believed to be the *nom de guerre* of Jose Ma. Sison. Sison was captured by security forces in November 1977. His work reflects both Leninist and Maoist concepts: Leninist, on the role of US 'monopoly capitalism', Maoist, on the role of peasant armed struggle and on the organisation of a 'national united front' of workers, peasants, petty and national bourgeoisie. The military wing of the Party is the 'New People's Army', an offshoot of the 'Huk' movement (see chapter 2 below).

9 Ibid., pp. 113–17.

10 Ibid., pp. 160–1, 168–9, 184–5, 199.

11 Ibid., pp. 205–7.

12 Carl Landé, *Leaders, Factions, and Parties: The Structure of Philippine Politics*, New Haven, Yale University Press, Southeast Asia Studies Monograph Series No. 6, 1965, p. 1.

13 Ibid., pp. 1–2.

14 Ibid., pp. 9–10, 12.

15 *The Senator Gravel Edition: The Pentagon Papers*, Boston, Beacon Press, 1971, vol. 2, p. 244.

16 Evidence of élite dominance is given in a detailed study of the leading office-holders in the Philippines since Independence. In two decades, 169 families provided nearly 600 public officials, including 7 presidents, 15 cabinet members, 42 senators, 127 house members and 10 justices. There is a mutually reinforcing network of political and economic power. Politicians at national level get much of their campaign funds from top economic groups – export–importers, manufacturers, tobacco and sugar 'blocs', etc. – which in turn receive favourable or protective legislation, liberal loans from government banks and financial institutions, official contracts and appointments to key public offices and public corporations. Dante C. Simbulan, 'A Study of the Socio-Economic Élite in Philippine Politics and Government, 1946–1963', Australian National University, unpublished doctoral thesis, 1965, pp. 13, 205–16, 295.

17 Landé, *Leaders, Factions and Parties*, pp. 102–4.

18 Guerrero, *Philippine Society and Revolution*, p. 206.

19 According to a recent assessment, martial law and the improvement in law and order have attracted foreign investment. It is still tacitly supported by many corporations, both foreign and local, because of the stability it has brought. Strikes in 'vital industries' are banned, thereby ensuring continuous labour at comparatively cheap wages. But this has done nothing to encourage the distribution of wealth, which still lies in the hands of a small number of families, including some of the old oligarchs, now politically docile, side by side with a new élite comprising relatives and loyal friends of the First Family (Rodney Tasker reporting from Manila, *Far Eastern Economic Review*, 30 September 1977. See also Robert B. Stauffer, 'Philippine Authoritarianism: Framework for Peripheral Development', *Pacific Affairs*, Fall 1977; and 'Testimony on the Philippines, by George McT. Kahin, before the U.S. House of Representatives', Subcommittee on International Organisations, 27 April 1978.

20 David Apter's summary of this thesis in his article, 'Government', reprinted in Apter, *Political Change: Collected Essays*, London, Frank Cass, 1973, p. 90.

21 Almond, 'Introduction', *Politics of the Developing Areas*, pp. 34–5.

22 Other types of interest groups are non-associational (kinship, ethnic, class, etc.), institutional (within legislatures, bureaucracies, etc., which properly have different functions to perform), and anomic (more or less spontaneous riots, demonstrations and so on); ibid., pp. 33–4.

23 Susanne Bodenheimer, *The Ideology of Developmentalism: The American Paradigm-Surrogate for Latin American Studies*, Beverly Hills, Sage, 1971.

24 Though Marxists deny this: see, for example, Ralph Miliband, *The State in Capitalist Society: Analyses of the Western System of Power*, London, Quartet, 1973.

25 This is implicit in Almond's recent 'Introduction' to the study of comparative politics, where he observes that 'the internal organisation and procedures of a political system need to be understood within the framework of a basic question: which structures are most suitable for the policies pursued by that system' (Gabriel Almond (ed.), *Comparative Politics Today: a World View*, Boston, Little, Brown, 1974, p. 6). The system, in other words, is taken for granted. What Almond is concerned with is how to fit the structures to the system – simply to make it more effective.

26 There are, of course, innumerable versions of 'Marxism', from dogmatism to revisionism, from economic determinism to acceptance of the autonomy of the superstructure, and from 'young' to 'old' Marx. What I have set out here is either the work of Marx himself, or is broadly acceptable to most Marxists.

27 Karl Marx, Preface to *A Contribution to the Critique of Political Economy*.

28 'The executive of the modern state is but a committee for managing the common affairs of the whole bourgeoisie' (Karl Marx and Frederick Engels, *Manifesto of the Communist Party*).

29 Ralf Dahrendorf resolves the contradiction between the two models of society in this way: 'There are sociological problems for the explanation of which the integration theory of society provides adequate assumptions; there are other problems which can be explained only in terms of the coercion theory of society; there are, finally, problems for which both theories appear adequate' (*Class and Class Conflict in Industrial Society*, quoted by W. F. Wertheim, in *Evolution and Revolution: The Rising Waves of Emancipation*, Harmondsworth, Penguin Books, 1974, p. 106). Wertheim himself takes the view that 'not only may value orientations among the members of one society diverge' but that 'conflicting value systems may operate within one and the same person'; this is his 'concept of ambivalence' (pp. 107–8).

30 Barrington Moore, for example, notes the 'unique' convergence between the landed and urban upper classes in England to 'favour the cause of freedom'; moreover the elimination of the 'peasant question from English politics' through the enclosure movement, which was part of the industrial revolution, meant that 'there was no massive reservoir of peasants to serve the reactionary ends of the landed upper-classes', as in Germany and Japan (*Social Origins of Dictatorship and Democracy: Lord and Peasant in the Making of the Modern World*, Harmondsworth, Penguin Books edn, 1973, pp. 424–6).

2 Revolutionary motivation

1 V. I. Lenin, *'Left-wing' Communism: An Infantile Disorder*, Moscow, Foreign Languages Publishing House, 1950, pp. 114–15. Lenin's italics.

2 Ibid., p. 115.

3 Eric R. Wolf, *Peasant Wars of the Twentieth Century*, London, Faber & Faber, 1973 edn., p. 295

4 Eric R. Wolf, 'Peasant Rebellion and Revolution', in Norman Miller and Roderick Aya (eds), *National Liberation: Revolution in the Third World*, New York, Free Press, 1971, pp. 52–3.

5 L. Trotsky, *History of the Russian Revolution*, trans. Max Eastman, London, Sphere, 1967, vol. 2, p. 12.

6 Wolf, 'Peasant Rebellion', pp. 54–5.

7 Hamza Alavi, 'Peasants and Revolution', *The Socialist Register*, London, Merlin, 1965, cited by John Wilson Lewis (ed.), *Peasant Rebellion and Communist Revolution in Asia*, Stanford University Press, 1974, 'Introduction' (with Kathleen J. Hartford), p. 12.

8 Mao Tse-tung, 'Report on an Investigation of the Peasant Movement in Hunan' (1927), *Selected Works*, Peking, Foreign Languages Press, 1965, vol. 1, pp. 31–3.

9 Ibid., p. 23.

10 Wolf, 'Peasant Rebellion', p. 55.

11 Many examples are given in the Bombay *Economic and Political Weekly*, cited by D. A. Low, 'The Asian Revolutions of the Mid-Twentieth Century', first national conference of the Asian Studies Association of Australia, Melbourne, May 1976.

12 Wolf, 'Peasant Rebellion', pp. 54–7.

13 Ibid., p. 58.

14 Mao Tse-tung, 'Why is it that Red Political Power can Exist in China?' (1928), *Selected Works*, vol. 1, Peking, Foreign Languages Press, 1965, pp. 64–5. See also 'The Struggle in the Chingkang Mountains' (1928), ibid., pp. 73, 87–9, 99; and 'A Single Spark can Start a Prairie Fire' (1930). On the advantages of bases in Kiangsi province: (1) 'the economy of Kiangsi is mainly feudal, the merchant-capitalist class is relatively weak, and the armed forces of the landlords are weaker than in any other southern province'; (2) Kiangsi is garrisoned by troops from other provinces who are unfamiliar with local conditions and 'usually lack enthusiasm'; and (3) the province 'is comparatively remote from imperialist influence' ('A Single Spark', p. 127).

15 Donald S. Zagoria, 'Asian Tenancy Systems and Communist Mobilisation of the Peasantry', in Lewis (ed.), *Peasant Rebellion and Communist Revolution in Asia*.

16 Hans-Dieter Evers, 'Group Conflict and Class Formation in South-East Asia' in Evers (ed.), *Modernisation in South-East Asia*, Kuala Lumpur, Oxford University Press/Institute of Southeast Asian Studies, Singapore, 1973, p. 110.

17 Rex Mortimer, 'Traditional Modes and Communist Movements: Change and Protest in Indonesia', in Lewis (ed.) *Peasant Rebellion and Communist Revolution in Asia*, pp. 113–14.

18 Barrington Moore, *Social Origins of Dictatorship and Democracy: Lord and Peasant in the Making of the Modern World*, Harmondsworth, Penguin Books, 1973.

19 Wolf, 'Conclusion', *Peasant Wars*, p. 289.

20 Derived from Zagoria, 'Asian Tenancy Systems', pp. 59–60. As Teodor Shanin puts it, the basic socio-political weaknesses of the peasants mean that they are no match for smaller, closely-knit, better organised and technologically superior groups; time and again, the peasants have been 'double-crossed' or

suppressed politically or by force of arms. Yet the peasants' chances of influencing the political sphere increase sharply in times of national crises. 'When non-peasant social forces clash, when rulers are divided or foreign powers attack, the peasantry's attitude and action may well prove decisive' ('Peasantry as a Political Factor', in Shanin (ed.), *Peasants and Peasant Societies*, Harmondsworth, Penguin Books, 1971, 1976, pp. 256–7).

21 Moore, *Social Origins of Dictatorship and Democracy*, p. 469.

22 Ibid., p. 470; and Jeffrey Race, 'Toward an Exchange Theory of Revolution', in Lewis (ed.), *Peasant Rebellion and Communist Revolution in Asia*.

23 Moore, *Social Origins of Dictatorship and Democracy*, p. 471.

24 James C. Scott, *Exploitation in Rural Class Relations: A Victim's Perspective*, New York, Southeast Asia Development Advisory Group (SEADAG) of the Asia Society: SEADAG Papers on Problems of Development in Southeast Asia, 1975. The paper was published, under the same title, in *Comparative Politics*, July 1975. See also James Scott, *The Moral Economy of the Peasant: Rebellion and Subsistence in Southeast Asia*, New Haven, Yale University Press, 1976.

25 Scott, *Exploitation in Rural Class Relations*, p. 47.

26 Ibid., pp. 46–7; see also James Scott, 'The Erosion of Patron–Client Bonds in Rural Southeast Asia', *Journal of Asian Studies*, November 1972.

27 Scott, *Exploitation in Rural Class Relations*, p. 47. In Burma, by 1939, 'nearly half of the farmed area of lower Burma . . . had passed into the hands of non-agricultural owners and most of the rest was mortgaged'; 59 per cent of farm land was under tenancy (less than one-third in upper Burma). There was great instability of tenure: nearly half the tenants in lower Burma changed holdings every year (H. V. Richter, 'The Union of Burma', in R. T. Shand (ed.), *Agricultural Development in Asia*, Canberra, Australian National University Press, 1960, pp. 149–50.

28 W. E. Wertheim, *Evolution and Revolution: The Rising Waves of Emancipation*, Harmondsworth, Penguin Books, 1974, pp. 190–9; he also cites Clifford Geertz, *The Social History of an Indonesian Town*, Cambridge, Mass., MIT Press, 1965.

29 Wolf, *Peasant Wars*, pp. 228–34; see also John Dunn, *Modern Revolutions: An Introduction to the Analysis of a Political Phenomenon*, Cambridge University Press, 1972, 'Algeria', esp. pp. 168–9. For the impact of the revolution, see ch. 3 below.

30 Peng Teh-huai, interviewed by Edgar Snow, *Red Star over China*, London, Gollancz, 1937, p. 284.

31 Vo Nguyen Giap, 'The Great Experiences Gained by our Party in Leading the Armed Struggle and Building Revolutionary Armed Forces' (1960), in *People's War, People's Army*, Hanoi, Foreign Languages Publishing House, 1961, p. 104.

32 Herbert Marcuse, *One Dimensional Man*, London, Sphere Books, 1970, p. 200.

33 Barrington Moore, *Social Origins of Dictatorship and Democracy*, p. 100.

34 'All such societies are governed by *necessity*, which is supplemented by and appears under the forms of accident' (Engels to Heinz Starkenburg, January 1894 in *Karl Marx: Selected Works*, London, Lawrence & Wishart, 1943, vol. 1, p. 392).

35 Karl Marx, Preface to *A Contribution to the Critique of Political Economy*, ibid., pp. 356–7.

36 Joseph Stalin, *The Foundation of Leninism* (1924), Peking, Foreign Languages

Press, 1965, reprint of Moscow 1953 edn, pp. 29, 73.

37 V. I. Lenin, *The Two Tactics of Social Democracy in the Democratic Revolution* (1905), in *Selected Works*, London, Lawrence & Wishart, 1946, vol. 3, pp. 110–11.

38 Stalin, *Foundations of Leninism*, pp. 58–9.

39 Lenin of course insisted – against the Left doctrinaires – that the 'specific features' which the revolutionary struggle assumes in each separate country must be taken into account (*'Left-Wing' Communism*, pp. 127–8).

40 Thomas H. Green, *Comparative Revolutionary Movements*, Englewood Cliffs, N.J., Prentice-Hall, 1974, pp. 146–8.

41 As Engels observed, the more the particular object of examination diverges from the economic foundation, the more its development is 'accidental' (i.e. the inner connection of things and events is remote or impossible to prove); but 'the longer the period considered' and the wider the field dealt with the more it will run parallel to the economic development (to Joseph Bloch (1890) and Starkenburg, in *Karl Marx: Selected Works*, vol. 1, pp. 381, 393).

42 'Peasants, Land Reform, and Revolutionary Movements': Rural Development Panel Seminar of SEADAG, held in Savannah, Georgia, 2–4 June 1974, New York, SEADAG, 1975.

43 SEADAG Summary of Proceedings. With regard to three other papers it was noted that: 'Disagreement arose over the relationship between tenancy and rural violence. It was suggested that in order to be able to predict peasant revolt the following factors, at a minimum, must be known: the characteristics of landlords; the distribution of wealth among the peasantry; the form and degree of stability of tenancy; the availability of a land frontier and of other economic opportunities for tenants; the mix of tenancy and other land systems; and the rights that tenants feel are customarily owed them. *However, there was disagreement as to the significance of these variables and to the priorities* to be assigned in investigating them' (SEADAG Summary, italics added). James Scott, too, refers to social science theories of peasant behaviour which tend to ignore the actual experience of 'intimidation and terror or the sense of injustice and exploitation' which move peasants to resist. Scott also discusses two books: F. L. Tullis, *Lord and Peasant in Peru* (Harvard University Press, 1970) which treats the theme of 'rising expectations' frustrated and turning towards aggression; and Joel S. Migdal, *Peasants, Politics, and Revolution* (Princeton University Press, 1974) based on the 'Bourgeois calculus' (Scott's phrase) of peasant organisational involvement predicated on material gains. Further, Scott qualifies the widely-held view that the 'atomised' peasantry depends on *external* organisation for effective cohesion; he notes that the 'informal social networks' created by villagers provide a basis on which revolutionary movements can build (Scott, 'Peasant Revolution: A Dismal Science', *Comparative Politics*, January 1977).

44 *Hukbalahab* (acronym), or 'Anti-Japanese People's Army', later 'Army of National Liberation', founded by Communist Party of the Philippines, 1942.

45 Dante C. Simbulan, 'A Study of the Socio-Economic Élite in Philippine Politics and Government', Australian National University, unpublished doctoral thesis, 1965, pp. 81–3. This situation will be little affected by President Marcos's land reforms: with a ceiling raised to 24 hectares (60 acres) for rice and corn fields, and with the exclusion of tenants farming other crops, the maximum effect of the reform is that 16 per cent of current tenant farmers 'might own land in fifteen

years'; landless labourers – perhaps the largest group of peasants – are offered nothing (Benedict J. Kerkvliet, 'Land Reform in the Philippines since the Marcos Coup', *Pacific Affairs*, Fall 1974).

As of July 1976 only 100,000 tenants had received 'certificates of land transfer' – a tentative promise of future benefit – about 25 per cent of the original programme goal; only 26,000 had actually stopped paying rent to landlords and started paying amortisation payments to the Land Bank – the crucial transaction that may accurately be called 'land reform' (David Wurfel, 'Martial Law in the Philippines: The Methods of Regime Survival', *Pacific Affairs*, Spring 1977).

46 Frank Golay, *The Philippines: Public Policy and National Economic Development*, Ithaca, Cornell University Press, 1961, pp. 23–4, 37–8.

47 Carl Landé, *Leaders, Factions, and Parties: The Structure of Philippine Politics*, Yale University Press, Southeast Asia Studies Monograph series No. 6, 1965, pp. 92–3, 96–7

48 N. D. Valeriano and C. T. R. Bohannan, *Counter-guerrilla Operations: The Philippines Experience*, New York, Praeger, 1962, pp. 33–4.

49 Carlos P. Romulo and Marvin Gray, *The Magsaysay Story*, New York, Pocket Books, 1957, pp. 92–3.

50 Eduardo Lachica, *Huk: Philippine Agrarian Society in Revolt*, Manila, Solidaridad Publishing House, 1971, pp. 14–15, 21, 25–6. But see also Benedict Kerkvliet, *The Huk Rebellion: A Study of Peasant Revolt in the Philippines* (Berkeley, University of California Press, 1977) who argues that the main aim of the peasant rebels – if not of the Communist Party, which played an ambiguous role – was to *re-establish* the traditional relationships that had been eroded by commercialisation: to reform the tenancy system, not to eliminate it.

51 Lachica, *Huk*, pp. 41–4.

52 David R. Sturtevant, 'Philippine Social Structure and its Relation to Agrarian Unrest' (unpublished Ph.D. thesis, Stanford University, 1958); quoted by Lachica, *Huk*, p. 61.

53 Lachica, *Huk*, pp. 11, 28–9, 31, 38. The New People's Army, whose commander was captured in August 1976, is in part an offshoot of the Huks operating north of Pampanga. Many years after the failure of the Huk rebellion, a communist critique emphasised: (1) Communist Party leaders 'erred in thinking that the Filipino people in general "could no longer endure the old rule" . . . [in fact] the people were susceptible to promises of "reform" '. (2) 'Once a revolutionary situation was declared, the party put almost all emphasis and cadres into the armed struggle, to the neglect of legal forms of struggle and to the neglect of allies . . . the party failed to project and build a united front. . . . The nationalist bourgeoisie was frightened and antagonised.' (3) 'Having become overconfident in 1950, the party became careless in its security measures': the entire party secretariat, with complete files of documents, was captured in Manila in October 1950: 'this blow resulted in dislocation and in loss of initiative, which was never recovered.' (4) The national liberation struggle was 'physically isolated from international allies' and received virtually no support from abroad. (Jorge Maravilla, *World Marxist Review*, November 1965; extracts in William J. Pomeroy (ed.), *Guerrilla Warfare and Marxism* (New York, International Publishers, 1968), pp. 240–1.) The insurgency in Mindanao, by contrast, is mainly the result of ethnic and religious grievances – aided, to a

certain extent, by Muslims abroad. Ironically, one of the reforms adopted to counter the Huk revolt – resettlement of landless peasants in the then underpopulated south – contributed, by creating competition for land between newcomers and settled villagers, to the Moro rebellion.

54 See 'The Ten Days', published by the *Bangkok Post*; Steward Meacham, 'The Ten Days That Shook Thailand', Quaker International Affairs Representatives Report (undated); J.-C. Pomonti, *Le Monde*, 17, 18, 19, 20, 25 October 1973; *Far Eastern Economic Review*, 10, 22 October, 26 November, 3 December 1973; R.-I. Heinze, 'Ten Days in October', and R. F. Zimmerman, 'Student Revolution in Thailand', *Asian Survey*, June 1974; Prudhisan Jumbala, 'The Emergence of the Thai Student Movement', *South East Asian Spectrum*, October 1975; Ross Prizzia and Narong Sinsawasdi, *Thailand: Student Activism and Political Change*, Bangkok, D.K. Books, 1974, chs 1–3.

55 Daniel and Gabriel Cohn-Bendit, *Obsolete Communism: The Left-Wing Alternative*, trans. A. Pomerans, Harmondsworth, Penguin Books, 1968, p. 137.

56 Ellen J. Hammer, *The Struggle for Indochina 1940–1955*, Stanford University Press, 1955, p. 71.

57 Ibid., p. 79.

58 Milton E. Osborne, *The French Presence in Cochinchina and Cambodia: Rule and Response (1859–1905)*, Ithaca, Cornell University Press, 1969, ch. 7.

59 Le Thanh Khoi, *Le Viet-Nam: Histoire et Civilisation*, Paris, Editions de Minuit, 1955, pp. 422–3.

60 Christine Pelser White, 'The Vietnamese Revolutionary Alliance: Intellectuals, Workers, and Peasants', in Lewis (ed.), *Peasant Rebellion and Communist Revolution in Asia*, pp. 79, 87–8.

61 David G. Marr, 'Concepts of Harmony and Struggle in Pre-Revolutionary Vietnam, 1925–1944', first national conference of Asian Studies Association of Australia, Melbourne, May 1976.

62 Philippe Devillers, *Histoire du Vietnam de 1940 à 1952*, Paris, Editions du Seuil, 1952, p. 61. See also David Marr, *Vietnamese Anticolonialism: 1885–1925*, Berkeley, University of California Press, 1971, ch. 10, 'Changing the Guard'.

63 Marr, 'Concepts of Harmony and Struggle'.

64 Paul Mus, *Viet-Nam: Sociologie d'une guerre*, Paris, Editions du Seuil, 1952, pp. 26, 31.

65 Vo Nguyen Giap, *People's War, People's Army*, Hanoi, Foreign Languages Publishing House, 1961, pp. 34–5. Party leaders, like Ho Chi Minh himself, were mostly of 'scholar-gentry' origins.

66 Ibid., p. 31.

67 Ho Chi Minh, *Selected Works*, Hanoi, Foreign Languages Publishing House, 1961, vol. 3, p. 378.

68 Ibid., pp. 421–2. However, once the French colonial regime had been defeated, the socialist aims of land reform in North Vietnam came to the fore: above all, to break the power of the landed, conservative class (landowners, rich peasants). This campaign went to extremes both in terms of classification (far too many were wrongly classified as landlords or rich peasants) and of methods – violence got out of hand. President Ho Chi Minh was forced to 'rectify' the programme.

69 *United States–Vietnam Relations 1945–1967*, Washington, D.C., U.S.

Government Printing Office, 1971, [The Pentagon Papers], vol. 10, pp. 935–6; quoted by Gareth Porter, *A Peace Denied: The United States, Vietnam, and the Paris Agreement*, Bloomington, Indiana University Press, 1975, p. 38.

70 Nguyen Thai, *Is South Vietnam Viable?*, Manila, Carmelo and Bauermann, 1962, pp. 43–4, 52–4, 86.

71 According to a RAND study in 1976, the Vietminh network had been virtually eliminated by Diem's anti-communist offensive. Ex-Vietminh prisoners or defectors 'spoke of terror, brutality and torture by GVN [Government of Vietnam] rural officials in carrying out the Communist Denunciation campaigns and of the arrest and slaying of thousands of old comrades from the "Resistance" ' (RAND study RM-5163-ISA (ARPA) by Joseph Zasloff, March 1967, summary in *United States–Vietnam Relations*, vol. 2, sec.IV A.5.Tab 2, p. 50).

72 General Earle Wheeler, Chairman of US Joint Chiefs of Staff, Department of State *Bulletin*, 6 February 1967.

73 Jeffrey Race, 'How They Won', *Asian Survey*, August 1970, pp. 639, 646: there is a similar analysis in his *War Comes to Long An: Revolutionary Conflict in a Vietnamese Village*, Berkeley, University of California Press, 1972, ch. 4. The Communist Party in the South was the 'People's Revolutionary Party', part of the NLF.

74 Race, 'How They Won', p. 648.

75 Robert L. Sansom, *The Economics of Insurgency in the Mekong Delta of Vietnam*, Cambridge, Mass., MIT Press, 1970, pp. 54–5.

76 Race, 'How They Won', p. 638.

77 Douglas Pike, *Viet Cong: The Organization and Techniques of the National Liberation Front of South Vietnam*, Cambridge, Mass., MIT Press, 1966, p. 60.

78 Sansom, *Economics of Insurgency*, p. 65. Several of these papers were reprinted in a 'Special Issue on Peasants and Revolution', *Comparative Politics*, April 1976; see Introduction by Donald Zagoria.

79 Race, 'How They Won', pp. 641, 648. Even the staunchly anti-communist member of the British Advisory Mission, Dennis J. Duncanson, reported that 'everywhere peasant grievances against authority, or feuds with other groups often identified with authority in the uniform of the militia or the Civil Guard, as well as credence for Vietcong offers of land, added their quota, if not a large one, of malcontents vulnerable to a sympathetic ear and a helping hand', Duncanson, *Government and Revolution in Vietnam*, London, Oxford University Press, 1968, p. 297.

80 Imports rose from 23 billion Vietnamese piastres in 1964 to 121 billion in 1969: Hla Myint, *Southeast Asia's Economy: Development Policies in the 1970s*, study sponsored by the Asian Development Bank, Harmondsworth, Penguin Books, 1972, pp. 118–20; also Sansom, *Economics of Insurgency*, pp. 164, 180–1.

81 Defense Secretary Schlesinger's estimate, *International Herald Tribune*, 3–4 May 1975.

3 Structural context

1 Letter to Vera Zasulich, quoted by Richard Gott, *Guerrilla Movements in Latin America*, London, Nelson, 1970, p. 14

2 Che Guevara, *Guerrilla Warfare*, Harmondsworth, Penguin Books, 1969, p. 13. However, experience shows that the destructive force of a protracted insurgency is more likely than an attempted insurrection to 'create' revolutionary conditions;

in addition, once the revolution is 'made', it is more likely to consolidate it.

3 Régis Debray, 'Castroism: The Long March in Latin America', written in 1965, in *Strategy for Revolution*, Harmondsworth, Penguin Books, 1973, pp. 39, 50, 51.

4 Ibid., p. 46.

5 Georges Sorel, *Reflections on Violence*, trans. T. E. Hulme, Chicago, Free Press, 1950, p. 58: 'A myth cannot be refuted, since it is, at bottom, identical with the conviction of a group.'

6 David C. Gordon, *The Passing of French Algeria*, London, Oxford Unversity Press, 1966, p. 57.

7 Hugh Tinker, *The Union of Burma*, London, Oxford University Press, 2nd edn, 1959, p. 34.

8 Eric R. Wolf, *Peasant Wars of the Twentieth Century*, London, Faber & Faber, 1973 edn, pp. 26, 28–32, 35–44.

9 Boris Goldenberg, *The Cuban Revolution and Latin America*, London, Allen & Unwin, 1965, p. 140.

10 Hugh Thomas, 'The Origins of the Cuban Revolution', *World Today*, October 1963.

11 See the previous chapter, 'Peasant participants'.

12 Ramon Eduardo Ruiz, *Cuba: The Making of a Revolution*, Amherst, University of Massachusetts Press, 1968, pp. 9–10.

13 Jacques Lambert, *Latin America: Social Structure and Political Institutions*, trans. Helen Kattel, Berkeley, University of California Press, 1967, table, pp. 26–7.

14 Samuel P. Huntington, *Political Order in Changing Societies*, New Haven, Yale University Press, 1969, p. 305.

15 Thomas, 'The Origins of The Cuban Revolution'. See also Ruiz, *Cuba*, pp. 142–7, 159.

16 Régis Debray, *La Critique des armes*, Paris, Editions du Seuil, 1974, vol. 1, p. 60.

17 Quoted by Richard L. Worsnop, 'Guerrilla Movements in Latin America', in *Editorial Research Reports on World in Ferment*, Congressional Quarterly, 1968. The US verdict is reminiscent of Acheson's report on the communist victory in China: 'The Nationalist armies did not have to be defeated; they disintegrated. History has proved again and again that a regime without faith in itself and an army without morale cannot survive the test of battle' (Secretary of State Dean Acheson's Foreword to *United States Relations with China, 1944–49*, August 1949).

18 Goldenberg, *The Cuban Revolution and Latin America*, p. 144.

19 Ibid., pp. 144, 146.

20 Ibid., pp. 159–60, 162–3.

21 Theodore Draper, *Castroism: Theory and Practice*, London, Pall Mall, 1965, pp. 23–5.

22 Ibid.

23 Che Guevara, *Reminiscences of the Cuban Revolutionary War*, London, Allen & Unwin, 1968, p. 208.

24 Tibor Mende, *From Aid to Re-Colonization: Lesson of a Failure*, London, Harrap, 1973, pp. 142–4.

25 Solon Barraclough, 'The Agrarian Problem', in Claudio Veliz (ed.), *Latin America and the Caribbean: A Handbook*, New York, Praeger, 1968, table, pp. 490–1.

26 The Report was released in November 1969; it recommended, *inter alia*, that

the USA provide more arms to Latin American governments to fight communist subversion (*New York Times* weekly review, 16 November 1969).

27 Alain-Marie Carron, 'Cuba: Revolution for Export', *Le Monde*, 2 March 1976 (translation in *Guardian Weekly*, 14 March 1976). After 1970 Cuba reduced its revolutionary pressure in Latin America. But the final resolution of the Havana Conference of Latin American Communist Parties in June 1975, while stating that 'the use of all legal possibilities is an unavoidable obligation', also affirmed the 'right and duty' of anti-imperialist forces to 'pave the way by the most varied means of popular action, including armed action' (ibid.).

28 Speech of 16 January 1963, quoted in Draper, *Castroism*, pp. 40–1.

29 Stephen Clissold, 'The Soviet Union and Latin America', in Veliz (ed.), *Latin America and the Caribbean*, pp. 452–4.

30 *Guerrilla Warfare*, pp. 123–4.

31 Juan de Onis, *International Herald Tribune*, 2 July 1968.

32 Jack Davis, *Political Violence in Latin America*, Adelphi Papers, No. 85, London, International Institute of Strategic Studies, February 1972, p. 11.

33 Samuel Huntington, *Civil Violence and the Process of Development*, Adelphi Papers, No. 83, London, International Institute of Strategic Studies, December 1971, p. 5. The chapter headings of Richard Gott's *Guerrilla Movements in Latin America* tell the story: 'Soldiers and Peasants in Guatemala', 'Revolutionary Failure in Venezuela', 'Violence in Colombia', 'Disaster in Peru', 'Tragedy in Bolivia' and finally 'Defeat of the Revolution?'.

34 Davis, *Political Violence*.

35 Hugh Thomas, *Cuba, or the Pursuit of Freedom*, London, Eyre & Spottiswoode, 1971, pp. 918, 946, 953, 1045.

36 Debray, *La Critique des armes*, p. 71.

37 Goldenberg, *The Cuban Revolution and Latin America*, pp. 73–4.

38 See Hugh Thomas, *Cuba, or the Pursuit of Freedom*, pp. 1054–5, 1215–29, 1323; and Debray, *La Critique des armes*, pp. 57–64. If the military and bureaucratic machine in Cuba had not been broken *before* carrying out the minimum programme of the revolution, Debray points out, the revolutionary process would itself have been broken by external military intervention or an internal coup, as in Guatemala in 1954, Brazil in 1964, Chile in 1973 (ibid., p. 67).

39 Alistair Hennessy, 'Bolivia', in Veliz (ed.), *Latin America and the Caribbean*, pp. 28–9.

40 Frances M. Foland, 'Agrarian Reform in Latin America', *Foreign Affairs*, October 1969.

41 Huntington, *Political Order in Changing Societies*, pp. 331–3; Hennessy, 'Bolivia', pp. 30–1.

42 Huntington, *Civil Violence and the Process of Development*.

43 Gott, *Guerrilla Movements in Latin America*, pp. 364–5.

44 Gino Germani, 'Stages of Modernisation in Latin America', in S. A. Halper and J. R. Sterling, *Latin America: The Dynamics of Social Change*, London, Allison & Busby, 1972, pp. 36–7.

45 Gott, *Guerrilla Movements in Latin America*, pp. 361, 363; Régis Debray, 'Problems of Revolutionary Strategy', *Strategy for Revolution*, pp. 156–7.

46 *Revolution in the Revolution?*, Harmondsworth, Penguin Books, 1968, pp. 28, 50, 60–2, 75, 81–2, 105.

47 Debray's *La Critique des armes* (1974) reveals a complete about-face. The facile but misleading brilliance of *Revolution in the Revolution?* gives way to a far more convincing, but also more pedestrian, analysis. Debray admits that his hypothesis of a military pyramid – constructed from the top downward – has been falsified by experience. Instead, the mixture of nationalism and social content in Latin American revolutionary struggles 'demands extreme flexibility'. The revolution, he writes, must combine political insurrection in the big industrial centres with the formation of a peasant or people's army in the countryside; it must work within the regular army (as in the Russia of 1917) and construct a new model army (as in China). See pp. 48–50, 95–107, 117–20.

48 Lambert, *Latin America: Social Structure and Political Institutions*, pp. 206, 208.

49 Amounting to not more than 8 per cent of the urban population in the most industrialised countries of Latin America; only 3 per cent in the least industrialised (ibid., pp. 81–2).

50 Ibid., p. 208.

51 Ibid., pp. 224–5.

52 Gott, *Guerrilla Movements in Latin America*, pp. 102–7.

53 Lambert, *Latin America: Social Structures and Political Institutions*, p. 226.

54 Debray, 'Problems of Revolutionary Strategy', pp. 142, 153.

55 V. I. Lenin. *What Is To Be Done?*, Moscow, Progress Publishers, 1973 edn, pp. 98–100.

56 From the Memorandum by President Bordaberry of Uruguay, dated 9 December 1975; it was intended to formalise the rule of the Uruguayan armed forces, which had taken power in 1973: report by Agence France-Presse (*Canberra Times*, 20 April 1976). The Memorandum did not save Bordaberry. He was forced by the military to resign in June 1976.

57 Ibid.

58 This is not to suggest that the armed forces are a monolith. On the contrary, personal and inter-service rivalries, and even conflict, are not unusual, while political tendencies vary from radical to reactionary.

59 G. I. Mirskii, *Armiya i Politika v Stranakh Azii i Afriki* (Army and Politics in the Countries of Asia and Africa), Moscow, Nauka, 1970, pp. 232, 238–9.

60 Even in such a 'European' country as Argentina, over two-thirds of more than 300 generals surveyed in the early 1960s are of recent immigrant origin, and less than one-third are descendants of old Argentine families; out of 114 of these generals, whose fathers' occupations are known, 69 are sons of businessmen, employees and military men; only ten are sons of landowners (Survey by José Luiz de Imaz in 1964, cited by Lambert, *Latin America: Social Structure and Political Institutions*, p. 241).

61 In Latin America only two governments effectively control their armed forces: in Costa Rica, where the army was disbanded in 1948, and Mexico, where it has become one of the functional groups subject to the authority of the one-party system. In all the other countries the armed forces determine their own strength, their equipment, the proportion of the budget to be spent on defence, and they impose the defence minister of their choice. In most countries, up to the 1960s, they have preferred indirect intervention, in the form of pressure on the government to comply with their demands, rather than direct assumption of power (Lambert, *Latin America: Social Structures and Political Institutions*, p. 246).

62 Mirskii, *Armiya i Politika*, pp. 315–16, 339; however, Mirskii is aware of the inadequacy of the 'psychological cast of mind' of the military with regard to political tasks and to work among the intelligentsia and the masses. Career officers, at best, may be efficient administrators; and that, as a rule, at low levels. Patriotism, loyalty to duty, will, decision, discipline, systematic organisation – all these are insufficient when it is a question, not just of producing order, but of the complicated decisions, and patient work, indispensable to the radical reconstruction of society (p. 307).

63 Huntington, *Political Order in Changing Societies*, 'Praetorianism and Political Decay', pp. 220–2.

64 In 1960 just over half the population of Latin America (total: 215 million) lived in rural areas: in Brazil nearly 50 million out of 70 million people; in Mexico 24 million out of a total of 34 million; in Colombia 11 million out of 16 million; in Argentina 8 million out of 20 million. However, by 1975 only 40 per cent of a total population of 327 million lived in the countryside; Brazil was 60 per cent urban, Mexico 63 per cent, Colombia 62 per cent, and Argentina 80 per cent: quoted by Daniel Bell, 'The Future World Disorder', *Foreign Policy*, September 1977.

65 Foland, 'Agrarian Reform in Latin America'.

66 Barraclough in Veliz (ed.), *Latin America and the Caribbean*, table, p. 490; 1960 figures, except for Guatemala, 1950, but here the proportion – after the reversal of the 1954 land reforms – is unchanged. One writer has estimated that 40 per cent of all Latin American farm families in the late 1960s were landless, while half of all farm land was controlled by 1 per cent of the people (Ernest Feder, '*Latifundia* and Agricultural Labour in Latin America', in Teodor Shanin (ed.), *Peasants and Peasant Societies*, Harmondsworth, Penguin Books, 1971, 1976, p. 83.

67 Foland, 'Agrarian Reform in Latin America'.

68 Lambert, *Latin America: Social Structures and Political Institutions*, pp. 67–9, 75–6, 83.

69 Ibid., p. 138.

70 Goldenberg, *The Cuban Revolution and Latin America*, p. 42.

71 Huntington, *Political Order in Changing Societies*, p. 280.

72 Ibid., p. 281. See also below, 'Urban insurgency'.

73 Miguel Arraes, *Brazil: The People and the Power*, trans. Lancelot Sheppard, Harmondsworth, Penguin Books, 1972, p. 104.

74 Ibid., p. 130.

75 Lambert, *Latin America: Social Structures and Political Institutions*, p. 214.

76 Ibid., pp. 215–16.

77 Frantz Fanon, 'Algeria Unveiled', *A Dying Colonialism*, Harmondsworth, Penguin Books, 1970.

78 Mao Tse-tung, 'Report on an Investigation of the Peasant Movement in Hunan' (1927), *Selected Works*, Peking, Foreign Languages Press, 1965, vol. 1, p. 44.

79 Frantz Fanon, *The Wretched of the Earth*, Harmondsworth, Penguin Books, 1967, p. 47. Fanon's celebrated study admittedly shows little concern either for the important role of Islam in Algeria and its cleavage with 'secular' France, or for the organisation, leadership and policies of the Nationalists, or the part played by the 'exterior' forces in Cairo during the war, or indeed the differences among resistance elements – rural, urban and external; liberal and radical; military and

civilian – which were to surface after independence.

80 Ibid., pp. 100–1.

81 Fanon's conviction of rural *authenticity* may well explain the ruggedness, strength and endurance of the great resistance movements; it may also partly account for the ruthlessly puritanical character of the Cambodian upheaval.

82 Fanon, *The Wretched of the Earth*, p. 74.

83 Ibid., p. 48.

84 Similar to Sorel's distinction between 'violence' – the act of justified revolt against an oppressive minority – and 'force', the 'illegitimate' action of these oppressors: *Reflections on Violence*, p. 194. But see also 'Urban insurgency', below.

85 See Fanon's scathing remarks, influenced by his experience of Nkrumah's Ghana, in 'The Pitfalls of National Consciousness', *The Wretched of the Earth*.

86 Proclaimed by the religious reformer, Sheikh Ben Badis, in 1931; quoted by Charles-Henri Favrod, *Le F.L.N. et l'Algérie*, Paris, Plon, 1962, p. 91.

87 Ibid., p. 101.

88 Ibid., p. 112.

89 Moses Moleira, quoted in Robert Moss, *Urban Guerrilla Warfare*, Adelphi Papers, No. 79, London, International Institute for Strategic Studies, August 1971, p. 7.

90 Varying from greater emphasis on the peasantry (Mexico, 1910) to proletarian revolt combined with peasant uprisings (Russia, 1917) and the virtual fusion of the two (China, especially after 1936, Vietnam 1945–75, Algeria 1954–62).

91 ILO Study: 'Changes in the Industrial Distribution of the World Labour Force, by Regions, 1880–1960' in *Essays in Employment* (ILO, 1971), quoted by Geoffrey Currey, 'The Definition of Development' in Rex Mortimer (ed.), *Showcase State: The Illusion of Indonesia's Accelerated Modernization*, Sydney, Angus & Robertson, 1973, table, pp. 34–5.

92 Sydney Goldstein, Visid Prachuabmoh, Alice Goldstein, *Urban–Rural Migration Differentials in Thailand*, Bangkok, Chulalongkorn University, Institute of Population Studies, 1974, the global setting, pp. 1–2.

93 Document prepared for the Conference, quoted by Gladwin Hill of the *New York Times: International Herald Tribune*, 1 June 1976.

94 Surveys of rural migrants to towns are virtually unanimous on this point: Joan M. Nelson, *Migration, Urban Poverty, and Instability in Developing Nations*, Boston, Mass., Harvard University, Occasional Papers in International Affairs, No. 22, 1969, p. 14.

95 Sorel, *Reflections on Violence*, pp. 142, 152.

96 Carlos Marighela, 'On Principles and Strategic Questions', quoted by Moss, *Urban Guerrilla Warfare*, p. 3.

97 Carlos Marighela, *Minimanual of the Urban Guerrilla*: the text is printed as an Appendix to Moss, *Urban Guerrilla Warfare*.

98 Nelson, *Migration, Urban Poverty, and Instability*, pp. 43–5.

99 Ibid., pp. 51–2, 62–5.

100 Fanon, *The Wretched of the Earth*, pp. 103, 106.

101 Debray, *La Critique des armes*, pp. 142–4.

102 Debray, 'Castroism: The Long March in Latin America', p. 56.

103 Régis Debray, *Les Epreuves du feu*, Paris, Seuil, 1974, Part II, 'A Propos des Tupamaros'.

104 Terrorism by a tiny number of radicals in West Germany, which has provoked an almost hysterial reaction among the 'law and order' majority, is a special case. Ralf Dahrendorf suggests that both spring from the insecurity and self-doubt that pervades Germany: 'In the absence of an entrenched tradition of social cohesion, of values that are accepted without dispute, the country is wavering between total indiscipline and total discipline, between the destructive desire to violate all rules and the dangerous desire to create rules for every contingency' (*International Herald Tribune*, 22–23 October 1977). It is no coincidence that terrorism should have made such an ominous appearance both in Germany and Italy – countries which were the last in Western Europe to be unified, where democracy had only precariously existed until recent times, and which were subjected to the traumatic experience of Nazi and fascist rule. Special circumstances, too, account for the spectacular emergence of the 'Red Brigades' in Italy. Among them are the vast numbers of unemployed, particularly affecting the youth, the corruption and incompetence of the ruling party, the bureaucratic and educational shambles, and (for radicals) the failure of the Italian Communist Party to present a revolutionary alternative.

105 Lin Piao, 'Long Live the Victory of People's War', *Peking Review*, 3 September 1965. This is an authoritative analysis (despite Lin Piao's later disgrace), to show that 'the establishment of rural revolutionary base areas and the encirclement of cities from the countryside is of outstanding and universal practical importance for the present revolutionary struggles of all the oppressed nations and peoples, and particularly . . . in Asia, Africa and Latin America' (ibid.).

106 The six necessary ingredients of the Chinese revolution, according to Ying-Mau Kau, are: political security, revolutionary base, socio-economic reforms, mass base, armed forces, and leadership with organisation. Except for the last, a *rural* environment provides the most favourable conditions. An urban environment is very *unfavourable* in terms of political security, revolutionary base, and the carrying out of socio-economic reforms: 'Urban and Rural Strategies in the Chinese Communist Revolution' in John Lewis (ed.), *Peasant Rebellion and Communist Revolution in Asia*, Stanford University Press, 1974, p. 270.

107 'Problems of Strategy in China's Revolution War' (1936), *Selected Works*, Peking, Foreign Languages Press, 1965, vol. 1, pp. 196–9.

108 Revolutionary war can only be carried on by mobilising the masses: i.e. leading the peasant struggle for land, safeguarding the workers' interests, establishing co-operatives, developing trade, solving questions of food, shelter, clothing and sickness. 'We should convince the masses that we represent their interests, that our lives are intimately bound up with theirs. We should help them to proceed from these things to an understanding of the higher tasks . . . so that they will support the revolution and spread it throughout the country' ('Be Concerned with the Well-Being of the Masses' (1934), *Selected Works*, vol. 1, pp. 147–9). Ying-Mau Kau underlines the critical importance of the mass-line technique in China: the deployment of cadres among the people to learn their problems (living, eating, working and studying together) ('Urban and Rural Strategies', p. 262).

109 This is not to rule out possible relaxations, from time to time, in the style of government – such as overtures to professionals, technocrats, intellectuals and organised workers; appropriately timed and managed elections; and other forms

of guided democracy – which do not disturb the substance of military, bureaucratic, landlord and business power.

4 General theory of revolution?

1 Edmund Burke, *Reflections on the Revolution in France*, edited and introduced by Conor Cruise O'Brien, Harmondsworth, Penguin Books, 1968, pp. 89–91. To Burke the 'circumstances' were hateful indeed: liberty leading to excess; a government which 'inspired false ideas and vain expectations'; 'laws overturned; tribunals subverted; industry without vigour, commerce expiring, the revenue unpaid' and all that follows of his magnificent tirade against the 'unnatural' overthrow of the established order (pp. 121, 126).

2 V. I. Lenin, 'Partisan Warfare' (1906) in *Marx-Engels-Marxism*, Moscow, Foreign Languages Publishing House, 1951, pp. 186–7.

3 Gunnar Myrdal, *An American Dilemma: The Negro Problem and Modern Democracy*, New York, Harper & Row, 1944, ch. 1.

4 Henry Bienen, *Violence and Social Change: A Review of Current Literature*, University of Chicago Press, 1968, p. 105.

5 Joseph Frankel, *Contemporary International Theory and the Behaviour of States*, London, Oxford University Press, 1973, p. 21.

6 Chalmers Johnson, *Revolutionary Change*, Boston, Little Brown, 1966, pp. 143, 149. Consider the analogy of artistic creation. 'In real art, theory does not precede practice but follows it,' writes Kandinsky. He refers to the 'many-sided genius' of Leonardo, who 'devised a system of little spoons with which different colours were to be used, thus creating a kind of mechanical harmony. One of his pupils, after trying in vain to use this system, in despair asked one of his colleagues how the master himself used the invention. The colleague replied: "The Master never used it at all" ' (Wassily Kandinsky, *Concerning the Spiritual in Art*, New York, George Wittenborn, 1966; original German edn, 1912, pp. 53–4).

7 Stanley Hoffmann, *Gulliver's Troubles, or the Setting of American Foreign Policy*, New York, McGraw-Hill, 1968, Introduction.

8 Myrdal, *An American Dilemma*, Appendix 1, p. 1033.

9 Burke, *Reflections on the Revolution in France*, p. 194. 'In events like these our passions instruct our reason' (p. 175).

10 Mao Tse-tung, 'On Contradiction' (1937), *Selected Works*, Peking, Foreign Languages Press, 1965, vol. 1, pp. 335, 338–9, italics added.

11 Truong Chinh, *The Resistance Will Win*, Hanoi, Foreign Languages Publishing Press, 1960, p. 95.

12 Ted Robert Gurr, *Why Men Rebel*, Princeton University Press, 1970, p. 326.

13 Carl von Clausewitz, *On War*, ed. Anatol Rapoport, Harmondsworth, Penguin Books, 1968, pp. 116–17, 121.

14 Bernard Brodie, *War and Politics*, New York, Macmillan, 1973, pp. 446, 452.

15 Quoted in *The Pentagon Papers*, *New York Times* edition, New York, Bantam Books, 1971, p. 150.

16 Ibid., p. 278.

17 For a more detailed discussion of the Thai situation, see John L. S. Girling, *Society and Politics in Thailand*, Ithaca, Cornell University Press, forthcoming.

18 Herman Kahn *et al.*, *Can We Win in Vietnam?*, New York, Praeger for Hudson

Institute, 1968, p. 178.
19 Barbara Salert, *Revolutions and Revolutionaries: Four Theories* (New York, Elsevier, 1976) includes two of the theories I discuss (those of Johnson and Gurr). The other two are 'rational choice' theory, derived from Mancur Olson Jr, *The Logic of Collective Action* (New York, Schocken Books, 1971); and Marx's theory of capitalist contradictions and class consciousness (this is a lucid and perceptive analysis, but confined to revolutionary possibilities in advanced industrialised countries). Salert's modified criteria for adequate explanations (of revolution) are 'that theories specify the relevant factors and the type of relationship that holds between these factors and the event being explained' (p. 15). Despite the reference to relevant factors, her critique is essentially a methodological one. Thus 'rational choice' meets her approval (while Johnson's functionalism and Gurr's wide-ranging psychological-sociological coverage do not) because it is 'based on assumptions that are far more restrictive than the ones used by Johnson' and Gurr. 'To obtain theories with strong explanatory power, we must usually rely on fairly restrictive assumptions' (p. 95) – in Olson's case, the rational assessment of costs and benefits. But if the assumption is so restrictive (as in her use of Olson's theory) it cannot possibly specify all the relevant factors, which is the first criterion for an adequate explanation of revolution. Nevertheless, her critique of Johnson's functionalism – 'the notion of a disequilibrated social system is so vague ... that its value as a theoretical construct is minimal' (p. 133) – is justified. Less so, because of the limitations of her approach, is her criticism of Gurr. With her overriding concern for theoretical rigor, Salert does not take sufficient account of Gurr's achievement in appraising such a variety of undeniably relevant factors, even though she correctly points out that he does not adequately explain the *relationship* between them. But this is a failing common to all theories of revolution.
20 Thomas Hobbes, *Leviathan*, ed. Michael Oakeshott, Oxford, Blackwell, n.d., p. 64.
21 'Does Modernisation Breed Revolution?', *Comparative Politics*, April 1973, Special Issue on Revolution and Social Change.
22 Ibid. See also Tilly, 'Town and Country in Revolution', in John Wilson Lewis (ed.), *Peasant Rebellion and Communist Revolution in Asia*, Stanford University Press, 1974.
23 Tilly, 'Does Modernisation Breed Revolution?'
24 Ibid.
25 *Why Men Rebel*, p. 357.
26 Which do not always inspire confidence: some examples of doubtful judgments are on pp. 71–2 (Vietnam), 108–9 (Indonesia), 117 (Ghana), 120 (Congo), 249 (Second World War resistance), 334 (independent occurrence of turmoil and 'internal war').
27 The 'frustration-anger-aggression' theory: the greater the frustration, the greater the quantity of aggression directed against the source of frustration (p. 9). But it is considered in its social context: 'The disposition to collective violence depends on how badly societies violate socially-derived expectations about the means and ends of human action' (p. 317). It is 'relative deprivation' – the discrepancy between value expectations and value capabilities; between what men believe they are rightfully entitled to and what they think they are capable of

attaining (p. 13) – that establishes the potential for violence. This includes perception of the situation (seen to be rising, falling or stable) of one social group relative to others.

28 Gurr, *Why Men Rebel*, p. 357.

29 Ibid., p. 149. Salert, *Revolutions and Revolutionaries*, considers that Gurr's psychological perspective 'focusses on the wrong sort of analysis [the frustration-aggression hypothesis is about the behaviour of individuals and does not necessarily apply to group behaviour as would be required by a theory of political violence], neglects considerations of interactions among individuals, and includes variables that have little, if anything, to do with frustration-aggression studies' (pp. 64, 136). But Salert suggests focusing the psychological inquiry 'on the conditions under which large numbers of people are likely to experience such severe relative deprivation that they would rationally join revolutionary movements' (p. 130); this is, actually, one of the achievements of Gurr's study.

30 *Why Men Rebel*, p. 321.

31 Ibid., pp. 322, 326.

32 Turmoil is unstructured mass violence; conspiracy is organised violence with limited support (typically coups d'état); and revolution or internal war is organised large-scale violence. Gurr rightly points out that structural conditions – the patterns of coercive control and institutional support as regards both regime and dissidents – finally determine the forms of violence (above) and their magnitude, in terms of scope (the proportion of the population intensely discontented), destructiveness and duration, but he states, rather than substantiates, the position: see *Why Men Rebel*, pp. 136, 154, 158–9, 201–2, 229–30, 320.

33 Ibid., p. 179.

34 Samuel P. Huntington, *Political Order in Changing Societies*, New Haven, Yale University Press, 1969, pp. 4–5.

35 Ibid., p. 55.

36 Ibid., p. 82.

37 Ibid., pp. 80–1.

38 Ibid., pp. 266, 277.

39 Ibid., pp. 267–8.

40 Ibid., pp. 268–70.

41 Ibid., pp. 336–8.

42 'Bases of Accommodation', *Foreign Affairs*, July 1968.

43 Jeffrey Race, *War Comes to Long An: Revolutionary Conflict in a Vietnamese Village*, Berkeley, University of California Press, 1972, p. 176, Race's italics.

44 *Revolutionary Change*, p. 56.

45 Talcott Parsons, 'Some Reflections on the Place of Force in Social Process', in Harry Eckstein (ed.), *Internal War: Problems and Approaches*, New York, Free Press, 1964, pp. 43, 47–8, 62.

46 *Revolutionary Change*, p. 91.

47 Ibid., p. 94.

48 Ted Gurr, 'The Revolution – Social-Change Nexus: Some Old Theories and New Hypotheses', *Comparative Politics*, April 1973, Special Issue on Revolution and Social Change. See also Salert's incisive criticism: for example, 'élite behaviour' is simply an overall label, referring to a wide variety of variables and

interrelationships; the theory does not specify the relationship between essential variables; and there is no way of determining how environmental changes will affect systemic variables (*Revolutions and Revolutionaries*, pp. 86–93).

49 The 'socio-psychological' needs of men, as Gurr emphasises, are security, welfare, the right to manage their own affairs, and a sense of identification – belonging to a community. On the importance of the latter, see also Bienen, *Violence and Social Change*, p. 17.

50 Johnson, *Revolutionary Change*, p. 143.

51 Revolutionary behaviour is 'open-optional' in the sense that each individual has many choices to make, as he considers the political alternatives before him (Thomas H. Greene, *Comparative Revolutionary Movements*, Englewood Cliffs, N.J., Prentice-Hall, 1974, p. 154).

5 US foreign policy: two perspectives

1 Robert S. McNamara, *The Essence of Security: Reflections in Office*, New York, Harper & Row, 1968, p. 149.

2 Ivan Illich, 'Outwitting the "Developed" Countries', in Henry Bernstein (ed.), *Underdevelopment and Development: The Third World Today*, Harmondsworth, Penguin Books, 1973, p. 363.

3 Gabriel A. Almond and G. Bingham Powell Jr, *Comparative Politics: A Developmental Approach*, Boston, Little, Brown, 1966, p. 35.

4 According to developmental pluralism, the goals of the system are assumed to be adaptation to environment and maintenance of equilibrium; 'unauthorised' violence, as opposed to 'legitimate' coercion by the state, is considered a 'deviant' phenomenon. As Lucian Pye explains: large numbers of 'restless' people', breaking with traditional ties, seek satisfaction, security and personal identification in political action; this 'creates a serious source of instability. . . . People guided by such considerations are now being recruited to the various deviant movements in Southeast Asia, and particularly to the Communist parties' (Pye, 'Southeast Asia', in Gabriel A. Almond and James S. Coleman (eds), *Politics of the Developing Areas*, Princeton University Press, 1960, pp. 133–4).

5 W. W. Rostow, 'Countering Guerrilla Attack', reprinted in Franklin M. Osaka (ed.), *Modern Guerrilla Warfare: Fighting Communist Guerrilla Movements, 1941–1961*, New York, Free Press, 1963, pp. 466–7.

6 Susanne Bodenheimer, 'Dependency and Imperialism', in K. T. Fann and Donald C. Hodges (eds), *Readings in U.S. Imperialism*, Boston, Porter, Sargent, 1971. The evidence is drawn from Latin America but the argument is applicable to the Third World in general.

7 As R. P. Dore puts it, the 'late starters' have to operate under the domination of the 'early starters'. Dore, 'The Late Development Effect', in Hans-Dieter Evers (ed.), *Modernisation in South-East Asia*, Kuala Lumpur, Oxford University Press for the Institute of Southeast Asian Studies, Singapore, 1973, pp. 67-8.

8 For example, Coleman, 'Conclusion', *Politics of the Developing Areas*, p. 535.

9 Henry Kissinger, 'Domestic Structure and Foreign Policy', *Daedalus*, no. 2, 1966, reprinted in *American Foreign Policy: Three Essays*, New York, Norton, 1969.

10 The UN Economic Commission for Latin America, cited by Susanne

Bodenheimer, *The Ideology of Developmentalism: The American Paradigm – Surrogate for Latin American Studies*, Beverly Hills, Sage Publications, 1971, p. 10.

11 B. S. Minhas, 'Rural Poverty, Land Redistribution and Development', *Indian Economic Review*, April 1970. Statistics are from 1960–1. The situation more than a decade later is either unchanged, or worse, as a result of increased population.

12 Robert S. McNamara, *Address to the Board of Governors* [of the World Bank], Nairobi, 24 September 1973, Washington, DC, 1973, p. 10. McNamara was reporting on the Bank's five year plan, 1974–8.

13 Osvaldo Sunkel, 'Transnational Capitalism and National Disintegration in Latin America', *Social and Economic Studies*, March 1973; Special Issue on Dependence and Under-Development in the New World and the Old. Sunkel was reporting research by Raymond Vernon and Neil Jacoby. Subsidiaries include those with minority control of up to 25 per cent. See also Joan E. Spero, *The Politics of International Economic Relations*, London, Allen & Unwin, 1977. The value added of all multinational corporations in 1971 has been estimated at about $500 billion, or one-fifth of world GNP, excluding communist countries: 'They are able to dominate markets because of their size, their access to financial resources, their control of technology' (p. 89).

14 Anibal Pinto and Jan Knakal, 'The Centre-Periphery System Twenty Years Later', *Social and Economic Studies*, March 1973. In terms of world trade, manufactured goods amounted to only just over one-fifth of the developing countries' exports in 1968 (compared to nearly three-quarters for the developed countries). The developing countries still depend largely on exports of primary products – amounting to some 70 or 80 per cent of the total – and the overwhelming bulk of their trade continues to be with the advanced countries: thus only one-fifth of develping countries' total trade is within its own 'zone', compared to the three-quarters of developed countries' trade which is 'intrazonal' (Pinto and Knakal; also Gunnar Myrdal, *The Challenge of World Poverty*, Harmondsworth, Penguin Books, 1971, p. 278). Evidently the quadrupled price of oil since 1973 has increased the share of the periphery in world trade; but this increase benefits only a small number of states (members of OPEC) and is at the expense of the great majority. See also Richard J. Barnet and Ronald E. Muller, *Global Reach: The Power of the Multinational Corporations* (New York, Simon and Schuster, 1974) on US corporate and banking expansion abroad, pp. 16–17, and the lack of bargaining power of the poor countries, pp. 137–43, 150–7. For a valuable bibliography, and discussion, see Richard L. Sklar, 'Postimperialism: A Class Analysis of the Multinational Corporation', *Comparative Politics*, October 1976.

15 McNamara, *Address to the Board of Governors*, pp. 13, 15, 17, 19. Access to credit is a further example. This is crucial for smallholders, McNamara reports, because they operate with practically no capital of their own. In countries as disparate as Bangladesh and Iran less than 10 per cent of institutional credit is available to rural areas; in Thailand, the Philippines and Mexico less than 15 per cent; in India less than 25 per cent. Yet only a fraction of that small proportion is available to the small farmer who 'is operating so close to the margin of survival that he is simply not as creditworthy as his more wealthy neighbours' (pp. 19–20). McNamara's advice is reinforced by that of Mahbul Ul Haq, *The Poverty Curtain: Choices for the Third World*, New York, Columbia University Press, 1976. A

professional economist, he argues that 'it is impossible to expect growth to filter down in societies where there is no equality of opportunity' (p. 61). The economic conditions of the poorest cannot be improved by short-lived welfare schemes, but only through increasing their productivity (e.g. of small farmers, landless labourers, and workers in the informal urban sector), by restructuring the pattern of investment through fundamental institutional reforms: 'a basic restructuring of the political, economic and social balance of power' (pp. 62, 64).

16 *Time* magazine quoted by Sunkel, 'Transnational Capitalism'.

17 Sunkel, 'Transnational Capitalism'.

18 Franz Schurmann's *The Logic of World Power* (New York, Pantheon Books, 1974) also provides a useful corrective to neo-Marxism. Schurmann emphasises the role of the state: 'The chief thrust of American imperialism, as this book argues, is control. The chief thrust of international capitalism is and has to be profit' (Prologue, p. xxvi). Rather than the state being the instrument of international capitalism, 'in fact, a complex struggle between government and business has made for much of the political history of the United States of America' (p. xxvii; see also pp. 114, 127–8). Schurmann points to the 'democratic origins' of US imperialism, the nationalist and internationalist 'currents' in the USA (each a combination of economic and political interests), and the role of government – rather than of the nationalist military or the internationalist corporations – in the anti-communist containment policy.

See also the shrewd, balanced, and generally persuasive, critique of neo-Marxist and radical theories of imperialism in Benjamin J. Cohen, *The Question of Imperialism: The Political Economy of Dominance and Dependence*, New York, Basic Books, 1973, particularly his excellent analysis of the positive and the negative aspects of capitalist trade with and investment in developing countries, pp. 168–85.

19 The autonomous behaviour of the Brazilian military is a case in point. The government, justifiably criticised in 1977 for its human rights record, cancelled its military assistance agreement with the USA. While Brazil was previously dependent on US aid, now the international banking community has become the underwriter of Brazil's military-economic development. (Whereas the USA provided 35–40 per cent of all arms sold in Latin America in the 1960s, today it provides only 14 per cent.) The shift to bank lending has sharply reduced American leverage. As Brazilians have pointed out: 'We are an important customer and it would hurt them [banks] to lose their client' (Don Oberdorfer, *International Herald Tribune*, 22 March 1977). Moreover, as one specialist points out, 'all over Latin America, the state has been strengthened enormously in recent years . . . Latin American governments tax more, spend more, regulate more, prohibit more, and control more than regimes in the region have ever done before. They have access to a rapidly expanding resource base. . . . Traditional élites favorably disposed toward the United States are being replaced by technocrats – civilian and military – often of a nationalistic bent. These new leaders, many of them well-trained (often in U.S. graduate schools), tend to identify their interests independently of and even through confrontation with the United States' (Abraham F. Lowenthal, 'The United States and Latin America: Ending the Hegemonic Presumption', *Foreign Affairs*, October 1976).

20 'Primacy' because in theory politics is a 'sovereign' function, capable of

regulating both political and economic activities; if it is also an autonomous function, i.e., not determined by economic structures, then the theory and practice of political primacy are united.

21 However, even one of the most generous forms of aid, under the 'Food for Peace Act', in which the USA has spent over $30 billion since 1954, has been inspired by at least four different purposes. 'It is a way to get rid of surplus food, and a way to help hungry people, an instrument of political and military policy, and a way to create markets for American food. Each of these purposes corresponds to a phase in the history of the program. . . . The United States now spends a little over a billion dollars a year on food aid. More than three-quarters of the aid – mostly wheat and rice – is sent under the P.L. 480 program. Eighty countries receive some food aid from the United States, although most of the aid each year goes to four or so countries. Quite prosperous countries are eligible for aid. Israel was the leading recipient of United States food aid in the 1976 fiscal year. In 1975, the largest recipient was India. South Vietnam was first in 1974 and 1973, and South Korea in 1972. . . . [However] in 1975 the United States more than doubled its food aid to the poorest countries' (Emma Rothschild, 'Is it Time to End Food for Peace?', *New York Times* weekly review, 20 March 1977).

22 The two are substantially the same, as can be seen from the following quotation: 'Peace must provide a durable structure of international relationships . . . built on partnership [with free nations], [America's] strength and willingness to negotiate [with adversaries]' (President Nixon, *A New Strategy for Peace*, A Report to the Congress, 18 February 1970). 'A leading American role in world affairs continues to be indispensable to the kind of world our own well-being requires. . . . Our friendships are constant, but the means . . . must be adjusted as world conditions change. . . . Our enmities are not immutable. . . . Agreements . . . have permanent significance only when they contribute to a stable structure of peace' (President Nixon, 'The Philosophy of a New American Foreign Policy', *The Emerging Structure of Peace*, Report to the Congress, 9 February 1972). See also J. L. S. Girling, 'Carter's Foreign Policy: Realism or Ideology?', *The World Today*, November 1977.

23 Note the similarity of Carter's recent foreign policy statements with those of Nixon and Kissinger. According to Carter, 'We will match, together with our allies and friends, any threatening power through a combination of military forces, political efforts and economic programs'; but 'we shall [also] seek the cooperation of the Soviet Union and other nations in reducing areas of tension.' Above all, 'we shall use our great economic, technological and diplomatic advantages to defend our interests and to promote American values' (President Carter, 'America's Position in a Changing World', address at Wake Forest University, North Carolina, 17 March 1978; United States Policy Statement Series, 1978, International Communication Agency).

24 The 'Alliance for Progress' in Latin America is the most spectacular example of liberal initiatives – launched with the grand design of creating a middle way between extremism of the Right and of the Left, and imbued with the faith that reform is the answer to revolution. So far from developing a progressive alternative in Latin America, the 'Alliance' came to an end with more authoritarian governments (duly recognised by the USA) than when it started. Even the show-piece, Chile under President Frei, achieved little either in the way

of social reform or economic growth, and the outcome of the build-up of frustration was to prove disastrous. The problem is this: although external proposals for reforms in Third World ruling systems are often sincerely advocated with the aim of transforming traditional into modern societies (in the US image), they have advantages and disadvantages; and the latter usually outweigh the former. The chief advantage is that urban or rural reforms, while not upsetting the basic structures of society, both improve their performance and make them more palatable to the mass of ordinary citizens. The great disadvantage is that attempts to induce change tend to undermine the power and confidence of entrenched élites; the latter are convinced that if they give way to pressures for reforms, even if to only a minor extent, this will open the floodgates of popular demands, which will sweep them away in a wave of unrest. (This sentiment is not unique to the Third World.) Only where external advocacy of change *coincides* with the emergence of powerful modernising groups in a given society may liberal expectations be fulfilled.

25 'For well over a century, the goals of industrialisation and democratisation have been taken for granted in the West. . . . [However] the success of communist industrialisation, as well as the collapse of democratic regimes among the new nations, has shaken faith in the inevitability of democracy in history. . . . [N]aive faith in the universal appeal of democracy and material welfare has given way to more sober second thoughts' (Gabriel A. Almond, *Comparative Politics Today: A World View*, Boston, Little, Brown, 1974, pp. 35, 38).

26 From the Vietnamese classic *Kim Van Kieu*, quoted by Truong Chinh, writing in 1946–7, in the darkest years of the war (*The Resistance Will Win*, Hanoi, Foreign Languages Publishing Press, 1960, p. 95).

6 America and the Third World: from involvement to intervention

1 William P. Bundy, 'Dictatorship and American Foreign Policy', *Foreign Affairs*, October 1975. William Bundy, editor of *Foreign Affairs* since 1972, was a career officer in the CIA (1951–61), Assistant and then Deputy Secretary of Defense for International Security Affairs (1961–4), Assistant Secretary of State for East Asian and Pacific Affairs (1964–9). Bundy's three objectives accord with six 'key principles' of US foreign policy enunciated by the American Ambassador in Thailand, Charles Whitehouse, evidently from a basic document circulated by the State Department: (1) Establishment of a stable, peaceful world order. (2) A conviction that while change is inevitable and desirable, that it should come through evolution. (3) The containment of totalitarianism in the bipolar world, and more recently a balance of power in the multipolar world. (4) The alleviation of human misery. (5) The active support of material progress. (6) An abiding belief in human freedom and the dignity of man. Reported in *Voice of the Nation* (Bangkok) 12 December 1975. Points (1) to (3) represent Bundy's first two objectives; (4) to (6) his third. This is not mere rhetoric. Schurmann, for example, emphasises the analogy with the New Deal, which provided social security for the American people and a measure of social justice: i.e. reforms to avert revolution. Similarly, the intention of US aid programmes is to provide security to overcome

chaos, to prevent nations turning revolutionary, and to bring them into the system (Franz Schurmann, *The Logic of World Power*, New York, Pantheon Books, 1974, pp. 42, 67).

2 Bundy, 'Dictatorship and American Foreign Policy'.

3 Robert S. McNamara, *Address to the Board of Governors* [of the World Bank] on the Bank's five year plan, 1974–8, Nairobi, September 1973.

4 Anibal Pinto and Jan Knakal, 'The Centre-Periphery System Twenty Years Later, *Social and Economic Studies*, March 1973.

5 Gunnar Myrdal, *The Challenge of World Poverty*, p. 389.

6 As the President of the Overseas Development Council points out, the experience of most developing countries over the last decade is that a rising growth rate alone is no guarantee against worsening poverty. He gives the example of Mexico, whose GNP has risen by 6–7 per cent p.a. over the last fifteen years; yet unemployment is increasing and the income gap between rich and poor is widening, because of very rapid population growth and government policies which bypass small labour-intensive producers and encourage production through large farms and urban-based factories. In the early 1950s the total income of the top one-fifth of the Mexican population was ten times that of the lowest one-fifth; in 1969 it was *sixteen* times (James P. Grant, 'Development: The End of "Trickle Down"?', *Foreign Policy*, Fall 1973).

Consider also the results in Morocco, a country which is actually more favoured than the average, because of its links with developed nations across the Mediterranean, and its vast reserves of potash. The capital, Casablanca, has two million inhabitants, skyscrapers, ultra-modern hotels, nightclubs and a busy port: 'business is booming here, traffic dense, and land prices are sky-rocketing'. But society is pyramidal: 'The base – 87 percent of the population – consists of peasant families (about 10 million people) living off approximately five hectares per family on the poorest 35 percent of the land, while 3 percent of the landowners hold the richest 33 percent. A sub-proletariat of three million lives in slums and looks for work it is unlikely to get. Then come 700,000 workers in industry, 200,000 cottage craftsmen, professional people, and technocrats. The apex consists of the rural middle classes, along with businessmen. This privileged group is also dominated by 200 – according to some, only 60 – top families' (Abdullah Ibrahim, former Prime Minister of Morocco, head of the new 'National Union of Popular Forces' (UNFP), reported by Paul Balta, *Le Monde*, in *Guardian Weekly*, 22 March 1975).

7 Raymond Vernon, *Sovereignty at Bay: The Multinational Spread of US Enterprises*, Harmondsworth, Penguin Books, 1973, p. 192.

8 Ibid., pp. 191–2.

9 See, for example, Geoffrey Barraclough, *An Introduction to Contemporary History*, Harmondsworth, Penguin Books, 1967, pp. 174–6, 191–3.

10 Vernon, *Sovereignty at Bay*, p. 193. In a later work, Vernon emphasises the tension between multinational enterprises and national interests. This is particularly acute when Third World nations undertake policies to create jobs, to reduce inequitable income differences between different classes and regions, to ensure the availability of scarce national supplies and the benign functioning of markets, to secure tax reserves, promote consumer safety, protect the environment and safeguard national security ('Storm over the Multinationals:

Problems and Prospects', *Foreign Affairs*, January 1977). The article is abridged from the concluding chapter of Vernon's *Storm over the Multinationals: The Real Issues*, Harvard University Press, 1977.

11 Thus Senator Frank Church, Chairman of the US Senate Foreign Relations Subcommittee of Multinational Corporations, has pointed to the 'evolution of complementary interests' between corporations and government as regards US policy towards the developing countries. The premise, especially in the 1960s, was that the 'United States had to be fully engaged in the international political, economic and social development of so-called Third World countries to avoid their domination by the Sino-Soviet bloc'; however, with the diminution of the Cold War, the single-minded focus of national policy is being replaced by a 'more diversified definition of national interests', including economic and financial, domestic and foreign (*Foreign Policy*, Fall 1973).

12 Note the Filipino example, referred to in chapter 1.

13 Richard Nixon, *US Foreign Policy for the 1970s: Shaping a Durable Peace*, Washington, DC, US Government Printing Office, 1973, p. 9.

14 *The Emerging Structure of Peace*, Report to the Congress, 1972, p. 45. The USA has provided the lion's share (46 per cent) of foreign economic assistance through the Inter-Governmental Group on Indonesia, from 1969 to 1972.

15 *Shaping a Durable Peace*, p. 43. In the two decades after 1949 the US Defense Department provided training for over 26,000 Latin American officers and men in the US Army School of the Americas in the Panama Canal Zone, and for nearly the same number in the United States (Michael T. Klare, *War Without End*, New York, Knopf, 1972, pp. 297, 301).

16 'Explanation' by the US official, visiting Kinshasa in December 1974 (Michael Kaufman, 'The U.S.A.–Zaire Connection', *New York Times* weekly review, 4 January 1975). US arms transfers to Zaïre rose from about $1 million in 1975 to $19 million in 1976 (Leslie Gelb, *New York Times* weekly review, 18 July 1976). In fiscal year 1977, the USA provided Zaïre with nearly $31 million, mainly in credits, to buy arms, and some $35 million in economic aid. Meanwhile private US investment in mining (copper, cobalt, industrial diamonds) amounts to nearly $1 billion (*New York Times* weekly review, 20 March 1977).

17 During the May 1978 Shaba crisis, the USA provided over $17 million in credits for arms sales to Zaïre, 'in the security interests of the United States' and because the Mobutu regime was 'basically supportive of our interests', according to the White House spokesman (*Australian*, 20–21 May 1978). The USA is backing the French President's policy of working with its francophone allies (such as Togo, Senegal, Gabon and Morocco) to bolster the security of the vulnerable Zaïre regime. France, with nearly 10,000 troops stationed in some half a dozen African countries, provides a foreign force second only to Cuba's 40,000-odd men.

18 Senate Foreign Relations Committee report, August 1976, quoted in *Guardian Weekly*, 8 August 1976.

19 Bernard Gwertzman, 'Saudi Arabia, Mideast Power Broker', *New York Times* weekly review, 23 October 1977. Saudi aid also flows to Syria, Jordan, the PLO, North Yemen; to Uganda, Mali, Nigeria, Zaïre and others in Africa; and to Pakistan in Asia (*Newsweek* special report, 6 March 1978).

However, Saudi Arabia is itself vulnerable to internal upheavals since, for example, half the labour force is made up of foreigners. Moreover the Saudis are 'formidable paymasters' only when other Arab governments are generally in agreement. Where there is disagreement, Saudis tend to go along with the majority (hence their disapproval of Camp David) (Joseph Kraft, *International Herald Tribune*, 27 December 1978). See Don Oberdorfer, *Guardian Weekly*, 20 May 1979.

20 Lyndon Johnson, *My Hope for America*, New York, Random House, 1964, p. 69.

21 *New York Times* weekly review, 14 July 1974. Britain and France, in comparison, sold $2 billion worth of arms in 1973; the Soviet bloc an estimated $2.5 billion in 1973.

22 John W. Finney, *New York Times* weekly review, 20 June 1976. US arms sales for fiscal year 1977 amount to $11.2 billion (including $8 billion for Iran, Saudi Arabia and Israel), compared with $12 billion in 1976 and an estimated $13.2 billion for fiscal 1978 (*Time*, 13 February 1978). Leslie Gelb, 'Arms Sales' (*Foreign Policy*, Winter 1976–7) points out that the USA has dominated the world arms trade over the decade 1965–74, with 49 per cent of world sales, compared to Russia with 29.2 per cent, France 4.4 per cent, China 3.3 per cent, and Britain 3.2 per cent. Total US military exports in 1979 are expected to be $14 billion.

23 Kenneth T. Young Jr, *The Southeast Asia Crisis: Law, Power and Policy in Search for Regional Order*, New York, Association of the Bar of the City of New York, 9th Hammarskjold Forum, 1965, p. 122; cited by Peter Dale Scott, 'The Vietnam War and the CIA-Financial Establishment', in Mark Selden (ed.), *Remaking Asia: Essays on the American Uses of Power*, New York, Pantheon Books, 1974, p. 150. Young was Ambassador to Thailand, and resigned in 1964; he then became President of the Asia Society.

24 Bundy, 'Dictatorship and American Foreign Policy'.

25 President Truman, announcing Military Security Program, 1 March 1952 (*Documents on American Foreign Policy, 1952*, New York, Harper, 1953, p. 33). Italics added.

26 Economic components derived from Vernon, *Sovereignty at Bay*, p. 115. Foreign policy components inferred from *US Foreign Policy for the 1970's*.

27 'We should intervene', urged the US Ambassador to the Dominican Republic in April 1965, 'to prevent another Cuba from arising out of the ashes of this uncontrollable situation' (Lyndon Johnson, *The Vantage Point: Perspectives of the Presidency 1963–1969*, New York, Holt, Rinehart & Winston, 1971, p. 197).

28 Vernon, *Sovereignty at Bay*, pp. 202, 208.

29 According to Vernon, 'deviations from the pattern' (*Sovereignty at Bay*, pp. 204, 208).

30 Gabriel Kolko, *The Roots of American Foreign Policy: An Analysis of Power and Purpose*, Boston, Beacon, 1969, ch. 3, 'The United States and World Economic Power'. The argument is similar to that of Robert Tucker and William Watts that US intervention in Vietnam was intended to maintain a stable world order under American leadership 'that would ensure the triumph of liberal-capitalist values and institutions' ('Introduction', *Beyond Containment: US Foreign Policy in Transition*, Washington, DC, Potomac Associates with *Foreign Policy*, 1973, p. xxv).

31 Kolko, *The Roots of American Foreign Policy*, p. 85.

32 Ibid. As Tucker and Watts put it, American opposition to revolutionary movements is not so much because they appear to threaten national security, but rather in 'the apprehension that they would prove resistant to American influence and control' (*Beyond Containment*, p. xxv).

33 D. K. Fieldhouse, ' "Imperialism", An Historiographical Revision', reprinted in K. E. Boulding and T. Mukerjee (eds), *Economic Imperialism*, Ann Arbor, University of Michigan Press, 1972, p. 118.

34 Kolko, *The Roots of American Foreign Policy*, pp. 86–7.

35 Mark Blaug, 'Economic Imperialism Revisited', reprinted in Boulding and Mukerjee, *Economic Imperialism*, p. 148.

36 Ibid., p. 149. In 1972, US direct investment abroad amounted to $94 billion, with Western Europe receiving 33 per cent, Canada 27 per cent, Latin America 18 per cent, Japan 2 per cent and other countries 20 per cent: Robert Gilpin, 'The Multinational Corporation and American Foreign Policy', in Richard Rosecrance (ed.), *America as an Ordinary Country: U.S. Foreign Policy and the Future*, Ithaca, Cornell University Press, 1976, pp. 176–7.

37 *Statistical Abstract of the United States 1971*, Washington, DC, US Department of Commerce Bureau of the Census, p. 755. See also Joan E. Spero, *The Politics of International Economic Relations*, London, Allen & Unwin, 1977, pp. 191–3.

38 Charles L. Schulze, former Director of the US Budget Bureau, 'The Economic Content of National Security Policy', *Foreign Affairs*, April 1973. See also Barrington Moore's discussion, 'Of Predatory Democracy: the U.S.A.', in his *Reflections on the Causes of Human Misery* (London, Allen Lane, The Penguin Press, 1972). Spero, *The Politics of International Economic Relations*, p. 72.

39. Kolko, *The Roots of American Foreign Policy*, pp. 51, 53; also J. P. Cole, *Geography of World Affairs*, Harmondsworth, Penguin Books, 1966, pp. 132, 148; James Reston, *New York Times* weekly review, 3 February 1974. The share of imports from all sources – as well as exclusively from developing countries – in American use of 12 important raw materials in 1950 and 1970, with estimates for 1985 and 2000, is given in official US studies, quoted by Richard J. Barnet and Ronald E. Muller, *Global Reach: The Power of the Multinational Corporations*, New York, Simon & Schuster, 1974, table, p. 126.

40 John Gallagher and Ronald Robinson, 'The Imperialism of Free Trade', *Economic History Review*, August 1953. In their study *Africa and the Victorians* (London, Macmillan, 1961) Robinson and Gallagher point out, contrary to Kolko's line of argument, that 'economic development was more a consequence than a motive of the "Scramble" ' for Africa and that, here at least, the theory of economic imperialism puts the cart before the horse (p. 409).

41 See, however, the discussion in *Foreign Policy*: C. Fred Bergsten, 'The Threat from the Third World', on control of oil, copper, tin, rubber and bauxite, Summer 1973; S. Mikdashi, 'Collusion Could Work', spells out the necessary conditions for effective co-operation among producers; but Stephen Krasner 'Oil is the Exception', concludes that so far only the oil exporters have been effective, thanks to three specific factors – enormous foreign exchange holdings, a common external enemy, and the tacit assistance of the multinationals (Spring 1974). See also Tony Smith, 'Changing Configurations of Power in North–South Relations since 1945', *International Organization*, Winter 1977.

42 Thirty-eight per cent of American imports of crude oil come from Arab states,

while imports from all sources now amount to nearly half of the total supply in the USA.

43 According to the list prepared by the American Embassy. However, the list was inaccurate, the individuals had nothing to do with initiating the revolt by the 'constitutionalists' against the military regime (prompting US intervention), and had very little prospect of 'taking it over', as President Johnson tried to argue: see Richard J. Barnet, *Intervention and Revolution: The United States in the Third World*, London, MacGibbon & Kee, 1970, pp. 171–2; Melvin Gurtov, *The United States against the Third World: Antinationalism and Intervention*, New York, Praeger, 1974, pp. 111–25.

44 Involvement of 'international communism': Iran had long been the object of great power attention, culminating in 1907 in a Russo-British spheres of influence agreement. During the Second World War the country was occupied by the armies of these two powers to forestall a possible Nazi intervention. The Soviet Union then backed a separatist rebellion in northern Iran in 1945, which collapsed with the entry of Iranian forces, backed by the USA. As to the non-involvement of international communism, in the 1951–3 crisis, see note 50 below.

45 President Eisenhower announced the act of US intervention in a nation-wide address as American troops were landing in Beirut: 'What we now see in the Middle East is the same pattern of conquest with which we became familiar in the period 1945 to 1950. This involves taking over a nation by means of indirect aggression; that is, under the cover of a fomented civil strife the purpose is to put into domestic control those whose real loyalty is to the aggressor. It was by such means that the communists attempted to take over Greece in 1947. That effort was thwarted by the Truman Doctrine. It was by such means that the communists took over the mainland of China in 1949.' Actually, as Gurtov points out, 'the United States intervened in a country where the issue was not communism but local and Arab politics; where the army was more eager to fight the [US] Marines than to subdue its own countrymen; where the countryside and most of the major cities were controlled by the rebels, not by forces loyal to the President; and where an opportunity was let pass to achieve a settlement without intervention on the same terms that were accepted after the intervention' – i.e. the replacement of President Chamoun, whose personal ambitions and divisive policies had sparked off the unrest (*The United States against the Third World*, pp. 36–7).

46 Kissinger's argument was that the balance of power in Africa hinged on the outcome of the war in Angola: if the USA failed to act, African nations would begin to think the only super-power that counted on the continent was the Soviet Union (Leslie Gelb, *New York Times* weekly review, 21 December 1975; see also ch. 8 below).

47 'The first real watershed in American policy towards Indonesia was the 1948 Madiun Rebellion, which destroyed the Dutch myth that the Republic's leadership was pro-communist and which demonstrated to certain elements in Washington "that the Indonesian revolutionaries could handle local communists". The second major element in the watershed was, of course, Dutch defiance of the United Nations; and the fact that this was the first major test case of the U.N.'s potential for viability' (communication from George McT. Kahin;

see also Kahin, *Nationalism and Revolution in Indonesia*, Ithaca, Cornell University Press, 1952).

48 Philip Jessup, Deputy US Representative to the United Nations Security Council, on 11 January 1949 (*Documents on American Foreign Relations*, vol. XI, p. 568). Italics added.

49 Joint US–French communiqué, 18 June 1952 (*Documents on American Foreign Relations 1952*, p. 284).

50 In the immediate post-war years circumstances did not favour US intervention in Asia: the global system of alliances and understandings was only in process of construction; isolationism was residual factor; the demobilisation of American troops from a war-time peak of eight million to less than one million in 1947 – including only 14,000 in the whole of the Far East – made intervention in China physically difficult, if not impossible, to sustain; the administration was absorbed in the struggle for Europe; and finally the problems of China were too enormous to manage even for a super-power. As Secretary of State Acheson pointed out, owing to the ineffectiveness of Kuomintang forces, the communists could probably only have been dislodged by American arms: 'It is obvious that the American people would not have sanctioned such a colossal commitment of our armies in 1945 or later' (Acheson's Letter of Transmittal, *United States Relations with China*).

51 In 1951 the Majlis (assembly) decided to nationalise the Anglo-Iranian Oil Company. The Leftist Tudeh Party aligned itself in effect with the nationalist Prime Minister Mossadegh against the Shah, who in turn had aligned himself with America, both to provide for his ambitious aid programme and to reorganise and re-equip the Iranian army. In November 1952, Secretary Acheson 'pressed the point' in talks with British Foreign Secretary Eden that 'Iran was on the verge of an explosion in which Mossadegh would break relations with the United States, after which nothing could save the country from the Tudeh Party and disappearance behind the Iron Curtain' (Dean Acheson, *Present at the Creation: My Years in the State Department*, New York, Norton, 1969, pp. 501, 503). Now although Mossadegh was a wealthy landowner, and therefore hardly likely to sell out to communism, the theory in American policy-making circles at this time was that indigenous communists, directed by the Soviet Union, were forming alliances with nationalist elements in the Middle East so that, in the midst of turmoil, they would be able to seize power: expounded by Parker Hart, Deputy Assistant Secretary of State for Near East and South Asian Affairs, in May 1959. Quoted by Herbert Tillema, *Appeal to Force: American Military Intervention in the Era of Containment*, New York, Thomas Y. Crowell, 1973, p. 76. In August 1973 the Shah fled, after his attempt to oust Mossadegh by staging a coup had failed. The first counter-move came when the army withheld help from the Prime Minister and 'then cast its decisive strength' against Mossadegh, whereupon the Shah returned in triumph (Acheson, *Present at the Creation*, p. 685). Bundy acknowledges the American role as one of 'decisive covert intervention' ('Dictatorship and American Foreign Policy').

52 Kissinger in a background briefing on the Chilean Presidential elections in 1970 predicted 'that if Allende wins, there is a good chance that he will establish over a period of years some sort of communist government. . . . In a major Latin American country you could have a communist government, joining, for

example, Argentina . . . Peru . . . and Bolivia. . . . I don't think we should delude
ourselves that an Allende takeover in Chile would not present massive problems
for us, and for democratic forces and for pro-U.S. forces in Latin America'
(briefing, 16 September 1970, quoted by Richard Fagen, 'The United States and
Chile: Roots and Branches', *Foreign Affairs*, January 1975).

53 In Guatemala the expropriation of plantations owned by the United Fruit
Company (under land reform legislation) was as much a *casus belli* as was the
growing influence of local communist leaders on the Arbenz government.

54 If the USA were unwilling to 'provide adequate assistance to allies fighting for
their lives', according to President Ford, this 'would seriously affect our
credibility throughout the world as an ally. And this credibility is essential to our
national security' (quoted by Leslie Gelb, *New York Times* weekly review,
2 February 1975). Ford was referring to Cambodia and South Vietnam.

55 Thus President Truman was so concerned about the possibility of the Italian
Communist Party winning the 1948 elections that he approved a top secret
National Security Council recommendation that the USA 'make full use of its
political, economic, and if necessary, military power' to prevent it (documents
published by the State Department, *Foreign Relations of the United States*, 'Western
Europe 1948', quoted in the *International Herald Tribune*, 13 February 1975).

The domestic backlash – resulting from the 'loss of territory to communism' –
against the administration that 'permitted' this loss should also be mentioned.
The 'loss' of China was viciously exploited by Republicans against Truman and
Acheson. Fear of such a backlash – over Vietnam – undoubtedly influenced the
Kennedy administration; but geopolitical considerations were more important.
Franz Schurmann, in *The Logic of World Power* (New York, Pantheon Books,
1974), argues that the 'New Deal ideology' of welfare plus security on a global
scale, motivating the executive and supported by the masses, was the driving
force behind US imperialism – and not the 'interests' of business corporations or
the bureaucracy (internationalist in the case of the State Department and
influential corporations, nationalist as far as the Pentagon is concerned). The
actual course of US foreign policy at a given time, according to Schurmann, has
been affected by the struggle between opposing nationalist and internationalist
'currents' – as in the Asia-first or Europe-first debate. However, the containment
policy not only reconciled these divergent interests, but also confirmed the
leading role of the executive. Schurmann's thesis is a brilliant, if controversial,
one argued in great detail.

56 Herbert Tillema, *Appeal to Force*, pp. 23–8.

57 Ibid., pp. 29–38, 105.

58 My analysis differs from that in Stanley Hoffmann's *Gulliver's Troubles, or the
Setting of American Foreign Policy* (New York, McGraw-Hill, 1968), a title which
refers to the existence of super-power and the restraints on the use of that power.
These restraints, according to Hoffmann, are the result of 'de facto polycentrism'
– the emergence of states lacking the traditional ingredients of military power but
possessing scarce resources, intangible assets of talent, capacity to mobilise, etc. –
which is tantamount to the 'devaluation' of coercive power. Hoffmann even
claims that what appears to be the global expansion of American power is merely
the 'denial' of such expansion to America's adversaries (pp. 26, 29–30, 34–8,
46–9). However, by limiting his analysis largely to political and strategic

considerations, Hoffmann misconceives the nature of the 'global' system: i.e. the collaborative relationship between élitist structures and imperial patron reflecting the economic (and at times military) dependence of most Third World countries, which is basic to the international hierarchy of patron–client relations. This is far removed from the situation of 'relative impotence' – the *inability* to exploit its superior force – attributed to the USA by Hoffmann (p. 73). The point is that the USA, in general, *does not need* to use outright force to protect the system: there are 'subtler mechanisms' continuously at work to maintain it. But when force is 'required', it has not hesitated to use it (apart from the qualifications already mentioned). This global role is certainly burdensome, but it is not exactly 'servitude'. Nevertheless, I support Hoffmann's plea for moderation, reduction of the need for clients, abstention from 'manipulation of another's domestic polity', and for flexibility, discrimination and acceptance of diversity ('Gulliver Untied', *Gulliver's Troubles*, pp. 343–4).

59 Raymond Aron, *The Imperial Republic: The United States and the World 1945–1973*, Englewood Cliffs, NJ, Prentice-Hall, 1974, p. 304. However, Aron makes clear, in opposition to the 'neo-isolationists', that such policies of global intervention differ from what he regards as 'the realistic diplomacy of containment', which is based on discrimination (p. 309).

60 'The new and long foreseen problem is that under conditions of nuclear balance our adversaries may be increasingly tempted to probe at the regional level. This temptation must be discouraged. . . . [Otherwise] the global balance of power and influence will inevitably shift to the advantage of those who care nothing about America's values or well-being' (Henry Kissinger, 'Foreign Policy and National Security' speech in Dallas, 22 March 1976; US Information Service, United States Policy Statements Series – 1976, p. 18).

61 The Truman Doctrine, message to joint session of Congress, 12 March 1947: 'At the present moment in world history nearly every nation must choose between alternative ways of life. . . . One way of life is based upon the will of the majority, and is distinguished by free institutions, representative government, free elections, guarantees of individual liberty, freedom of speech and religion, and freedom from political oppression. The second way of life is based upon the will of a minority forcibly imposed upon the majority. . . . It relies upon terror and oppression, a controlled press and radio, fixed elections, and the suppression of personal freedoms. . . . I believe that it must be the policy of the United States to support free peoples who are resisting attempted subjugation by armed minorities or by outside pressures' (*Documents on American Foreign Relations*, vol. IX, p. 7).

The Eisenhower Doctrine, message to Congress, 5 January 1957: 'The reason for Russia's interest in the Middle East is solely that of power politics. Considering her announced purpose of communising the world, it is easy to understand her hope of dominating the Middle East. . . . The action I propose would . . . authorise such assistance and cooperation [with a nation or group of nations in the Middle East] to include the employment of the armed forces of the United States to secure and protect the territorial integrity and political independence of such nations, requesting such aid, against overt armed aggression from any nation controlled by International Communism' (Arthur M. Schlesinger Jr (general editor), *The Dynamics of World Power: A Documentary of*

United States Foreign Policy 1945–1973, New York, Chelsea House Publishers, 1973, vol. II, ed. Walter LaFeber, pp. 567–71).

62 As Kissinger puts it: 'If leaders around the world come to assume that the United States lacks either the forces or the will to resist while others intervene to impose solutions, they will accommodate themselves to what they will regard as the dominant trend. And an unopposed super-power may draw dangerous conclusions when the next opportunity for intervention beckons. . . . It is time that the world be reminded that America remains capable of forthright and decisive action' ('Foreign Policy and National Security', Dallas, 22 March 1976). Compare President Kennedy's address, 'The Lessons of Cuba', 20 April 1961: 'Should it ever appear that the inter-American doctrine of non-interference merely conceals or excuses a policy of non-action – if the nations of this hemisphere should fail to meet their commitments against outside communist penetration – then I want it clearly understood that this Government will not hesitate in meeting its primary obligations, which are to the security of the Nation' (quoted by Gurtov, *The United States against the Third World,* p. 88).

63 *U.S. Foreign Policy for the 1970's,* especially *Building for Peace* (1971) p. 4. The Carter administration, in spite of differences with the Nixon–Kissinger line, essentially adheres to this three-part formula. See Carter's speech at Notre Dame University, 22 May 1977. (The similarities and differences in foreign policy between Nixon–Kissinger and Carter–Brzezinski are discussed in the 'Conclusion' of this study.)

64 This is the point of the 'Sonnenfeldt Doctrine' with regard to Eastern Europe: 'It must be our policy to strive for an evolution that makes the relationship between the Eastern Europeans and the Soviet Union an organic one . . . a more autonomous existence within the context of a strong Soviet geopolitical influence.' As for the rest of Europe, in Kissinger's words, 'the dominance of communist parties in the West is unacceptable' (text of speeches by Sonnenfeldt and Kissinger, *International Herald Tribune,* 12 April 1976).

However, note present National Security Adviser Brzezinski's cautious qualification: 'I think if we eventually move toward a more accommodated [co-operative] world, the notion of narrow, somewhat watertight spheres of influence will become increasingly antiquated – as a consequence of historical process and not as the deliberate objective of foreign policy' (interview with *U.S. News & World Report,* 30 May 1977).

7 Limited war

1 Quoted by Conor Cruise O'Brien, Introduction to Edmund Burke, *Reflections on the Revolution in France,* Harmondsworth, Penguin Books, 1968, p. 61.

2 Excerpts in *SEATO Record* (Bangkok), April 1966.

3 Raymond Aron, *The Evolution of Modern Strategic Thought,* Adelphi Papers, No. 54, London, International Institute for Strategic Studies, February 1969. Aron's italics.

4 'Limited Retaliation as a Bargaining Process' in Klaus Knorr and Thornton Read (eds), *Limited Strategic War,* New York, Praeger, 1962, pp. 151–4.

5 Robert Osgood, *Limited War: The Challenge to American Security,* University of Chicago Press, 1957, p.1.

6 Ibid., p. 5.

7 Ibid., p. 235.

8 *Foreign Affairs*, July 1947, reprinted in George Kennan, *American Diplomacy 1900–1950*, New York, Mentor Books, 1952, p. 99. Kennan later argued in favour of a political response rather than a 'call to arms'. See interview with Kennan, and 'What Containment Really Meant' by Charles Gati, *Foreign Policy*, Summer 1972.

9 Osgood, *Limited War*, p. 4.

10 Ibid., pp. 28–9, 35.

11 An excellent example is Thomas Schelling, *Arms and Influence*, Yale University Press, 1966, particularly 'The Manipulation of Risk' and 'The Idiom of Military Action'. Schelling states that 'a loyal group at the Institute for Defense Analyses [of the Defense Department] in Washington spent eleven weekly seminars with me while the first draft was taking shape'.

12 'The Military Establishment (or How Political Problems become Military Problems)', *Foreign Policy*, Winter 1970–1.

13 *The Senator Gravel Edition: The Pentagon Papers*, Boston, Beacon Press, 1971, vol. 2, p. 98.

14 Arthur Schlesinger Jr, *A Thousand Days: John F. Kennedy in The White House*, London, Mayflower-Dell Paperback, 1967, pp. 256–7.

15 Morton Halperin, *Limited War in the Nuclear Age*, New York, John Wiley, 1963, pp. 123, 129. Italics added.

16 As General Collins, 'Special United States Representative in Vietnam', announced on his arrival in Saigon in November 1954, 'an American mission will soon take charge of instructing the Vietnam army with special American methods which have proved effective in Korea, Greece, Turkey and other parts of the world' (*New York Times*, 18 November 1954, quoted by Geoffrey Warner, 'The United States, France and Vietnam in the Year after Geneva', unpublished seminar paper, Australian National University, September 1972).

17 Roger Hilsman, *To Move a Nation: The Politics of Foreign Policy in The Administration of John F. Kennedy*, New York, Doubleday, 1967, p. 129.

18 Terence Smith, *International Herald Tribune*, 28 July 1969.

19 Osgood, *Limited War*, p. 190. General MacArthur had urged 'neutralising' the sanctuary north of the Yalu, intensifying the economic blockade of China, imposing a naval blockade of the Chinese coast, removing restrictions on US air reconnaissance of China's coastal areas and of Manchuria, and of removing the restraints on the use of Nationalist Chinese forces (speech to joint session of Congress, 19 April 1951; *Documents on American Foreign Relations*, the Council on Foreign Relations, vol. XIII, p. 28).

20 Osgood, *Limited War*, p. 147.

21 Dean Acheson, *Present at the Creation: My Years in the State Department*, New York, Norton, 1969, p. 219. Italics added.

22 'A feeling is widely and strongly held that "the Establishment" is out of its mind. The feeling is that we are trying to impose some U.S. image on distant peoples we cannot understand (any more than we can the younger generation here at home) and we are carrying the thing to absurd lengths. Related to this feeling is the increased polarisation that is taking place in the United States with seeds of the worst split in our people in more than a century' (note by Assistant Secretary of Defense John McNaughton to Secretary McNamara, 6 May 1967;

quoted in *The Pentagon Papers, New York Times* edition, New York, Bantam Books, 1971, pp. 534–5).

23 Memorandum by the Special Assistant to the President for National Security Affairs, McGeorge Bundy, 1 April 1965 (*Senator Gravel Edition: The Pentagon Papers*, vol. 3, pp. 360–1; italics added). (The phrase 'bargaining trade-offs' was used by the Pentagon analyst quoting the memorandum.)

24 Schelling, *Arms and Influence*, pp. vi, 2.

25 Especially Charles Wolf Jr, 'Insurgency and Counterinsurgency: New Myths and Old Realities', *Yale Review*, Winter 1967: 'At a broad conceptual level, the main concern of insurgency efforts should be to influence the behavior and action of the populace rather than their loyalty and attitudes.' See also Nathan Leites and Charles Wolf Jr, *Rebellion and Authority: An Analytical Essay on Insurgent Conflicts*, Chicago, Markham, 1970.

26 Schelling, *Arms and Influence*, p. 3.

8 Counter-insurgency: analysts and operators

1 Text in *Congressional Record*, 10 May 1972, 'Summary of Responses', pp. E4976–81.

2 Such as the 'American creed' which, as Myrdal puts it, expresses the 'higher' valuations of 'liberty, equality, justice and fair opportunity', Christian principles and 'ideals of human brotherhood', Gunnar Myrdal, *An American Dilemma: The Negro Problem and Modern Democracy*, New York, Harper & Row, 1944, p. lxxii.

3 Henry Kissinger, 'Domestic Structure and Foreign Policy', *Daedalus*, no. 2, 1966; reprinted in *American Foreign Policy: Three Essays*, New York, Norton, 1969.

4 Bernard Brodie, *War and Politics*, New York, Macmillan, 1973, pp. 482–6.

5 Dr Stephen Lukasik, Director of Defense Advanced Research Projects Agency, in US House of Representatives, Committee on Appropriations, Sub-Committee, *Department of Defense Appropriations for 1974, Hearings*, 93rd Congress, 1st Session, Washington, DC, US Government Printing Office, 1973, Part 9, p. 1025.

6 Dr Malcolm Currie, Director of Defense Research and Engineering, *Department of Defense Appropriations for 1976, Hearings*, 94th Congress, 1st Session, Part 4, p. 360. Italics added. Development of 'integrated intelligence and target engagement systems represents the great challenge and opportunity of the next decade for DoD' (Dr Currie, *Department of Defense Appropriations for 1977, Hearings*, 94th Congress, 2nd Session, Part 3, p. 18). Currie was speaking in the context of 'general purpose forces' – applicable to counter-guerrilla as well as conventional war.

7 Quoted in Irving Louis Horowitz (ed.), *The Rise and Fall of Project Camelot: Studies in the Relationship between Social Science and Practical Politics*, Cambridge, Mass., MIT Press, 1967, pp. 47–8. For a defence of Camelot, see Seymour J. Deitchman, *The Best Laid Schemes: A Tale of Social Research and Bureaucracy*, Cambridge, Mass., MIT Press, 1976. Deitchman was Special Assistant for Counter-Insurgency Programs in the Defense Department's Office of Defense Research and Engineering. He was directly involved in Camelot, and was later director of Project Agile – see below.

8 Quoted by Dante Fascell, member of the US House of Representatives'

Sub-committee on International Organizations, in *Rise and Fall of Project Camelot*, p. 189.

9 Budgeted Behavioral and Social Science Research Funds, Department of Defense; reported, *Rise and Fall of Project Camelot*, p. 364. In 1970 the Defense Department provided three-fifths (or $162 million) of *total* Federal obligations for Research and Development to Federally-funded R. & D. Centres. Among those whose work included research in the behavioural and social sciences, RAND (Air Force) received $20 million, the Research Analysis Corporation (Army) received $9½ million, and the Army-financed 'Human Resources Research Organisation', which was separated from George Washington University in October 1969 after student demonstrations, well over $4 million (*Federal Support to Universities, Colleges and Selected Nonprofit Institutions*, Fiscal Year 1969 (NSF70-27) and Fiscal Year 1970 (NSF71-28), National Science Foundation, Washington, DC, 1970, 1971). RAND, SORO, RAC, and 'HumRo' provided for well over half the social, behavioural and operational research in counter-insurgency in 1965; add the Defense Department's Institute for Defense Analyses, with $10 million budget in 1970, and the Stanford Research Institute (sold off by Stanford University, after student protests, in January 1970), with an annual budget of $60 million (including some $25 million in defence contracts), and the great bulk of work in this field is accounted for (Michael T. Klare, *War Without End*, New York, Knopf, 1972, pp. 77, 79, 81). Ironically, on the non-military 'non-profit' research side, funds for foreign area programmes were drastically reduced by Congress from 1970. The US Office of Education's aid for Asian studies, for instance, was cut by more than half from over $7 million to just over $3 million (*New York Times*, 10 July 1971). The Nixon administration in 1971 set up a sub-committee of the National Security Council to co-ordinate all federally-financed research on foreign affairs, i.e. the 'full range of needs of the national security foreign affairs process ... from research involving the application or advancement of the social-behavioural sciences or humanistic studies'. This involved research financed by the State Department, Defense Department, US AID (Agency for International Development), US Information Agency and the Arms Control and Disarmament Agency. Taking into account only security-related (software) research proper, planned expenditure for fiscal years 1974–5 amounted to some $12.5 million. Nearly $7 million went to the Defense Department (a considerable reduction from the $22.6 million spent in fiscal years 1968–9); it was divided more or less equally into research on 'international conflict situations', including 'external counter-insurgency measures'; Soviet technology, strategies and forces; Chinese strategies and forces; and East Asia (*Third USC/FAR* [Under-Secretaries Committee of the National Security Council on Foreign Affairs Research] *Consolidated Plan for Foreign Affairs Research FY-1974-75*, US Government Printing Office, August 1973, Appendix pp. 1–2, 18, 21–9, 36, 38, 45–6.

10 *Defense Department Sponsored Foreign Affairs Research*, Hearings before the Senate Committee on Foreign Relations, 9 May 1968 ('The American Asian Studies Establishment', *Bulletin of Concerned Asian Scholars*, Summer–Fall 1971).

11 RAND Corporation, *Annual Report 1969*, Santa Monica, April 1970, p. 8.

12 Johann Galtung, 'After Camelot', in Horowitz (ed.), *The Rise and Fall of Project Camelot*, p. 293.

13 RM-5163-ISA/ARPA, March 1967.

14 *Viet Cong Motivation and Morale in 1964: A Preliminary Report*, John C. Donnell, Guy J. Pauker, Joseph J. Zasloff (RAND) RM -4507/3-ISA, March 1965, pp. viii, 3–4, 20–4, 27.

15 Henry Rowen, Interview in Canberra, 15 June 1972.

16 Quoted in *The University – Military Complex: A Directory and Related Documents*, North American Congress on Latin America, 1969, p. 40.

17 Roger Trinquier, *La Guerre Moderne*, Paris, La Table Ronde, 1961, pp. 31, 51.

18 Alf Heggoy, *Insurgency and Counterinsurgency in Algeria*, Bloomington, Indiana University Press, 1972, pp. 176–87, 235–44.

19 Trinquier, *La Guerre Moderne*, p. 102.

20 Ibid., p. 61.

21 Ibid., pp. 132, 135.

22 Ibid., p. 111.

23 Andrew R. Molnar, John D. Lenoir, Jerry M. Tinker, 'Counter-measure Techniques' in Tinker (ed.), *Strategies of Revolutionary Warfare*, New Delhi, S. Chand, 1969, especially pp. 295–314.

24 R. W. Komer, *Bureaucracy Does Its Thing: Institutional Constraints on U.S./GVN Performance in Vietnam*, RAND R-967-ARPA, August 1972, p. 114. Komer has returned to official prominence, in the field of security (NATO affairs), with the advent of the Carter administration.

25 Ibid., Preface, p. iii. According to RAND report R-957-ARPA, February 1972, 'Four major real-life cases – Malaya, Laos, Thailand, and Vietnam – have been analysed'. Komer is also author of one of these studies, *The Malayan Emergency in Retrospect: Organisation of a Successful Counter-Insurgency Effort*. The Preface to this work states that 'a related RAND study is Douglas S. Blaufarb's R-19-ARPA, *Organising and Managing Unconventional War in Laos, 1962–1972* (U), January 1972- Secret' (p. iii). Presumably the study of insurgency in Thailand is also secret. A further RAND study, revealed in Congressional *Hearings* of the *Defense Department's Appropriations for 1971*, is the *VC Infrastructure Handbook*, written in English and Vietnamese and used by the police to 'root out' the NLF administrative apparatus (Klare, *War Without End*, pp. 224–5). See also Douglas S. Blaufarb, *The Counterinsurgency Era: U.S. Doctrine and Performance – 1950 to the Present*, New York, Free Press, 1977.

26 Komer, *Bureaucracy Does Its Thing*, pp. 7, 151.

27 Ibid., pp. 5, 10, 21.

28 Alain C. Enthoven and K. Wayne Smith, *How Much is Enough?*, New York, Harper & Row, 1971, p. 294; quoted in Komer, *Bureaucracy Does Its Thing*, p. 40.

29 Ibid., p. 151.

30 Benedict Anderson, 'Western Values and Research on Indonesia', paper delivered to the Association of Asian Studies Conference, April 1971.

31 The social science component of defence research, contrary to the situation in the 1960s, barely makes an appearance in the current defence appropriations. Instead the emphasis is on maintaining the 'technological initiative' as a 'priceless asset' of the USA: 'For decades we have based our security and economic vitality on technology. Today we find ourselves in an uncertain world. . . . In this increasingly competitive, often hostile and rapidly changing world, Americans seem to have only one real choice. . . . Technology thus

appears to offer us our place in the sun – the means to insure our security and economic vitality. . . . I am urging today the clear articulation of a national policy. We must maintain the broad technological initiatives' (Malcolm Currie, Director of Defense Research and Engineering, *Department of Defense Appropriations for 1976, Hearings*, 94th Congress, 1st Session, Part 4, p. 352). The striking decline in social science funding is evident after fiscal year 1972. Funds for 1973 were reduced almost by half – to $1.6 million out of total Department of Defense outlay on research by university and non-profit institutions of over $230 million. Within the social sciences, funds for political studies were reduced from $567,000 to $9,000, and for sociology from over $1 million to $72,000 (*Federal Support to Universities, Colleges, and Selected Nonprofit Institutions*, FY 72 (NSF74–313) and FY73 (NSF75-304)). In fact the Mansfield Amendment in 1969 prohibited the military from carrying out research not specifically related to military functions.

32 '*C'est pire qu'un crime: c'est une faute*': attributed to Napoleon's police chief, Fouché.

33 Eqbal Ahmed, 'Revolutionary Warfare and Counterinsurgency', in Norman Miller and Roderick Aya (eds), *National Liberation: Revolution in the Third World*, New York, Free Press, 1971, pp. 148–50.

34 Quoted by Alex Carey, 'The Clockwork Vietnam: Psychology of Pacification', unpublished seminar paper, Australian National University, Canberra, October 1972. Carey interviewed Vann in August 1970.

35 John Pustay, *Counterinsurgency Warfare*, New York, Free Press, 1965, pp. 16–18. Pustay was an Air Force Captain at the time he wrote this 'controversial' work; he is now Major General, Deputy Chief of Intelligence for the Air Force (communication from Vincent Davies, University of Kentucky).

36 Ibid., pp. 36–40.

37 Ibid., pp. 6, 8.

38 Pustay quotes Khrushchev's 1961 national-liberation wars speech to conclude, incorrectly: 'In other words, communist doctrine prescribes active Societ involvement in insurgency wars' (p. 13). It is for this reason that the US 2counter-insurgency mission is 'obligatory'.

39 *The Senator Gravel Edition: The Pentagon Papers*, Boston, Beacon Press, 1971, vol. 2, pp. 636–7.

40 Edward Lansdale, *In the Midst of Wars: An American's Mission to Southeast Asia*, New York, Harper & Row, 1972, pp. 368–9; Lansdale's italics.

41 Lansdale's report on the Saigon Military Mission (*The Pentagon Papers*, *New York Times* edition, New York, Bantam Books, 1971, p. 60).

42 Lansdale, *In the Midst of Wars*, pp. 168–9.

43 *Pentagon Papers*, *New York Times* edn, pp. 136–7.

44 Lansdale, *In the Midst of Wars*, pp. 372–3.

45 Memorandum VN 091, to Defense Secretary McNamara, 17 January 1961, quoted in *United States–Vietnam Relations 1945–1967*, Book 2, p. 74.

46 Lansdale, *In the Midst of Wars*, p. 375.

47 Ibid., p. 373.

48 Tad Szulc, reporting data from US Defense Department, *International Herald Tribune*, 5 October 1972.

49 Senator Kennedy's Sub-Committee for Refugees; figures given in Cornell

University's Center for International Studies, *The Air War in Indochina*, reported in the *New York Times* weekly review, 21 November 1971.

50 Investigation of Kien Hoa province by correspondent Kevin Buckley, reported in *Newsweek*, 19 June 1972.

51 Report to President Johnson, early in 1967; quoted in *The Senator Gravel Edition: The Pentagon Papers*, vol. 2, p. 575.

52 *International Herald Tribune*, 19 October 1972. Military experts from 50 countries agreed in October 1974, at a meeting organised by the International Committee of the Red Cross in Lucerne, that incendiary and fragmentation weapons, among others, caused unnecessary suffering and should be limited in use. A further conference, to update the 1949 Geneva Conventions on Warfare, took place in Geneva in April–May 1976. In May 1977 a majority of delegates voted to prevent the use of napalm, landmines, booby traps and incendiary bombs, but failed to win the necessary two-thirds majority. The debate continues.

53 Sir Robert Thompson, *No Exit from Vietnam*, London, Chatto & Windus, 1969, p. 164.

54 Deryck Viney, *Guardian Weekly*, 19 January 1974.

55 US House of Representatives, *Department of Defense Appropriations for 1964*, *Hearings*, 88th Congress, 1st Session, Washington, 1963, Part 1, pp. 483–4; quoted by Klare, *War Without End*, p. 136.

56 Statement before the Senate Committee on Armed Services, *Hearings*, 91st Congress, 2nd Session, Washington, 1971, pp. 3–38; quoted by Klare, *War Without End*, p. 167; on SMASH, p. 177.

57 The evidence, used to answer these questions, is drawn almost entirely from official or technical sources. I am much indebted, in this regard, to the tireless research of Michael Klare published in his book *War Without End*. There is no need to accept all his arguments (I do not), for in most of his chapters his comments are kept to a minimum: the facts speak for themselves.

58 US House of Representatives, *Department of Defense Appropriations for 1968*, *Hearings*, Washington, 1967, Part 3, pp. 176–7, quoted by Klare, *War Without End*, p. 168.

59 *Congressional Record*, 11 August 1969, pp. S9589–91; Klare, *War Without End*, p. 139.

60 'Research and Development for Vietnam', *Science and Technology*, October 1968; Klare, *War Without End*, p. 209.

61 US House of Representatives, *Department of Defense Appropriations for 1974*, *Hearings*, Part 9, p. 895.

62 US House of Representatives, *Department of Defense Appropriations for 1971*, *Hearings*, Part 6, p. 750; Klare, *War Without End*, pp. 215, 218. Italics added.

63 'As countries from Taiwan to Brazil and Zaire to Malaysia stock up on sophisticated American weaponry, U.S. civilian arms experts are taking top jobs in their armed forces. . . . Pentagon statistics show that 7,700 arms experts – most recruited from the U.S. armed services – are stationed in 34 countries', and especially the Persian Gulf (Pacific News Service, San Francisco *Sunday Examiner and Chronicle*, 14 March 1976). Among products potentially available for use are 'unattended ground sensors' – 'derivatives of equipment used in Southeast Asia' – and 'tactical all-weather reconnaissance and intelligence processing

capabilities', essential for accurate targeting for strike operations, as shown by 'our own experience in Southeast Asia' and the Middle East war (Currie, *Department of Defense Appropriations for 1976*, Part 4, pp. 455, 471).

64 It was announced in May 1975 that the Government of Iran had contracted with Rockwell International to establish an intelligence complex (Ibex) to monitor military and civilian electronic communications throughout the Persian Gulf (Associated Press, 1 June 1975). American cryptographers, cryptoanalysts, computer programmers and electrical engineers from the National Security Agency were being recruited for Ibex (*Sunday Examiner and Chronicle*, 14 March 1976).

65 *Aviation Week*, 25 November 1963, quoted by Klare, *War Without End*, p. 226.

66 US House of Representatives, *Department of Defense, Appropriations for 1968, Hearings*, Part 3, pp. 175–6; quoted by Klare, *War Without End*, pp. 227–8.

67 US House of Representatives, *Hearings on Thailand and the Philippines*, 16 June 1969, quoted in Al McCoy, 'Subcontracting Counter-insurgency', *Bulletin of Concerned Asian Scholars*, December 1970.

68 Testimony by Robert Nooter, acting Assistant Administrator for East Asia, US Agency for International Development (AID), 16 June 1969, quoted in Eric R. Wolf and Joseph G. Jorgensen, 'Anthropology on the Warpath in Thailand', *New York Review of Books*, 19 November 1969.

69 Harry Cleaver, *Counterinsurgency Research in Thailand*, Pacific Studies Center, 1970, quotes the 'Abstract' of the project (Klare, *War Without End*, p. 230).

70 US Senate, Committee on Government Operations, Permanent Investigations Subcommittee, *Riots, Civil and Criminal Disorders, Hearings*, 91st Congress, 1st Session, Washington, 1969, Part 21, p. 4667; Klare, *War Without End*, p. 230.

71 US House of Representatives, *Department of Defense Appropriations for 1971, Hearings*, Part 6, pp. 750, 730, 728; Klare, *War Without End*, pp. 236–8.

72 US House of Representatives, *Department of Defense Appropriations for 1974, Hearings*, Part 9, pp. 1025–9, 1035.

73 *Far Eastern Economic Review*, 3 December 1973. See also Puey Ungphakorn, *Sia chip ya sia sin* ('Lose Your Life, Don't Lose All'), Bangkok, Klett Thai, 1974, pp. 12–13. His views are borne out by a recent survey of Thai élite attitudes: 40 per cent of respondents 'feel that the major cause for communist insurgencies stems from abuses of power on the part of the officials'; 16 per cent attribute the insurgencies to external support; 16 per cent to ignorance and deception; only 10 per cent to ideological beliefs (report of preliminary findings, *Prachachart Weekly Digest* (Bangkok), 24 December 1975).

74 Jeffrey Race, 'The War in Northern Thailand', *Modern Asian Studies*, January 1974.

75 Excerpts from J. L. S. Girling, 'Politics Amalgamated: The Thai Example', *Australian Outlook*, December 1970.

76 US House of Representatives, *Department of Defense Appropriations for 1971, Hearings*, Part 6, p. 728; Klare, *War Without End*, p. 239. RAND is still employing some 550 experts on the 'DoD effort', mostly directed toward long-range issues (Currie, *Department of Defense Appropriations for 1976, Hearings*, Part 4, p. 409).

77 George Kennan, *American Diplomacy 1900–1950*, p. 59.

78 *New York Times* weekly review, 28 May 1978.

79 Quotations from Leonard Sullivan (in 1974 he was promoted to Assistant
Secretary of Defense) and General Westmoreland; Klare, *War Without End*, pp.
139, 209, 203–4; research activities, Klare, *War Without End*, pp. 130–3, 160, 166,
170–8, 180, 187, 192–4.

9 Implications of involvement

1 Thus Edwin O. Reischauer: the year 1968 saw 'the beginning of a great change
in the tide of policy'; the return to a classic US stance ('Back to Normalcy', *Foreign
Policy*, Fall 1975).
2 'Official State Department non-verbatim summary of remarks', made by
Secretary of State Henry Kissinger at a meeting in London in December 1975 of
US Ambassadors to Europe (text in *International Herald Tribune*, 12 April 1976).
For a perceptive analysis of détente, and its 'balance of ambivalences', see Coral
Bell, *The Diplomacy of Detente: The Kissinger Era*, London, Martin Robertson, 1977.
Détente is the 'management of adversary power' through 'conscious and
deliberate reduction of tensions' in the central (or local) balance; this is in
contrast to the maintenance of tensions at a relatively high level in the Cold War
period. Détente is discussed in the context of nuclear strategy, the 1973 Middle
East war, European security, US disengagement from Southeast Asia, the
Cyprus crisis, Portugal and South Africa, etc.
   A persuasive view of détente is put forward by Secretary of State Cyrus
Vance's special adviser on Soviet affairs, Marshall D. Shulman. He points out
that 'in thinking about United States–Soviet relations, we tend in this country to
think of there being only two attitudes, hard and soft. What is desirable is to
develop an understanding that there needs to be a policy which is neither hard
nor soft, that is based on a realistic understanding of the nature of the Soviet
system and the problem presented by Soviet policies, but at the same time has a
clear view of what our own self-interest requires. That means, in the first
instance, the stabilisation of the military competition, and over the longer run an
effort to enlarge the cooperative rather than the competitive side of relations'
(interview with Bernard Gwertzman, *New York Times* weekly review, 16 April
1978). However, the National Security Council, under Brzezinski, is more
alarmed by Soviet 'lack of restraint' (in its arms build-up, and in Africa) which
adversely affects détente; Carter veers towards the NSC on these issues, and
towards the State Department on the importance of negotiating SALT.
3 Speech by Kissinger, San Francisco, 3 February 1976. Note the similarity with
the Carter administration's attitude toward détente. President Carter has
emphasised the 'real and deeply rooted' competition between the Soviet Union
and America. 'But it is also true that our two countries share many important
overlapping interests. Our job is to explore those interests and use them to
enlarge the areas of cooperation between us. . . . We search for areas of
agreement where our real interests and those of the Soviets coincide. . . . [In this
way] we both should have a greater stake in the creation of a constructive and
peaceful world order' (Speech to the Southern Legislative Conference,
Charleston, 21 July 1977).
4 See chapter 6 above, 'America in a "bind"'. Coral Bell makes a similar point.
The essential stability of the central balance, she writes, is threatened on the one
hand by changes in nuclear technology and strategy and, on the other, by the

destabilising impact either of revolution or the parliamentary access to power of communists, leading to the gain or loss of allies or fellow-travellers (Bell, *The Diplomacy of Detente*, p. 227).

5 This section is based on excerpts from my ' "Kissingerism": The Enduring Problems" ', *International Affairs*, July 1975.

6 Richard Nixon, *U.S. Foreign Policy for the 1970's: A New Strategy for Peace*, Washington DC, US Government Printing Office, 1970, pp. 55–6.

7 Richard Nixon, *U.S. Foreign Policy for the 1970's: Building for Peace*, Washington DC, US Government Printing Office, 25 February 1971, p. 5.

8 The crucial lesson of Vietnam is 'that America shall never again over-extend and exhaust itself by direct involvement in remote wars with no clear strategic significance' (Kissinger, Boston, 11 March 1976: Department of State *Bulletin*, 5 April 1976).

9 This is precisely the problem with the Carter administration's plan for phased withdrawal from South Korea. Washington prefers to reduce direct military commitments to a minimum so as to keep its options open in the event of an emergency. But the very fact of withdrawal reduces America's capacity to deter the North Koreans, who may take advantage of resulting instability in the South. Without a troop commitment, the deterrent that remains to the USA is either too little to be effective (air power) or too big to use (nuclear weapons). Taiwan is a rather different case, since it does not face a direct military threat: its military power in the area is formidable. However, Chinese pressure on the USA to abrogate the security treaty with Taiwan is also a destabilising factor. This obstacle to US recognition of Peking – which took effect from January 1979 – was overcome by Peking's *de facto* acquiescence in the US decision to continue arms supply to Taiwan.

10 Speech, St Louis World Affairs Council, 17 May 1975 (Department of State *Bulletin*, 2 June 1975).

11 John Gallagher and Ronald Robinson, 'The Imperialism of Free Trade', *Economic History Review*, August 1953.

12 ' "Internal War": The New Communist Tactic', in Franklin Mark Osanka (ed.), *Modern Guerrilla Warfare: Fighting Communist Guerrilla Movements*, New York, Free Press, 1962, p. 453.

13 Harlan Cleveland, Assistant Secretary of State for International Organisation Affairs (quoted by Melvin Gurtov, *The United States against the Third World*, New York, Praeger, 1974, pp. 58–9).

14 Dr Currie, Director of Defense Research and Engineering, *Department of Defense Appropriations for 1977, Hearings*, Part 3, p. 7.

15 Ibid., p. 5; Currie's italics.

16 Speech at San Francisco, 3 February 1976. See NATO statement, 16 May 1979.

17 St Louis World Affairs Council, 12 May 1975.

18 Ibid. However, note Paul Warnke's reminder that 'it is a mistake to over-estimate the importance of the Soviet Union as a world power. Militarily, it approaches the strength of the United States. But in terms of economic weight and political influence, and as a promising source of materials and technology, it is still a long way from first rank' (Warnke, 'We Don't Need a Devil (to Make or Keep our Friends)', *Foreign Policy*, Winter 1976–7). Warnke was Director of the

Arms Control and Disarmament Agency in the Carter administration. Moreover, Robert Legvold argues that Soviet leaders, on the basis of their own assessment of the 'correlation of forces', have a long-term commitment to détente. By détente, they mean three things: (a) nurturing processes that restrain changes they fear and those that ease the changes they desire; (b) sanctifying their global status; and (c) securing the economic and technological benefits of the international division of labour. Legvold points out that Soviet global policy has less to do with the application of power (toward control), as in Western conceptions of military–political strategy, than it does with status and access. Soviet leaders seek to participate in international decisions of concern to them; this depends in part on Soviet military power, in part on the nature of local circumstances, as in the Middle East (Legvold, 'The Nature of Soviet Power', *Foreign Affairs*, October 1977).

19 The danger of American involvement is brought out by the Senate Foreign Relations Committee report in US arms sales in the Middle East (Simon Winchester, *Guardian Weekly*, 8 August 1976).

20 Speech at St Louis, 'The Challenge of Peace', 12 May 1975.

21 Reports from Lima, 'Peruvians Bury the Revolution', by Joanne Omag, and from Washington, 'Banks Start Pulling the Strings', by Don Oberdorfer, *Washington Post*; reprinted in *Guardian Weekly*, 12 September 1976. More 'tough' measures were demanded, following the visit of an IMF mission, as a condition for further loans: to cut government expenditures, reduce subsidies on staple items, devalue the currency still further, and increase taxation (Reuters report, *International Herald Tribune*, 27 May 1977). In March 1978, President Morales said he was putting all his efforts into a 'maximum austerity plan' beyond which he could not go without 'risking a grave deterioration in the social and economic conditions of the Peruvian people'. Rioting broke out after the government had ordered large price increases for petrol, wheat, milk and cooking oil; and on 20 May 1978 the President imposed martial law.

22 Hobart Rowen, 'Kickbacks are Kid's Stuff', *Washington Post*; reprinted in *Guardian Weekly*, 5 September 1976. The ruling party in 1971 was the investment-oriented Jamaican Labor Party, which had been in power for almost ten years; it was defeated in the 1972 general elections by Michael Manley's social-democratic People's National Party.

23 Interview with Oriana Fallaci, 'The CIA's Mr Colby', *New Republic*, 13 March 1976. Ironically, the CIA may be trying to 'do it' *both* ways: there have been outbreaks of 'unexplained' violence in Jamaica coinciding with press reports that the country was 'unstable and mismanaged' and about to become a Cuban satellite (Saul Landau, 'What Future for Jamaica?', *Washington Post*; and John Hatch, 'Jamaica on a Knife Edge'; both in *Guardian Weekly*, 12 September 1976). However, the Carter administration has reversed US policy to one of reconciliation with the Jamaican government, increasing aid from $10 to $63 million: *International Herald Tribune*, 19 December 1977.

24 President Truman's announcement of 6 March 1952 on communist designs in Asia (*Documents on American Foreign Relations 1952*, New York, Harper Bros for Council on Foreign Relations, 1953, p. 33).

25 As the House Select Committee on Intelligence (hereafter Pike Committee) points out, 'all evidence in hand suggests that the CIA, far from being out of

control, has been utterly responsive to the instructions of the President and the Assistant to the President for National Security Affairs' (Report dated 19 January 1976). The second section of the Report, 'The Select Committee's Investigative Record', was published in *Village Voice*, Special Supplement, 20 February 1976, p. 36.

26 As Colby told Fallaci: 'You know, those people [Soviet agents] are serving their government and I disagree with their philosophy, but about their professional side I must say that they can do a good job' (bugging, atom spies, double agents) (*New Republic*, 13 March 1976).

27 At the Pacem in Terris conference, 1973 (Department of State *Bulletin*, 29 October 1973).

28 'Foreign Policy, Public Opinion and Secrecy', *Foreign Affairs*, October 1973. Similarly, the Church Committee recommends a ban on 'all political assassinations, efforts to subvert democratic governments and support for police or other internal security forces which engage in systematic violation of human rights.' Institutional reforms for the intelligence community were promulgated by the Ford administration in 1976 and Carter in January 1978. The CIA reduced the number of its clandestine operatives from 8,500 to 4,500. Ninety per cent of intelligence, according to Admiral Turner, is now gathered by technical means, including spy satellites, radio monitoring and transmission deciphering (David Binder, *New York Times* weekly review, 14 May 1978).

29 Interview with Fallaci, *New Republic*, 13 March 1976. Thus Brzezinski, according to Washington sources, 'wants the United States to shake free from the Vietnam war-inspired curbs on presidential power enough to permit US aid for clandestine operations in Africa "to pin down the Cubans" and limit their ability to stretch into other adventures' (Murrey Marder, *Washington Post*; in *Guardian Weekly*, 28 May 1978).

30 Interview with Fallaci, *New Republic*, 13 March 1976.

31 'Alleged Assassinations': plots against Lumumba, Castro, Trujillo, Diem and Schneider (Chile).

32 See below, on Chile; also evidence by Philip Agee, *Inside the Company: CIA Diary* (Harmondsworth, Penguin Books, 1975) on forged documents planted in Peru and Ecuador, pp. 146, 279. Agee was a CIA agent in Ecuador, Uruguay and Mexico in the 1960s. According to the review of the book by William Bundy [WPB], *Foreign Affairs*, October 1975, 'what the author knows first-hand seems unquestionable, if occasionally tinted . . . this remains a deeply disturbing book about the lengths to which American policy in Latin America went during this period'.

33 In Ecuador, the CIA financed an anti-communist 'National Defense Front' of Conservatives and Social Christians, including a Social Christian bomb squad of provocateurs; it manipulated organised labour activities under the guise of 'adult education' (Agee, *Inside the Company*, pp. 158–9, 216, 243–5).

34 CIA Africa Division to Leopoldville, 27 October 1960 (the plot to assassinate Lumumba, apparently authorised by President Eisenhower himself) ('Alleged Assassinations', p. 46; italics added).

35 American policy toward Cambodia comprised two main objectives: (1) US efforts to prop up a discredited and hopeless regime – from 1971 it was facing military disaster and was only 'preserved' by external support at the cost of

immense destruction – so that the 'US side' would not have to negotiate out of weakness; and related to this, (2) massive American bombing (until Congress put a stop to it in 1973) which could be turned on or off as an 'incentive' for the adversary to negotiate. In fact these two points apply to the whole of Indochina.

36 Interview with Fallaci, *New Republic*, 13 March 1976,

37 See Dennis J. Duncanson, *Government and Revolution in Vietnam*, London, Oxford University Press for the Royal Institute of International Affairs, 1968, ch. 6, 'The Bounty of America'.

38 National Security Study – 1 (February 1969), CIA assessment; *Congressional Record*, 10 May 1972, p. E5005.

39 Ibid.

40 A CIA representative in Saigon, Lucius Conein, testified that he had known the generals involved in the coup for many years. 'Some of them I had known back even in World War II. Some of them were in powerful positions and I was able to talk to them on a person to person basis' ('Alleged Assassinations', p. 218).

41 Report of committee headed by General James Doolittle to President Eisenhower; quoted by Anthony Lewis, *New York Times* weekly review, 2 May 1976.

42 Details of Senate report, quoted by Laurence Stern, 'CIA Role in Chile', *Washington Post*; *Guardian Weekly*, 14 December 1975.

43 'Alleged Assassinations', p. 229.

44 Ibid., p. 225.

45 Ibid., p. 227.

46 Statement reported in *Multinational Corporations and United States Foreign Policy*, Hearings before the Subcommittee on Multinational Corporations of the US Senate Foreign Relations Committee, 93rd Congress, Washington, 1973, part 2, pp. 542–3; quoted by Richard Fagen, 'The United States and Chile: Roots and Branches', *Foreign Affairs*, January 1975.

47 'Alleged Assassinations', p. 231.

48 Ibid., p. 228.

49 Ibid., pp. 225, 231, 234.

50 Ibid., p. 232.

51 Cable from CIA headquarters, 7 October 1970; 'Alleged Assassinations', p. 234; italics added.

52 Cable, 19 October 1970, 'Alleged Assassinations', p. 234.

53 Statement of 6 August 1975; 'Alleged Assassinations', p. 254.

54 The World Bank and the International Development Bank refused to act on Chile's request for loans – although Bangladesh and Haiti were considered to be either sufficiently credit-worthy or deserving cases (Elizabeth Farnsworth, 'Chile', *Foreign Policy*, Fall 1974). The covert aim of the economic campaign, according to reports by the International Telephone and Telegraph Corporation (ITT), later revealed by US Congressional Hearings on Multinational Corporations, was that 'a swiftly deteriorating economy (bank runs, plant bankruptcies, etc.) will touch off a wave of violence resulting in a military coup'. And again: 'massive unemployment and unrest might produce enough violence to force the military to move' (Peter Jenkins, quoting the 'Anderson Papers' on Chile, *Guardian Weekly*, 22 September 1973; *New York Times* weekly review, 22 September 1974; Seymour Hersh, *International Herald Tribune*, 12 September

1974).

55 Incessant opposition attacks and crippling strikes forced the Allende government 'so much on to the defensive that no coherent set of objectives could be obtained'. After June 1972, 'inflation soared out of control, growth halted, and correspondingly the political situation turned far more ugly. Encouraged by the growing intransigence of the opposition majority in Congress . . . those who had lost from the income redistribution and property seizures determined to . . . bring the government (and the socialist economy) to its knees' (Laurence Whitehead, 'Why Allende Fell', *The World Today*, November 1973).

56 Régis Debray, *La Critique des armes*, Paris, Editions du Seuil, 1974, vol. I, p. 293.

57 In Chile's precarious economic situation (dependence on exports of primary products, especially copper; limited domestic market because of the highly unequal distribution of income, and small but backward agrarian sector) the American threat in 1970 not to allow one 'nut or bolt' to reach Allende's Chile, and to 'condemn' the people of Chile to the 'utmost deprivation and poverty' proved to be grimly effective.

58 The political, economic and social forces of Left and Right in Chile were set on a collision course from at least 1971 onwards. The efforts to compromise, after Allende's election as President in 1970, after the first 'businessmen's strike' in October 1972 and even a few weeks before the end, proved abortive. Electoral strength was almost equally divided among three separate 'coalitions': the Left, or 'Popular Unity', comprising communists (the most moderate and responsible), Allende's Socialists, non-Marxist elements among Catholics and Radicals, and an extremist fringe; the Christian Democrats, divided into the Left wing, under the 1970 Presidential candidate Tomic, and the Right led by former President Frei; and the far Right 'National Party', which included its own brand of extremists. The essence of the Left strategy was to use its position of power under the Presidency to expand to the limits of its 'natural' constituency (from the residual one-third to at least half the electorate) by socialist measures demonstrating to the masses where their 'true' interests lay. This was achieved at one stage in 1971, during the municipal elections. Similarly, the very survival of the Right as an electoral force – that is the Frei Christian Democrats and the National Party – depended on using their power base in Congress, where together they could rally a majority, to frustrate the socialist objectives of Popular Unity.

59 The so-called 'Frei gambit': 'Alleged Assassinations', p. 231

60 The Chile coup has also had the opposite effect – chiefly outside Latin America – of encouraging a more subtle communist 'penetration' of the system by readiness to take part in 'Centre-Left' coalitions in order to forestall the possibility of Right-wing violence.

61 The erosion of America's economic primacy is clearly shown by these figures. Whereas Latin America's exports to the USA were nearly 50 per cent of total exports in 1950, they are down to 32 per cent today. Latin American imports from the USA, too, have fallen from 57 to 37 per cent in 25 years, and are still declining. In 1964 the USA provided more than half the total of foreign investment in Brazil; by now the share is less than 30 per cent. In 1973 new Japanese investment in Brazil exceeded that of the USA for the first time (Lowenthal, 'The

United States and Latin America', *Foreign Affairs*, October 1976). America's declining share of total foreign aid to developing countries is another indication. The USA supplied 60 per cent of the total of under $10 billion in economic aid in 1965; but less than 25 per cent of a total of $20 billion in 1977. France, West Germany and Japan have each more than tripled their foreign development aid over the last ten years (Clyde Farnsworth 'Overseas Aid Seems Less Political', *New York Times* weekly review, 18 September 1977).

62 See Mihajlo Mesarovic and Eduard Pestel, *Mankind at the Turning Point*, London, Hutchinson, 1975, especially pp. 57–8 (gap between rich and poor countries), 75 (population increase), 76, 80 (unemployment) and 116, 122 (food supply).

10 Conclusion: the global condition

1 US commitments, in Samuel P. Huntington's view, 'will be maintained if they serve the dual purposes of morality and security' (Huntington's survey of current foreign policy and future prospects, 'Beyond Isolationism', *Dialogue*, US Information Agency, vol. 9. 1976, no. 2).

2 Promoted in particular by Saul H. Mendlovitz and Richard A. Falk. As Falk puts it, 'governments cannot hope to effectuate such a consensus [a redistributive consensus premised on justice for all sectors of *global* society] without prior social and economic transformations on a national level – the domestic disparities are too great, the scarcities are too pronounced, the capital surplus too restricted, the capacities for disruption too dispersed and potent . . . and the energies of the entrenched elites too formidable to reach any kind of workable consensus among governments as to what is fair and just in the world.' Yet 'the evidence available suggests a monumental absence of *will* on the part of leadership groups to achieve a redistributive consensus'; and even if a consensus were reached on goals, 'it could not be successfully implemented by the state system'. Instead, an 'awakening of consciousness' is required to build the foundation for a social movement dedicated to the creation of a peaceful and just system of world order, structured around 'a system of non-territorial central guidance' (Falk, *Statecraft in an Era of World Order, Decay and Renewal*, Yencken Memorial Lectures, Australian National University, Canberra, 1974, pp. 48–50; see also Falk, *A Study of Future Worlds*, New York, Free Press, 1975, ch. IV; and Jagdish Bhagwati (ed.), *Economics and World Order*, London, Macmillan, 1972).

3 Earl C. Ravenal, 'The Case for Strategic Disengagement', *Foreign Affairs*, April 1973.

4 Ibid.

5 Areas and stages of withdrawal are elaborated in Earl C. Ravenal, 'After Schlesinger: Something Has to Give', *Foreign Policy*, Spring 1976, e.g. Asia half a decade, Western Europe one decade. In Asia, withdrawal would mean no military assistance to Asian clients; in Europe, however, this would require 'most exacting and patient diplomacy'. Ravenal's thesis is criticised by Amos Jordan, Acting Assistant Secretary of Defense, in the same issue of *Foreign Policy*.

6 Ravenal, 'The Case for Strategic Disengagement'.

7 Ravenal, 'After Schlesinger'.

8 President Nixon, Department of State *Bulletin*, 15 October 1973.

9 Reportedly 'under consideration' to deter a possible North Korean thrust

following the fall of Saigon (*International Herald Tribune*, 15 May 1975).

10 Statement by Elliot Richardson, Secretary of Commerce: although it would be 'catastrophic', another oil embargo could 'force' the USA into a 'major military struggle' (*Reuter*, Washington, 28 July 1976). Carter's Defense Secretary, Harold Brown, warned in his 'guidance' to service chiefs that events in the Persian Gulf could undermine the NATO powers by obstructing the production and transportation of vital oil supplies. He speculated in his budget presentation that local clashes in the Gulf aggravated by Soviet intervention 'might require the dispatch of appropriate U.S. forces to the scene in support of friends' (Stephen S. Rosenfeld, *Washington Post*, in *Guardian Weekly*, 19 March 1978). See also Richard Burt's report that the Defense Department is putting together a 'quick reaction' force of Army and Marine units for possible deployment in the Persian Gulf (*New York Times* weekly review, 17 March 1978). President Carter in his address of 17 March 1978 also emphasised America's 'important historical responsibilities to enhance peace in East Asia, in the Middle East, in the Persian Gulf' and spoke of the Defense Department preparing 'quick deployable forces – air, land and sea – to defend our interests throughout the world'. See also Brown, 25 February 1979.

11 Interview with *U.S. News and World Report*: quoted by *Reuter*, 19 May 1975. Schlesinger also pointed to 'major Soviet advances' under way in tactical air and mobility forces which, unless countered, could give 'the Soviets the capacity rapidly to intrude into the Middle East toward the Persian Gulf – with all that that implies. The overall assessment is that the United States and its allies face a serious deficit of conventional strength in the Eastern Hemisphere. Thus, in order to deter, we remain highly dependent on the threat of introducing nuclear weapons into combat. This is not a threat to be lightly made or lightly implemented' (*Foreign Policy*, Fall 1976).

12 Huntington, 'Beyond Isolationism'. Huntington was brought in by Brzezinski as Co-ordinator of Security Planning in the National Security Council. He was chief author of the controversial presidential review memorandum PRM-10, assessing the global balance of power for the Carter administration, which takes the view that we are in a 'second era' of the Cold War. The second part of the study, prepared by the Office of International Security Affairs in the Defense Department, considered 'force postures' in five areas: a possible conflict in Central Europe involving NATO and the Warsaw Pact; an East–West war outside Europe; possible conflicts in East Asia; 'national' wars (wars that might be fought by choice – 'I don't want to say more Vietnams, but that's what we're talking about', according to one source); and all-out nuclear war with the Soviet Union (Robert G. Kaiser, 'Global Strategy Memo Divides Carter's Staff', *Washington Post* in *International Herald Tribune*, 7 July 1977).

13 A US Army officer on the destruction of Ben Tre during the Tet offensive in South Vietnam, 1968; quoted by Don Luce and John Sommer, *Viet Nam – The Unheard Voices*, Ithaca, Cornell University Press, 1969, p. 201.

14 John McNaughton, Assistant Secretary of Defense under McNamara, had anticipated an 'exit by negotiations' from the Vietnam conflict and listed various 'bargaining counters' available to the USA as well as 'techniques to minimise impact of bad outcomes'; but the memorandum ended by rejecting the possibility: 'With the physical situation and the trends as they are the fear is overwhelming that an exit negotiated now would result in humiliation for the

U.S.' (Draft Memorandum for McNamara, 24 March 1965; reported in *Pentagon Papers*, *New York Times* edition, New York, Bantam Books, 1971, pp. 437–8).

15 An example: It is 'abundantly clear' that Soviet policy anticipates unrelenting class struggle, world-wide support of revolutionary forces, efforts to restrict US influence, trade, investment and procurement of raw materials in the Third World, and 'permanent, positive conflict between the communist and capitalist social systems until the latter collapses in a "world crisis of capitalism" '. The USA should therefore recognise that far-reaching US–Soviet co-operation is an illusion or deception; the USA should 'counter each Soviet challenge in strategic areas [undefined] crucial to the United States at any necessary level – from diplomacy . . . to security guarantees and the deployment abroad of military forces for defense of threatened territory or regimes' (Ray S. Cline, *New York Times* weekly review, 18 April 1976). Cline was formerly director of the Bureau of Intelligence and Research in the State Department; now executive director of studies, the Center for Strategic and International Studies, Georgetown University.

16 Perhaps the most penetrating critique is by Stanley Hoffmann, 'The Hell of Good Intentions', *Foreign Policy*, Winter 1977–8. The key problem, Hoffmann writes, is to establish an order of priorities – not all at once – within an 'overall coherent vision of the desirable world'. Instead of this, he notes the contrary aspects of Carter's policies on human rights (subordinated to security interests), arms control (and arms sales), preventing nuclear proliferation (and confronting important allies), intervening in the Arab-Israeli conflict (half-way between 'good offices' and an imposed solution), the ambivalent attitude toward the North–South economic dialogue, and so forth. As to policy management, Hoffmann bitingly refers to the Carter administration's 'overdose of activism', the successive improvisations and 'quick, poorly prepared initiatives', and the frequent 'painful changes in direction'. He concludes that, without a clear rationale or overall design, neither the American public nor the Congress will support Carter's policies or be convinced of their urgency. Hoffmann's indictment is correct; but missing from the catalogue of errors is any indication of just *what* overall policy, conception or vision he thinks Carter should promote. Carter's methods, or lack of method, are not the real problem: they only reflect the problem of America's role in a changing world.

17 Kissinger's reply to a Senator who had warned against American involvement in Angola (reported by Tom Wicker, *New York Times* weekly review, 14 March 1976).

18 Pike Committee, p. 40, note 477. The former head of the CIA's Angola task force later revealed that, in spite of Congressional prohibitions, CIA advisers had supported Holden Roberto's pro-Western faction in the guise of 'intelligence gatherers'. He also claimed that the USA was first to intervene covertly (in July 1974) to which the Soviet reacted – not the other way round (*Newsweek*, 22 May 1978, quoting John Stockwell's account, *In Search of Enemies: A CIA Story*, New York, Norton, 1978).

19 David B. Ottaway, 'Administration Split on Africa Policy', *Washington Post*, reprinted *Guardian Weekly*, 26 February 1978. But note Vance's more moderate approach (Jonathan Steele, 'Vance Changes Tack on Angola', *Guardian Weekly*, 2 July 1978).

20 Kissinger's speech at Dallas, 22 March 1976.
21 Kissinger, Boston, 11 March 1976.
22 Interview with Oriana Fallaci, 'Otis Pike and the CIA', *New Republic*, 3 April 1976.
23 Objective from the point of view of a super-power: subjective from that of social forces in the Third World; i.e. people whose will, determination and awareness have effected changes.

Index

Academic Advisory Council for Thailand, 180
Acheson, Dean, 158, 232, 251–2
Advanced Research Projects Agency, 170, 178–9,
　180–1
Afghanistan, 130, 141
Agile, Project, 178, 181
Alavi, Hamza, 22
Algeria, 21, 28, 39, 47–8, 64–7, 73, 87, 96, 131, 141,
　143, 156, 169, 172–3, 176, 215, 235
Allende, Salvador, 202–4, 267
Alliance for Progress, 244–5
Almond, Gabriel, 108–9, 225, 245
Angola, 15, 64, 140–1, 143, 186, 196, 216–18, 270
Argentina, 49, 51, 56, 58, 70, 76, 125, 130, 137,
　141–2, 192, 203, 234
Aron, Raymond, 148–9, 152
Australia, 84, 137

Bangladesh, 57, 124, 141–2, 222, 242
Bao Dai, 43, 144
Batista, 50–3, 58, 83
Bell, Coral, 262–3
Biafra, 66
Bodenheimer, Susanne, 111, 225
Bolivia, 54–5, 62, 82, 130, 141–2, 203
Bourgeoisie (national), 17, 32, 57, 63, 92, 112
Brazil, 51–2, 60, 62, 64, 70–3, 76, 112, 125, 127–8,
　130, 138, 141–2, 192, 206, 215, 243, 267
Britain (British), 65, 127, 130, 136–8, 144, 156,
　172, 189, 211, 225, 248
Brodie, Bernard, 83, 164
Brown, Harold, 222, 269
Brzezinski, Zbigniew, 119, 149, 214–15, 218, 262,
　265
Bundy, William, 122–3, 152
Bureaucracy, 4, 30, 57, 61, 113, 125
Burke, Edmund, 78, 81, 152, 238
Burma, 26, 48, 61, 65, 85–6, 140, 227

Cambodia, 38–9, 54, 140–1, 186, 199–200, 216,
　236, 265–6
Camelot, Project, 165–7, 169
Caribbean, 145, 189
Carter, President, 119–20, 127–9, 130, 132, 149,

151, 185, 214–18, 244, 254, 262–3, 265
Castro, Fidel, 50, 52, 53–4, 83, 87, 98
Chad, 142
Chile, 9, 49, 51, 55, 60, 62, 73, 76, 125, 130, 135,
　138, 140, 142–3, 145, 193, 198, 201–5, 216, 244,
　266–7
China, 17, 21–4, 27, 28, 31, 41, 52, 56, 64–6, 74–6,
　82, 87–8, 96, 104, 114, 119, 135–7, 141, 143–4,
　152–3, 156, 160, 164, 169–70, 185, 190, 193–4,
　215, 222, 232, 234, 237, 248, 250–2, 263
Church, Frank (also Committee), 195–6, 201–2,
　204, 247, 265
CIA, 175, 191, 195–9, 201–4, 217, 264–6
Clausewitz, Carl von, 83, 100
Clifford, Clark, 174
Cohn-Bendit, Daniel and Gabriel, 39
Colby, William, 194, 197–8, 264–5
Colombia, 51, 53, 55–6, 62, 77, 141
Colonialism, 26–7, 40, 57, 65–7, 77, 82, 92, 125
Congo, 140–1, 156, 205
Counter-Insurgency, 56, 162–84, 256, 258
Cuba, 17, 21, 46–56, 60, 64, 68, 104, 129, 130, 140,
　142–3, 148, 156, 203, 218, 222, 233
Currie, Malcolm, 165, 258–9
Cyprus, 73, 146

Dahrendorf, Ralf, 225, 237
Davis, Jack, 53
Debray, Régis, 47–8, 51, 53, 56, 233–4
Defense Department (US), 165–8, 177–8, 183–4,
　217
Developmental Theory, 4, 8, 10, 113–14, 122, 241
Diem, President, 39, 43, 85–6, 150, 170, 200, 213,
　231
Dominican Republic, 140, 142–3, 155, 165
Domino theory, 84
Dos Santos, T., 2, 223
Dulles, John F., 120, 154
Dutch, 64, 143

Ecuador, 56, 62, 141, 265
Egypt, 61, 96, 127–31, 141–2, 159, 177, 192
Eisenhower, President, 84, 123, 149–50, 174, 201,
　250, 253

Engels, Frederick, 47
Eritrea, 66
Ethiopia, 128–31, 141–2

Falk, Richard, 268
Fanon, Frantz, 16, 65–7, 71, 235, 236
foco, 48, 56
Ford, President, 202, 204, 265
France (French), 23, 28–9, 38–9, 40–3, 48, 64–7, 73, 81, 86–7, 96–7, 127–8, 130, 136–8, 144, 156, 159, 172, 176–7, 211, 247, 248, 268
Frei, Eduardo, 201, 203, 244, 267

Gallagher, John, 189, 249
Germany, 137–8, 169, 172, 206–7, 237, 268
Ghana, 125, 130
Giap, Vo Nguyen, 29, 42, 169
Gilpin, Robert, 223
Gott, Richard, 56
Goulart, 64
Greece, 158–9, 199, 216, 250
Guatemala, 53, 54, 56, 60, 62, 123, 140–3, 145, 193, 252
Guerrero, Amado, 223–4
Guevara, Che, 47, 51–2, 69, 80, 82
Gurr, Ted, 89–90, 92–5, 99–100, 239–40

Halberstam, David, 172
Halperin, Morton, 157
Helms, Richard, 202
Herzfield, Charles, 178–9
Hilsman, Roger, 190
Ho Chi Minh, 20, 41–3, 85, 230
Hoffmann, Stanley, 80, 252–3, 270
Huntington, Samuel, 56, 61, 89–90, 95–100, 213, 269

India, 9, 22, 24, 57, 71, 76, 84, 114, 124, 130–1, 137, 143, 157, 192, 222, 242–3
Indochina, 39–41, 65, 86–7, 132, 137, 143, 159, 161, 169, 172, 177, 197
Indonesia, 24, 39, 57, 64–5, 76, 84, 125, 127, 130, 140–4, 157, 250
International Peace Research Institute, 177
Iran, 53–4, 64, 76, 123, 127–8, 140–1, 143, 145, 159, 179, 192, 196, 206, 217, 222, 242, 250–1, 261
Iraq, 131, 141–3, 196
Ireland, 73
Israel, 16, 129–30, 143, 177, 192, 217, 243
Italy, 196, 201, 237, 252

Jamaica, 138, 194–5, 264
Japan (Japanese), 7, 23, 27, 36, 38, 41–2, 64–5, 74–5, 84, 86, 115, 119, 127, 138, 159, 169, 172, 205–7, 267–8
Java, 24, 27
Johnson, Chalmers, 79–80, 89–91, 98–9, 100, 239
Johnson, President, 84–9, 120, 123, 129, 149, 155, 159, 161, 170, 176, 185
Jordan, 130–1, 141

Kabyles, 28
Kahin, George, 224, 250
Kandinsky, Wassily, 238
Kaplan, Morton, 152–3
Katanga, 128
Katzenbach, Nicholas, 197–9
Kennan, George, 153, 183, 255
Kennedy, President, 6, 84, 120, 123, 134, 149, 155–6, 174
Kenya, 130, 157
Kerala, 24
Khomeini, Ayatollah, 222
Khrushchev, 156–7
Kissinger, Henry, 114, 119–20, 127, 134, 185, 189, 191, 193, 196, 197, 199, 202–3, 212, 214–18, 254, 262
Klare, Michael, 179, 260
Kolko, Gabriel, 135–8
Komer, R. W., 170, 176
Korea (South), 15, 54, 84, 115, 123, 125, 130, 132, 139, 143, 154, 158–9, 177, 193, 205, 215, 243, 262–3
Kuomintang, 23, 60, 74–5
Kurds, 196
Ky, Nguyen Cao, 200

Landé, Carl, 224
Landlords (landowners), 34–5, 40–1, 51, 62
Land problems, 5, 25–6, 44, 61–3, 96, 116
Landsberger, Henry, 32–3
Lansdale, Maj.-Gen., 175–6
Laos, 85, 140, 154, 156, 158, 160, 174, 180, 182, 186, 190, 199–200
Lebanon, 9, 130, 140, 142–3, 250
Lenin, 20, 29, 31–2, 39, 40, 46–7, 59, 69, 72, 78, 81, 97–8, 135–7, 224, 228
Libya, 131
Lon Nol, 141
Lukasik, Stephen, 165, 181
Luzon, 33–5

MacArthur, Gen., 255
McNamara, Robert, 84, 110, 115, 155, 160, 194, 269
McNaughton, John, 160, 168, 255, 269
Magsaysay, President, 169, 175
Malaya (Malaysia), 76, 87, 125, 130, 142–4, 165, 169–70
Manila, 34–5
Mao Tse-tung (Maoist), 7, 22–3, 46–7, 51, 60, 65, 68, 74–6, 82, 98, 157, 169, 173, 223, 226
Marcos, President, 7, 141
Marcuse, Herbert, 30
'Marginals', 19, 34, 63. 71–2, 77
Marx (Marxism, Marxists), 1–12, 16, 30–1, 46, 78, 97, 103, 107, 113–20, 208, 218, 223, 225
Massu, Gen., 169
Mekong Delta, 24, 44
Meo, 180, 182
Mexico, 21, 48, 51, 64, 96, 125, 234, 242, 246

Middle class (strata), 7, 17, 30, 34, 35, 49, 53, 56, 58, 61, 63–4, 75, 77, 96, 113, 117
Miliband, Ralph, 225
Military, 30, 36, 59–61, 72, 75
Mirskii, G., 61, 234–5
Modernisation, 27, 76–7
Moore, Barrington, 24–5, 225, 227
Morocco, 128, 130, 143, 246
Mozambique, 64, 141, 218
Mus, Paul, 42
Myrdal, Gunnar, 80, 117, 124, 215

Nasser, President, 60
Nationalism (nationalist), 27–8, 64–7, 85, 96, 125
National Liberation Front of South Vietnam (NLF), 43–4, 85, 98, 173, 176
Nazis, 169
New People's Army, 35, 229
New Zealand, 84, 137
Nicaragua, 53, 141
Nigeria, 128, 142
Nixon, President, 119–20, 123, 134, 137, 149, 162, 170, 176, 185–6, 187–90, 193, 196, 199, 201, 202, 203, 205, 215

Oman, 142
Osgood, Robert, 153–4

Pakistan, 54, 57, 124, 130, 143, 157, 192, 222
Palestine, 73, 141
Pampanga, 35
Panama, 56, 141–2
Paraguay, 168
Park, President, 141
Patron–Client, 3, 5–7, 11
Peasantry, 17, 19, 21–33, 34–5, 42–3, 57, 61–3, 66–9, 72, 74, 77, 86, 96, 182, 226–7, 228–9, 237, 242
Persian Gulf, 127–9, 212, 269
Peru, 55–6, 58, 62, 112, 125, 138, 141–2, 194, 203, 264
Philippines, 1, 2–7, 8, 12, 21, 26, 33–5, 84, 87, 114, 130, 140–1, 165, 167, 169–70, 175, 215, 223–4, 228–9
Phoumi Nosavan, 174
Phumiphon Adunyadet, King, 37–8
Pike (Committee), 196, 219, 264–5
Pluralism, 1–12, 107–11, 113, 118–21, 122, 222, 228–9, 242
Portugal (Portuguese), 64, 141
Prapat, Gen., 37–8, 141, 182–3
Puey Ungphakorn, 181–2
Pustay, John, 173
Pye, Lucian, 223, 241

Race, Jeffrey, 43, 98, 227
RAND Corporation, 167, 170, 183, 257
Ravenal, Earl, 210, 268
Rechtin, Eberhardt, 180–4
Rhodesia, 138, 142, 217–18
Robinson, Ronald, 189, 249

Rosecrance, Richard, 223
Rousseau, 9
Rowen, Henry, 167–8
Rusk, Dean, 84, 142, 167–8
Russia (pre-1917), 21, 31–2, 46, 58, 69, 96, 104, 234
Rwanda-Burundi, 142

Salert, Barbara, 240
Sarit, Field Marshal, 37–8, 141
Saudi Arabia, 127, 129–30, 206, 247–8
Schelling, Thomas, 159–60
Schlesinger, Arthur, 156
Schlesinger, James, 212–13, 269
Schurmann, Franz, 243, 245, 252
Scott, James, 26, 71, 228
Shah of Iran, 54, 128, 196, 251
Shanin, Teodor, 226–7
Shulman, Marshall, 262
Sihanouk, Prince, 38–9, 54
Simbulan, Dante, 224, 228
Somalia, 129, 142
Sorel, Georges, 66, 70, 236
Soustelle, Jacques, 67
South Africa, 193, 217
Soviet Union ('Russia'), 87, 97, 119, 127, 129, 131–2, 136, 143–4, 145, 148, 151, 153, 155–9, 164, 172, 185, 190–1, 203, 205, 213–14, 218, 222, 248, 262–4, 269–71
Spain, 50
Sri Lanka, 76, 130, 142
Stalin, 15, 145
Stanford Research Institute, 180, 257
Students, 36–9, 43, 58–9, 72, 75
Sukarno, President, 9, 125, 143–4
Sullivan, Leonard, 178
Sunkel, Osvaldo, 116–17
Syria, 61, 130–1

Taiwan, 84, 115, 125, 130, 139, 153, 193, 263
Taylor, Gen. Maxwell, 156, 160, 168, 175, 177
Templar, Gen., 169
Tenancy, 23, 26–7, 34–5
Terrorism, 66–7, 70–1, 73
Thailand, 1, 9, 21, 35–9, 54, 85–6, 105, 130, 140, 161, 165, 167, 179–82, 218, 242, 261
Thanom Kittikachorn, 37, 141
Thieu, President, 200
Thompson, Sir Robert, 177
Tillema, Herbert, 145
Tilly, Charles, 89–92, 94, 99–100
Trinquier, Roger, 169
Trotsky, 22
Truman, President, 122, 132, 144, 149–50, 158, 250, 252–3
Truong Chinh, 83
Tucker, Robert W., 223, 248–9
Tupamaros, 70, 72
Turkey, 158
Turner, Admiral, 191

UN, 68, 177
Unger, Leonard, 180
Urban Insurgency, 16, 68–73
Urbanisation (urban), 19, 29, 55, 65, 68, 92, 95, 111, 125
Uruguay, 9, 49, 51, 53, 58, 70, 72–3, 76, 141, 215, 234

Vance, Cyrus, 215, 262
Vann, J. P., 172–3
Vargas, President, 63
Venezuela, 53, 55, 58, 60, 62, 68, 138, 141–2
Vernon, Raymond, 125, 133, 246–7
Vietminh, 41–2, 85–7, 144
Vietnam, 1, 12, 15, 17, 21, 22, 23, 26, 27, 31, 38–9, 39–45, 48, 56, 64, 76, 84–8, 96, 98, 103–4, 106, 131, 134–8, 140–1, 143–4, 148, 152, 154, 156, 158, 160–1, 162–5, 167–8. 170, 172–6, 179–80, 185–6, 190, 193, 197, 199–201, 205, 212, 216, 219, 222, 230–1, 243, 252, 269

Watts, William, 223, 248–9
Wertheim, W. F., 27–8
Westmoreland, Gen., 168
Wolf, Eric, 21–2, 49
Workers (working class), 19, 29–30, 49, 58, 117, 222
World Bank, 114–16, 124, 194, 266

Yarmolinsky, Adam, 155
Yemen, 131, 177

Zaïre, 125, 127–8, 130, 138, 247
Zapata, Emiliano, 48
Zasloff, Joseph, 167–8

For Product Safety Concerns and Information please contact our EU
representative GPSR@taylorandfrancis.com
Taylor & Francis Verlag GmbH, Kaufingerstraße 24, 80331 München, Germany